400 SAUCES

DIPS, DRESSINGS, SALSAS, JAMS, JELLIES & PICKLES

400 SAUCES

DIPS, DRESSINGS, SALSAS, JAMS, JELLIES & PICKLES

HOW TO ADD SOMETHING SPECIAL TO EVERY DISH FOR EVERY OCCASION, FROM CLASSIC COOKING SAUCES TO FUN PARTY DIPS

Featuring over 400 step-by-step recipes shown in more than
1400 stunning photographs – everything from cordon bleu sauces
to spicy relishes, chutneys or delicious jams and jellies

CATHERINE ATKINSON,
CHRISTINE FRANCE
AND MAGGIE MAYHEW

HERMES
HOUSE

This edition is published by Hermes Housee

Hermes House is an imprint of Anness Publishing Ltd
Hermes House, 88–89 Blackfriars Road, London SE1 8HA
tel. 020 7401 2077; fax 020 7633 9499
www.hermeshouse.com; www.annesspublishing.com

If you like the images in this book and would like to investigate using them for publishing,
promotions or advertising, visit our website www.practicalpictures.com for more information.

Publisher: Joanna Lorenz
Editorial Director: Helen Sudell
Contributing Editor: Bridget Jones
Project Editor: Catherine Stuart
Production Controller: Ben Worley
Page Design: Adelle Morris
Cover Design: Chloe Steers

ETHICAL TRADING POLICY
At Anness Publishing we believe that business should be conducted in an ethical and ecologically
sustainable way, with respect for the environment and a proper regard to the replacement of the
natural resources we employ.
As a publisher, we use a lot of wood pulp to make high-quality paper for printing, and that wood
commonly comes from spruce trees. We are therefore currently growing more than 750,000 trees
in three Scottish forest plantations: Berrymoss (130 hectares/320 acres), West Touxhill
(125 hectares/305 acres) and Deveron Forest (75 hectares/185 acres). The forests we manage
contain more than 3.5 times the number of trees employed each year in making paper for the books
we manufacture.
Because of this ongoing ecological investment programme, you, as our customer, can have the
pleasure and reassurance of knowing that a tree is being cultivated on your behalf to naturally
replace the materials used to make the book you are holding.
Our forestry programme is run in accordance with the UK Woodland Assurance Scheme (UKWAS) and
will be certified by the internationally recognized Forest Stewardship Council (FSC). The FSC is a
non-government organization dedicated to promoting responsible management of the world's forests.
Certification ensures forests are managed in an environmentally sustainable and socially responsible
way. For further information about this scheme, go to www.annesspublishing.com/trees

A CIP catalogue record for this book is available from the British Library.

Parts of this edition previously appeared in *Sauces* and *The Complete Book of Preserves
and Pickles*.

NOTES
Bracketed terms are intended for American readers.
    For all recipes, quantities are given in both metric and imperial measures and, where appropriate,
in standard cups and spoons. Follow one set, but not a mixture, because they are not
interchangeable.
    Standard spoon and cup measures are level. 1 tsp = 5ml, 1 tbsp = 15ml, 1 cup = 250ml/8fl oz.
    Australian standard tablespoons are 20ml. Australian readers should use 3 tsp in place of 1 tbsp
for measuring small quantities of gelatine, flour, salt, etc.
    American pints are 16fl oz/2 cups. American readers should use 20fl oz/2.5 cups in place of 1
pint when measuring liquids.
    Electric oven temperatures in this book are for conventional ovens. When using a fan oven, the
temperature will probably need to be reduced by about 10–20°C/20–40°F. Since ovens vary, you
should check with your manufacturer's instruction book for guidance.
    Medium (US large) eggs are used unless otherwise stated.
    The nutritional analysis given for each recipe is calculated per portion (i.e. serving or item), unless
otherwise stated. If the recipe gives a range, such as Serves 4–6, then the nutritional analysis will
be for the smaller portion size, i.e. 6 servings. Measurements for sodium do not include salt added
to taste.

CONTENTS

INTRODUCTION

Like the accessory that turns an ordinary outfit into a stunner, or the painting that provides the perfect focal point for a room, a sauce can transform the simplest dish into something unforgettable. It may be integral to the dish, drawing all the elements together into a harmonious whole, or it may be served on the side, providing a complementary or contrasting flavour. The aim may be to offer an alternative texture: a crisp salsa with a salmon steak, for instance, or pickled red cabbage with sausages. Colour has a role to play, too. A simple sweet treat, such as a spoonful of ruby-red plum and cardamom jelly, can look superb alongside a slice of quiche or a portion of deep-fried Camembert. A sauce can also soothe, as when guacamole is offered alongside a fiery chilli, or it can challenge the palate. Think horseradish sauce with roast beef, or wasabi – such an innocent-looking fire-raiser – spooned alongside sushi.

Sauces have been central to culinary tradition for centuries. The word evolved from the Latin *salsus*, which means salted, and they were

originally conceived by cooks, not to add piquancy to food, but to disguise the fact that the meat or fish that formed the basis of the dish was past its best. To mask suspect flavours, strongly flavoured spice rubs were popular. Subtlety wasn't a strong point until the Italian Renaissance, when inspired chefs at the court of the Medici family began to develop dishes renowned for their fine flavour and flamboyant presentation.

Left: Add herbs such as thyme and bay leaves to sauces and preserves for maximum freshness and flavour.

Above: The classic French white onion sauce is traditionally enjoyed with rare, juicy steak.

When Catherine de Medici travelled to France in 1533 to marry the future King Henry II, she took her personal chefs with her and introduced her hosts to a range of new and delicious dishes, often married with delicate sauces. These were adopted and adapted by the French. Just over a century later, Francois La Varenne developed the roux-based sauce, and for almost three hundred years successive French chefs, including the great

Marie-Antoine Carême, created and classified complex sauces with the kind of energy usually reserved for main course meals!

By the mid-1950s, just as the taste for rich, heavy sauces was declining, Paul Bocuse tossed his chef's hat into the ring and introduced nouvelle cuisine. Sauces became lighter, complementing beautifully presented food made from the finest fresh ingredients.

Cooks have learned that, while classic sauces still have a vital role to play, it is okay to loosen up a little. Sauces can be a simple stock reduction, a fruit coulis, a savoury jelly, a relish made of raw, chopped vegetables. They can be creamy or crisp, hot or cold, sweet or savoury.

Below: Jams and jellies marry up all kinds of fruits and vegetables, and can be savoury or sweet.

They can start out as a marinade or end as a dip. A sauce might be an old favourite, like the apple sauce that always accompanied your grandmother's roast pork, or a more modern blend. Sun-dried tomatoes with radicchio, perhaps, or a Thai-style basil and chilli mixture. Then there are the sauces you store – like chutneys, pickles and other preserves. The art of preserving is as old a tradition as sauce-making, but this too is experiencing a renaissance, thanks to cross-cultural influences and all kinds of new serving ideas. Some classic "spreads" can even work as super-fast sauces: try, for instance, spooning jam or marmalade onto a hot, steamed pudding.

Both reference sections to the book are outstanding, outlining all any cook needs to know about basic ingredients, equipment and

Above: Many preserves are stored using the same, simple methods: tried and tested for centuries!

techniques for making sauces and preserves. Over 400 inspiring recipes are clearly explained, with step-by-step pictures to encourage and inspire. In short, when it comes to classic condiments, this is the only guide you'll ever need.

classic savoury sauces, salsas and dips, sauces for main course meat, fish and vegetable dishes, dressings and marinades and sweet sauces

SAUCES

SUCCESS WITH SAUCES

A sauce can be many things to many meals – from the simplest aside to accentuate the taste of plain cooking, to the integral part of a more complex dish. Savoury or sweet, fragile or full of punch, the one characteristic shared by all sauces is their liquid content. Unlike dry toppings, spice mixes or rubs, sauces include some form of liquid, even if this is a fat, such as butter, that becomes liquid on heating. There may be hundreds of brands and types to buy but nothing competes with home-made sauce – and it doesn't have to be complicated to be brilliant.

CLASSICAL STANDARDS

Old-school culinary experts still classify sauces by techniques (thickening, reducing or concentrating, or emulsifying methods), uses or colour, highlighting "mother" or foundation sauces that could be varied to create a range of recipes. While classical methods and

Above: Fresh-tasting salsas combine handfuls of herbs with full, ripe and flavourful fruit and vegetables

combinations are still the essence of many sauces, there is now a more relaxed approach. The basic laws may still apply, but they have given rise to new, exciting interpretations.

FRESH COMBINATIONS

Not only has the approach lightened up, but so have the recipes and sauce partnerships.

Heavy coating sauces and fat-rich liquors that once flooded plates are no longer the norm. New-generation sauces enhance, not mask, good ingredients; gravies bring out the best in meats; and butters moisten rather than render greasy. Light stocks and base liquids, simple reductions, restraint with creams and butter, and fine (rather than heavy) thickening are popular. Marrying sauces with main ingredients has been opened up in simple partnerships that are easy to prepare, and bursting with colour and vitality.

WORLD INFLUENCES

The international food scene has changed sauces and their use dramatically. Whereas previous generations may have introduced the occasional spice to European ingredients with timidity, twenty-first century recipes refine the use of international ingredients to an eclectic art.

Hot or cold, sweet-sour or savoury-sweet, we are all aware of brilliant sauces that transform everyday foods into exciting international meals. Whether based on stock, milk or vegetables, classic methods are now fused with all kinds of cross-cultural influences, and can be enlivened in seconds by an instinctive seasoning twist, or unconventional combinations of ingredients.

Left: There are many delightful twists on the classic tomato sauce, which will work equally well in meat and vegetarian dishes.

COOK IN OR SERVE ON

Many of the recipes in this section of the book concentrate on the integration of a main dish with a complementary sauce. There are variations and suggestions for the different ways in which the sauce can be served, and the ingredients it will suit. As a general rule, 'serve on' sauces added at the very end of the recipe are separated from the main dish in both the listed ingredients and in the method.

Some dishes, such as casseroles and braised dishes, generate their own sauce during cooking, which makes the cook's life a little easier; others involve adding food to a prepared sauce for cooking. While cooking in a sauce is a great way of making full-flavoured dishes that are rounded, with a certain depth and complexity, serve-on sauces can bring different culinary personality.

Cooked in advance and often served with plain cooked foods, sauce accompaniments can be prepared using the cooking residue from roasting, pan-frying or braising. They may be based on a marinade or basting mixture. The simplest flavoured butters or oils can be served as sauces or dressings for cooked foods.

HOT-COLD COMBINATIONS

Cold dressings and fresh, uncooked sauces should not be set aside only for use with salads or as dips – they are also fantastic with hot foods. Oils and vinegars, mayonnaise-based sauces, or yogurt mixtures are all terrific with freshly cooked fish, poultry, meat or vegetables. Smooth purées, finely chopped salsas or chunky vegetable and fruit mixtures do not have to be cooked to be classed as a sauce. Pepped up with spices, tart with citrus, or aromatic with fresh herbs, all sorts of uncooked sauces are packed with nutrients. They are often low in fat and can be very quick to make.

COOK-AHEAD SIMPLICITY

Making your own sauces does not have to be laborious. Instead of buying mixtures laden with hidden fats, sugars, seasoning and artificial flavourings, pick up a few favourite recipes and some sure-winner tips from the chapters that follow. Use them as your everyday, hassle-free flavour makers. Soon you will gain the confidence to experiment with a whole host of exciting new twists on your culinary repertoire.

The majority of sauces can be made in advance, cooled and chilled in a covered container. Some can be made one or two days in advance, while others can be prepared up to a week ahead. All

Below: Spices such as nutmeg are essential additions to many savoury and sweet sauces.

Above: A light, fruity sauce is the perfect accompaniment to all kinds of egg-based puddings.

sorts of sauces freeze well, ready for thawing at the last minute in the microwave. Making a big batch of a favourite simple sauce (tomato or basic white sauce, for example) and freezing it in portions is an excellent way to save time and eat well. Try freezing salsas and dips in little pots.

Seasonal fruit and vegetables can be used for sauces when they are at their best and least expensive. 'Fresh' sauces can be frozen for year-round use. Don't limit yourself to savoury sauces. Fruit purées, chocolate sauces and syrups are all suitable for chilling or freezing.

There is just one simple rule when making sauces ahead, and that's labelling. Always label your pot of sauce with its name, quantity and date. It is also worth stocking up on cook-in bags or containers that can go from freezer to microwave, steamer, double boiler or oven. Creative and cost-effective, successful sauce-making can literally transform your approach to everyday cooking.

a guide to
making sauces

There is no great secret to sauces – it's simply a matter of marrying tried and tested techniques with good ingredients, and partnering the right sauce with the main food. A little know-how goes a long way, so it's worth learning the sauce-making basics – when to boil, simmer or barely warm, why some mixtures are whisked hard and others gently stirred, which sauces can be whizzed up in seconds, and when to cook ahead for last-minute perfection.

FLOURS

There is a wide range of flours and thickening agents on the market. It is important to select the right product, since the choice of flour used for a sauce will determine not only the cooking method used, but the final texture and flavour of the finished sauce. These general guidelines should help remove any mystique involved.

Below from left to right: Brown flour, wholemeal (whole-wheat) flour.

Below: Sauce flour

PLAIN WHITE FLOUR

Also known as all-purpose flour, this is the standard choice for making roux-based sauces and gravies. Its fine, smooth texture combines easily with melted fat for a sauce with a roux base, so that when heated, the starch grains burst and cook, thickening the sauce liquid.

White flour usually contains 70–75 per cent of the wheatgrain. Most of the bran and wheatgerm have been removed during milling, leaving it almost white, so it is excellent for thickening white sauces. White flour is chemically bleached, making it pale in colour and therefore more suitable for white sauces than unbleached, stoneground flours.

Below: Plain (all-purpose) flour.

STRONG AND SOFT FLOURS

These are flours designed for specific baking uses, not for sauces, but could be used in an emergency if you run out of plain flour. Self-raising (self-rising) flour has chemical agents added during milling which react with heat to make cake mixtures rise during cooking. Strong flour, or bread flour, has a higher proportion of gluten, making it most suitable for bread making. Soft flours, or sponge flours, have a lower gluten content, and are designed for cakes, but they also make good thickeners for light sauces.

WHOLEMEAL, WHEATMEAL AND BROWN FLOURS

All of these flours contain more of the bran and wheatgerm, between 80 and 90 per cent of the grain, which gives them a nutty flavour and coarse texture, and a darker colour than white flour. Because of this, they are not usually chosen for making sauces, but if you don't mind the texture and colour, there's no reason why any of these flours should not be used for thickening sauces. The bonus is that they will add a little extra dietary fibre and nutrients to the dish.

SAUCE FLOUR

This flour has been recently introduced, and has a lower protein level than ordinary wheat flour, so that sauces made with it are less likely to go lumpy. It is designed specifically for making cooked white sauces and gravies. It is also a good choice for making low-fat sauces, since it is suitable for use in recipes made by the all-in-one, or blending method, in which no fat is used to mix the flour to a paste.

CORNFLOUR

Also known as cornstarch, this fine maize flour is gluten-free. It is light and smooth, producing velvety-textured sauces, usually made by the blending method. For smooth results it has to be mixed to a smooth paste with a little cold liquid (a technique known as slaking) before adding hot liquid. It is widely used in Chinese sauces, and its light, slightly jellied, texture makes it particularly suitable for sweet sauces and blancmange, or light sauces for coating foods.

POTATO FLOUR

Also known as *farine de fécule*, potato flour is made from pure potato starch. It is very fine and smooth and is bright white in colour. It makes a light, clear thickener for sauces without affecting the flavour. You will need to use slightly less potato flour than ordinary plain flour for thickening. It is most suited to the blending method of sauce making, and is often used as a thickener in Chinese and Asian dishes and stir-fry sauces, so it is easily available from Oriental stores.

ARROWROOT

This is a white, finely ground powder made from the root of a tropical tree, which is grown in Central America. It is used as a thickening agent, in the same way as cornflour, for sauces made by the blending method. Whereas cornflour makes an opaque sauce, arrowroot clears when boiled. It is often used in sweet glazes.

Below, clockwise from top left: Cornflour (cornstarch), custard powder, potato flour, arrowroot.

CUSTARD POWDER

Useful for quick custard sauces, this is an unsweetened cornflour-based mix flavoured with vanilla.

A similar result can be achieved by enriching a cornflour sauce with egg yolks and adding vanilla essence. Make up with milk by the blending method. Sweeten to taste.

STORING FLOUR

Store flour in a cool, dark, dry, airy place, away from steam or damp. Place the flour into a clean tin or a storage jar with a close-fitting lid, and always make sure you wash and dry the container thoroughly before refilling it. Check the "use by" dates, and use up the flour within the recommended pack date, or replace it. Don't add new flour to old in a storage jar – it is always best to use up the older flour first.

Once opened, plain white (all-purpose) flour can be stored under the right conditions for about six months, but

wholemeal (whole-wheat) and brown flours have a higher fat content so these are best used within two months. Like all food, flour is best used while fresh – it develops "off" flavours, ultimately becoming rancid, when old. If stored in damp conditions, it tastes musty, so buy in small quantities.

FATS AND OILS

Fats make sauces palatable, and improve their flavour and texture. The ones usually used in sauces are "yellow" fats, such as butter or margarine, or oils. Many are combined with flour in sauces, for example in a roux, a cooked paste, or in beurre manié, a raw paste. Heating flour with fat allows liquid to be incorporated without forming lumps. The classic emulsified sauces, such as hollandaise or mayonnaise, use either melted butter or liquid oils, beaten with eggs until combined and thickened in an emulsion. The same principle is used in reduced sauces, such as beurre blanc, or in oil-based salad dressings such as vinaigrette, where the fat is whisked into a reduced or well-flavoured liquid base to make a smooth emulsion. In salsas and purées, oil is added for flavour by stirring into, or drizzling over, the other ingredients.

Clockwise from top left: Ghee, clarifed butter, concentrated butter.

TYPES OF FAT

Saturated fats are solid at room temperature, and are the ones that can raise cholesterol levels in the blood. Polyunsaturated fats can help lower cholesterol levels; mono-unsaturated fats, which are beneficial in regulating cholesterol levels, are liquid but can be made solid by a process known as hydrogenation. This is the process used to make margarines and spreads.

butter

A natural product made by churning cream, butter has an 80 per cent fat content, which is saturated fat. Butter is made in two basic types, sweetcream and lactic, and both are available salted, lightly salted or unsalted. The choice will depend largely on flavour, according to whether you are making a sweet or savoury sauce. There are other alternatives, however. Clarified butter, ghee or concentrated butters, which can be made at home, will withstand higher temperatures than untreated butter, and will not burn as easily.

margarine

Soft (tub) margarines, made from a blend of vegetable oils and/or animal oils, have a soft, spreadable texture. Hard (packet) margarines have a firmer texture and are made from animal and vegetable fats. Both types have the same fat content as butter, and can be used as a direct substitute for butter in making sweet and savoury sauces. As the flavour is inferior to butter, margarines are best chosen for more robustly flavoured sauces where their own flavour will not be as noticeable.

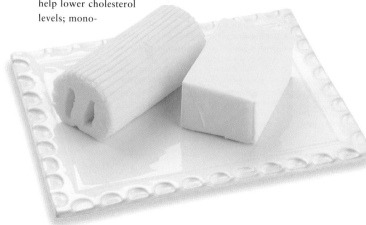

Left: Lactic unsalted butter (left), sweetcream salted butter.

spreads

The wide choice of different spreads on the market is confusing to say the least, but as a rough guide, unless they are labelled "low-fat", or "very low-fat", they are generally suitable for sauce-making. After that, choice is very much a matter of personal preference.

Polyunsaturated vegetable oil spreads: Products described in this way are made either from a single vegetable oil or sunflower oil alone, or from a blend of different vegetable oils. They vary in fat content from 61 to 79 per cent.

Monounsaturated vegetable oil spreads: Made from olive oil or rapeseed oil, these vary in fat content from 60 to 75 per cent.

Below: Margarine tub (left) and block.

Dairy spreads: These contain cream or buttermilk to retain a buttery flavour and smooth texture, while providing a lower-fat alternative to butter. The fat content varies between 61 and 75 per cent.

Reduced-fat spreads: These products are either made from vegetable oils alone or may also contain some dairy or animal fat. Their fat content is between 50 and 60 per cent.

Low-fat spreads and very low-fat spreads: These spreads, popular with the weight-conscious, contain less than 40 per cent fat, and are often as low as 25 per cent. They are not recommended for cooking, although they can be added to all-in-one method sauces.

STORING FAT

All solid fats should be stored in the refrigerator, below 4°C/39°F. They should be covered or closely wrapped to protect them from light and air. Keep them away from strong-smelling foods as they can absorb other flavours easily. (The section used for storing butter in most refrigerators is in the door, and is not quite so cold as other parts, so the butter should not become too hard.) Oils tend to

Above, from left: Polyunsaturated, olive, dairy, and reduced-fat spreads.

solidify at low temperatures, so are best kept in a cool cupboard with a temperature of 4–12°C/39–54°F. Keep them away from light, which will cause them to become rancid quickly.

OILS

These fats are liquid at room temperature. They are used in emulsion sauces, such as mayonnaise or salad dressings, usually balanced with vinegar or other acids, such as citrus juices. However, they can also be used as a

Below, left to right: Very low-fat and low-fat spreads.

direct replacement for butter or hard fats in roux or similar flour-thickened sauces, with good results. With the exception of coconut oil and palm oil, they are mostly rich in unsaturated fat, which helps reduce cholesterol levels. The choice of individual oils for a particular sauce depends largely on flavour and personal taste.

Groundnut (peanut) oil: Made from peanuts, this is usually used where a mild flavour is required.

Sesame seed oil: Usually used for flavouring Oriental sauces at the end of cooking, as it has an intense, rich flavour and burns easily when heated. However it can be heated with care, or mixed half and half with another oil, such as groundnut, if necessary.

Soya oil: A mild-flavoured oil

Below, from left: Groundnut (peanut) oil, sunflower oil, soya oil, sesame oil, walnut oil.

which will withstand high temperatures, this keeps well and is economical to use.

Sunflower oil: A little more expensive to use than soya oil, this versatile, light-flavoured oil is good for sauces or dressings, as it does not mask other flavours.

Nut oils: Walnut and hazelnut oils are the most commonly used nut oils for dressings, lending their rich, distinctive flavours to salads. Use in moderation, perhaps combined with a milder oil, as the flavours can be strong.

olive oils

The characteristics and quality of olive oils vary and depend on variety, growing region and method of production. Many are blended, but the best-quality oils are produced on individual estates. For most sauces, including mayonnaise, it's best to choose

virgin or pure olive oil, and keep the more expensive extra virgin ones for salad dressings, or for drizzling directly over foods. It is more economical to buy olive oils in larger quantities.

Extra virgin first pressed or cold pressed olive oils: These oils are made from the first pressing of the olives, with no extra treatment, such as heat or blending. By law, these oils never have more than 1 per cent acidity, ensuring a fine flavour. They have a distinctive flavour and pungent aroma. They are usually a deep green colour and are sometimes cloudy, although both of these factors vary according to the area where the oil was produced.

Virgin olive oil: This is also cold pressed and unrefined, but has a higher acidity content than extra virgin oil, with a maximum level of 1 to 1.5 per cent.

Pure olive oil: This comes from the third or fourth pressing of the olives, and is usually blended. It has a maximum acid content of 2 per cent. It is mild, rather than overpowering, and therefore widely used in cooking.

Light olive oil: This is a product created during the last pressing of the fruit. The term "light" refers to the clear colour and delicate flavour, not the calorie count.

STORE CUPBOARD

A well-stocked store cupboard (pantry) makes every cook's life a lot easier, and when it comes to sauce making, it really makes sense. Just by keeping a few basic ingredients in stock, you will always be able to whip up an impromptu sauce when the occasion demands, transforming a simple dish into something special.

STOCK CUBES AND POWDERS

There is a wide choice of commercial stock (bouillon) cubes and powders, and these vary in flavour and quality. Good-quality products make adequate substitutes for fresh stock, and certainly they are very convenient to use. However, some tend to be quite salty, so allow for this when adding other seasonings. Follow the pack directions for quantities to use. Generally speaking, it is worth paying a little more for good-quality stock cubes or powder, and it is worth choosing one that is made with natural ingredients for a more natural flavour.

Many supermarkets also now sell cartons of basic ready-made fresh stocks on the chilled foods counter, including beef, chicken, fish and vegetable stock. These are a good substitute for home-made if you're short of time.

Canned consommé makes an excellent substitute for a good brown stock in rich savoury sauces, so is well worth keeping handy in the store cupboard. If you need a light stock, the colour of consommé may be too dark to use, but brands do vary widely.

CANNED TOMATOES AND BOILED SAUCES

Since many of the plum tomatoes we buy out of season are lacking in

Above: Consommé
Left: Stock cubes and powder
Below, clockwise from left: Passata, sugocasa, whole plum tomatoes, tomato purée, chopped tomatoes in tomato juice.

flavour, it's a safer bet to go for good-quality canned tomatoes in recipes, either whole or chopped. The best are from Italy, so check the label carefully. Polpa di pomodoro are finely chopped or crushed. Avoid those with added herbs or spices, which are best added fresh.

Crushed or creamed tomatoes: Sold as sugocasa, polpa and passata (bottled strained tomatoes), and usually packed in convenient jars, long-life packs or bottles, these products are invaluable for sauces.

Below, top row from left: Oyster sauce, soy sauce, Worcestershire sauce, fish sauce, hot pepper sauce.
Bottom row:
Red pesto,
green pesto,
English
mustard.

COOK'S TIP
Chopped canned tomatoes are usually more expensive than whole ones, so you can save valuable pennies by simply chopping them yourself.

Sugocasa and polpa both have a chunky texture, while passata is sieved to a creamy smooth, sauce-like purée.

Tomato purée (paste): This is concentrated, cooked tomato pulp in a strong, thick paste, and is sold in tubes or cans. The strength of different brands varies, so use with care or the flavour can overpower a sauce. Sun-dried tomato paste has a sweet, rich flavour, and is milder than ordinary tomato purée.

COMMERCIAL SAUCES

The huge range of commercially-made flavouring sauces or condiments now available is a boon to the creative cook. The following are some of the most useful to keep in your store cupboard.

Hot pepper sauces: Widely used in West Indian and South American cooking, there are many versions of pepper sauce, the most famous being Tabasco. Use with caution, as they can be fiery hot. These sauces will pep up almost any savoury sauce, marinade or dressing.

Mustards: Ready-made mustards are a blend of ground mustard seeds with flour and salt, often with wine, herbs and other spices. Dijon is often used for classic French sauces and for dressings such as vinaigrette and mayonnaise – it also helps to stabilize the emulsion. Yellow English mustard is a good choice to give colour and bite to cheese sauce or to flavour rich gravies for meat. Milder German mustard is good for a barbecue sauce to serve with chops or sausages. Mild, creamy American mustard is squeezed on hotdogs or burgers. Wholegrain mustard gives a pleasant texture, particularly to creamy savoury sauces and dressings.

Oyster sauce: A thicker-textured

sauce made with the extract of real oysters, this adds a delicious sweet-savoury flavour to sauces for accompanying meat, fish or vegetables (in non-vegetarian dishes).
Pesto: Commercially made pesto is sold in jars, either the traditional green basil pesto, or a red pesto made from sun-dried tomatoes. Use it just as it is as a replacement for fresh pesto sauce to stir into pasta, pepped up with a little freshly grated Parmesan cheese or an extra drizzle of olive oil. You can also add it by the spoonful to enrich and enhance the flavour of tomato sauces, salsas and dressings. Once the jar is opened, this type of product should be treated as fresh and stored in the refrigerator.
Soy sauce: Although this is traditionally used for Chinese and Japanese foods, there is no need to limit its use to Oriental dishes. Use it to flavour and colour all kinds of savoury sauces, marinades and dressings. Light soy sauce is good in light, sweet-and-sour or stir-fry sauces for fish or vegetables, and the richer, sweeter dark soy sauce is best with rich meat sauces, such as satays, or for barbecue sauces.
Thai fish sauce or nam pla: This is a classic Thai sauce made from fermented fish. It has a pungent flavour and is best in cooked sauces. It adds a richness to sauces for both meat and fish.
Worcestershire sauce: This classic English sauce has its origins in India. Its spicy, mellowed, but piquant, flavour enhances savoury sauces, marinades and dressings of any type. It is often used to bring out meaty flavours in gravies and long-cooked casserole sauces.

COCONUT MILK AND CREAM
Coconut milk and cream are used widely in Oriental dishes, particularly those based on spicy and curried sauces. They can be used rather like dairy products, for thickening, enriching and flavouring.
Coconut milk: This is available in cans and long-life packs. It is similar in thickness to single cream.
Coconut cream: This has the thickness of double cream. Creamed coconut is solid and

white; it is sold in solid blocks, so you can cut off just the amount you need and melt it into sauces or in a little hot water.

VINEGARS

These aromatic vinegars are based on malt, wine, beer, cider, rice wine and sugar, and are often used to enhance flavour in sauces or as emulsifiers. Dark, long-matured sherry or balsamic vinegars have intense, powerful flavours and you may only need a few drops.

Below: Red and white wine vinegars and fruit vinegars are useful for salad dressings.

HERBS AND SPICES

Many sauce recipes call for herbs and spices to add flavour and colour, and there's no end to the variety you can buy nowadays, especially in the larger supermarkets and good grocers. Generally speaking, herbs are the leafy tops and stems of an edible plant, and spices are from the berries, seeds, bark and roots.

CULINARY HERBS

It's worth growing a few of the more useful common herbs yourself. Some herbs grown in pots on the kitchen windowsill, will always be handy when you need to snip off a few sprigs. It is considerably cheaper, too, as supermarket fresh herbs, even the ones in pots, have a limited life and can be quite costly. A useful basic selection to grow at home would include parsley, chives, thyme,

mint, oregano, sage, bay and dill.

When cooking with herbs, you don't need to be too precise. Treat the measurements quoted in recipes as a general guide, and add the herbs according to your personal preference.

dried and frozen herbs

Dried herbs are useful to keep in the cupboard for emergencies, but always plump for fresh in preference if you can get them – it will make a noticeable difference to the flavour of the dish. Many of the delicate-leafed herbs, such as basil, coriander or chervil, do not dry successfully, but the ones that are worth buying dried are thyme, rosemary, parsley, mint, oregano,

Above, clockwise from top left: Chopped and frozen herbs – coriander, parsley, chives.

tarragon and dill. Store dried herbs in airtight containers in a cool place away from light, and use them quickly as their flavour is soon lost.

Below, clockwise from bowl: Curry paste, nutmeg, cinnamon sticks, vanilla pods (beans), salt, whole coriander, cumin seeds, black, green, white peppercorns.

Left, clockwise from top: Freeze-dried mint, freeze-dried parsley, freeze-dried dill, freeze-dried tarragon, dried thyme, dried rosemary. Centre: Freeze-dried oregano.

Above, clockwise from left: Mint, bay, thyme.

Frozen herbs, such as parsley, chives and coriander, retain more of the flavour of fresh herbs and can be very useful and convenient – they can be added to a sauce or dressing straight from the freezer.

SALT AND PEPPER

Good-quality sea salt has a more intense flavour than "table" or "cooking" salt. There are different varieties of sea salt with distinctive flavours. Strong black peppercorns, mild white and very mild green are all worth storing.

CULINARY SPICES

Keep a good store of spices in the kitchen. A useful selection includes whole nutmeg, cinnamon sticks, vanilla pods, coriander seeds, cumin seeds and curry paste (curry pastes keep longer than powders). **Cinnamon sticks:** These have a sweet, spicy flavour and are widely used in sweet sauces and chutneys. They can be crushed or used whole and removed at the end of cooking. **Coriander:** These seeds are valued for seasoning pickles and chutneys; they have a mild sweet flavour. **Cumin:** A key ingredient in chutneys and curries, these seeds have a pronounced and slightly bitter taste. **Curry paste:** This is sold in a range of strengths and flavours. It keeps for much longer than curry powder. **Vanilla pods (beans):** Infuse these dried pods in milk or cream for sweet sauces and custards. Store in a jar of caster sugar to make vanilla sugar. **Whole nutmeg:** Freshly grated whole nutmeg is much better than the powdered variety, which quickly loses its flavour.

EXTRACTS AND FLOWER WATERS

Vanilla or other flavouring extracts can be very convenient, but choose carefully, as some are inferior artificial flavourings. Check the label – it should describe the contents as pure vanilla extract or extract of vanilla, not vanilla flavouring.

Flower waters are a delightful way to flavour cold sweet sauces, syrups and creams in particular, but occasionally they are used in Middle Eastern savoury sauces. The best known are rose and orange flower water, and should be used in small amounts – the best quality flower waters are triple-distilled, so just a few drops will add a delicately exotic scent to a creamy sauce.

Right, from left: Flower essences, vanilla extract, almond essence.

YOGURT

Yogurt and other lower-fat dairy products, such as fromage frais, make excellent lighter replacements for cream in many sauces, savoury or sweet. In cooking, stabilize yogurt with cornflour (cornstarch).

Greek (US strained plain) yogurt: This may be made from either cow's or sheep's milk. It is richer in flavour and texture than most yogurts, but still only has a fat content of around 8–10 per cent, so it makes a light substitute for cream in sauces.

Low-fat yogurt: Semi-skimmed (low-fat) or skimmed milk are used to make low-fat yogurt. Both types are quite sharp and tangy, which can be refreshing in light sauces. Low-fat yogurt is also used as a base for many dips and dressings.

EGGS

As a general rule, medium eggs are the size to use for recipes, unless the recipe states otherwise, but you may find it useful to have small eggs for using to enrich or thicken modest quantities of sauces.

The freshness of supermarket eggs is easily checked, as most are individually marked with a date stamp on their shells. Fresh eggs should store well for 2 weeks,

Below, clockwise from top: Parmesan, mascarpone, ricotta, Cheddar, Gruyère.

Left: Eggs.

providing that the shell is not damaged or dirty. Egg shells are porous, so they are best stored at the bottom of the refrigerator away from strong-smelling foods. As a general rule, before use, eggs should be left at room temperature for about 30 minutes.

SAFETY TIP

Because of the slight risk of contamination in raw eggs, it is recommended that pregnant women, young children, elderly people or anyone weakened by chronic illness should avoid eating raw or lightly cooked eggs.

CHEESES

Many hard cheeses can be grated and melted into sauces.

Strong, hard cheeses: Mature cheeses such as Cheddar, Gruyère and Parmesan will grate easily and melt into hot sauces. Their fine flavour complements pasta sauces or a creamy white sauce to pour over vegetables. Always grate these cheeses freshly as you need them. Once cheese is added to a sauce, heat it gently without boiling, or it will overcook and become stringy.

Soft, fresh cheeses: Those of a creamier consistency such as ricotta or mascarpone are used to enrich sauces and dips, from tomato sauces to fruit purées or custards. Ricotta is light and mild, and makes a good base for dips. Mascarpone is rich, creamy and high in fat, and can be used in the same way as thick cream.

SAUCE-MAKING EQUIPMENT

Making sauces requires very little in the way of specialist items, but a carefully selected set of basic equipment will help make tasks such as boiling, whisking and straining much easier. You may even find that most of these items are already in your kitchen. Shop around for those you still need, as quality varies enormously.

PANS

The rule here is to choose the right pan for the job, which means that your pans do not necessarily have to be a matching set. Some pans may be suitable for more than one task, but you will need a variety of sizes and types. Look for solid, heavy pans that are stable when empty, and have tight-fitting lids and firmly riveted handles. Buying good-quality pans is an investment, as they will last for years, but cheap, thin pans will not only wear out quickly, but also conduct heat unevenly and cause burnt spots. The following examples will cover most culinary requirements.
• Milk pan with high sides and a lip. This may be non-stick, but this is not essential.

• Three pans with lids, ranging in size from about 1 litre/1¼ pints/4 cups to 7 litres/12⅓ pints/30 cups. They should be deep and straight-sided to minimize the amount of evaporation.
• Sauté pan – this is a deep pan with straight sides.
• Double boiler – a useful pan for making delicate creams and custards, and melting ingredients such as chocolate. If you don't have one, you can improvise by placing a heatproof bowl over a pan of gently boiling water.

Top: Double boiler and heatproof bowl placed over pan
Right, clockwise from left: Enamelled, anodized aluminium and copper pans.

materials for saucepans

Stainless steel: This is attractive and hard-wearing, and providing they have a thick base with aluminium or copper, the pans will conduct heat evenly and efficiently.

Anodized aluminium: Light and easy to clean, this conducts the heat well and does not corrode. The metal reacts when in contact with acid and alkaline, so food should not be left to stand for too long in these pans.

Copper: These pans are expensive but conduct heat very efficiently and are attractive and durable. Choose pans with a stainless steel lining, which is harder-wearing than tin.

Enamelled cast iron: This is heavy, but conducts the heat well, evenly and slowly. These pans retain the heat for a long time, and are hard-wearing and durable.

WOODEN SPOONS

A good assortment of wooden spoons is essential, and it is a good idea to keep them for individual uses. You might reserve one for spicy sauces, one for creams and custards, and so on; then there is no risk of flavour transfer. A good selection includes a wooden spoon, a wooden corner spoon with an edge to reach into the rims of pans, and a flat-edged wooden spatula.

WHISKS

Balloon whisks and spiral sauce whisks are efficient for blending or whisking. It is useful to have two different sizes.

LADLES

Available in various sizes, ladles are very useful for spooning and

Below, from left: Draining spoon, ladles with variable cup shapes.

Above, from left: Spiral sauce whisks, balloon whisk, wooden spoons.

pouring sauces over foods. Some smaller ones have a useful lip for more precise pouring. Stainless steel ladles are the best. A slotted stainless steel draining spoon is invaluable for skimming and removing small pieces of ingredients from sauces.

Above: Measuring jug and spoons

MEASURING JUG

Choose a solid jug (pitcher) marked with standard measurements. Heatproof glass is ideal, as it is easy to see the liquid level and can take boiling liquids, yet the handle remains cool as it is a poor heat conductor. Stainless steel jugs are attractive and hard-wearing.

MEASURING SPOONS

A set of measuring spoons, either imperial or metric (select the type to correspond to the instructions you prefer to follow) is essential for accurate measuring the small amounts of sauce ingredients. Ordinary table cutlery varies widely in capacity and should not be used for measuring. Spoon measurements given in recipes are always level.

SIEVE AND CHINOIS

A fine-meshed stainless steel sieve is essential for sauce making; look for a double-mesh, hard-wearing sieve. It can also be very useful to have a chinois, a cone-shaped sieve that is used for straining and puréeing. range of ingredients.

Above, from left: Chinois and sieve.

ELECTRICAL EQUIPMENT

Although not essential for making sauces, a blender, food processor, hand blender or whisk can take much of the hard work out of many sauces and dressings. A food processor is brilliant for chopping and slicing. Hand-held electric blenders are perhaps more versatile and convenient than larger machines for sauces, as they can be used to blend or purée mixtures in a pan or jug (pitcher), and are easy to clean by simply swishing in hot soapy water after use. A hand-held electric whisk is also useful for quick beating and whisking.

Left: Hand-held electric whisk.
Below: Hand blender.

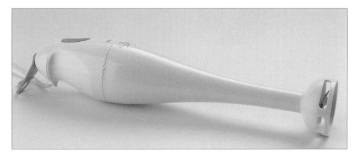

STERILIZING AND STORING

Many sauces based on flour, cheese or vegetables will keep for at least two weeks. Store in a sterilized glass jar. Jars can be boiled on top of the stove or heated in the oven.
• Stove-top sterilizing calls for a large deep pan with a wide bottom.
• For oven sterilizing, the jars are arranged on a roasting pan or baking tray, which should be level on the bottom (so the jars do not slide about) and have at least a shallow rim to prevent them from sliding off when lifted.
• Special tongs are available for lifting hot jars.
• Filling jars is easy using a wide-topped jam funnel and a small ladle or small heatproof jug.

storing fresh sauces

A wide variety of fresh sauces can be prepared ahead and chilled or frozen. White sauces, wine sauces and tomato-based sauces are all excellent freezer candidates: make a big batch and freeze useable portions ready for thawing and reheating in the microwave.
• Airtight plastic freezer containers are ideal for chilling or freezing. Remember to allow a little headspace rather than filling the container to the brim.
• Foil freezer bags are brilliant for sauces. They have a gusset and base, so they stand up filling, and the top folds over to seal.
• Alternatively, supporting a freezer bag in a freezerproof bowl or jug to fill and freeze it is a good idea. When the sauce is solid, lift the bag out of the container and place in the freezer for long-term storage.

MAKING BASIC STOCKS

Commercial stock cubes and bouillon powder won't match the flavour of home-made stock; however, they can be useful for enriching a stock that lacks flavour. Heat it until boiling, then stir in a stock cube or a teaspoonful of bouillon powder. Each recipe makes about 1 litre/1¾ pints/4 cups.

BEEF STOCK

INGREDIENTS
675g/1½lb shin (shank) of beef, diced
1 large onion, chopped
1 large carrot, chopped
1 celery stick, chopped
bouquet garni
6 black peppercorns
2.5ml/½ tsp sea salt
1.75 litres/3 pints/7½ cups water

1 Place all the ingredients in a large pan and slowly bring to the boil.

2 Cover the pan and simmer very gently for 4 hours, skimming occasionally to remove scum. Strain the stock and cool.

FISH STOCK

INGREDIENTS
1kg/2¼lb white fish bones and trimmings
1 large onion, sliced
1 large carrot, sliced
1 celery stick, sliced
bouquet garni
6 white peppercorns
2.5ml/½ tsp sea salt
150ml/¼ pint/⅔ cup dry white wine
1 litre/1¾ pints/4 cups water

1 Place the ingredients in a pan and bring to the boil.

2 Skim any scum from the surface, cover the pan and simmer for 20 minutes. Strain and allow to cool.

CHICKEN STOCK

INGREDIENTS
1 chicken carcass
chicken giblets
1 leek, chopped
1 celery stick, chopped
bouquet garni
5ml/1 tsp white peppercorns
2.5ml/½ tsp sea salt
1.75 litres/3 pints/7½ cups water

1 Break up the carcass, place in a pan with the remaining ingredients. Bring to the boil.

2 Reduce the heat, cover and simmer for 2½ hours, skimming off scum occasionally. Strain and cool.

MAKING A BOUQUET GARNI
A traditional bouquet garni usually contains a bay leaf, a sprig of thyme and a few sprigs of parsley, but this can be varied according to taste, and to suit the dish you are making. Other vegetables or herbs you may like to include are a piece of celery for poultry dishes; a rosemary sprig for beef or lamb; a piece of fennel or leek, or a strip of lemon rind, for fish dishes.

Tie the herbs together firmly with fine cotton string, so the bundle is easy to remove from the stock after cooking.

Alternatively, tie the herbs in a clean muslin (cheesecloth) square. Leave a long length of the string to tie to the pan handle.

VEGETABLE STOCK

INGREDIENTS

500g/1¼lb chopped mixed vegetables, such as onions, carrots, celery, leeks
bouquet garni
6 black peppercorns
2.5ml/½ tsp sea salt
1 litre/1¾ pints/4 cups water

1 Place all the ingredients in a large pan and slowly bring to the boil.

2 Skim any scum from the surface, then reduce the heat and cover the pan. Simmer gently for 30 minutes. Strain the stock and allow it to cool before chilling.

KEEPING STOCK CLEAR

For a clear soup it is important to keep the stock clear; avoid boiling the stock but cook it very gently, and skim the top from time to time.

1 Trim any fat from the meat or bones before adding to the stock pan, as excess fat will affect the clarity of the stock.

2 Keep the heat at a low simmer, and skim off any scum as it gathers on the surface during cooking. Most vegetables can be added to stock for flavour, but potatoes tend to break down and make the stock cloudy so it's best to avoid these.

3 Strain the stock through a sieve lined with muslin (cheesecloth), and avoid pressing the solids, as this may spoil the stock's clarity.

REMOVING FAT FROM STOCK

Excess fat should be removed to improve the look and taste; it also helps keep the stock clear.

1 Let the stock stand until the fat surfaces, then skim off the fat with a large, shallow spoon. To absorb more grease, blot the surface with several layers of kitchen paper.

2 Then, drop in a few ice cubes. The fat will set around the ice so it can be simply spooned off.

3 Alternatively, cool then chill until the fat layer rises to the surface and sets. Then the fat can simply be lifted off. Use a large spoon to remove the solidified fat.

HOW TO STORE STOCK

Stock will keep for a week in the refrigerator or freezes well. Reduce it to take up less freezer space.

1 To freeze, pour into airtight containers, allowing 2.5cm/1in headspace for expansion, then seal and freeze for up to 3 months.

2 To freeze stock in convenient portions to add to sauces, pour into ice cube trays for freezing.

COOK'S TIPS
• Do not salt stock: season in later use.
• For a brown stock from beef or veal bones, roast the bones in a hot oven for 40 minutes. Add vegetables half-way through. Deglaze the pan with water and then simmer as usual.
• For concentrated stock, simmer until reduced and syrupy enough to coat the back of a spoon. At its most concentrated it will set to a solid jelly that will richly flavour sauces and soups.

FLOUR-BASED SAUCES

The standard way to adjust the consistency of a sauce is to thicken it with a flour. There are three basic methods for this – roux, blending, or all-in-one.

Many of the classic white sauces are based on a "roux" – a cooked mixture of flour and fat. The most basic white sauce uses milk, but by varying the liquid used, other well-known white sauces can be made. For a classic béchamel sauce, the milk is flavoured with vegetables and herbs. For velouté sauce, the milk is replaced with stock, giving it a more opaque appearance, and the cooked sauce may be enriched with cream. Brown sauces or gravy are made by browning the roux, usually with onions, before adding stock or other liquid such as wine.

BASIC RECIPE FOR WHITE ROUX SAUCES

Using the classic roux method, you can adjust the amount of thickening to create varying consistencies. A pouring sauce is poured directly over foods when serving. The slightly thicker coating sauce is used to make a smooth covering for fish or vegetables.

For a pouring consistency:
15g/½ oz/1 tbsp butter
15g/½ oz/2 tbsp plain (all-purpose) flour
300ml/½ pint/1¼ cups liquid

For a coating consistency:
25g/1oz/2 tbsp butter
25g/1oz/¼ cup plain (all-purpose) flour
300 ml/½ pint/1¼ cups liquid

MAKING A ROUX-BASED WHITE SAUCE

When making a roux, stir the paste over the whole pan base, and add the liquid gradually; heating the liquid first helps to avoid lumps.

1 Melt the butter in a pan, then add the flour. Cook on a low heat and stir for 1–2 minutes. Allow the mixture to bubble until it resembles a honeycomb in texture but does not brown. It is important to cook well at this point, to allow the starch grains to swell and burst, and avoid lumps forming later.

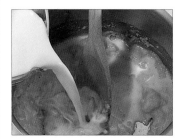

2 Off the heat, gradually stir in the liquid, which may be either hot or cold. Return to the heat and stir until boiling. Reduce the heat and simmer, stirring constantly, for 2 minutes, until the sauce is thickened and smooth.

BLENDING METHOD

Blending-method sauces are usually made with cornflour (cornstarch), arrowroot, potato flour or sauce flour. Cornflour and sauce flour make light, glossy sauces that are good for freezing. If you need a crystal-clear result for glazing, use arrowroot or potato flour. The liquid may be milk, stock, fruit juice or syrup from canned or poached fruit. As a guide, you will need about 20g/¾oz/3 tbsp cornflour or sauce flour to thicken 300ml/½ pint/1¼ cups liquid to a pouring consistency. Arrowroot or potato flour are slightly stronger, so use approximately 15g/½oz to 300ml/½ pint/1¼ cups liquid to obtain the same consistency.

1 Place the flour in a bowl and add just enough liquid to make a smooth, thin paste. Heat the remaining liquid in a pan until almost boiling.

2 Pour a little hot liquid on to the blended mixture, stirring. Pour the mixture back into the pan, whisking, to avoid lumps. Return to the heat and stir until boiling, then simmer gently for 2 minutes, stirring until thickened and smooth.

ALL-IN-ONE METHOD

This uses the same ingredients and proportions as the roux method, but the liquid must be cold. Place the flour, butter and liquid in a pan and whisk over a moderate heat until boiling. Stir for 2 minutes, until thickened and smooth.

USING AN EGG YOLK LIAISON

This is a simple way to lightly thicken milk, stock, cream or reduced liquids. It is good for enriching savoury white or velouté sauces. Two egg yolks enrich and thicken about 300ml/½ pint/1¼ cups liquid. A mixture of egg yolk and cream has the same effect: add it off the heat to avoid curdling.

Stir 30ml/2 tbsp hot liquid or sauce into two yolks in a bowl. Return it to the rest of the sauce. Heat gently, stirring, without boiling.

MAKING BEURRE MANIÉ

Literally translated as "kneaded butter", this is a mixture of flour and butter. It can be stirred into a simmering sauce, poaching liquid or cooked dish to thicken the juices. It's a convenient way to adjust a sauce or dish at the end of cooking, and easy to control as you can add the exact amount required. Any leftover beurre manié can be chilled, covered, for two weeks.

1 Place equal amounts of butter and flour in a bowl and knead together with your fingers or a wooden spoon to make a smooth paste.

2 Drop teaspoonfuls of the beurre manié paste into the simmering sauce, whisking thoroughly to incorporate each spoonful before adding the next, until the sauce is thickened and smooth and the desired consistency is achieved.

INFUSING FLAVOURS

To infuse flavours into milk, stock or other liquids before using in sauces such as béchamel, pour the liquid into a saucepan and add thin slices or dice of onion, carrot and celery, a bouquet garni, peppercorns or a mace blade. Bring the liquid slowly to the boil, then remove the pan from the heat. Cover and leave to stand for about 10 minutes. Strain the milk to remove the flavourings before use.

ADDING FLAVOURINGS TO FLOUR-BASED SAUCES

The follow variations and add variety to a basic sauce.
• Stir 50g/2oz/½ cup grated Cheddar or other strong cheese into a basic white sauce with 5ml/1 tsp wholegrain mustard and a generous dash of Worcestershire sauce.
• Wine livens up the flavour of most stock-based sauces – boil 60ml/4 tbsp red or white wine in a pan until well-reduced, then stir into the finished sauce with a grating of nutmeg or black pepper.
• Add chopped herbs a few minutes before the end of the cooking time.

FIXING A LUMPY SAUCE

If a flour-thickened sauce is lumpy, don't despair – it can be corrected.

1 First, whisk the sauce hard with a light wire whisk to smooth out lumps, then reheat gently, stirring.

2 If the sauce is still not smooth, rub it through a fine sieve, pressing firmly with a wooden spoon. Reheat gently, stirring.

3 Alternatively, process the sauce in a food processor until smooth. Reheat gently, stirring.

KEEPING SAUCES HOT

1 Pour into a heatproof bowl and place over a pan of very gently simmering water.

2 To avoid a skin, place lightly oiled or wetted greaseproof or non-stick baking paper on the sauce.

DEGREASING SAUCES

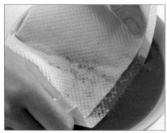

Remove any fat from a hot sauce or gravy with a flat metal spoon. Drag the flat surface of a piece of kitchen paper over the surface to absorb final traces of grease.

MAKING A ROUX-BASED BROWN SAUCE

The base for many sauces for meat, brown onions and vegetables before adding flour. The fat can be butter and oil, or dripping. Butter alone is unsuitable as it burns easily at high temperatures. Use about 30ml/2 tbsp oil and 25g/1oz/¼ cup flour to 600ml/1 pint/2½ cups brown stock. At the last moment, stir in 15g/½ oz/1 tbsp chilled butter.

1 Melt the fat and fry 1 small, finely chopped onion until soft and brown. Sprinkle on the flour and stir over a low heat for 4–5 minutes, until rich brown.

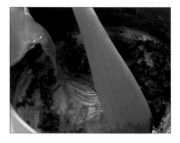

2 Remove from the heat and gradually stir in the liquid, either hot or cold. Return to the heat and stir until boiling. Simmer gently, stirring, for 2 minutes, until thick and smooth. The sauce may be strained to remove the onions.

DEGLAZING FOR SAUCE

Deglazing means adding a little liquid after roasting or pan-frying to dilute rich juices into sauce. Spoon off excess fat and scrape sediment from the pan as you stir in liquid.

1 Tilt the pan and spoon off excess fat from the surface of the juices.

2 Stir in a few tablespoons of wine, stock or cream.

3 Simmer, stirring and scraping as the sauce boils. Boil rapidly until syrupy, then pour over the food.

MAKING GRAVY

Good gravy should be smooth and glossy, never heavy and floury. It's usually best to use the minimum of thickening, but this can be adjusted to taste. Providing the meat has been roasted to rich brown, the meat juices will have enough colour. If it is pale, a few drops of gravy browning can be stirred in.

1 For thickened gravy, skim off all except about 15ml/1 tbsp fat from the juices in the roasting pan. Gradually stir in about 15ml/1 tbsp flour, scraping sediment and juices.

2 Place the pan on the heat and stir until bubbling. Cook, stirring constantly, for 1–2 minutes until browned and the flour is cooked.

3 Gradually stir in the liquid, until the gravy is the desired thickness. Simmer for 2–3 minutes, stirring, and adjust the seasoning.

VEGETABLE SAUCES AND SALSAS

Many sauces use vegetables for flavour, colour and texture. There are endless opportunities for different sauces from the basic techniques. Puréed or chopped vegetables are used for cooked sauces or fresh salsas. Vegetable sauces and salsas are often the fresh and light alternatives to classic rich sauces, and they are invariably very easy and quick to make.

BASIC TOMATO SAUCE

Fresh tomatoes must be ripe and plum tomatoes are best. Canned should be plain not flavoured. Peel fresh tomatoes before using and use about 500g/1¼lb tomatoes instead of each 400g/14oz can in these, and other, recipes.

Makes about 450ml/¾ pint/scant 2 cups

INGREDIENTS

1 clove garlic, finely chopped
1 small onion, finely chopped
1 celery stick, finely chopped
15ml/1tbsp olive oil
15g/½ oz/1 tbsp butter
400g/14oz can chopped tomatoes
handful of basil leaves
salt and ground black pepper

1 Cook the onion, garlic and celery in the oil and butter.

2 Continue cooking the onion mixture over low heat, stirring occasionally, for about 15–20 minutes or until the onions soften and are just beginning to colour.

3 Stir in the tomatoes and bring to the boil. Reduce the heat, cover and cook gently for 10–15 minutes, stirring occasionally, until thick.

4 Tear or roughly chop the basil leaves and stir into the sauce. Adjust the seasoning with salt and pepper and serve hot.

COOK'S TIP
A soffritto (Italian), or sofrito (Spanish), is the base of many Mediterranean meat or tomato sauces. Recipes may list "soffritto" as an ingredient. For basic soffritto, finely chopped onion, garlic, green (bell) pepper and celery, perhaps with carrot or pancetta, are sautéed slowly until soft and caramelized.

QUICK SALSA CRUDO

This is literally a "raw sauce" of vegetables or fruits, and it's easy to create your own combinations of flavour. A good basic start for a salsa crudo is chillies, peppers, onions, and garlic. Serve with grilled chicken, pork, lamb or fish.

1 Peel, deseed or trim the vegetables as necessary, then use a sharp knife to cut them into small, even dice. Try to combine texture and colour as well as flavours, and use chillies and other very spicy ingredients sparingly. Put all the diced ingredients into a bowl.

2 Add 15–30ml/1–2 tbsp olive oil and a squeeze of lime or lemon juice and stir in finely chopped fresh basil, coriander (cilantro), flat leaf parsley or mint. Season to taste and toss well before serving.

HOW TO PEEL TOMATOES

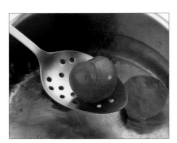

Cut crosses in the tomatoes. Add to a pan of boiling water. Turn off the heat and leave for 30 seconds. Transfer to a bowl of cold water. Peel using a small knife.

Alternatively, skewer a tomato firmly on a fork and hold in a gas flame until the skin blisters and splits. When cool enough to handle, peel using a small knife.

GRILLED VEGETABLES FOR PURÉES AND SAUCES

Chargrilled vegetables are used in many sauces or salsas. Rapid grilling on a barbecue gives full flavour, especially with peppers, aubergines (eggplants), tomatoes, garlic or onions, retaining juices while caramelizing the flesh. This is not always practical, so the best alternative is to roast the vegetables on a baking sheet under a grill.

ROAST VEGETABLE SAUCE

Serve with poultry, meat or game. For a sauce with more texture, simply process for a shorter time.

Makes about 300ml/¹/₂ pint/1¹/₄ cups

INGREDIENTS
2 red or orange (bell) peppers, halved
1 small onion, halved
1 small aubergine (eggplant), halved
2 tomatoes with skins removed
2 garlic cloves, unpeeled
30–45ml/2–3 tbsp olive oil
15ml/1 tbsp lemon juice
25g/1oz/½ cup fresh white breadcrumbs

1 Place the vegetables and garlic cut-sides down on a baking sheet. Cook under a very hot grill, or in a hot oven, until the skins are black and charred, and the flesh is tender.

2 Remove from the heat and leave until cool enough to handle, then peel the peppers and onions.

3 Scoop the flesh from the aubergines, and squeeze the flesh from the garlic.

4 Place all the vegetables in a blender or food processor and process to a smooth purée, adding oil and lemon juice to taste. If you prefer a very smooth sauce, rub the purée through a fine sieve.

5 To thicken a vegetable purée, stir in a small quantity of fresh breadcrumbs and process for a few seconds. The mixture will thicken further when left to stand, so do not add too much bread.

SAVOURY BUTTER SAUCES

The simplest sauce is melted butter flavoured with lemon juice or herbs. A more refined version uses clarified butter, which has moisture and added ingredients removed. Emulsions of butter with vinegar or other flavourings make rich beurre blanc or hollandaise sauce. Cold flavoured butters flavour and moisten hot foods, and can be shaped prettily for extra garnish.

BLENDER HOLLANDAISE

This rich butter sauce is quick and easy to make in a blender.

Makes 250ml/8fl oz/1 cup

INGREDIENTS
60ml/4 tbsp white wine vinegar
6 peppercorns
1 bay leaf
3 egg yolks
175g/6oz/¾ cup clarified butter
salt and ground black pepper

1 Simmer the vinegar, peppercorns and bay leaf in a small pan until reduced to about 15ml/1 tbsp. Discard the flavourings.

2 Place the egg yolks in a blender and start the motor. Add the reduced liquid through the feeder tube and blend for 10 seconds.

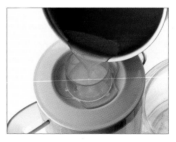

3 Heat the butter until hot. With the motor running, pour the butter through the feeder tube in a thin, steady stream until the sauce is thick and smooth. Season to taste with salt and pepper, and serve warm with poached fish, eggs or vegetables.

CORRECTING CURDLING

If hollandaise sauce is overheated, or if the butter is added too quickly, it may curdle and become slightly granular in texture. If this happens, remove it from the heat immediately, before the sauce separates.

Quickly drop an ice cube into the sauce, then beat hard until the cube melts and cools the sauce. It also helps to stand the base of the pan in a bowl of iced water whilst whisking in the ice cube.

BEURRE BLANC

This is one of the simplest sauces to make. White wine and vinegar are reduced in volume over a high heat to produce an intense flavour. Butter is whisked into the liquid to enrich and thicken it. This is good with poached or grilled fish or chicken.

1 Place 45ml/3 tbsp each of white wine vinegar and dry white wine in a small pan with a finely chopped shallot. Bring to the boil and boil until reduced to about 15ml/1 tbsp.

2 Cut 225g/8oz/1 cup chilled unsalted (sweet) butter into small cubes. On a low heat, gradually whisk in the butter, piece by piece, allowing each piece to melt and be absorbed before adding the next. Season to taste and serve at once.

HOW TO CLARIFY BUTTER

Clarified butter is heated until the moisture evaporates and ingredients other than fat (for example, salt) separate out, leaving clear rich fat. Clarified butter, ghee in Indian cooking, keeps well and can be heated to higher temperatures than ordinary butter without burning. It can be used for sautéing, and in sauces it gives a mild flavour and a high gloss. There are two main methods of clarifying.

Heat the butter in a pan with an equal quantity of water until it melts. Remove from the heat and leave to cool until the butter sets. Carefully lift out the fat, leaving the water and solids behind.

Alternatively, melt the butter over low heat. Cook gently until it stops spitting and a sediment forms. Skim off scum. Strain through a sieve lined with muslin (cheesecloth).

MAKING SAVOURY BUTTERS

Flavoured butters can be shaped or piped decoratively to serve with steaks or poached or grilled fish.

To make a herb-flavoured butter, finely chop your choice of fresh herbs. Beat the butter until softened then stir in the herbs to mix evenly.

MAKING SHAPED SLICES

To make butter slices, chill the softened herb butter lightly. With your hands, roll the butter into a long sausage-shape and wrap in baking parchment or clear film (plastic wrap). Chill and cut off slices of the butter as required.

PIPING BUTTER

Soften the butter before filling the pipe then, using a star nozzle, squeeze on to baking parchment.

MAKING SHAPED BUTTERS

Chill lightly, then roll out the butter between sheets of baking parchment. Chill until firm, then remove the top sheet and stamp out small shapes with a cutter.

FLAVOURINGS FOR SAVOURY BUTTERS

Flavoured butters can be rubbed or spread on meat before roasting, grilling or barbecuing; used on foil-wrapped fish; or used for hot breads instead of garlic butter.
• Finely chopped herbs, such as chives, parsley, dill, mint, thyme or rosemary. Use one herb or a combination and add as much as the butter will comfortably absorb, or to achieve the required flavour.
• Finely grated lemon, lime or orange rind and juice.
• Finely chopped canned anchovy fillets.
• Finely chopped gherkins or capers.
• Crushed, dried chillies or finely chopped fresh chillies.
• Crushed, fresh garlic cloves, or roasted garlic purée.
• Ground coriander seeds, curry spices or paste.

SAVOURY EGG SAUCES

Eggs are widely used for thickening and enriching sauces, or for making an emulsion, such as mayonnaise. Freeze spare egg yolks (left from meringue for sauces: stir in a pinch of salt or sugar before freezing to prevent them from thickening.

MAYONNAISE

Hand-whisked mayonnaise is smooth, glossy and perfect with delicately poached salmon or a chicken salad. The choice of oil depends on taste: extra virgin olive oil is often too strong. It's a good idea to use either light olive oil or half olive oil with half sunflower oil, or another lighter-flavoured oil. All ingredients should be at room temperature for a good sauce and to help avoid curdling.

Makes about 300ml/½ pint/1¼ cups

INGREDIENTS

2 egg yolks
15ml/1 tbsp lemon juice
5ml/1 tsp Dijon mustard
300ml/½ pint/1¼ cups light olive oil
salt and ground black pepper

1 Place the egg yolks, lemon juice, mustard, salt and pepper in a bowl and beat the mixture until smooth and evenly combined.

2 Pouring with one hand and whisking with the other, add the oil gradually, drop by drop, making sure that each drop is whisked in before adding more.

3 Once a thick emulsion has formed, the oil can be poured faster, in a fine, steady stream, whisking until the mixture becomes smooth and thick. Season to taste.

BLENDING MAYONNAISE

A food processor or blender wil speed up the process of making mayonnaise. Use a whole egg instead of the yolks.

Process the egg and flavourings for a few seconds then slowly pour in the oil through the feeder tube in a thin, steady stream with the motor running, until the mixture forms a smooth, creamy texture.

CORRECTING CURDLING

If oil is added too quickly, the mayonnaise will separate; this can be corrected if you stop as soon as the mixture begins to separate. Break a fresh egg yolk into a clean bowl. Gradually whisk in the separated mayonnaise, a small spoonful at a time, whisking constantly until it thickens. Keep going until all the mixture is used.

MAYONNAISE VARIATIONS
• Garlic Mayonnaise: add 3–6 crushed garlic cloves.
• Spicy Mayonnaise: add 15ml/1 tbsp mustard, 7–15ml/1½ tsp–1 tbsp Worcestershire sauce and, if you like, a dash of Tabasco sauce.
• Green Mayonnaise: combine 25g/1oz each of parsley and watercress sprigs in a blender or food processor. Add 3–4 chopped spring onions (scallions) and 1 garlic clove. Blend until finely chopped. Add 120ml/4fl oz mayonnaise and blend until smooth. Season to taste.
• Blue Cheese Dressing: mix 8oz/225g crumbled Danish blue cheese into the mayonnaise.

SWEET EGG SAUCES

Sweet egg sauces are often rich and creamy and include fine pouring or thick and creamy custard. Light and fluffy sabayon can be served on its own or as a luxurious sauce.

CUSTARD SAUCE

Crème anglaise is traditional vanilla pouring custard sauce. It is quite different from custard made with cornflour (cornstarch) or custard powder – thinner, richer and more delicate. As well as being served as a classic sauce, either warm or cold, crème anglaise is often used as the base for creams or ice creams. It may be enriched by using cream instead of milk, or flavoured with liqueurs. This must be heated slowly and gently or it will curdle.

Makes about 400ml/14fl oz/1²/₃ cups

INGREDIENTS

300ml/½ pint /1¼ cups milk
1 vanilla pod (bean)
3 egg yolks
15ml/1 tbsp caster (superfine) sugar

1 Heat the milk and vanilla pod until just boiling, then remove from the heat. (To intensify the flavour split the pod lengthways.) Cover and leave to infuse for 10 minutes then strain into a clean pan.

2 Beat the eggs and sugar lightly and pour in the milk, whisking.

3 Heat gently, stirring, until the custard thickens enough to lightly coat a wooden spoon. Remove from the heat and pour into a jug (pitcher) to arrest the cooking.

CORRECTING CURDLING

At first signs of curdling, plunge the pan base into cold water. Whisk in a teaspoonful of cornflour (cornstarch) smoothly, then reheat.

SABAYON SAUCE

1 Whisk 1 egg yolk and 15ml/ 1 tbsp caster (superfine) sugar per portion in a bowl over a pan of simmering water. Whisk in 30ml/ 2 tbsp sweet white wine, liqueur or fruit juice, for each egg yolk. Whisk until frothy and the sauce holds the trail of the whisk. Serve at once or whisk until cool.

BAKED CUSTARD

A classic partner for cooked fruit. Preheat the oven to 180°C/350°F/ Gas 4. Grease an ovenproof dish. Beat 4 large (US extra large) eggs, a few drops of vanilla extract and 15–30ml/1–2 tbsp caster (superfine) sugar. Whisk in 600ml/1 pint/2½ cups hot milk. Strain into the prepared dish. Place in a roasting pan. Pour in warm water to half fill the tin. Bake for 50–60 minutes.

CLASSIC DESSERT SAUCES

As well as the popular custards and flavoured white sauces, quick and easy dessert toppings can be made almost instantly from ready-made ingredients, and these are ideal to serve over scoops of ice cream. They could also be served with pancakes and are particularly popular with children.

HOW TO USE VANILLA

Vanilla pods (beans) are commonly used in sweet dessert sauces, but they are occasionally used to flavour savoury cream sauces.

To flavour sugar, bury a vanilla pod in a jar of caster (superfine) sugar. It can be used as vanilla-flavoured sugar to add to sweet sauces and desserts.

To infuse (steep) milk or cream with vanilla, heat it gently with the vanilla pod over a low heat until almost boiling. Remove, cover and stand for 10 minutes. Remove the pod, rinse and dry; it may be re-used several times in this way.

To get maximum flavour from the pod, use a sharp knife to slit the pod lengthways and open out. Use the tip of the knife to scrape out the sticky black seeds inside and add to the hot sauce.

SPEEDY SAUCES FOR TOPPING ICE CREAM

Lots of store-cupboard ingredients can be quickly transformed into irresistible sauces.

marshmallow melt

Melt 90g/3½oz marshmallows with 30ml/2 tbsp milk or cream in a small pan. Add a little grated nutmeg and spoon over ice cream.

black forest sauce

Drain canned black cherries and blend a little of the syrup with a little arrowroot or cornflour (cornstarch). Add to the remaining syrup in a pan. Heat gently, stirring, until boiling and slightly thick. Add the cherries and a dash of kirsch. Bubble for a few seconds, then use hot, warm or cool.

chocolate-toffee sauce

Chop a Mars bar and heat very gently in a pan, stirring until just melted. Spoon over ice cream and sprinkle with chopped nuts.

marmalade whisky sauce

Heat 60ml/4 tbsp marmalade with 30ml/2 tbsp whisky, until melted and bubbling. Spoon on ice cream.

whisky sauce

Measure 600ml/1 pint/2½ cups milk. Mix 15ml/1 tbsp of the milk with 30ml/2 tbsp cornflour (cornstarch). Bring the remaining milk to the boil and pour a little on the cornflour mixture. Return all to the pan and heat gently, stirring, until thickened. Simmer for 2 minutes. Off the heat, stir in 30ml/2 tbsp sugar and 60–90ml/4–6 tbsp whisky.

PRESENTATION IDEAS

When you've made a delicious sauce for a special dessert, why not make more of it by using it for decoration on the plate, too? Try one of the following simple ideas to make your sauce into a talking point. Individual slices of desserts, cakes or tarts, or a stuffed baked peach, look especially good like this.

MARBLING

Use this technique when you have two contrasting sauces of similar thickness, such as a fruit purée with custard or cream. Spoon alternate spoonfuls of the sauces into a bowl or on to a serving plate, then stir the two sauces lightly together, swirling to create a marbled effect.

YIN-YANG SAUCES

This is ideal for two contrasting colours of purée or coulis, such as a raspberry and a mango fruit coulis. Spoon one sauce on each side of a serving plate and push them together gently with a spoon, swirling one around the other, to make a yin-yang shape.

DRIZZLING

Pour a smooth sauce or coulis into a jug with a fine pouring lip. Drizzle the sauce in droplets or a fine wavy line on to the plate around the food.

PIPING OUTLINES

Spoon a small amount of fruit coulis or chocolate sauce into a piping (pastry) bag fitted with a plain writing nozzle. Pipe the outline of a shape on to a serving plate, then spoon in sauce to fill the inside.

FEATHERING HEARTS

Flood the plate with a smooth sauce, such as chocolate sauce or a fruit purée. Drop in small droplets of pouring (half-and-half) cream from a teaspoon at even intervals. Draw the tip of a small knife through the cream, to drag each drop into a heart.

QUICK SAUCES FOR CRÊPES

rich butterscotch sauce

Melt 75g/3oz/6 tbsp butter, 175g/6oz/1½ cups brown sugar and 30ml/2 tbsp golden (light corn) syrup in a pan over a low heat. Off the heat, add 75ml/5 tbsp double (heavy) cream, stirring until smooth. If you like, add about 50g/2oz/½ cup chopped walnuts. Serve hot with ice cream or crêpes.

orange sauce

Melt 25g/1oz/2 tbsp unsalted (sweet) butter in a heavy pan. Stir in 50g/2oz/¼ cup caster (superfine) sugar and cook until golden. Stir in the juice of 2 oranges and ½ lemon until the caramel has dissolved.

summer berry flambé

Melt 25g/1oz/2 tbsp butter in a frying pan. Add in 50g/2oz/¼ cup caster (superfine) sugar and cook until golden brown. Add the juice of 2 oranges and the grated rind of ½ orange, and cook until syrupy. Add 350g/12oz/3 cups mixed berries and warm through. Add 45ml/3 tbsp of Grand Marnier and set alight in a safe place. When the flames have died, spoon the syrup over the crêpes.

FRUIT SAUCES

From the simplest fresh fruit purée, to a cooked and thickened fruit sauce, there are hundreds of ways to add flavour to puddings, tarts and pies. The addition of a little liqueur or lemon juice can bring out the fruit flavour and prevent discoloration. Some fruit sauces, notably apple and cranberry, also partner meat and poultry, and fresh fruit salsas can cool spicy dishes.

MAKING A FRUIT COULIS

A delicious fruit coulis will add a sophisticated splash of colour and flavour to desserts and ices. It can be made from either fresh or frozen fruit, in any season. Soft fruits and berries such as raspberries, blackcurrants or strawberries, are ideal, and tropical fruit, such as mango and kiwi, can be quickly transformed into aromatic coulis. A few drops of orange flower water or rose water add a scented flavour, but use it with caution – too much will overpower delicate ingredients.

1 Remove any hulls, stems, peel or stones from the fruit.

2 Place the prepared fruit in a blender or food processor and process until smooth.

3 Press the purée through a fine sieve to remove the pips (seeds) or any fibrous parts and create a silk-smooth coulis. Sweeten the coulis to taste with icing (confectioners') sugar, and if necessary add a squeeze of lemon or lime juice to sharpen and intensify the flavour.

COOK'S TIP

For cooked peeled fruit, mash with a potato masher for a coarser purée.

peach sauce

Purée a 400g/14oz can of peaches in light syrup, together with their juice and 1.5ml/¼ tsp of almond essence in a blender or food processor. Transfer to a jug (pitcher) and chill before serving with sponge puddings, tarts, ice creams or mousses. This can be made with other canned fruit.

passion fruit coulis

This coulis is superb with skewered fruit. For example, cut 3 ripe papayas in half and scoop out the seeds. Peel them and cut the flesh into chunks. Thread the chunks on bamboo skewers.

1 Halve eight passion fruit and scoop out the flesh. Purée in a blender for a few seconds.

2 Press the pulp through a sieve and discard the seeds. Add 30ml/ 2 tbsp of lime juice, 30ml/2 tbsp of icing (confectioners') sugar and 30ml/2 tbsp of white rum. Stir well until the sugar has dissolved.

3 Spoon some of the coulis on plates. Place the fruit skewers on top. Drizzle the remaining coulis over the skewers and garnish with a little toasted coconut, if liked.

CHOCOLATE SAUCES

Chocolate sauces are enduringly popular, from simple custards to richly indulgent versions combined with liqueur or cream. They can be served with ice cream and other frozen desserts, but are also delicious with poached pears and a wide range of puddings. Flavoured liqueurs can be chosen to echo the flavour of the dessert, and coffee, brandy and cinnamon all go especially well with chocolate.

The more cocoa solids chocolate contains, the more chocolatey the flavour will be. Plain (semisweet) chocolate may have between 30–70 per cent of cocoa solids. Plain dark (bittersweet) chocolate has around 75 per cent, so if you're aiming at a really rich, dark sauce, this is the best choice. Milk chocolate has 20 per cent cocoa solids. White chocolate contains no cocoa solids, so strictly speaking it is not a chocolate at all, but gets its flavour from cocoa butter.

The best method of melting chocolate is in a double boiler or in a bowl over a pan of hot water. Never allow water or steam to come into contact with the chocolate as this may cause it to stiffen. Overheating will also spoil the flavour and texture.

Plain chocolate should not be heated above 49°C/120°F, and milk or white chocolate not above 43°C/110°F.

For sauce recipes where the chocolate is melted with a quantity of other liquid such as milk or cream, the chocolate may be melted with the liquid in a pan over direct heat, providing there is plenty of liquid. Heat gently, stirring until melted.

Cocoa is ground from the whole cocoa mass after most of the cocoa butter has been extracted.

CREAMY CHOCOLATE SAUCE

Place 120ml/4fl oz/½ cup double (heavy) cream in a pan and add 130g/4½oz chocolate in pieces. Stir over low heat until the chocolate melts. Serve warm or cold.

CHOCOLATE CUSTARD SAUCE

1 Melt 90g/3½oz plain dark (bittersweet) chocolate in a bowl over a pan of hot water.

2 Heat 200ml/7fl oz/scant 1 cup crème anglaise until hot but not boiling and stir in the melted chocolate until evenly mixed. Serve hot or cold.

RICH CHOCOLATE BRANDY SAUCE

Break 115g/4oz plain (semisweet) chocolate into a bowl. Place over a pan of hot water to heat gently until melted. Remove from the heat and add 30ml/2 tbsp brandy and 30ml/2 tbsp melted butter, then stir until smooth. Serve hot.

MAKING MARINADES AND DRESSINGS

Marinades can be savoury or sweet, spicy, fruity or fragrant, to flavour or enhance to all kinds of foods. They're also useful for tenderizing; moistening during cooking; and as the basis of a sauce to serve with the finished dish.

OIL-BASED MARINADES

Choose an oil-based marinade for low-fat foods, such as lean meat, poultry or white fish, which may dry out during cooking. Oil-based marinades are especially useful for grilling and barbecuing, and at their simplest consist of oil with crushed garlic and chopped herbs. Add crushed chillies for a hot and spicy marinade. Do not salt marinades as this draws the juices out of food.

1 Place the marinade ingredients in a measuring jug (pitcher) and beat well with a fork to mix thoroughly. Arrange the food in a single layer in a non-metallic dish and pour the marinade over.

2 Turn the food to coat evenly in the marinade. Cover and leave in the fridge to marinate from 30 minutes to several hours, depending on the recipe. Turn the food occasionally.

3 When ready to cook, remove the food from the marinade. The marinade can be poured into a small pan and simmered for several minutes until thoroughly heated, then served spooned over the cooked food.

WINE- OR VINEGAR-BASED MARINADES

Wine- or vinegar-based mixtures are best with rich foods such as game or oily fish, to add flavour, and to contrast and balance richness. Use herb-flavoured vinegars for oily fish and add chopped fresh herbs, such as tarragon, parsley, coriander (cilantro) and thyme for flavour.

The acid in the wine or vinegar starts the tenderizing process well before cooking. For game, which can have a tendency to be tough, leave in the marinade overnight. Add lemon juice, garlic, black pepper and herbs, and even sherry, cider or orange juice according to your preference.

Yogurt is a good marinade and can be flavoured with crushed garlic, lemon juice, and handfuls of chopped mint, thyme or rosemary for lamb or pork. For fish, use a marinade based on lemon juice with a little oil and lots of black pepper.

1 Measure the ingredients into a jug (pitcher) and beat with a fork.

2 Arrange the food in a wide, non-metallic dish in a single layer and spoon over the marinade. Turn the food to coat evenly. Cover and chill for 30 minutes up to several hours, depending on the recipe.

3 Drain the food of excess marinade before cooking. If the food is to be griddled or grilled (broiled), brush with the marinade during cooking for flavour and to keep it moist.

MAKING A VINAIGRETTE-STYLE DRESSING

A good vinaigrette can do more than dress a salad. It can also be used to baste meat, poultry, seafood or vegetables during cooking. Many classic dressings, such as vinaigrette or French dressing, are based on an oil and acid mixture. The basic proportions are 3 parts oil to 1 part acid beaten together to form an emulsion. This can be done by simply whisking with a fork in a jug (pitcher), or the ingredients can be placed in a screw-topped jar and shaken thoroughly. The oil you choose for a dressing adds character to the flavour, and which one you use for which dressing depends upon your own taste and upon the salad ingredients. A strongly flavoured extra virgin olive oil adds personality to a simple green leaf or potato salad, but can overpower more delicate ingredients. Pure olive oil or sunflower oil adds a lighter flavour. Nut oils, such as walnut or hazelnut, are expensive, but can add a distinctive unusual flavour to a salad when used in small quantities.

The acid in a dressing may be vinegar or lemon juice, and this can define the flavour of the finished salad. Choose from wine, sherry or cider vinegars, herb, chilli or fruit vinegars, to balance or contrast with the salad ingredients and the type of oil. Matured vinegars such as balsamic can be strong

Right: Bottled dressings make pleasing kitchen ornaments and excellent gift ideas.

VARIATIONS

• Use red or white wine vinegar, or use a herb-flavoured vinegar.
• Replace 1 tablespoon of the vinegar with wine.
• Use olive oil, or a mixture of vegetable and olive oils.
• Use 4fl oz/120ml olive oil and 30ml/2 tbsp walnut or hazelnut oil.
• Add 15–30ml/1–2 tbsp Dijon mustard to the vinegar before whisking in the oil.
• Add 15–30ml/1–2 tbsp chopped herbs (parsley, basil, chives, thyme, etc) to the vinaigrette.

in flavour. Balsamic has a strong flavour, because of its ageing in wooden barrels and so the basic proportions of 3 parts oil to 1 of vinegar should be amended to 5 parts oil and 2 of balsamic vinegar.

Lemon juice adds a lively tang. Other fruit juices, such as orange or apple juice can be used for a sweeter, less acid flavour.

classic vinaigrette

To ensure the ingredients blend in a smooth emulsion, they should all be at room temperature.

Put 30ml/2 tbsp vinegar in a bowl with 10ml/2 tsp Dijon mustard, salt and ground black pepper. Add 1.5ml/¼ tsp caster (superfine) sugar if you like. Whisk to combine. Slowly drizzle in 90ml/6 tbsp oil, whisking until the vinaigrette is smooth and well blended. Check the seasoning and adjust if necessary.

creamy orange dressing

This is sufficiently versatile to go with a mixed salad with orange segments and tomatoes; grilled chicken; smoked duck breasts; or chicken kebabs on rice salad.

Serves 4

45ml/3 tbsp half-fat crème fraîche
15ml/1 tbsp white wine vinegar
finely grated rind and juice of 1 small orange
salt and ground black pepper

1 Measure the crème fraîche and wine vinegar into a screw-topped jar with the orange rind and juice.

2 Shake well until evenly combined, then adjust the seasoning to taste as desired.

classic savoury sauces

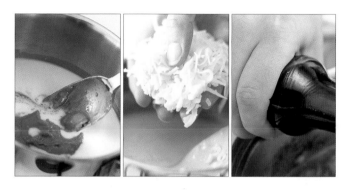

Hot or cold, cooked or raw, master these influential savoury sauces and you'll have countless variations at your disposal. As well as homely white sauces and gravy, there are lightly whisked sauces, juicy tomato or vegetable concoctions, a speedy technique for making satay sauce and the essential mayonnaise recipe. Use this section as a quick reference for checking technique, finding the right proportions of ingredients and seeking out the right accompaniment.

béchamel sauce

This is a creamy white sauce with an excellent, mellow flavour, which makes it ideal for lasagne as well as a suitable base or accompaniment for many fish, egg and vegetable dishes.

2 Over a gentle heat, melt the butter in a pan, remove from the heat and stir in the flour. Return to the heat and cook for 1–2 minutes, stirring, to make a roux.

3 Reheat the flavoured milk until almost boiling. Strain into a jug (pitcher), pressing the vegetables with a spoon to extract the juices.

4 Off the heat, gradually add the milk to the roux, stirring constantly until smooth. Return to the heat, bring to the boil and cook gently until the sauce thickens, stirring constantly. Simmer the sauce gently for 3–4 minutes.

5 Remove the pan from the heat. Season the sauce to taste and stir in the cream.

Serves four

INGREDIENTS

1 small onion
1 small carrot
1 celery stick
bouquet garni
6 black peppercorns
pinch of freshly grated nutmeg or a blade of mace
300ml/½ pint/1¼ cups milk
25g/1oz/2 tbsp butter
25g/1oz/¼ cup plain (all-purpose) flour
30ml/2 tbsp single (light) cream
salt and ground black pepper

1 Peel and finely chop the vegetables. Put the vegetables, flavourings and milk in a pan. Bring to the boil. Remove from the heat

Energy 117kcal/488kJ; Protein 3.4g; Carbohydrate 8.6g, of which sugars 3.8g; Fat 7.9g, of which saturates 5g; Cholesterol 22mg; Calcium 107mg; Fibre 0.2g; Sodium 73mg.

basic white sauce

This white sauce is wonderfully adaptable for all kinds of savoury dishes, but it can be bland so always taste and season carefully.

Serves six

INGREDIENTS

600ml/1 pint/2½ cups milk
25g/1oz/2 tbsp butter
25g/1oz/¼ cup plain (all-purpose) flour
salt and ground black pepper

1 Warm the milk in a pan over a low heat, but do not boil.

2 In a separate pan melt the butter, then stir in the flour and cook gently over low heat for 1–2 minutes to make a roux. Do not allow the roux to brown.

VARIATIONS

This classic white sauce is the "mother" recipe to countless variations, all of which can be prepared by adding one or two ingredients to the base sauce just before it is ready to serve.
• Parsley sauce is traditionally served with bacon, fish or broad (fava) beans. Stir in 30–60ml/2–4 tbsp chopped fresh parsley (to taste) before serving.
• Cheese sauce makes delicious egg and vegetable gratins. Stir in 50g/2oz/½ cup finely grated mature Cheddar and 2.5ml/½ tsp prepared mustard when the sauce has simmered.

3 Remove the pan from the heat, gradually pour in the milk, stirring constantly to make a smooth sauce. Stop adding milk occasionally and stir vigorously to prevent lumps from forming.

4 Return to the heat and bring to the boil slowly, stirring constantly until the sauce thickens.

5 Simmer gently for a further 3–4 minutes until thickened and smooth. Season with salt and ground black pepper to taste.

COOK'S TIPS

• For a thicker, coating sauce, increase the amount of flour to 50g/2oz/½ cup and the butter to 50g/2oz/¼ cup.
• If you aren't using a non-stick pan, use a small whisk to incorporate the flour and milk smoothly.

Energy 91kcal/383kJ; Protein 3.8g; Carbohydrate 8g, of which sugars 4.8g; Fat 5.2g, of which saturates 3.3g; Cholesterol 15mg; Calcium 127mg; Fibre 0.1g; Sodium 68mg.

velouté sauce

This savoury pouring sauce is named after its smooth, velvety texture. It's based on a white stock made from fish, vegetables or meat, so it can easily be adapted to the dish you are serving.

Serves four

INGREDIENTS

600ml/1 pint/2½ cups stock
25g/1oz/2 tbsp butter
25g/1oz/¼ cup plain (all-purpose) flour
30ml/2 tbsp single (light) cream
salt and ground black pepper

1 Heat the stock until almost boiling, but do not boil. In another pan melt the butter and stir in the flour. Cook, stirring, over a moderate heat for 3–4 minutes, or until a pale, straw colour, stirring continuously.

2 Remove the pan from the heat and gradually blend in the hot stock, stirring constantly. Return to the heat and bring to the boil, still stirring constantly, until the sauce thickens.

3 Continue to cook at a very slow simmer, stirring occasionally, until reduced by about a quarter.

4 Skim the surface of the sauce occasionally during cooking to remove any scum, or pour it through a very fine strainer at the end of the simmering time.

5 Just before serving, remove the pan from the heat and stir in the cream. Season to taste.

VARIATIONS

• For a richer flavour in a special dish, replace 30–45ml/2–3 tbsp of the stock with dry white wine or vermouth.
• For a sherry velouté, add 60ml/4 tbsp dry sherry with the stock, reducing the quantity of stock by 60ml/4 tbsp.

Energy 130kcal/538kJ; Protein 1.1g; Carbohydrate 5.2g, of which sugars 0.3g; Fat 11.8g, of which saturates 7.4g; Cholesterol 31mg; Calcium 19mg; Fibre 0.2g; Sodium 130mg.

lemon sauce with tarragon

The sharpness of lemon and the mild aniseed flavour of tarragon transform the delicate flavours of chicken, egg or steamed vegetable dishes.

Serves four

INGREDIENTS

1 lemon
a small bunch of fresh tarragon
1 shallot, finely chopped
90ml/6 tbsp white wine
1 quantity Velouté sauce
45ml/3 tbsp double (heavy) cream
30ml/2 tbsp brandy
salt and ground black pepper

1 Thinly pare the rind from the lemon, taking care not to remove any white pith. Squeeze the juice from the lemon and pour it into a pan. Discard the lemon.

2 Discard the coarse stalks from the tarragon. Chop the leaves and add all but 15ml/1 tbsp to the pan with the lemon rind and shallot.

COOK'S TIP

This sauce goes well with an easy lunch of boiled eggs, or will accompany a range of suitably simple suppers. Try serving with pieces of boned chicken breast, wrapped with streaky (fatty) bacon rashers (strips) and grilled (broiled) or pan-fried.

3 Add the wine and simmer gently until reduced by half. Strain the liquid into a clean pan and return to the hob.

4 Add the Velouté sauce, cream, brandy and reserved tarragon. Heat through, taste and adjust the seasoning if necessary.

Energy 172kcal/713kJ; Protein 1.3g; Carbohydrate 5.6g, of which sugars 0.8g; Fat 12.8g, of which saturates 7.9g; Cholesterol 33mg; Calcium 39mg; Fibre 0.6g; Sodium 46mg.

espagnole sauce

Espagnole is a classic rich brown sauce, ideal for serving with red meat and game. It also makes a delicious, full-flavoured base for other sauces.

2 Gradually stir in the flour and cook for 5–10 minutes over a medium heat until the roux has become a rich brown colour.

3 Remove the pan from the heat and gradually blend in the stock.

Serves four to six

INGREDIENTS

25g/1oz/2 tbsp butter
50g/2oz bacon, chopped
2 shallots, unpeeled and chopped
1 carrot, chopped
1 celery stick, chopped
mushroom trimmings (if available)
25g/1oz/¼ cup plain (all-purpose) flour
600ml/1 pint/2½ cups hot brown stock
bouquet garni
30ml/2 tbsp tomato purée (paste)
15ml/1 tbsp sherry (optional)
salt and ground black pepper

1 Melt the butter in a heavy pan and fry the bacon for 2–3 minutes. Add the shallots, carrot, celery and mushroom trimmings, if using, and cook the mixture for a further 5–6 minutes, or until golden.

4 Slowly bring to the boil, stirring until the sauce thickens. Add the bouquet garni, tomato purée, sherry, if using, and seasoning. Reduce the heat and simmer gently for 1 hour, stirring occasionally.

5 Strain the Espagnole sauce, and gently reheat before serving.

COOK'S TIP

This sauce can be covered and stored in the refrigerator for up to 4 days, or it can be frozen for up to 1 month.

Energy 49kcal/204kJ; Protein 0.8g; Carbohydrate 4g, of which sugars 0.8g; Fat 3.6g, of which saturates 2.2g; Cholesterol 9mg; Calcium 9mg; Fibre 0.3g; Sodium 159mg.

chasseur sauce

This excellent mushroom and wine sauce will transform simple pan-fried or grilled chicken, grilled or roast pork, or rabbit dishes. To give the sauce more flavour use chestnut mushrooms.

Serves three to four

INGREDIENTS

25g/1oz/2 tbsp butter
1 shallot, finely chopped
115g/4oz/2 cups mushrooms, sliced
120ml/4fl oz/½ cup white wine
30ml/2 tbsp brandy
1 quantity Espagnole sauce
15ml/1 tbsp chopped fresh tarragon
 or chervil

3 Pour in the wine and brandy, and simmer over a medium heat until reduced by half.

4 Add the Espagnole sauce and herbs and heat through, stirring occasionally. Serve hot.

1 Melt the butter in a medium or large pan over a medium heat, and fry the shallot, stirring often, until soft but not brown.

2 Add the mushrooms and sauté, stirring occasionally until they just begin to brown.

Energy 166kcal/687kJ; Protein 2g; Carbohydrate 7.5g, of which sugars 2.3g; Fat 10.7g, of which saturates 6.6g; Cholesterol 27mg; Calcium 22mg; Fibre 0.9g; Sodium 279mg.

mustard and dill sauce

Serve this fresh-tasting sauce with any cold, smoked or raw marinated salmon. Note that it contains raw egg yolk, so, as with hollandaise sauce, it is best to avoid serving it to children, pregnant women, the elderly or anyone with a weakened immune system.

Makes about 120ml/4fl oz/½ cup

INGREDIENTS

1 egg yolk
30ml/2 tbsp brown French mustard
2.5–5ml/½–1 tsp soft dark brown sugar
15ml/1 tbsp white wine vinegar
90ml/6 tbsp sunflower or vegetable oil
30ml/2 tbsp finely chopped fresh dill
salt and ground black pepper

1 Put the egg yolk in a small bowl and add the mustard with a little soft brown sugar to taste. Beat with a wooden spoon until smooth.

2 Stir in the white wine vinegar, then whisk in the oil, drop by drop at first, then in a steady stream. As the oil is added, the dressing will start to thicken and emulsify.

3 When the oil has been completely amalgamated, season the sauce with salt and pepper, then stir in the finely chopped dill. Cover and chill for 1–2 hours before serving.

Energy 716kcal/2950kJ; Protein 5.9g; Carbohydrate 6.3g, of which sugars 5.6g; Fat 74.3g, of which saturates 9.6g; Cholesterol 202mg; Calcium 106mg; Fibre 1.5g; Sodium 904mg.

olive oil, tomato and herb sauce

This aromatic sauce is served warm, rather than hot, with grilled or poached salmon or trout. It tastes so great you'll want to provide plenty of good bread or boiled new potatoes to mop up any sauce remaining on the plate.

Makes about 350ml/12fl oz/1½ cups

INGREDIENTS

225g/8oz tomatoes
15ml/1 tbsp finely chopped shallot
2 garlic cloves, finely sliced
120ml/4fl oz/½ cup extra virgin olive oil
30ml/2 tbsp cold water
15ml/1 tbsp lemon juice
caster (superfine) sugar
15ml/1 tbsp chopped fresh chervil
15ml/1 tbsp chopped fresh chives
30ml/2 tbsp torn fresh basil leaves
salt and ground black pepper

COOK'S TIP

It is essential to the flavour of this sauce that you use the best quality olive oil.

1 Peel and seed the tomatoes, then cut them into fine dice.

2 Place the shallot, garlic and oil in a small pan over a very gentle heat and infuse for a few minutes. The ingredients should warm through, but definitely not fry or cook.

3 Whisk in the cold water and lemon juice. Remove from the heat and stir in the tomatoes. Add a pinch of salt, pepper and caster sugar, then whisk in the chervil and chives. Leave to stand for 10–15 minutes. Reheat gently to warm, then stir in the basil before serving.

Energy 776kcal/3200kJ; Protein 3g; Carbohydrate 9.2g, of which sugars 8.7g; Fat 81.1g, of which saturates 11.7g; Cholesterol 0mg; Calcium 100mg; Fibre 4.5g; Sodium 34mg.

mousseline sauce

A truly luscious sauce, that is subtly flavoured, rich and creamy. Try serving it as a dip for prepared artichokes or artichoke hearts, or with shellfish.

Serves four

INGREDIENTS

2 egg yolks
15ml/1 tbsp lemon juice
75g/3oz/6 tbsp softened butter
90ml/6 tbsp double (heavy) cream
extra lemon juice (optional)
salt and ground black pepper

VARIATION

If you like, substitute the lemon juice in this recipe with an equal amount of freshly squeezed lime juice.

1 To make the sauce, whisk the yolks and lemon juice in a bowl over a pan of barely simmering water, or a double boiler, until very thick and fluffy.

2 Whisk in the butter, a very little at a time, allowing each piece to melt before adding the next, until completely absorbed and the sauce has the consistency of mayonnaise.

3 In a separate bowl, whisk the cream until it forms stiff peaks. Fold the whipped cream into the warm sauce and adjust the seasoning to taste. You can also add a little more lemon juice for extra sharpness, depending on the food the sauce is to accompany.

VARIATION

For a lavish accompaniment to special fish dishes such as lobster or Dover sole, stir in 30–45ml/2–3 tbsp caviar before serving as a Caviar Mousseline.

Energy 282kcal/1159kJ; Protein 1.9g; Carbohydrate 0.5g, of which sugars 0.5g; Fat 30.3g, of which saturates 18.1g; Cholesterol 172mg; Calcium 26mg; Fibre 0g; Sodium 123mg.

béarnaise sauce

For classic, plain meat dishes, this herby butter sauce adds a note of sophistication without swamping grilled or pan-fried steak. It also enhances plain vegetables.

Serves two to three

INGREDIENTS

45ml/3 tbsp white wine vinegar

30ml/2 tbsp water

1 small onion, finely chopped

a few fresh tarragon and chervil sprigs

1 bay leaf

6 crushed black peppercorns

115g/4oz/½ cup butter

2 egg yolks

15ml/1 tbsp chopped fresh herbs, such as tarragon, parsley, chervil

salt and ground black pepper

1 Place the vinegar, water, onion, herb sprigs, bay leaf and peppercorns in a pan. Simmer gently until the liquid is reduced by half. Strain and cool.

2 In a separate bowl, cream the butter until soft.

3 In a bowl over a saucepan of gently simmering water, or a double boiler, whisk the egg yolks and liquid until paler in colour and light and fluffy in texture. Do not allow the water to boil rapidly or overheat the egg mixture or it will cook and curdle.

4 Gradually add the butter, half a teaspoonful at a time. Whisk until all the butter has been incorporated before adding any more.

5 Add the chopped fresh herbs and stir in seasoning to taste.

6 Serve warm, not hot, on the side of a grilled steak or allow a good spoonful to melt over new potatoes.

VARIATION

To make Choron sauce, which is very good with roast or grilled lamb, stir in 15ml/1 tbsp tomato purée (paste) to the sauce at the end of step 1.

Energy 335kcal/1378kJ; Protein 2.6g; Carbohydrate 1.9g, of which sugars 1.5g; Fat 35.3g, of which saturates 21g; Cholesterol 216mg; Calcium 38mg; Fibre 0.5g; Sodium 241mg.

newburg sauce

This creamy Madeira-flavoured sauce originated in America. Its rich flavour will not mask delicate foods and it is ideal for serving with shellfish. It also goes well with pan-fried chicken.

3 Add the cayenne and all but 60ml/4 tbsp of the cream. Leave over the simmering water for 10 minutes to heat through.

4 Stir in the Madeira. Beat the yolks with the remaining cream and stir into the hot sauce. Continue stirring the sauce over barely simmering water until thickened. Season to taste. Serve immediately.

Serves four

INGREDIENTS

15g/½ oz/1 tbsp butter

1 small shallot, finely chopped

pinch of cayenne pepper

300ml/½ pint/1¼ cups double (heavy) cream

60ml/4 tbsp Madeira

3 egg yolks

salt and ground black pepper

1 Melt the butter in a pan then cook the shallot until transparent.

2 Place a heatproof bowl over a pan of simmering water and add the cooked shallot.

VARIATIONS

• For a classic lobster newburg, add 200g/8oz/2 cups lobster meat to the pan with the shallot at the beginning of the recipe and proceed as above.

• For a twist in the tail, add 15–30ml/ 1–2 tbsp pink or black lumpfish roe towards the end of cooking. It will colour the sauce beautifully too.

Energy 469kcal/1930kJ; Protein 3.6g; Carbohydrate 3.4g, of which sugars 3g; Fat 47.5g, of which saturates 28.2g; Cholesterol 262mg; Calcium 60mg; Fibre 0.2g; Sodium 51mg.

rich vegetable sauce

For a full tomato flavour and rich red colour, fresh Italian plum tomatoes are an excellent choice if they are available. This makes a delightful topping for plain-cooked fresh pasta.

Serves four to six

INGREDIENTS

30ml/2 tbsp olive oil

1 large onion, chopped

2 garlic cloves, crushed

1 carrot, finely chopped

1 celery stick, finely chopped

675g/1½lb tomatoes, peeled and chopped

150ml/¼ pint/⅔ cup red wine

150ml/¼ pint/⅔ cup vegetable stock

bouquet garni

2.5–5ml/½–1 tsp sugar

15ml/1 tbsp tomato purée (paste), or to taste

salt and ground black pepper

4 Remove the bouquet garni from the sauce. Taste the sauce and adjust the seasoning, if necessary, adding salt and pepper, and an extra pinch of sugar with a little more tomato purée if the flavour is too weak or slightly sharp.

5 Serve the sauce as it is or, for a smoother texture, press it through a sieve. Alternatively, purée the sauce in a blender or food processor. This is delicious spooned over barely blanched sliced courgettes or cooked whole French (green) beans.

1 Heat the oil in a pan, add the onion and garlic and sauté until soft and pale golden brown. Add the carrot and celery and continue to cook, stirring occasionally, until all the vegetables are golden.

2 Stir in the tomatoes, wine, stock and bouquet garni. Season with salt and ground black pepper to taste.

3 Bring the tomato mixture to the boil. Reduce the heat, cover and simmer gently for 45 minutes, stirring occasionally.

Energy 81kcal/338kJ; Protein 1.2g; Carbohydrate 6.2g, of which sugars 5.9g; Fat 4.1g, of which saturates 0.7g; Cholesterol 0mg; Calcium 18mg; Fibre 1.7g; Sodium 24mg.

cumberland sauce with duck

*Orange, redcurrant jelly and red wine make this vibrant sauce perfect with duck. Traditionally
it is served with boiled or baked ham, but this classic recipe pairs it with roasted duck.*

Serves eight

INGREDIENTS

4 minneolas or oranges, segmented, with
rind and juice reserved

2 x 2.25kg/5lb oven-ready ducks,
with giblets

salt and ground black pepper

fresh parsley sprig, to garnish

For the Cumberland sauce

30ml/2 tbsp plain (all-purpose) flour

300ml/½ pint/1¼ cups chicken or
duck stock

150ml/¼ pint/⅔ cup port or red wine

15ml/1 tbsp redcurrant jelly

1 Preheat the oven to 180°C/
350°F/Gas 4. Tie the minneola or
orange rind with string and place it
inside the cavities of the two ducks.

2 Place the ducks on a rack in one
large or two smaller roasting pans,
prick the skin well with a fork or a
skewer, season with salt and pepper
and cook for 30 minutes per every
450g/1lb (about 2½ hours) until the
tender and the juices run clear.

3 Halfway through cooking, pour
off the fat from the roasting pan(s)
into a heatproof bowl.

4 When the ducks are cooked,
transfer them to a carving place or
board. Cover lightly with foil and
leave to rest. Remove the orange
rind from the cavities. Finely chop
the rind or cut it into fine shreds
and set it aside for the sauce.

5 To make the sauce, remove any
fat from the roasting pan(s), leaving
the sediment and juices. If using two
pans, scrape the sediment and juices
into one pan. Add the flour and
cook gently, stirring, for 2 minutes.

6 Add the reserved rind to the
roasting pan with the stock, port or
red wine and redcurrant jelly. Stir
well to blend, then bring to the boil
and simmer, stirring frequently, for
about 10 minutes. Strain the sauce
into a pan. Add the orange segments
with their juices.

7 To carve the ducks, remove the
legs and wings, cutting through the
joints. Cut the two end joints off
the wings and discard them. Cut the
breast meat off the carcass in one
piece and slice it thinly. Serve with a
little of the hot sauce poured over
and serve the rest separately.

COOK'S TIP

When the sauce is made to accompany
ham or grilled meats, without the roast
orange and roasting juices, cook the
finely shredded rind of 1 orange in a
little boiling water and drain. Make the
sauce in a pan, adding the orange.

Energy 244kcal/1028kJ; Protein 31.3g; Carbohydrate 4.3g, of which sugars 1.4g; Fat 10.2g, of which saturates 3.4g; Cholesterol 169mg; Calcium 24mg; Fibre 0.1g; Sodium 176mg.

blue cheese and walnut sauce

This is a very quick but indulgently creamy sauce. The blue cheese melts easily with cream to make a simple sauce to serve with vegetables or pasta for a delicious lunch or supper.

Serves two

INGREDIENTS

50g/2oz/¼ cup butter

50g/2oz/¾ cup button (white) mushrooms, sliced

150g/5oz hard blue cheese, such as Gorgonzola, Stilton or Danish Blue

150ml/¼ pint/⅔ cup sour cream

25g/1oz/⅓ cup grated Pecorino cheese

50g/2oz/½ cup broken walnut pieces

salt and ground black pepper

1 Melt the butter in a saucepan, add the mushrooms and cook gently for 3–5 minutes, stirring occasionally until lightly browned.

2 Crumble the blue cheese into a bowl and add the cream. Add seasoning to taste and mash together well using a fork, until thoroughly combined.

3 Stir the cheese cream into the mushroom mixture and heat gently, stirring, until melted.

4 Finally, stir in the Pecorino cheese and the walnut pieces. Remove from the heat. Serve warm.

Energy 828kcal/3420kJ; Protein 26.8g; Carbohydrate 3.9g, of which sugars 3.7g; Fat 78.5g, of which saturates 40.8g; Cholesterol 167mg; Calcium 616mg; Fibre 1.2g; Sodium 1237mg.

quick satay sauce

There are many versions of this tasty peanut sauce. This one is very speedy and it tastes delicious drizzled over grilled or barbecued skewers of chicken. For parties, spear chunks of chicken with cocktail sticks and arrange around a bowl of warm sauce.

3 Add the Worcestershire sauce and a dash of Tabasco, to taste. Pour into a serving bowl.

4 Use a potato peeler to shave thin curls from a piece of fresh coconut, if using. Scatter the coconut over the dish of your choice and serve immediately with the sauce.

Serves four

INGREDIENTS

200ml/7fl oz/scant 1 cup creamed coconut
60ml/4 tbsp crunchy peanut butter
1 tsp Worcestershire sauce
Tabasco sauce, to taste
fresh coconut, to garnish (optional)

2 Add the peanut butter and stir vigorously until it is blended into the creamed coconut. Continue to heat until the mixture is warm but not boiling hot.

1 Pour the coconut cream into a small pan and heat it gently over a low heat, stirring occasionally, for about 2 minutes.

COOK'S TIP

Thick coconut milk can be substituted for creamed coconut, but take care to buy an unsweetened variety for this recipe. Look out for instant coconut milk powder, often available from Asian stores, as it is an excellent and versatile, practical alternative to creams or canned coconut milk.

Energy 108kcal/451kJ; Protein 3.6g; Carbohydrate 5.8g, of which sugars 4.9g; Fat 8g, of which saturates 2.1g; Cholesterol 0mg; Calcium 30mg; Fibre 0.8g; Sodium 150mg.

green peppercorn sauce

This creamy sauce is excellent with pasta, pork or lamb steaks, or grilled chicken. The green peppercorns in brine are a better choice than the dry-packed type because they tend to give this piquant, creamy sauce a more rounded, fuller flavour.

Serves three to four

INGREDIENTS

15ml/1 tbsp green peppercorns in
   brine, drained
1 small onion, finely chopped
25g/1oz/2 tbsp butter
300ml/½ pint/1¼ cups light stock
juice of ½ lemon
15ml/1 tbsp beurre manié
45ml/3 tbsp double (heavy) cream
5ml/1 tsp Dijon mustard
salt and ground black pepper

3 Whisk in the beurre manié a piece at a time, whisking until the sauce is thick and smooth.

4 Reduce the heat and stir in the peppercorns, cream and mustard. Heat gently without boiling, then season to taste and serve.

VARIATION

For a lighter sauce, use crème fraîche instead of the double (heavy) cream.

COOK'S TIP

For beurre manié, cream equal quantities of butter and plain (all-purpose) flour together. Chill until firm.

1 Dry the peppercorns on kitchen paper, then crush lightly under a knife or in a mortar and pestle.

2 Soften the onion in the butter. Add the stock and lemon juice. Bring to the boil, reduce the heat and simmer for 15 minutes.

Energy 129kcal/533kJ; Protein 0.8g; Carbohydrate 2.5g, of which sugars 1.2g; Fat 13.1g, of which saturates 8.1g; Cholesterol 33mg; Calcium 19mg; Fibre 0.3g; Sodium 86mg.

peanut sauce

This is based on the famous Indonesian sauce that accompanies grilled pork, chicken or seafood satay. Slightly thinned down with water, it is also used to dress gado-gado, a wonderful salad of mixed raw or cooked vegetables and fruit.

Serves four to six

INGREDIENTS

30ml/2 tbsp peanut oil

75g/3oz/¾ cup unsalted peanuts, blanched

2 shallots, chopped

2 garlic cloves, chopped

15ml/1 tbsp chopped fresh root ginger

1–2 green chillies, seeded and thinly sliced

5ml/1 tsp ground coriander

1 lemon grass stalk, chopped

5–10ml/1–2 tsp light brown muscovado
  sugar

15ml/1 tbsp dark soy sauce

105–120ml/3–4 fl oz/scant ½ cup
  coconut milk

15–30ml/1–2 tbsp Thai fish sauce (nam pla)

15–30ml/1–2 tbsp tamarind purée

lime juice

salt and ground black pepper

1 Heat the oil in a small, heavy frying pan and gently fry the peanuts, stirring frequently, until they are evenly and lightly browned. Use a draining spoon to remove the nuts from the pan and drain thoroughly on kitchen paper. Set aside to cool.

2 Add the shallots, garlic, ginger, most of the sliced chillies and the ground coriander to the oil remaining in the pan, and cook over a low heat, stirring occasionally, for 4–5 minutes, until the shallots are softened but not at all browned.

3 Transfer the spice mixture to a food processor or blender and add the peanuts, lemon grass, 5ml/1 tsp of the sugar, the soy sauce and 105ml/3fl oz of coconut milk and the fish sauce. Blend to form a fairly smooth sauce.

4 Taste and add more fish sauce, tamarind purée, seasoning, lime juice and/or more sugar to taste.

5 Stir in the extra coconut milk and a little water if the sauce seems very thick, but do not let it become too runny.

6 Serve cool or reheat the sauce gently, stirring all the time to prevent it from separating. Garnish with the remaining sliced chilli before serving.

COOK'S TIP

To make tamarind purée, soak 25g/1oz tamarind pulp in 120ml/4fl oz/½ cup boiling water in a non-metallic bowl for about 30 minutes, mashing the pulp occasionally with a fork. Then press the pulp through a stainless steel sieve. This purée will keep for several days in a covered container in the refrigerator.

Energy 123kcal/513kJ; Protein 3.9g; Carbohydrate 5.8g, of which sugars 4.7g; Fat 9.6g, of which saturates 1.6g; Cholesterol 0mg; Calcium 34mg; Fibre 1.3g; Sodium 557mg.

apple sauce

Really more of a condiment than a sauce, this tart purée is usually served warm or cold, rather than hot. It is the classic accompaniment for roast pork, duck or goose, but is also good with grilled sausages, cold meats and savoury pies.

Serves six

INGREDIENTS

225g/8oz tart cooking apples
30ml/2 tbsp water
thin strip of lemon rind
15ml/1 tbsp butter
15–30ml/1–2 tbsp caster (superfine)
   sugar

1 Peel, quarter, core and thinly slice the apples.

3 Remove and discard the lemon rind. Beat the apples until smooth or press them through a sieve.

4 Stir the butter into the apple sauce and then add sugar to taste.

2 Place the apples in a pan with the water and lemon rind. Cook gently, stirring frequently, until pulpy.

VARIATIONS
• Stir in 15ml/1 tbsp Calvados with the butter and sugar.
• To make a creamy sauce, stir in 30ml/2 tbsp sour cream or crème fraîche at the end of cooking

Energy 42kcal/175kJ; Protein 0.1g; Carbohydrate 6g, of which sugars 6g; Fat 2.1g, of which saturates 1.3g; Cholesterol 5mg; Calcium 3mg; Fibre 0.6g; Sodium 16mg.

salsa verde

There are many versions of this classic green salsa. Try this one drizzled over chargrilled squid, or with jacket potatoes served with a green salad.

2 Use your fingers to rub the excess salt off the capers. Add them, with the tarragon and parsley, to the food processor and pulse again until the ingredients are quite finely chopped.

3 Transfer the mixture to a bowl. Mix in the lime rind and juice, lemon juice and olive oil, stirring lightly so the citrus juice and oil do not emulsify.

4 Gradually add the Tabasco sauce and black pepper to taste. Chill the salsa, but do not prepare it more than 8 hours in advance.

Serves four

INGREDIENTS

2–4 green chillies, halved
8 spring onions
2 garlic cloves
60ml/4 tbsp salted capers
sprig of fresh tarragon
bunch of fresh parsley
grated rind and juice of 1 lime
juice of 1 lemon
90ml/6 tbsp olive oil
about 15ml/1 tbsp green Tabasco sauce
ground black pepper

1 Halve and seed the chillies and trim the spring onions. Halve the garlic cloves. Place in a food processor and pulse briefly.

COOK'S TIP

Salted capers can be strong and may need rinsing before use. If you prefer, you may use pickled capers instead.

Energy 158kcal/652kJ; Protein 0.9g; Carbohydrate 1.1g, of which sugars 1g; Fat 16.8g, of which saturates 2.4g; Cholesterol 0mg; Calcium 35mg; Fibre 1g; Sodium 6mg.

coriander pesto salsa

This aromatic salsa is delicious over fish, chicken or pasta, or used to dress an avocado and tomato salad. To transform it into a dip, simply mix with a little mayonnaise or sour cream.

Serves four

INGREDIENTS

50g/2oz fresh coriander (cilantro) leaves

15g/½oz fresh parsley

2 red chillies

1 garlic clove

50g/2oz/⅓ cup shelled pistachio nuts

25g/1oz/⅓ cup finely grated Parmesan cheese, plus extra to garnish

90ml/6 tbsp olive oil

juice of 2 limes

salt and ground black pepper

VARIATION

Any number of different herbs or nuts may be used to make a similar salsa to this one – try a mixture of rosemary and parsley, or add a handful of black olives for a Mediterranean flourish.

1 Process the fresh coriander and parsley in a food processor or blender until finely chopped.

2 Halve the chillies lengthways and remove their seeds. Add to the herbs together with the garlic, and process until finely chopped.

3 Add the pistachio nuts to the herb mixture and pulse the power until they are roughly chopped. Stir in the Parmesan cheese, olive oil and lime juice.

4 Add salt and pepper to taste. Spoon the mixture into a serving bowl, then cover and chill until ready to serve. Garnish with a little extra Parmesan.

Energy 263kcal/1083kJ; Protein 5.4g; Carbohydrate 2.5g, of which sugars 1.9g; Fat 25.7g, of which saturates 4.6g; Cholesterol 6mg; Calcium 123mg; Fibre 1.8g; Sodium 140mg.

classic tomato salsa

This is the traditional tomato-based salsa that most people associate with Mexican food. There are innumerable recipes for it, but the basic ingredients of onion, tomato and chilli are common to all. Serve this salsa as a condiment. It goes well with a wide variety of dishes.

Serves six as an accompaniment

INGREDIENTS

3–6 fresh Serrano chillies

1 large white onion

grated rind and juice of
   2 limes, plus strips of lime rind,
   to garnish

8 ripe, firm tomatoes

large bunch of fresh coriander (cilantro)

1.5ml/¼ tsp sugar

salt

VARIATIONS

• Use spring onions (scallions) or mild red onions instead of white onion.

• For a smoky flavour, use chipotle chillies instead of Serrano chillies.

1 Use 3 chillies for a salsa of medium heat; up to 6 if you like it hot. To peel the chillies, spear them on a long-handled metal skewer and roast them over the flame of a gas burner until the skins blister and darken. Do not let the flesh burn. Alternatively, dry-fry them in a griddle pan until the skins are scorched and blackened.

2 Place the roasted chillies in a strong plastic bag and tie the top of the bag to keep the steam in. Set aside for about 20 minutes.

3 Meanwhile, chop the onion finely and put it in a bowl with the lime rind and juice. The lime juice will soften the onion considerably.

4 Remove the chillies from the bag and peel off the skins. Cut off the stalks, then slit the chillies and scrape out the seeds. Chop the flesh and set it aside in a small bowl.

5 Cut a small cross in the base of each tomato. Place in a heatproof bowl and pour over boiling water to cover. Leave for 30 seconds.

6 Lift out the tomatoes and plunge them into a bowl of cold water. Drain well. Remove the skins.

7 Dice the peeled tomatoes and put them in a bowl. Add the chopped onion, which should by now have softened, together with any remaining lime juice and rind. Chop the coriander finely.

8 Add the chopped coriander to the salsa, with the chillies and the sugar. Mix gently until the sugar has dissolved and all the ingredients are coated in lime juice. Cover and chill for 2–3 hours to allow the flavours to blend. Garnish with the extra strips of lime rind just before serving.

Energy 47kcal/199kJ; Protein 1.8g; Carbohydrate 9.1g, of which sugars 7.9g; Fat 0.6g, of which saturates 0.1g; Cholesterol 0mg; Calcium 39mg; Fibre 2.6g; Sodium 16mg.

fragrant tomato and chilli salsa

Roasting the tomatoes gives a greater depth to the flavour of this salsa, which also benefits from the warm, rounded flavour of roasted chillies.

Serves six as an accompaniment

INGREDIENTS

500g/1¼lb tomatoes, preferably
  beefsteak tomatoes

2 fresh Serrano chillies or other fresh
  red chillies

1 onion

juice of 1 lime

large bunch of fresh coriander (cilantro)

salt

1 Preheat the oven to 200°C/400°F/ Gas 6. Cut the tomatoes into quarters and place them in a roasting pan. Add the chillies. Roast for 45 minutes to 1 hour, until the tomatoes and chillies are charred and softened.

2 Place the roasted chillies in a strong plastic bag. Tie the top to keep the steam in and set aside for 20 minutes. Leave the tomatoes to cool slightly, then use a small, sharp knife to remove the skins and dice the flesh.

3 Chop the onion finely, then place it in a bowl and add the lime juice and the diced tomatoes. Mix well.

4 Remove the chillies from the bag and peel off the skins. Cut off the stalks, then slit the chillies and scrape out the seeds with a sharp knife. Chop the chillies roughly and mix them into the onion mixture.

5 Chop the coriander and add most of it to the salsa. Add salt to season, cover and chill for at least 1 hour before serving, sprinkled with the remaining chopped coriander. This salsa will keep in the refrigerator for 1 week.

Energy 25kcal/104kJ; Protein 1.1g; Carbohydrate 4.4g, of which sugars 4.1g; Fat 0.4g, of which saturates 0.1g; Cholesterol 0mg; Calcium 26mg; Fibre 1.6g; Sodium 11mg.

smoky tomato salsa

The smoky flavour in this recipe comes from the smoked bacon and the commercial liquid smoke marinade. Served with sour cream, this salsa makes a great baked potato filler.

Serves four

INGREDIENTS

450g/1lb tomatoes

4 rindless smoked streaky (fatty)
bacon rashers (strips)

15ml/1 tbsp vegetable oil

45ml/3 tbsp chopped fresh coriander
(cilantro) leaves or parsley

1 garlic clove, finely chopped

15ml/1 tbsp liquid smoke marinade

freshly squeezed juice of 1 lime

salt and ground black pepper

1 Place the tomatoes in a heatproof bowl. Pour over boiling water and leave for 30 seconds. Remove with a slotted spoon, dunk in cold water and then peel. Halve the tomatoes, scoop out and discard the seeds, then finely dice the flesh.

2 Cut the bacon into small pieces. Heat the oil in a frying pan and cook the bacon for 5 minutes, stirring occasionally, until crisp and browned.

3 Remove the cooked bacon from the heat and drain and pat dry on kitchen paper. Leave to cool for a few minutes then place in a bowl.

4 Add the tomatoes and the chopped fresh coriander or parsley to the bacon. Stir in the garlic, then add the liquid smoke and freshly squeezed lime juice. Season the salsa with salt and pepper to taste and mix well, using a wooden spoon or plastic spatula.

5 Spoon the salsa into a serving bowl, cover with clear film (plastic wrap) and chill until ready to serve.

VARIATION

Give this smoky salsa an extra kick by adding a dash of Tabasco sauce or a pinch of dried chilli flakes.

Energy 82kcal/343kJ; Protein 3.1g; Carbohydrate 3.8g, of which sugars 3.8g; Fat 6.2g, of which saturates 1.5g; Cholesterol 8mg; Calcium 31mg; Fibre 1.7g; Sodium 171mg.

fresh tomato and tarragon salsa

Plum tomatoes, garlic, olive oil and balsamic vinegar make for a very Mediterranean salsa – try serving this with grilled lamb cutlets or toss it with freshly cooked pasta.

3 Using a sharp knife, crush or finely chop the garlic.

4 Whisk together the oil, balsamic vinegar and plenty of salt and pepper to make a dressing.

5 Add the chopped fresh tarragon to the dressing and stir lightly.

6 Mix the tomatoes and garlic in a bowl and pour the tarragon dressing over. Leave to infuse (steep) for at least 1 hour before serving at room temperature. Garnish with more shredded tarragon leaves.

Serves four

INGREDIENTS

8 plum tomatoes, or 500g/1¼lb sweet cherry tomatoes

1 small garlic clove

60ml/4 tbsp olive oil or sunflower oil

15ml/1 tbsp balsamic vinegar

30ml/2 tbsp chopped fresh tarragon, plus extra shredded leaves, to garnish

salt and ground black pepper

1 Plunge the tomatoes into boiling water for 30 seconds. Remove with a slotted spoon; cool in cold water.

2 Use a sharp knife to peel the tomatoes (the skins slip off easily if they have stood in the water long enough) and finely chop the flesh.

COOK'S TIP

Be sure to serve this salsa at room temperature as the tomatoes taste less sweet, and rather acidic, when chilled.

Energy 125kcal/517kJ; Protein 1.3g; Carbohydrate 4.4g, of which sugars 4.1g; Fat 11.5g, of which saturates 1.5g; Cholesterol 0mg; Calcium 29mg; Fibre 1.8g; Sodium 15mg.

grilled corn on the cob salsa

*This unusual salsa is full of deliciously sweet vegetables. Use cherry tomatoes for an extra
special flavour, and combine them with the ripest and freshest corn on the cob.*

Serves four

INGREDIENTS

2 corn on the cob
30ml/2 tbsp melted butter
4 tomatoes
8 spring onions (scallions)
1 garlic clove
30ml/2 tbsp fresh lemon juice
30ml/2 tbsp olive oil
Tabasco sauce, to taste
salt and ground black pepper

1 Remove the husks and silky
threads covering the corn on the
cob. Brush the cobs with the melted
butter and gently barbecue or grill
(broil) them for 20–30 minutes,
turning occasionally, until tender
and tinged brown.

2 To remove the kernels, stand
each cob upright on a chopping
board and use a large, heavy knife
to slice down the length of the cob.

3 Plunge the tomatoes into boiling
water for 30 seconds. Remove with
a slotted spoon and plunge into
cold water to cool. Then peel the
tomatoes (the skins should slip off
easily) and finely dice the flesh.

4 Place 6 spring onions on a
chopping board and chop finely.
Crush and chop the garlic, and then
mix together with the corn and
tomato in a small bowl.

5 Stir the lemon juice and olive oil
together, adding Tabasco sauce, salt
and pepper to taste.

6 Pour this mixture over the salsa
and stir well. Cover the salsa and
leave to steep at room temperature
for 1–2 hours before serving.
Garnish with the remaining
spring onions.

COOK'S TIP

Make this salsa in summer when fresh
cobs of corn are readily available.

Energy 188kcal/785kJ; Protein 2.6g; Carbohydrate 17.1g, of which sugars 8.5g; Fat 12.7g, of which saturates 4.9g; Cholesterol 16mg; Calcium 18mg; Fibre 2g; Sodium 191mg.

fiery salsa

This is a scorchingly hot salsa for only the very brave! Spread it sparingly on to cooked meats and burgers or add a tiny amount to a curry or pot of chilli.

Serves four to six

INGREDIENTS

6 Scotch bonnet chillies
2 ripe tomatoes
4 standard green jalapeño chillies
30ml/2 tbsp chopped fresh parsley
30ml/2 tbsp olive oil
15ml/1 tbsp balsamic vinegar or sherry
  vinegar
salt

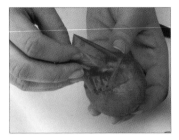

1 Skin the Scotch bonnet chillies, either by holding them in a gas flame for 3 minutes until the skins blacken and blister, or by plunging them into boiling water. Then, using rubber gloves, rub off the skins from the chillies.

2 Hold each tomato on a fork in a gas flame for 3 minutes until the skin blisters. (Or plunge them into boiling water for 30 seconds, if you prefer.) Once cool enough to touch, remove the skins, halve the tomatoes, and remove the seeds. Chop the flesh very finely.

3 Try not to touch the Scotch bonnet chillies with your bare hands: use a fork to hold them and slice them open with a sharp knife. Scrape out and discard the seeds, then finely chop the flesh.

4 Halve the jalapeño chillies, remove their seeds and finely slice them widthways into tiny strips. Mix both types of chillies, the tomatoes and the chopped parsley in a bowl.

5 In a small bowl, whisk the olive oil with the vinegar and a little salt. Pour this over the salsa and cover the dish. Chill for up to 3 days.

Energy 52kcal/215kJ; Protein 0.8g; Carbohydrate 3.4g, of which sugars 3.2g; Fat 4g, of which saturates 0.6g; Cholesterol 0mg; Calcium 20mg; Fibre 1.3g; Sodium 7mg.

bloody mary salsa

This salsa is perfect for parties – serve it with sticks of crunchy celery or fingers of refreshing cucumber or, on a really special occasion, with freshly shucked oysters.

Serves two

INGREDIENTS

4 ripe tomatoes
1 garlic clove
1 celery stick
2 spring onions (scallions)
45ml/3 tbsp tomato juice
Worcestershire sauce, to taste
Tabasco sauce, to taste
10ml/2 tsp horseradish sauce
15ml/1 tbsp vodka
juice of 1 lemon
salt and ground black pepper

VARIATION

Blend 1–2 seeded, fresh red chillies with the tomatoes, instead of stirring in the Tabasco sauce.

1 Halve the tomatoes, garlic and celery. Trim the spring onions.

2 Put the tomatoes, garlic, celery and spring onions in a blender or food processor. Process until the vegetables are finely chopped, then transfer the mixture to a small serving bowl.

3 Stir in the tomato juice, a little at a time, then add a few drops of Worcestershire sauce and Tabasco sauce to taste. Mix well and set aside for 10–15 minutes.

4 Stir in the horseradish sauce, vodka and lemon juice. Add salt and ground black pepper, to taste. Serve immediately, or cover and chill for 1–2 hours.

Energy 65kcal/275kJ; Protein 2g; Carbohydrate 8.2g, of which sugars 8.1g; Fat 1.1g, of which saturates 0.3g; Cholesterol 1mg; Calcium 29mg; Fibre 2.6g; Sodium 125mg.

chilli and coconut salsa

This fruity sweet-and-sour salsa, spiked with chillies, goes well with grilled or barbecued fish, lamb, pork or sausages. It is also excellent with baked sweet potatoes.

Serves six to eight

INGREDIENTS

1 small coconut

1 small pineapple

2 green Kenyan chillies

5cm/2in piece lemon grass stalk

60ml/4 tbsp natural (plain) yogurt

2.5ml/½ tsp salt

30ml/2 tbsp chopped fresh coriander (cilantro)

coriander (cilantro) sprigs, to garnish

1 Puncture two of the coconut eyes with a screwdriver. Drain out the coconut water from inside the shell.

2 Crack the coconut shell, prise away the flesh, and then coarsely grate the pieces of coconut into a mixing bowl.

3 Peel the pineapple and remove the eyes with a potato peeler. Finely chop the flesh and add to the coconut together with any juice.

4 Halve the chillies and remove the stalks, seeds and pith. Chop very finely and stir into the coconut.

5 Finely chop the lemon grass with a very sharp knife. Add to the coconut mixture with the remaining ingredients and stir well. Spoon into a serving dish and garnish with coriander sprigs.

COOK'S TIP

When buying a coconut, check its freshness by shaking gently – you should hear the liquid swishing about inside. If not, it's dried out and stale.

Energy 104kcal/434kJ; Protein 1.4g; Carbohydrate 7.2g, of which sugars 7.2g; Fat 8g, of which saturates 6.7g; Cholesterol 0mg; Calcium 27mg; Fibre 2.5g; Sodium 134mg.

berry salsa

This unusual, richly coloured fruit salsa is the perfect choice for a summer al fresco meal. It tastes terrific with barbecued fish or poultry, or baked gammon (cured or smoked ham).

Serves four

INGREDIENTS

1 fresh jalapeño chilli

½ red onion, finely chopped

2 spring onions (scallions), chopped

1 tomato, finely diced

1 small yellow (bell) pepper, seeded and finely chopped

45ml/3 tbsp chopped fresh coriander (cilantro)

1.5ml/¼ tsp salt

15ml/1 tbsp raspberry vinegar

15ml/1 tbsp fresh orange juice

5ml/1 tsp honey

15ml/1 tbsp olive oil

175g/6oz/1½ cups strawberries, hulled

175g/6oz/1½ cups blueberries or blackberries

200g/7oz/generous 1 cup raspberries

3 In a small bowl, whisk together the salt, vinegar, orange juice, honey and olive oil until thoroughly combined. Pour this dressing over the chilli and pepper mixture and stir well.

4 Coarsely chop the strawberries. Then stir them into the mixture with the blueberries or black berries and the raspberries. Allow to stand at room temperature for 3 hours before serving.

1 Wearing rubber gloves, finely chop the jalapeño chilli (discard the seeds and pith if a less-hot flavour is preferred). Place the pepper in a mixing bowl.

2 Add the red onion, spring onions, tomato, pepper and coriander, and stir until well mixed.

COOK'S TIP

Defrosted frozen berries can be used in the salsa, but the texture will be softer.

Energy 94kcal/392kJ; Protein 2.7g; Carbohydrate 13.7g, of which sugars 13.1g; Fat 3.5g, of which saturates 0.5g; Cholesterol 0mg; Calcium 71mg; Fibre 4.9g; Sodium 14mg.

orange, tomato and chive salsa

Fresh chives and sweet oranges create a very cheerful combination of flavours in this unusual salsa that is a very good accompaniment to cheese or meat salads.

3 Roughly chop the orange segments and add them to the bowl with the collected juice. Halve the tomato and use a teaspoon to scoop the seeds and soft middle into the oranges mixture. With a sharp knife, finely dice the flesh and add to the mixture in the bowl.

4 Hold the bunch of chives neatly together and use a pair of kitchen scissors to snip them into the bowl.

Serves four

INGREDIENTS

2 large, sweet oranges
1 beefsteak tomato or 2 plum tomatoes
bunch of fresh chives
1 garlic clove
30ml/2 tbsp extra virgin olive oil
  or grapeseed oil
sea salt

1 Slice the base off 1 orange so that it will stand firmly. Using a sharp knife, remove the peel in strips by slicing from the top to the bottom of the orange, cutting just below the pith. Repeat with the second orange.

2 Over a bowl, remove the orange segments: cut to the middle and close to the membrane on one side of a segment. Gently twist the knife and scrape the segment off the other membrane. Repeat, squeezing juice from the leftover membrane.

5 Thinly slice the garlic and stir it into the orange and tomato mixture. Pour the olive oil into the salsa, season it to taste with sea salt and stir well to mix and serve.

VARIATION
It is best to serve the salsa within 2 hours, or it may become too juicy.

Energy 90kcal/376kJ; Protein 1.6g; Carbohydrate 8.3g, of which sugars 8.2g; Fat 5.9g, of which saturates 0.8g; Cholesterol 0mg; Calcium 64mg; Fibre 2.4g; Sodium 13mg.

fiery citrus apple salsa

This very unusual apple salsa is laced with garlic and mint. It makes a fantastic marinade for shellfish, and it is also delicious drizzled over barbecued meat.

Serves four

INGREDIENTS

1 orange
1 green eating apple
2 fresh red chillies, halved and seeded
1 garlic clove
8 fresh mint leaves
juice of 1 lemon
salt and ground black pepper

VARIATION

For a super-fiery flavour, don't seed the chillies: the seeds will make the salsa particularly hot and fierce.

3 Peel the apple, slice it into wedges and remove the core by slicing through the centre.

4 Place the chillies in a blender or food processor with the orange segments and juice, apple wedges, garlic and fresh mint. Process for a few seconds until smooth. Then, with the motor running, slowly pour the lemon juice into the mixture.

5 Season to taste with a little salt and ground black pepper. Pour the salsa mixture into a bowl or small jug (pitcher) and serve immediately.

1 Slice the bottom off the orange so that it will stand firmly on a chopping board. Using a sharp knife, remove the peel by slicing from the top to the bottom of the orange.

2 Hold the orange in one hand over a bowl. Slice towards the middle of the fruit, to one side of a segment, and then gently twist the knife to ease the segment away from the membrane and out of the orange. Remove all the segments. Squeeze any juice from the remaining membrane into the bowl.

Energy 24kcal/104kJ; Protein 1g; Carbohydrate 5.3g, of which sugars 4.2g; Fat 0.1g, of which saturates 0g; Cholesterol 0mg; Calcium 16mg; Fibre 1.1g; Sodium 2mg.

creamy pineapple-passion fruit salsa

Pineapple and aromatic passion fruit create a salsa that's bursting with fruit flavour – great with barbecued pork or baked smoked ham. It also makes a luxurious dessert!

Serves six

INGREDIENTS

1 small pineapple

2 passion fruit

150ml/¼ pint/⅔ cup Greek (US strained plain) yogurt

30ml/2 tbsp light brown muscovado sugar

1 Cut off the top and bottom of the pineapple so that it will stand firmly on a chopping board. Using a large, sharp knife, slice off the peel, working down the fruit.

2 Use a small, sharp knife to carefully cut out the eyes. Slice the peeled pineapple and use a small pastry cutter to cut out the tough core. Finely chop the flesh.

3 Halve the passion fruit and use a spoon to scoop out the seeds and pulp into a bowl.

4 Stir in the chopped pineapple and the Greek yogurt. Cover and chill until required.

5 Stir in the muscovado sugar just before serving the salsa – if you add the sugar too soon, the salsa will become too thin and juicy.

VARIATION

For a spicy twist, add 45ml/3 tbsp finely chopped fresh root ginger to the fruit and leave it to steep for 1 hour. Season the salsa with plenty of ground black pepper and a little freshly grated nutmeg when stirring in the sugar.

Energy 78kcal/328kJ; Protein 2g; Carbohydrate 12.8g, of which sugars 12.8g; Fat 2.7g, of which saturates 1.3g; Cholesterol 0mg; Calcium 53mg; Fibre 1g; Sodium 20mg.

mixed melon salsa

A combination of two very different melons gives this salsa an exciting flavour and texture. Try it with thinly sliced Parma ham or smoked salmon.

Serves ten

INGREDIENTS

1 small orange-fleshed melon, such as Charentais

1 large wedge watermelon

2 oranges

1 Quarter the orange-fleshed melon and use a large spoon to scoop out the seeds. Discard them. Use a large, sharp knife to cut off the skin. Dice the melon flesh.

2 Pick out the seeds from the watermelon, then remove the skin. Dice the flesh into small chunks.

3 Use a zester to pare long fine strips of rind from both oranges. Halve the oranges and squeeze out all their juice.

4 Mix both types of the melon and the orange rind and juice together in a bowl. Chill for about 30 minutes and serve.

VARIATION
Other melons can be used for this salsa. Try cantaloupe, Galia or Ogen.

Energy 58kcal/250kJ; Protein 1.1g; Carbohydrate 13.5g, of which sugars 13.5g; Fat 0.4g, of which saturates 0.1g; Cholesterol 0mg; Calcium 30mg; Fibre 0.9g; Sodium 25mg.

mango and red onion salsa

A very simple tropical salsa, which is livened up by the addition of passion fruit pulp. This salsa goes well with salmon and poultry.

3 Score the mango halves deeply in both directions, taking care to avoid cutting through the skin. Carefully turn the skin inside out so the flesh stands out and slice the dice off the skin. Place in the bowl.

4 Place the red onion in the bowl with the mango. Halve the passion fruit, scoop out the pulp, and add to the mango mixture in the bowl.

Serves four

INGREDIENTS

1 large ripe mango
1 red onion, finely chopped
2 passion fruit
6 large fresh basil leaves
juice of 1 lime, to taste
sea salt

5 Tear the basil leaves coarsely and stir them into the mixture with lime juice and a little sea salt to taste. Mix well and serve the salsa immediately.

1 Holding the mango upright on a chopping board, use a large knife to slice from top to bottom on either side of the large central stone, so that you are left with two sizeable portions of the flesh.

2 Using a smaller knife, trim away any flesh still clinging to the top and bottom of the stone. Peel and dice these trimmings and place in a bowl ready to mix with the rest of the mango flesh for the salsa.

VARIATION

Freshly cooked sweetcorn kernels are a delicious addition to this salsa.

Energy 42kcal/178kJ; Protein 1.1g; Carbohydrate 9.7g, of which sugars 8.4g; Fat 0.2g, of which saturates 0.1g; Cholesterol 0mg; Calcium 18mg; Fibre 1.9g; Sodium 4mg.

peach and cucumber salsa

Angostura bitters add an unusual and very pleasing flavour to this salsa. The distinctive, sweet taste of the mint complements chicken and other meat dishes.

Serves four

INGREDIENTS

2 peaches
1 mini cucumber
2.5ml/½ tsp Angostura bitters
15ml/1 tbsp olive oil
10ml/2 tsp fresh lemon juice
30ml/2 tbsp chopped fresh mint
salt and ground black pepper

1 Using a small, sharp knife, carefully score a line right around the centre of each peach, taking care to cut just through the skin.

2 Bring a large pan of water to the boil. Add the peaches and blanch them for 1 minute. Drain and briefly refresh in cold water. Peel off and discard the skin. Halve the peaches and remove their stones (pits). Finely dice the flesh and place in a bowl.

3 Trim the ends off the cucumber. Slice it lengthways into strips, then finely dice the flesh and stir it into the peaches. Stir the Angostura bitters, olive oil and lemon juice together and then stir this dressing into the peach mixture.

4 Stir in the mint with salt and pepper to taste. Chill and serve within 1 hour.

VARIATION

Use diced mango in place of the peaches for an alternative.

COOK'S TIP

The texture of the peach and the crispness of the cucumber will fade fairly rapidly, so try to prepare this salsa as close to serving time as possible.

Energy 49kcal/203kJ; Protein 1.1g; Carbohydrate 4.8g, of which sugars 4.7g; Fat 3g, of which saturates 0.4g; Cholesterol 0mg; Calcium 28mg; Fibre 1.4g; Sodium 5mg.

guacamole

One of the best-loved Mexican salsas, this blend of creamy avocado, tomatoes, chillies, coriander and lime now appears on tables the world over. Bought guacamole usually contains mayonnaise, but this is not an ingredient that you are likely to find in traditional recipes.

Serves six to eight

INGREDIENTS

4 tomatoes

4 ripe avocados, preferably fuerte

juice of 1 lime

½ small onion

2 garlic cloves

small bunch of fresh coriander (cilantro), chopped

3 fresh red fresno chillies

salt

tortilla chips or breadsticks, to serve

COOK'S TIP

To crush a garlic clove, roughly chop it and sprinkle with sea salt, then work in using the side of a large knife blade.

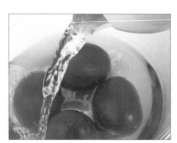

1 Cut a cross in the base of each tomato. Place the tomatoes in a heatproof bowl and pour over boiling water to cover. (If you prefer, add the tomatoes to a pan of boiling water, taking the pan off the heat.)

2 Leave the tomatoes in the water for 30 seconds, then lift them out using a slotted spoon and plunge them into a bowl of cold water. Drain and peel. Cut the tomatoes in half, remove the seeds, then chop the flesh roughly and set it aside.

3 Cut the avocados in half, then remove the stones (pits). Scoop out the flesh and process it in a food processor or blender until almost smooth, then scrape into a bowl and stir in the lime juice.

4 Chop the onion finely, then crush the garlic. Add both to the avocado and mix well. Stir in the coriander.

5 Remove the stalks and seeds from the chillies, then finely chop them and mix them into the avocado mixture, with the tomatoes.

6 Taste the guacamole and add salt if needed. Cover closely with clear film (plastic wrap) and chill for 1 hour. Serve with tortilla chips or breadsticks to dip. If well covered, guacamole will keep in the refrigerator for 2–3 days.

COOK'S TIP

Smooth-skinned fuerte avocados are native to Mexico, so would be ideal for this dip. If they are not available, use any avocados, but make sure they are ripe. To test, gently press the top of the avocado; it should give a little.

Energy 156kcal/645kJ; Protein 2.1g; Carbohydrate 3.7g, of which sugars 2.5g; Fat 14.7g, of which saturates 3.1g; Cholesterol 0mg; Calcium 26mg; Fibre 3.5g; Sodium 11mg.

guacamole with lime

Guacamole is often served as a first course with corn chips for dipping. The chunky texture of this version makes it more versatile and it makes a great accompaniment for grilled fish, poultry or meat, especially steak. It is also very good in baked potatoes or butternut squash.

Serves four

INGREDIENTS

2 large ripe avocados

1 small red onion, very finely chopped

1 red or green chilli, seeded and very finely chopped

½–1 garlic clove, crushed with a little salt

finely shredded rind of ½ lime and juice of 1–1½ limes

pinch of sugar

3 tomatoes, seeded and chopped

30ml/2 tbsp roughly chopped fresh coriander (cilantro)

2.5–5ml/½–1 tsp ground toasted cumin seeds

15ml/1 tbsp olive oil

15–30ml/1–2 tbsp sour cream (optional)

salt and ground black pepper

lime wedges dipped in sea salt, and fresh coriander (cilantro) sprigs, to garnish

1 Cut 1 avocado in half and lift out and discard the stone (pit). Scrape the flesh from both halves into a bowl and mash it to a coarse paste with a fork.

2 Stir in the onion, chilli, garlic, lime rind, sugar, tomatoes and coriander. Add the ground cumin and seasoning to taste, then stir in the olive oil.

3 Halve and stone (pit) the remaining avocado. Dice the flesh and stir it into the guacamole.

4 Squeeze in fresh lime juice to taste, mix well, then cover and leave to stand for 15 minutes so that the flavour develops. Stir in the sour cream, if using. Serve with lime wedges dipped in sea salt, and fresh coriander sprigs.

Energy 189kcal/781kJ; Protein 2.4g; Carbohydrate 5.2g, of which sugars 3.8g; Fat 17.6g, of which saturates 3.6g; Cholesterol 0mg; Calcium 37mg; Fibre 4g; Sodium 15mg.

garlic mayo

This can be as easy to make as stirring crushed garlic into good quality, ready-made mayonnaise; but do make your own mayo if possible – it will make all the difference.

3 When the mayonnaise is as thick as soft butter, stop adding oil. Season the mayonnaise to taste and add more lemon juice or vinegar as required.

4 Crush the garlic with the blade of a knife and stir it into the mayonnaise. For a milder flavour, blanch the garlic cloves twice in boiling water, then purée them before beating into the mayonnaise.

Serves four to six

INGREDIENTS

2 large egg yolks
pinch of dried mustard
up to 300ml/½ pint/1¼ cups mild olive oil or olive oil and grapeseed oil, mixed
15–30ml/1–2 tbsp lemon juice
white wine vinegar or warm water
2–4 garlic cloves
salt and ground black pepper

1 Make sure the egg yolks and oil have come to room temperature before you start. Place the yolks in a bowl with the mustard and a pinch of salt, and whisk.

2 Gradually whisk in the oil, drops at a time at first, then in a trickle. As the mayonnaise starts to thicken, thin it down with a few drops of lemon juice or vinegar, or a few teaspoons of warm water.

VARIATIONS

• For Provençal aioli, crush 3–5 garlic cloves with a pinch of salt, then whisk in the egg yolks. Omit the mustard. Continue as above, using all olive oil.
• For spicy garlic mayonnaise, omit the mustard and stir in 2.5ml/½ tsp harissa or red chilli paste and 5ml/1 tsp sundried tomato paste with the garlic.
• Use roasted garlic purée or puréed smoked garlic for a different flavour.
• Beat in 15g/½ oz mixed herbs, such as tarragon, parsley, chervil and chives. Blanch the herbs in boiling water for 20–30 seconds, then drain and dry them on kitchen paper before finely chopping them.

Energy 327kcal/1344kJ; Protein 1.5g; Carbohydrate 1.1g, of which sugars 0.1g; Fat 35.2g, of which saturates 5.3g; Cholesterol 67mg; Calcium 9mg; Fibre 0.3g; Sodium 3mg.

basil and lemon mayo

This fresh mayonnaise is flavoured with lemon and two types of basil. Serve as a dip with potato wedges or crudités, or as an accompaniment to salads and jacket potatoes.

Serves four to six

INGREDIENTS

2 large egg yolks
15ml/1 tbsp lemon juice
150ml/¼ pint/⅔ cup olive oil
150ml/¼ pint/⅔ cup sunflower oil
handful of green basil leaves
handful of dark opal (purple) basil leaves
4 garlic cloves, crushed
salt and ground black pepper
green and dark opal basil leaves and
    sea salt, to garnish

3 Once half the oil has been added, the remainder can be incorporated more quickly. Continue processing the mixture to form a thick and creamy mayonnaise.

4 Tear both types of basil into small pieces and stir into the mayonnaise with the crushed garlic and seasoning. Transfer to a serving dish, cover and chill until ready to serve, garnished with basil leaves and sea salt.

1 Place the egg yolks and lemon juice in a food processor or blender and process them briefly together.

2 In a jug (pitcher), stir the two oils together. With the machine running, pour in the oil very slowly, a drop at a time.

COOK'S TIP

If you can only find green basil leaves, simply use double the amount in the recipe, but it is worth seeking out the dark opal variety. It is quite distinctive in its appearance, with crinkled, dark purple leaves and a richly scented flavour, with a hint of blackcurrants that adds a fruity tang to the mayo.

Energy 329kcal/1355kJ; Protein 1.8g; Carbohydrate 1.3g, of which sugars 0.3g; Fat 35.3g, of which saturates 4.9g; Cholesterol 67mg; Calcium 26mg; Fibre 0.7g; Sodium 6mg.

creamy aubergine dip

Spread this velvet-textured dip thickly on to toasted rounds of bread, then top them with slivers of sun-dried tomato to make wonderful, Italian-style crostini.

Serves four

INGREDIENTS

1 large aubergine (eggplant)
30ml/2 tbsp olive oil
1 small onion, finely chopped
2 garlic cloves, finely chopped
60ml/4 tbsp chopped fresh parsley
75ml/5 tbsp crème fraîche
Red Tabasco sauce, to taste
juice of 1 lemon, to taste
salt and ground black pepper

1 Preheat the grill (broiler) to medium-high. Place the aubergine on a non-stick baking sheet and grill (broil) it for 20–30 minutes, turning, until it is blackened and wrinkled, and soft when squeezed.

2 Remove the aubergine from the oven, cover with a clean dish towel and set aside. It should take around five minutes to cool.

3 Heat the oil in a frying pan and cook the onion and garlic for five minutes, until they are softened, but not browned.

4 Peel the skin from the aubergine. Then mash the flesh with a large fork or potato masher to make a pulpy purée.

5 Stir in the onion and garlic, parsley and crème fraîche. Add Tabasco, lemon juice and salt and pepper to taste.

6 Transfer the dip to a serving bowl and serve warm or leave to cool and serve at room temperature.

COOK'S TIP

The aubergine (eggplant) can also be roasted in the oven at 200°C/400°F/ Gas 6 for 20 minutes or until tender.

Energy 137kcal/566kJ; Protein 1.4g; Carbohydrate 3.1g, of which sugars 2.5g; Fat 13.4g, of which saturates 5.9g; Cholesterol 21mg; Calcium 42mg; Fibre 1.8g; Sodium 9mg.

artichoke and cumin dip

This dip is so easy to make and is unbelievably tasty. Serve with olives, hummus and wedges of pitta bread as an informal summery snack selection.

Serves four

INGREDIENTS

2 x 400g/14oz cans artichoke
  hearts, drained

2 garlic cloves, peeled

2.5ml/½ tsp ground cumin

olive oil

salt and ground black pepper

VARIATION

Grilled (broiled) artichokes bottled in oil have a fabulous flavour and can be used instead of canned artichokes. Try adding a handful of basil leaves to the artichokes before blending.

1 Put the artichoke hearts in a food processor with the garlic and ground cumin, and add a generous drizzle of olive oil. Process to a smooth purée and season with plenty of salt and ground black pepper to taste.

2 Spoon the purée into a serving bowl and serve with an extra drizzle of olive oil swirled on the top and slices of warm pitta bread or wholemeal (whole-wheat) toast fingers and carrot sticks for dipping.

Energy 76kcal/315kJ; Protein 1.6g; Carbohydrate 3.9g, of which sugars 3.5g; Fat 6.2g, of which saturates 1g; Cholesterol 0mg; Calcium 18mg; Fibre 3.5g; Sodium 4mg.

taramasalata

This delicious smoked mullet roe speciality is one of the most famous Greek dips. (Smoked cod's roe is often used as a less-expensive alternative.) It is ideal for a buffet or for handing round with drinks. Fingers of warm pitta bread, breadsticks or crackers are good dippers.

Makes 1 bowl

INGREDIENTS

115g/4oz smoked mullet or cod's roe
2 garlic cloves, crushed
30ml/2 tbsp grated onion
60ml/4 tbsp olive oil
4 slices white bread, crusts removed
juice of 2 lemons
30ml/2 tbsp milk or water
ground black pepper
warm pitta bread, breadsticks or
crackers, to serve

1 Place the smoked roe, garlic, onion, oil, bread and lemon juice in a blender or food processor and process briefly until just smooth.

2 Add the milk or water and process again for a few seconds. (This will give the taramasalata a creamier texture.)

3 Pour the taramasalata into a serving bowl, cover with clear film (plastic wrap) and chill for 1–2 hours in the refrigerator before serving. Sprinkle the dip with freshly ground black pepper just before serving.

Energy 761kcal/3178kJ; Protein 33.7g; Carbohydrate 51.7g, of which sugars 4.3g; Fat 48.1g, of which saturates 6.8g; Cholesterol 380mg; Calcium 130mg; Fibre 1.9g; Sodium 647mg.

hummus

This classic Middle Eastern dish is made from cooked chickpeas, ground to a paste and flavoured with garlic, lemon juice, tahini, olive oil and cumin. It is delicious served with wedges of toasted pitta bread or crudités.

Serves four to six

INGREDIENTS

400g/14oz can chickpeas, drained

60ml/4 tbsp tahini

2–3 garlic cloves, chopped

juice of ½ –1 lemon

cayenne pepper

small pinch to 1.5ml/¼ tsp ground cumin, or more to taste

salt and ground black pepper

VARIATION

Process 2 roasted red (bell) peppers with the chickpeas, then continue as above. Serve sprinkled with lightly toasted pine nuts and paprika.

1 Using a potato masher or food processor, coarsely mash the chickpeas. If you prefer a smoother purée, process them in a food processor or blender until smooth and creamy.

2 Mix the tahini into the chickpeas, then stir in the garlic, lemon juice, cayenne, cumin, and salt and pepper to taste. If needed, add a little water. Serve at room temperature.

Energy 142kcal/596kJ; Protein 7.1g; Carbohydrate 11.6g, of which sugars 0.4g; Fat 7.9g, of which saturates 1.1g; Cholesterol 0mg; Calcium 98mg; Fibre 3.7g; Sodium 149mg.

cream and walnut sauce

This walnut and cream pesto is a simplified version of one traditionally served with pansotti in Liguria. The sauce would go equally well with any pasta stuffed with ricotta or spinach, or with plain pasta shells for a less rich alternative.

Serves six to eight

INGREDIENTS

500g/1¼lb herb-flavoured pasta dough with eggs
50g/2oz/¼ cup butter
freshly grated Parmesan cheese, to serve
salt and ground black pepper

For the filling

250g/9oz/generous 1 cup ricotta cheese
115g/4oz/1¼ cups freshly grated Parmesan cheese
1 large handful fresh basil leaves, finely chopped
1 large handful fresh flat leaf parsley, finely chopped
a few sprigs of fresh marjoram or oregano, leaves removed and finely chopped
1 garlic clove, crushed
1 small egg

For the cream and walnut sauce

90g/3½oz/1 cup shelled walnuts
1 garlic clove
60ml/4 tbsp extra virgin olive oil
120ml/4fl oz/½ cup double (heavy) cream

1 To make the filling, put the ricotta cheese, Parmesan cheese, basil, parsley, marjoram or oregano, garlic and egg in a bowl. Season with salt and ground black pepper to taste, and beat well until thoroughly mixed.

COOK'S TIP

To make herb pasta, add chopped fresh oregano, chives and parsley when mixing in the eggs. Take care not to overfill the pansotti, or they will burst open during cooking.

2 To make the sauce, put the walnuts, garlic clove and oil in a food processor and process to a paste, adding up to 120ml/4fl oz/½ cup warm water, through the feeder tube, to thin down the paste.

3 Spoon the mixture into a bowl and add the cream. Beat well to mix, then season to taste.

4 Using a pasta machine, roll out one-quarter of the pasta into a 90–100cm/36–40in strip. Cut the strip with a sharp knife into two 45–50cm/18–20in lengths (you can do this during rolling if the strip gets too long to manage).

5 Using a 5cm/2in square ravioli cutter, cut eight to ten squares from one of the pasta strips.

6 Using a teaspoon, put a mound of filling on each pasta square.

7 Brush a little water around the edge of each square, then fold the square diagonally in half over the filling to make a triangle. Press gently to seal.

8 Spread out the pansotti on clean floured dish towels, sprinkle lightly with flour and set aside to dry, while repeating the process with the remaining dough, to make a total of 64–80 pansotti.

9 Cook the pansotti in a large pan of boiling salted water for 4–5 minutes, until tender.

10 Meanwhile, put the walnut sauce in a large, warmed bowl and add a ladleful of the pasta cooking water to thin it down. Melt the butter in a small pan until sizzling.

11 Drain the pansotti and tip them into the bowl of walnut sauce. Drizzle the butter over them, toss well, then sprinkle with grated Parmesan. Alternatively, toss the pansotti in the melted butter, spoon into warmed individual bowls and drizzle over the sauce. Serve the dish immediately, with extra Parmesan handed round separately.

Energy 535kcal/2228kJ; Protein 17.3g; Carbohydrate 30.9g, of which sugars 2.3g; Fat 39g, of which saturates 16.3g; Cholesterol 157mg; Calcium 271mg; Fibre 1.9g; Sodium 483mg.

squid sauce

What better partner for a delicious squid sauce than squid ink tagliatelle? The tastes blend perfectly, but the sauce will enhance any plain pasta.

2 Add 30ml/2 tbsp of the parsley to the pan, stir, then add the squid and stir again. Cook for 3–4 minutes, then add wine.

3 Simmer for a few seconds, then add the tomatoes and chilli.

4 Season the mixture. Cover and simmer gently for about 1 hour, until the squid is tender. Add more water if necessary.

5 Cook the pasta in plenty of boiling, salted water, according to the instructions on the packet, until *al dente*. Drain and return the tagliatelle to the pan. Add the squid sauce and mix well.

6 Serve at once, sprinkled with the remaining chopped parsley.

Serves four

INGREDIENTS

450g/1lb squid ink tagliatelle

For the squid sauce

105ml/7 tbsp olive oil
2 shallots, chopped
3 garlic cloves, crushed
45ml/3 tbsp chopped fresh parsley
675g/1½ lb cleaned squid, cut into rings and rinsed
150ml/¼ pint/⅔ cup dry white wine
400g/14oz can chopped plum tomatoes
2.5ml/½ tsp dried chilli flakes or powder
salt and ground black pepper

1 Heat the oil in a pan and add the shallots. Cook until pale golden, then add the garlic and cook for a few more minutes until it colours a little.

Energy 746kcal/3145kJ; Protein 40.8g; Carbohydrate 90.2g, of which sugars 8.1g; Fat 24.6g, of which saturates 3.8g; Cholesterol 380mg; Calcium 87mg; Fibre 5g; Sodium 204mg.

clam and tomato sauce

Clam and tomato sauce is a regular dish in Neopolitan restaurants, where it is often served with vermicelli or spaghetti. Fresh mussels could be substituted for the clams.

Serves four

INGREDIENTS

350g/12oz vermicelli

For the clam and tomato sauce

1kg/2¼ lb fresh hard-shell clams

250ml/8fl oz/1 cup dry white wine

2 garlic cloves, bruised

1 large handful fresh flat leaf parsley

30ml/2 tbsp olive oil

1 small onion, finely chopped

8 ripe plum tomatoes, peeled, deseeded and finely chopped

½–1 fresh red chilli, deseeded and finely chopped

salt and ground black pepper

1 Scrub the clams thoroughly under cold running water and discard any that are open and that do not close when they are sharply tapped against the work surface.

2 Pour the wine into a large pan, add the garlic cloves and half the parsley, then the clams. Cover tightly and bring to the boil over high heat. Cook for about 5 minutes, shaking frequently, until the clams have opened.

3 Tip the clams into a large colander over a bowl to drain. Set aside until cool enough to handle, then remove about two-thirds of them from their shells, pouring the clam liquid into the bowl of cooking liquid. Discard any clams that have failed to open. Set both shelled and unshelled clams aside, keeping the unshelled clams warm in a bowl covered with a lid.

4 Heat the oil in a pan, add the onion and cook gently, stirring frequently, for about 5 minutes until softened and lightly coloured. Add the tomatoes, then strain in the clam cooking liquid. Add the chilli and salt and pepper to taste. Chop the remaining parsley finely and set aside.

5 Bring to the boil, half-cover the pan and allow to simmer gently for 15–20 minutes.

6 Meanwhile, cook the pasta according to the instructions on the packet, until it is *al dente*. Drain the pasta well and tip it into a warmed bowl.

7 Meanwhile, add the shelled clams to the tomato sauce, stir well and heat very gently for 2–3 minutes.

8 Taste the sauce for seasoning, then pour the sauce over the pasta and toss everything together well. Serve garnished with the reserved clams and sprinkled with parsley.

Energy 493kcal/2064kJ; Protein 19.6g; Carbohydrate 77.8g, of which sugars 7.7g; Fat 7g, of which saturates 1.1g; Cholesterol 42mg; Calcium 114mg; Fibre 2.8g; Sodium 782mg.

prawn and vodka sauce

The combination of prawns, vodka and pasta has become a modern classic in Italy. Here the sauce is served with two-coloured pasta, but it also goes well with short shapes such as penne.

Serves four

INGREDIENTS

350g/12oz fresh or dried paglia e fieno

For the prawn and vodka sauce

30ml/2 tbsp olive oil

¼ large onion, finely chopped

1 garlic clove, crushed

15–30ml/1–2 tbsp sun-dried tomato purée (paste)

200ml/7fl oz/scant 1 cup double (heavy) cream

12 large raw prawns (shrimp), peeled and chopped

30ml/2 tbsp vodka

salt and ground black pepper

1 Soften the onion and garlic gently in the oil, stirring, for 5 minutes.

2 Add the tomato purée and stir for 1–2 minutes, then add the cream and bring to the boil, stirring. Season the sauce with salt and pepper to taste, and allow it to bubble gently until it starts to thicken slightly. Then remove the pan from the heat.

3 Cook the pasta according to the packet instructions, until *al dente*. When it is almost ready, add the prawns and vodka to the sauce; toss over a medium heat for 2–3 minutes, until the prawns are pink.

4 Drain the pasta and turn it into a warmed bowl. Pour the sauce over and toss well. Divide among warmed bowls and serve at once.

COOK'S TIP

This sauce is best as soon as it is ready, otherwise the prawns (shrimp) overcook and toughen. Make sure that the pasta is very nearly cooked before adding the prawns to the sauce.

Energy 641kcal/2682kJ; Protein 16.1g; Carbohydrate 67.4g, of which sugars 5.1g; Fat 34.1g, of which saturates 17.7g; Cholesterol 117mg; Calcium 71mg; Fibre 2.9g; Sodium 71mg.

smoked salmon and cream sauce

This modern way of serving pasta is popular all over Italy. The three essential ingredients combine beautifully, and the dish is very quick and easy to make.

Serves four

INGREDIENTS

350g/12oz penne

For the smoked salmon and cream sauce

115g/4oz thinly sliced smoked salmon

2–3 fresh thyme sprigs

30ml/2 tbsp butter

150ml/¼ pint/⅔ cup double (heavy) cream

salt and ground black pepper

1 Cook the pasta in boiling salted water until it is *al dente*.

2 Meanwhile, using kitchen scissors, cut the smoked salmon into thin strips, about 5mm/¼in wide. Strip the leaves from the thyme sprigs.

3 Melt the butter in a large pan. Stir in the cream with a quarter of the salmon and thyme leaves, then season with pepper. Heat gently for 3–4 minutes, stirring constantly. Do not allow to boil. Taste for seasoning.

4 Drain the pasta and toss it in the cream and salmon sauce. Divide among four warmed bowls and top with the remaining salmon and thyme leaves. Serve immediately.

Energy 582kcal/2441kJ; Protein 18.5g; Carbohydrate 65.5g, of which sugars 3.6g; Fat 29.2g, of which saturates 16.8g; Cholesterol 77mg; Calcium 47mg; Fibre 2.6g; Sodium 597mg.

salsa picante for chicken enchilladas

This "hot" salsa is actually a low-heat version using seeded green chillies, and is also cooled down by the soured cream. It also makes a good side dish with kebabs of chicken or pork.

3 Preheat the oven to 180°C/350°F/ Gas 4 and butter a shallow ovenproof dish. Take one tortilla and sprinkle with a good pinch of cheese and chopped onion, about 40g/1½oz of the chicken and 15ml/ 1 tbsp of salsa picante.

4 Pour over 15ml/1 tbsp of sour cream, roll up and place, seam-side down, in the dish. Make seven more enchilladas.

Serves four

INGREDIENTS

8 wheat tortillas

175g/6oz/1½ cups grated Cheddar cheese

1 onion, finely chopped

350g/12oz cooked chicken, cut into small chunks

300ml/½ pint/1¼ cups sour cream

1 avocado, sliced and tossed in lemon juice, to garnish

For the salsa picante

1–2 green chillies

15ml/1 tbsp vegetable oil

1 onion, chopped

1 garlic clove, crushed

400g/14oz can chopped tomatoes

30ml/2 tbsp tomato purée (paste)

salt and ground black pepper

1 To make the salsa picante, cut the chillies in half lengthways and carefully remove the cores and seeds. Slice the chillies very finely. Heat the oil in a frying pan and fry the onion and garlic for about 3–4 minutes until softened. Add the tomatoes, tomato purée and chillies. Simmer gently, uncovered, for 12–15 minutes, stirring the mixture frequently.

2 Pour the sauce into a food processor or blender, and process until smooth. Return to the heat and cook very gently, uncovered, for a further 15 minutes. Season to taste then set aside.

5 Pour the remaining salsa over the top and sprinkle with cheese and onion. Bake in the oven for 25–30 minutes until golden. Serve with the remaining cream. Garnish with the sliced avocado.

Energy 665kcal/2778kJ; Protein 39.8g; Carbohydrate 39.8g, of which sugars 9.4g; Fat 38.7g, of which saturates 20.6g; Cholesterol 149mg; Calcium 472mg; Fibre 3.7g; Sodium 569mg.

cajun-style tomato sauce for chicken

Sizzling fried chicken served in a hot and tasty tomato sauce is irresistibly good with plain rice mixed with corn and chives. The sauce is also good with pan-fried pork.

Serves four

INGREDIENTS

1 chicken, 1.6kg/3½ lb, cut into 8 pieces

90g/3½ oz/¾ cup plain (all-purpose) flour

250ml/8fl oz/1 cup buttermilk or milk

vegetable oil, for frying

salt and ground black pepper

chopped spring onions (scallions), and fresh coriander (cilantro) sprigs, to garnish

For the cajun-style tomato sauce

115g/4oz/½ cup lard or vegetable oil

2 onions, chopped

2–3 celery sticks, chopped

1 large green (bell) pepper, seeded and chopped

2 garlic cloves, finely chopped

65g/2½ oz/9 tbsp plain (all-purpose) flour

225g/8oz tomatoes

250ml/8fl oz/1 cup passata (bottled strained tomatoes)

450ml/¾ pint/scant 2 cups red wine or chicken stock

2 bay leaves

15ml/1 tbsp soft brown sugar

5ml/1 tsp grated orange rind

2.5ml/½ tsp cayenne pepper

1 For the sauce, heat the lard or oil in a large pan. Add the onions, celery, green pepper and garlic and cook, stirring, until softened. Stir in the flour. Cook over a medium heat, stirring for 15–20 minutes.

2 Plunge the tomatoes into boiling water for 30 seconds, then refresh in cold water. Peel and chop the tomatoes, then stir them into the onion mixture with the remaining sauce ingredients and seasoning. Boil, then simmer gently for 1 hour.

3 Meanwhile, prepare the chicken. Put the flour in a plastic bag and season with salt and pepper. Dip each piece of chicken in buttermilk or milk, then dredge in the flour to coat lightly all over. Shake off the excess flour. Set the chicken aside for 20 minutes to let the coating set before frying.

4 Heat the vegetable oil 2.5cm/1in deep in a large pan until it is very hot and starting to sizzle. Fry the chicken pieces, turning them once, for about 30 minutes, or until deep golden brown all over and cooked through.

5 Drain the chicken on kitchen paper and add them to the sauce. Serve immediately, garnished with a sprinkling of spring onion and coriander sprigs.

Energy 796kcal/3295kJ; Protein 33.2g; Carbohydrate 18.8g, of which sugars 5.9g; Fat 65.7g, of which saturates 12.5g; Cholesterol 160mg; Calcium 57mg; Fibre 2.2g; Sodium 147mg.

curried apricot sauce for turkey kebabs

This is a South African way of cooking poultry in a delicious sweet-and-sour spiced sauce.

Serves four

INGREDIENTS
675g/1½lb turkey breast fillet60ml/4 tbsp
crème fraîche

For the curried apricot sauce
15ml/1 tbsp oil
1 onion, finely chopped
1 garlic clove, crushed
2 bay leaves
juice of 1 lemon
30ml/2 tbsp curry powder
60ml/4 tbsp apricot jam
60ml/4 tbsp apple juice
salt

1 Heat the oil in a pan. Add the onion, garlic and bay leaves and cook over low heat until the onions are soft. Add the lemon juice, curry powder, jam, apple juice and salt. Cook for 5 minutes, then cool.

2 Cut the turkey into 2cm/¾in cubes and add to the marinade. Mix well, cover and leave in a cool place to marinate for at least 2 hours or chill overnight.

3 Prepare a barbecue or preheat the grill (broiler). Thread the turkey on to four metal skewers, allowing the marinade to run back into the bowl. Cook the kebabs for 6–8 minutes, turning often, until done.

4 Meanwhile, transfer the marinade to a pan and simmer for 2 minutes. Stir in the crème fraîche and serve.

Energy 411kcal/1733kJ; Protein 60.4g; Carbohydrate 15.4g, of which sugars 13g; Fat 12.5g, of which saturates 5.5g; Cholesterol 142mg; Calcium 72mg; Fibre 1.9g; Sodium 197mg.

sambal kecap for chicken kebabs

A spicy marinade makes tender chicken exotic. The satays can be barbecued or grilled.

Serves four

INGREDIENTS
4 chicken breast fillets, about 175g/6oz
  each, skinned
30ml/2 tbsp deep-fried onion slices

For the sambal kecap
1 fresh red chilli, seeded and finely
  chopped
2 garlic cloves, crushed
60ml/4 tbsp dark soy sauce
20ml/4 tsp lemon juice or 15–25ml/
  1–1½ tbsp tamarind juice
30ml/2 tbsp hot water

1 Soak eight wooden skewers in water for at least 30 minutes. Drain the skewers just before using them – this prevents them from burning during cooking.

2 To make the sambal kecap, mix the chilli, garlic, soy sauce, lemon or tamarind juice and hot water. Leave to stand for 30 minutes.

3 Cut the chicken into 2.5cm/1in cubes and add to the sambal kecap. Mix thoroughly. Cover and leave in a cool place to marinate for 1 hour.

4 Turn the chicken and marinade into a sieve placed over a pan and leave to drain for a few minutes. Set the sieve aside.

5 Add 30ml/2 tbsp hot water to the marinade and bring to the boil. Lower the heat and simmer for 2 minutes, then pour into a bowl and leave to cool. When cool, add the deep-fried onions.

6 Prepare a barbecue or preheat the grill (broiler). Thread the skewers with the chicken and cook for about 10 minutes, turning regularly, until the chicken is golden and cooked through. Serve with the sambal kecap as a dip.

Energy 265kcal/1120kJ; Protein 55.2g; Carbohydrate 3.5g, of which sugars 2g; Fat 3.4g, of which saturates 1g; Cholesterol 158mg; Calcium 19mg; Fibre 0.6g; Sodium 1204mg.

marsala cream for turkey

Marsala and cream make a very rich and opulent sauce. The addition of lemon juice gives it a refreshing tang, which offsets the richness just perfectly.

Serves six

INGREDIENTS

6 turkey breast steaks
45ml/3 tbsp plain (all-purpose) flour
30ml/2 tbsp olive oil
25g/1oz/2 tbsp butter
salt and ground black pepper

For the Marsala cream sauce
175ml/6fl oz/¾ cup dry Marsala
60ml/4 tbsp lemon juice
175ml/6fl oz/¾ cup double (heavy) cream

To serve
lemon wedges and chopped fresh
  parsley, to garnish
mangetouts (snowpeas) and green beans

1 Put each turkey steak between clear film (plastic wrap) and pound with a rolling pin to flatten out evenly. Cut each steak in half or into quarters, cutting away and discarding any sinew.

2 Spread out the flour in a shallow bowl. Season well with salt and pepper and coat the meat.

COOK'S TIP
To make this sauce without using the pan drippings, omit the oil and heat the butter in a pan before adding the other ingredients.

3 Heat the oil and butter in a wide, heavy pan or frying pan until sizzling. Add as many pieces of turkey as you can, and sauté over a medium heat for about 3 minutes on each side until crispy and tender.

4 Using tongs or a spoon and fork, transfer the turkey to a warmed serving dish and keep hot. Cook the remaining turkey in the same way and remove from the pan. Tent the turkey loosely with foil and keep hot while making the sauce.

5 To make the sauce, mix the Marsala and lemon juice in a jug (pitcher), add to the oil and butter remaining in the pan. Bring to the boil, stirring in the sediment, then add the cream.

6 Heat gently until simmering, then continue to simmer, stirring constantly, until the sauce is reduced and glossy. Taste for seasoning before serving.

7 Spoon the sauce over the turkey, garnish with the lemon wedges and parsley and serve at once.

Energy 391kcal/1625kJ; Protein 29.7g; Carbohydrate 6.8g, of which sugars 1.1g; Fat 23.8g, of which saturates 12.8g; Cholesterol 115mg; Calcium 32mg; Fibre 0.2g; Sodium 93mg.

tarragon and parsley sauce for chicken

The aniseed-like flavour of tarragon has a particular affinity with chicken, especially in creamy sauces. Serve seasonal vegetables and boiled red Camargue rice with the chicken.

Serves four

INGREDIENTS

30ml/2 tbsp light olive oil

4 chicken breast portions (about 250g/9oz each), skinned

3 shallots, finely chopped

2 garlic cloves, finely chopped

115g/4oz/1½ cups wild mushrooms (such as chanterelles or ceps) or shiitake mushrooms, halved

150ml/¼ pint/⅔ cup dry white wine

300ml/½ pint/1¼ cups double (heavy) cream

15g/½oz/¼ cup chopped mixed fresh tarragon and flat leaf parsley

salt and ground black pepper

sprigs of fresh tarragon and flat leaf parsley, to garnish

1 Heat the olive oil in a frying pan and add the chicken, skin side down. Cook for 10 minutes, turning the chicken until it is a golden brown colour on both sides.

2 Reduce the heat and cook the chicken for 10 minutes more, turning occasionally. Remove from the pan and set aside.

3 Add the shallots and garlic to the pan and cook gently, stirring, until the shallots are soft but not brown.

4 Increase the heat, add the mushrooms and stir-fry for 2 minutes. Replace the chicken, then pour in the wine. Simmer for 5–10 minutes, or until most of the wine has evaporated.

5 Add the cream and gently mix the ingredients together. Simmer for 10 minutes, or until the sauce has thickened. Stir the herbs into the sauce and season to taste. Arrange the chicken on warm plates and spoon the sauce over. Garnish with tarragon and parsley.

SAFETY TIP

Unless you're an expert, or know of one who will identify them for you, it's safer not to pick mushrooms in the wild, but buy them instead from a reliable source.

Energy 722kcal/3003kJ; Protein 62.1g; Carbohydrate 2.9g, of which sugars 2.5g; Fat 48.8g, of which saturates 26.6g; Cholesterol 278mg; Calcium 66mg; Fibre 0.7g; Sodium 171mg.

cashew nut sauce for chicken

The nut sauce for this chicken dish is deliciously thick and nutty. The sauce is also good with cooked pork or turkey. It is best served with fluffy, plain boiled rice.

Serves four

INGREDIENTS

2 onions

30ml/2 tbsp tomato purée (paste)

50g/2oz/½ cup cashew nuts

7.5ml/1½ tsp garam masala

5ml/1 tsp crushed garlic

5ml/1 tsp chilli powder

15ml/1 tbsp lemon juice

1.5ml/¼ tsp ground turmeric

5ml/1 tsp salt

15ml/1 tbsp natural (plain) low-fat yogurt

30ml/2 tbsp corn oil

15ml/1 tbsp chopped fresh
   coriander (cilantro)

15ml/1 tbsp sultanas (golden raisins)

450g/1lb/3¼ cups cubed chicken

175g/6oz/2¼ cups button (white)
   mushrooms, halved

300ml/½ pint/1¼ cups water

chopped fresh coriander (cilantro),
   to garnish

1 Cut the onions into quarters then place them in a food processor or blender and process for about 1 minute, until very finely chopped.

2 Add the tomato purée, cashew nuts, garam masala, garlic, chilli powder, lemon juice, turmeric, salt and yogurt. Process for a further 1–1½ minutes.

3 In a pan, heat the oil, lower the heat to medium and pour in the spice mixture from the food processor. Fry for about 2 minutes, turning down the heat if necessary.

4 Add the fresh coriander, sultanas and cubed chicken and continue to stir-fry for a further 1 minute.

5 Add the mushrooms, pour in the water and bring to a simmer. Cover and cook over a low heat for about 10 minutes, or until the chicken is cooked through and the sauce is thick. Cook for a little longer if necessary.

6 Serve garnished with chopped fresh coriander.

Energy 297kcal/1244kJ; Protein 32g; Carbohydrate 12.5g, of which sugars 9g; Fat 13.6g, of which saturates 2.5g; Cholesterol 79mg; Calcium 51mg; Fibre 2.4g; Sodium 131mg.

orange and pepper sauce for chicken

Orange, ginger, coriander, garlic and black pepper make a deliciously zesty sauce for chicken in this low-fat curry. The sauce is also a good choice for turkey or duck.

Serves four

INGREDIENTS

225g/8oz low-fat fromage frais or
  ricotta cheese

50ml/2fl oz/¼ cup natural (plain)
  low-fat yogurt

120ml/4fl oz/½ cup orange juice

7.5ml/1½ tsp grated fresh root ginger

5ml/1 tsp crushed garlic

5ml/1 tsp freshly ground black pepper

5ml/1 tsp salt

5ml/1 tsp ground coriander

1 chicken, about 675g/1½lb, skinned and
  cut into 8 pieces

15ml/1 tbsp oil

1 bay leaf

1 large onion, chopped

15ml/1 tbsp fresh mint leaves

1 green chilli, seeded and chopped

1 In a small bowl whisk together the fromage frais or ricotta cheese, yogurt, orange juice, ginger, garlic, pepper, salt and coriander.

COOK'S TIP

If you prefer the taste of curry leaves, you can use them instead of the bay leaf, but you need to double the quantity.

2 Pour the sauce over the chicken, turn the pieces to coat them evenly, and set aside for 3–4 hours.

3 Heat the oil with the bay leaf in a wok or heavy frying pan and fry the onion until soft.

4 Pour in the chicken mixture and stir-fry for 3–5 minutes over a medium heat. Lower the heat, cover and cook for 7–10 minutes, until the chicken is cooked. Add a little water if the sauce is too thick. Add the mint and chilli, and serve.

Energy 362kcal/1525kJ; Protein 58.4g; Carbohydrate 13.3g, of which sugars 11.9g; Fat 8.7g, of which saturates 3.1g; Cholesterol 169mg; Calcium 117mg; Fibre 0.3g; Sodium 171mg.

classic korma sauce for chicken

Although kormas are traditionally rich, this recipe uses yogurt instead of cream, which lightens the sauce. To prevent the yogurt from curdling, add it very slowly, stirring until it is mixed.

3 Heat the oil in a large, heavy pan and cook the chicken cubes for 8–10 minutes, or until browned on all sides. Remove the chicken cubes with a slotted spoon and set aside.

4 Add the cardamom pods and fry for 2 minutes. Add the onion and fry for a further 5 minutes.

5 Stir in the garlic and ginger paste, cumin and salt, and cook, stirring, for a further 5 minutes.

6 Add half the yogurt, stirring in a tablespoonful at a time, and cook over a low heat, until it has all been absorbed. Return the chicken to the pan.

7 Cover and simmer over a low heat for 5–6 minutes, or until the chicken is tender. Add the remaining yogurt and simmer for a further 5 minutes. Garnish with toasted flaked almonds, if using, and coriander. Serve with rice.

Serves four

INGREDIENTS

675g/1½lb chicken breast fillet, skinned

2 garlic cloves, crushed

2.5cm/1in piece fresh root ginger, roughly chopped

15ml/1 tbsp oil

3 green cardamom pods

1 onion, finely chopped

10ml/2 tsp ground cumin

1.5ml/¼ tsp salt

300ml/½ pint/1¼ cups natural (plain) low-fat yogurt

toasted flaked (sliced) almonds (optional) and a fresh coriander (cilantro) sprig, to garnish

plain rice, to serve

1 Remove any visible fat from the chicken fillets and cut the meat into 2.5cm/1in cubes.

2 Put the garlic and ginger into a food processor or blender with 30ml/2 tbsp water and process to a smooth, creamy paste.

COOK'S TIP

Traditionally, kormas are spicy dishes with a rich, creamy texture. They are not meant to be very hot curries.

Energy 251kcal/1059kJ; Protein 44.5g; Carbohydrate 6.8g, of which sugars 6.5g; Fat 5.4g, of which saturates 1.3g; Cholesterol 119mg; Calcium 155mg; Fibre 0.2g; Sodium 164mg.

hara masala sauce for chicken

This fruity chicken dish has a creamy sauce, enlivened with a kick of chilli balanced by a twist of mint and coriander flavours. It tastes terrific and looks attractive too.

Serves four

INGREDIENTS

1 crisp green eating apple, peeled, cored and cut into small cubes

60ml/4 tbsp fresh coriander (cilantro) leaves

30ml/2 tbsp fresh mint leaves

120ml/4fl oz/½ cup natural (plain) low-fat yogurt

45ml/3 tbsp low-fat fromage frais or ricotta cheese

2 medium green chillies, seeded and chopped

1 bunch spring onions (scallions), chopped

5ml/1 tsp salt

5ml/1 tsp sugar

5ml/1 tsp crushed garlic

5ml/1 tsp grated fresh root ginger

15ml/1 tbsp oil

225g/8oz chicken breast fillet, skinned and cubed

25g/1oz/2 tbsp sultanas (golden raisins)

1 Process the apple, 45ml/3 tbsp of the coriander, the mint, yogurt, fromage frais or ricotta, chillies, spring onions, salt, sugar, garlic and ginger in a food processor for about 1 minute, pulsing the power.

2 Heat the oil in a frying pan, pour in the yogurt mixture and cook over a low heat for 2 minutes.

3 Next, add the chicken cubes and blend everything together. Cook over a medium-low heat for 12–15 minutes, or until the chicken is fully cooked through.

4 Finally, just before serving the chicken, add the sultanas and the remaining 15ml/1 tbsp fresh coriander leaves. Stir lightly to mix, and serve.

Energy 150kcal/630kJ; Protein 16.8g; Carbohydrate 10.7g, of which sugars 10.5g; Fat 4.8g, of which saturates 1.3g; Cholesterol 41mg; Calcium 111mg; Fibre 1.4g; Sodium 561mg.

pomegranate and nut sauce for duck

This exotic sweet-and-sour sauce originally comes from Iran. Walnuts are nutty but slightly tender when cooked and their mellow flavour is the perfect match for sweet pomegranates.

2 Transfer to a pan, add the walnuts and stock, then season with salt and pepper. Stir, then bring to the boil and simmer the mixture, uncovered, for 20 minutes.

3 Cut the pomegranates in half and scoop out the seeds. Reserve the seeds of one pomegranate. Transfer the remaining seeds to a blender and process to break them up. Strain through a sieve, to extract the juice, and stir in the sugar and lemon juice.

4 Score the skin of the duck breasts in a diamond pattern with a sharp knife. Heat the remaining oil in a frying pan or griddle and place the duck breasts in it, skin-side down.

5 Cook gently for 10 minutes, pouring off the fat, until the skin is dark golden and crisp. Turn the duck breasts over and cook for a further 3–4 minutes. Transfer to a plate and leave to rest. Deglaze the frying pan with the pomegranate juice, then add the walnut and stock mixture and simmer for 15 minutes until thickened.

6 Slice the duck and serve drizzled with a little sauce, and garnished with the reserved pomegranate seeds. Serve the remaining sauce separately.

COOK'S TIP
Choose pomegranates with shiny, brightly coloured skins. Only the seeds are used in cooking; pith is discarded.

Serves four

INGREDIENTS
4 duck breasts, about 225g/8oz each

For the pomegranate and nut sauce
30ml/2 tbsp olive oil
2 onions, very thinly sliced
2.5ml/½ tsp ground turmeric
400g/14oz/2½ cups walnuts, roughly chopped
1 litre/1¾ pints/4 cups duck or chicken stock
6 pomegranates
30ml/2 tbsp caster (superfine) sugar
60ml/4 tbsp lemon juice
salt and ground black pepper

1 To make the sauce, heat half the oil in a frying pan. Add the onions and turmeric, and cook gently for a few minutes until soft.

Energy 1052kcal/4366kJ; Protein 59.6g; Carbohydrate 13.2g, of which sugars 12.2g; Fat 88.7g, of which saturates 9.3g; Cholesterol 248mg; Calcium 131mg; Fibre 4.2g; Sodium 258mg.

spicy plum sauce for duck sausages

These rich duck sausages – which are better baked in their own juices than fried – are perfectly complemented by the spiciness of the plum sauce. Add sweet potato mash for a fabulous meal.

Serves four

INGREDIENTS

8–12 duck sausages

For the sweet potato mash

1.5kg/3¼lb sweet potatoes, cut into chunks

25g/1oz/2 tbsp butter

60ml/4 tbsp milk

salt and ground black pepper

For the plum sauce

30ml/2 tbsp olive oil

1 small onion, chopped

1 small red chilli, seeded and chopped

450g/1lb plums, stoned (pitted) and chopped

30ml/2 tbsp red wine vinegar

45ml/3 tbsp clear honey

1 Preheat the oven to 190°C/375°F/ Gas 5. Arrange the duck sausages in a single layer in a large, shallow ovenproof dish and bake, uncovered, for 25–30 minutes, until browned and crisp. Turn the sausages two or three times during cooking, to ensure that they brown and cook evenly.

2 Meanwhile, put the sweet potatoes in a pan and pour in enough water to cover them. Bring to the boil, reduce the heat and simmer for 20 minutes, or until tender. Drain and mash, then place the pan over a low heat. Stir frequently for about 5 minutes to dry out the mashed potato. Beat in the butter and milk, season.

3 Heat the oil in a small pan and fry the onion and chilli gently for 5 minutes. Stir in the plums, vinegar and honey, then simmer gently for 10 minutes.

4 Serve the freshly cooked sausages with the mash and plum sauce.

Energy 1058kcal/4434kJ; Protein 21.9g; Carbohydrate 114.6g, of which sugars 43.6g; Fat 60.3g, of which saturates 22.9g; Cholesterol 85mg; Calcium 190mg; Fibre 11.8g; Sodium 1338mg.

cranberry sauce for venison

Venison steaks are a healthy choice for a special occasion and delicious with this sauce of cranberries, port and ginger. The sauce also complements roast duck, pork, lamb or turkey.

Serves four

INGREDIENTS

30ml/2 tbsp sunflower oil

4 venison steaks

2 shallots, finely chopped

salt and ground black pepper

fresh thyme sprigs, to garnish

creamy mashed potatoes and broccoli, to serve

For the cranberry sauce

1 orange

1 lemon

75g/3oz/¾ cup fresh or frozen cranberries

5ml/1 tsp grated fresh root ginger

1 fresh thyme sprig

5ml/1 tsp Dijon mustard

60ml/4 tbsp redcurrant jelly

150ml/¼ pint/⅔ cup ruby port

1 For the sauce, use a vegetable peeler to pare the rind thinly from half the orange and half the lemon, then cut into very fine strips.

2 Blanch the citrus rind strips in a small pan of boiling water for about 5 minutes until tender. Strain the strips and refresh in cold water.

3 Squeeze the juice from the orange and lemon and then pour into a small pan. Add the cranberries, ginger, thyme, mustard, redcurrant jelly and port. Cook over a low heat until the jelly melts.

4 Bring to the boil, stirring occasionally, then cover and cook gently, for about 15 minutes, or until the cranberries are just tender.

5 Heat the oil in a heavy frying pan, add the venison and cook over a high heat for 2–3 minutes.

6 Turn the steaks and add the shallots. Cook for 2–3 minutes, depending on whether you like rare or medium cooked meat.

7 Just before the end of cooking, pour in the sauce and add the citrus strips. Cook for a few seconds to thicken slightly, then remove the thyme and add seasoning to taste.

8 Transfer the venison steaks to warmed plates and spoon over the sauce. Garnish with thyme sprigs and serve accompanied by creamy mashed potatoes and broccoli.

COOK'S TIP

When frying venison, always remember the briefer the better – venison will turn to leather if subjected to fierce heat after it has reached the medium-rare stage. If you dislike any hint of pink, cook it to this stage and then let it rest in a low oven for a few minutes.

Energy 315kcal/1328kJ; Protein 33.7g; Carbohydrate 17.8g, of which sugars 17.8g; Fat 8.9g, of which saturates 1.9g; Cholesterol 75mg; Calcium 16mg; Fibre 0.4g; Sodium 106mg.

redcurrant sauce for lamb burgers

The sweet-sour redcurrant sauce is the perfect complement to the taste of lamb and would go equally well with grilled or roast lamb steaks.

Serves four

INGREDIENTS

500g/1¼lb minced (ground) lean lamb
1 small onion, finely chopped
30ml/2 tbsp finely chopped fresh mint
30ml/2 tbsp finely chopped fresh parsley
115g/4oz mozzarella cheese
30ml/2 tbsp oil, for basting
salt and ground black pepper

For the redcurrant sauce

115g/4oz/1 cup fresh or frozen
  redcurrants
10ml/2 tsp clear honey
5ml/1 tsp balsamic vinegar
30ml/2 tbsp finely chopped mint

1 To make the sauce, place all the ingredients in a bowl and mash them together with a fork. Season with salt and ground black pepper. Set aside at room temperature.

2 Mix the lamb, onion, mint and parsley with plenty of salt and pepper. Divide the mixture into eight and press into a flat rounds.

3 Cut the mozzarella into four chunks. Place a chunk of cheese on half of the lamb rounds. Top each with another round of meat.

4 Press the two rounds of meat together firmly, making four fairly flat burgers. Use your fingers to pinch and blend the edges, and seal in the cheese completely. If the edges are not well sealed, the cheese will flow out as it melts during cooking.

VARIATION

For a store-cupboard (pantry) sauce, melt a jar of redcurrant jelly in a small pan over low heat. Stir in the balsamic vinegar and mint but omit the honey. Add a handful of fresh or frozen rapsberries (if available), lightly crushed.

5 Brush the lamb burgers with olive oil and cook over a moderately hot barbecue for about 15 minutes, or grill for 10 minutes turning once, until golden brown. Serve with the sauce.

Energy 393kcal/1637kJ; Protein 30.1g; Carbohydrate 5.3g, of which sugars 4.9g; Fat 28.2g, of which saturates 12.4g; Cholesterol 113mg; Calcium 172mg; Fibre 1.9g; Sodium 206mg.

cook-in tomato sauce for meatballs

For a quick tomato sauce, passata can be enlivened with a little sugar, bay leaves and onions.
This makes an ideal "cook-in" sauce for fish, poultry or meat – little Greek-style meatballs
flavour the smooth sauce as they simmer gently in this recipe.

Serves four

INGREDIENTS

50g/2oz/1 cup fresh breadcrumbs
150ml/¼ pint/⅔ cup milk
675g/1½ lb minced (ground) lamb
30ml/2 tbsp grated onion
3 garlic cloves, crushed
10ml/2 tsp ground cumin
30ml/2 tbsp chopped fresh parsley
flour, for dusting
olive oil, for frying
salt and ground black pepper
fresh flat leaf parsley, to garnish

For the tomato sauce

600ml/1 pint/2½ cups passata (bottled
  strained tomatoes)
5ml/1 tsp sugar
2 bay leaves
1 small onion, peeled

1 Mix together the breadcrumbs
and milk. Add the lamb, onion,
garlic, cumin and parsley and
season with salt and pepper.

2 Shape the mixture into little fat
sausages, about 5cm/2in long, and
roll them in flour. Place on a plate
and chill briefly, if possible, so the
sausages firm up slightly.

3 Meanwhile, prepare the sauce.
Put the passata, sugar, bay leaves
and whole onion in a pan. Bring to
the boil, reduce the heat and cover
the pan. Simmer for 20 minutes.

4 Heat a little olive oil in a frying
pan. Fry the sausages for about 8
minutes, turning, until evenly
browned. Spoon out any excess fat.

5 Pour the sauce over the sausages
and simmer gently for 10 minutes.
Serve garnished with parsley.

VARIATION

Lamb is more commonly used in
Greece for these sausages, but as an
alternative you could try using minced
(ground) turkey.

Energy 530kcal/2212kJ; Protein 36.8g; Carbohydrate 19.6g, of which sugars 9.5g; Fat 34.5g, of which saturates 12.4g; Cholesterol 132mg; Calcium 128mg; Fibre 2g; Sodium 576mg.

baked pesto for lamb

The intense aromas of fresh basil and garlic in classic pesto sauce combine irresistibly with lamb, and the pine nuts and Parmesan create a delectable crunchy crust during roasting. This is an unusual way of using the simple sauce that is so good with plain cooked pasta.

Serves six

INGREDIENTS

2.25–2.75kg/5–6lb leg of lamb

For the pesto

90g/3½oz/1¾ cups fresh basil leaves

4 garlic cloves, coarsely chopped

45ml/3 tbsp pine nuts

150ml/¼ pint/⅔ cup olive oil

50g/2oz/⅔ cup freshly grated Parmesan cheese

5ml/1 tsp salt, or to taste

1 To make the pesto, combine the basil, garlic and pine nuts in a food processor, and process until finely chopped. With the motor running, slowly add the oil in a steady stream. Scrape the mixture into a bowl. Stir in the Parmesan and salt.

2 Set the lamb in a roasting dish. Use a small pointed knife to make several slits into the meat. Spoon pesto into each slit.

3 Coat the surface of the lamb in a thick, even layer of the remaining pesto. Cover the meat and leave to stand for 2 hours at room temperature, or chill overnight.

4 Preheat the oven to 180°C/350°F/ Gas 4. Place the lamb in the oven and roast, allowing about 20 minutes per 450g/1lb if you like rare meat, or 25 minutes per 450g/1lb if you prefer it medium-rare. Turn the lamb occasionally during roasting.

5 Remove the leg of lamb from the oven, cover it loosely with foil, and let it rest for about 15 minutes before carving and serving.

VARIATION

Lamb steaks or lamb chops could be coated with this delicious pesto. It is also good as a filling for baked butternut squash or potatoes.

Energy 1006kcal/4206kJ; Protein 116.2g; Carbohydrate 0.7g, of which sugars 0.6g; Fat 60g, of which saturates 18.7g; Cholesterol 383mg; Calcium 157mg; Fibre 0.9g; Sodium 332mg.

red onion relish for lamb burgers

A sharp-sweet relish of red onions, ripe little tomatoes and red peppers works well with burgers based on Middle-Eastern style lamb. Serve with pitta bread, fries and a green salad.

Serves four

INGREDIENTS

25g/1oz/3 tbsp bulgur wheat

500g/1¼lb lean minced (ground) lamb

1 small red onion, finely chopped

2 garlic cloves, finely chopped

1 fresh green chilli, seeded and finely chopped

5ml/1 tsp ground toasted cumin seeds

2.5ml/½ tsp ground sumac

15g/½oz fresh flat leaf parsley, chopped

30ml/2 tbsp chopped fresh mint

olive oil, for frying

salt and ground black pepper

For the red onion relish

2 red (Italian) onions, cut into 5mm/¼in thick slices

75ml/5 tbsp extra virgin olive oil

2 red (bell) peppers, halved and seeded

350g/12oz cherry tomatoes, chopped

1 fresh red or green chilli, seeded and finely chopped

30ml/2 tbsp chopped fresh mint

30ml/2 tbsp chopped fresh parsley

15ml/1 tbsp chopped fresh oregano

2.5–5ml/½–1 tsp ground sumac

15ml/1 tbsp lemon juice

sugar, to taste

1 Pour 150ml/¼ pint/⅔ cup hot water over the bulgur wheat in a bowl and leave to stand for 15 minutes, then tip into a sieve lined with a clean dish towel. Drain, then squeeze out the excess moisture.

2 Place the bulgur wheat in a bowl and add the lamb, onion, garlic, chilli, cumin, sumac, parsley and mint. Mix thoroughly together by hand, season with salt and ground black pepper, then mix again.

3 Using your hands, form the mixture into 8 burgers and set aside while you make the relish.

4 For the relish, brush the onions with 15ml/1 tbsp of the oil and grill (broil) for 5 minutes each side, until brown. Cool, then chop. Grill the peppers, skin-side up, until charred. Place in a bowl, cover and leave for 10 minutes. Peel, seed and finely dice the peppers.

5 Mix the onions and peppers in a bowl. Add the tomatoes, chilli, herbs and sumac. Stir in the remaining oil and the lemon juice. Season with salt, pepper and sugar.

7 Heat a heavy frying pan or a ridged, cast-iron grill (broiling) pan over a high heat and grease lightly with olive oil. Cook the burgers for about 5–6 minutes on each side, or until just cooked at the centre.

8 While the burgers are cooking, taste the relish and adjust the seasoning. Serve the burgers freshly cooked, with the relish.

COOK'S TIP

Sumac is a sweet-sour spice made from berries. Substitute grated (shredded) lemon rind, if you prefer.

Energy 514kcal/2135kJ; Protein 27.4g; Carbohydrate 19.1g, of which sugars 13.5g; Fat 37g, of which saturates 10.7g; Cholesterol 96mg; Calcium 96mg; Fibre 4.5g; Sodium 107mg.

onion and caper sauce with bacon

Onions and capers make a piquant sauce that is traditional with boiled mutton, but it is also delicious with boiled bacon or gammon.

Serves six

INGREDIENTS

1.8–2kg/4–4½lb piece of gammon (smoked ham) or bacon, soaked if necessary

1 onion, quartered, stuck with 4 cloves

1 large carrot, sliced

1 celery stick

1 fresh bay leaf

fresh thyme sprig

30ml/2 tbsp Dijon mustard

45–60ml/3–4 tbsp demerara (raw) sugar

For the onion and caper sauce

50g/2oz/¼ cup butter

225g/8oz onions, chopped

25g/1oz/¼ cup plain (all-purpose) flour

250ml/8fl oz/1 cup milk

1 fresh bay leaf

30ml/2 tbsp small salted capers, rinsed and roughly chopped

30ml/2 tbsp chopped fresh parsley (optional)

15–30ml/1–2 tbsp Dijon mustard

salt and ground black pepper

1 Place the meat in a pan and cover with water. Bring to the boil and simmer for 5 minutes. Drain, rinse, then return to the pan. Cover with water. Add the onion, carrot, celery, bay leaf and thyme. Bring to the boil, then simmer very gently for 25 minutes per 450g/1lb.

2 Preheat the oven 200°C/400°F/ Gas 6. Drain the meat, reserving 475ml/16fl oz/2 cups of the cooking liquid. Place the meat in a roasting pan and strip off and discard the skin, leaving an even layer of fat on the meat. Spread the mustard over the fat and press the sugar all over the mustard.

3 Cook the gammon in the oven for 20–25 minutes, until glazed and browned. Remove from the oven and keep warm, covered loosely in foil, until ready to serve.

4 Start making the sauce just before the meat has finished boiling. Melt 40g/1½oz/3 tbsp of the butter in a pan and cook the onions very gently, half-covered, for about 20 minutes, until they are soft and yellow but not browned. Stir occasionally, to prevent them sticking to the pan.

5 Stir in the flour and cook, stirring constantly, for 2–3 minutes. Gradually stir in 300ml/½ pint/1¼ cups of the hot reserved cooking liquid. Cook until the sauce is thick and smooth, then gradually stir in the milk. Add the bay leaf and cook very gently for 20–25 minutes, stirring frequently.

6 Gradually stir in a little more of the reserved cooking liquid to make a sauce of pouring consistency and cook for a further 5 minutes. Remove the bay leaf.

7 Stir in the chopped capers and parsley, if using. Add 15ml/1 tbsp mustard, then taste for seasoning. Add salt, pepper and more mustard to taste. Stir in the remaining butter and serve immediately with the sliced meat, small new potatoes, tossed a little butter, and garlic, and broad (fava) beans.

Energy 529kcal/2204kJ; Protein 55.2g; Carbohydrate 8.7g, of which sugars 4.6g; Fat 30.5g, of which saturates 12.3g; Cholesterol 89mg; Calcium 106mg; Fibre 1.1g; Sodium 2786mg.

classic white onion sauce

This is the classic French white onion sauce. It is excellent with veal, chicken, pork or lamb –
but also poured over poached eggs and grilled. It can be left chunky with onion, or puréed.

4 Remove and discard the bay leaf
and parsley, then process the sauce
in a blender or food processor if
you want a smooth sauce.

5 Stir in the cream and reheat the
sauce gently, then season to taste
with salt and pepper. Add a little
more milk or stock if the sauce is
very thick. Season with the nutmeg.
before serving.

VARIATIONS

• For leek sauce, substitute leeks for
onions, using the white part of the
leeks. Cook for just 4–5 minutes in the
butter before adding the flour. Omit the
nutmeg and stir in 15ml/1 tbsp Dijon
mustard just before serving.

• Season the sauce with about 30ml/
2 tbsp Dijon mustard at the end of
cooking to make *sauce Robert* – a
classic French sauce traditionally served
with pork chops. It also goes very well
with ham or rabbit.

Serves four

INGREDIENTS

40g/1½oz/3 tbsp butter
350g/12oz onions, chopped
25g/1oz/¼ cup plain (all-purpose) flour
500ml/17fl oz/generous 2 cups hot milk
  or stock, or a mixture of both
1 fresh bay leaf
a few parsley stalks
120ml/4fl oz/½ cup double (heavy) cream
freshly grated nutmeg
salt and ground black pepper

1 Melt the butter in a large heavy
pan. Add the onions and fry gently
over a low heat, stirring, for 10–12
minutes, until they are soft and
golden yellow, but not browned.

2 Stir in the flour and cook gently,
stirring constantly, for 2–3 minutes.

3 Gradually stir in the hot milk,
stock, or milk and stock mixture
and bring to the boil. Add the bay
leaf and parsley. Cook very gently,
stirring often, for 15–20 minutes.

COOKS' TIP

The sauce should be cooked for this
length of time to cook out the raw flour
flavour. A heat diffuser mat is very useful
to keep the heat as low as possible
when cooking delicate sauces.

Energy 334kcal/1384kJ; Protein 6.4g; Carbohydrate 18.2g, of which sugars 11.5g; Fat 26.7g, of which saturates 16.6g; Cholesterol 70mg; Calcium 197mg; Fibre 1.4g; Sodium 124mg.

onion and mustard sauce for pork

The piquant sauce adds punch and flavour to this simple supper dish. Serve favourite creamy
potato mash and buttery broccoli or cabbage for the perfect feel-better meal.

Serves four

INGREDIENTS

4 pork loin chops, 2cm/¾in thick
30ml/2 tbsp plain (all-purpose) flour
45ml/3 tbsp olive oil
2 Spanish (Bermuda) onions, thinly sliced
2 garlic cloves, finely chopped
250ml/8fl oz/1 cup dry (hard) cider
150ml/¼ pint/⅔ cup vegetable, chicken
  or pork stock
generous pinch of brown sugar
2 fresh bay leaves
6 fresh thyme sprigs
2 strips lemon rind
120ml/4fl oz/½ cup double (heavy) cream
30–45ml/2–3 tbsp wholegrain mustard
30ml/2 tbsp chopped fresh parsley
salt and ground black pepper

1 Preheat the oven to 200°C/400°F/
Gas 6. Trim the chops of excess fat.
Season the flour with salt and
pepper and use to coat the chops.
Heat 30ml/2 tbsp of the oil in a
frying pan and brown the chops on
both sides, then transfer them to an
ovenproof dish.

2 Add the remaining oil to the pan
and cook the onions over a fairly
gentle heat until they soften and
begin to brown. Add the garlic and
cook for 2 minutes more.

3 Stir in any left-over flour, then
gradually stir in the cider and
stock. Season well with salt and
pepper and add the brown sugar,
bay leaves, thyme sprigs and lemon
rind. Bring the sauce to the boil,
stirring constantly, then pour over
the chops.

4 Cover and cook in the oven for
20 minutes. Reduce the heat to
180°C/350°F/Gas 4 and continue
cooking for another 30–40 minutes.
Remove the foil for the last 10
minutes of the cooking time.

5 Use a spoon and fork to lift the
chops from the sauce and transfer
them to a serving dish. Keep warm,
covered with foil.

6 Pour the sauce from the roasting
dish into a pan. Alternatively, if the
dish is flameproof, place it over a
direct heat. Discard the herbs and
lemon rind, then bring the sauce to
the boil, stirring.

7 Add the cream and continue to
boil, stirring constantly. Taste for
seasoning, adding a pinch more
sugar if necessary. Finally, stir in
the mustard to taste and pour the
sauce over the braised chops.
Sprinkle with the chopped parsley
and serve immediately.

sweet and sour sauce for pork

Sweet-and-sour pork must be one of the most popular dishes served in Chinese restaurants and take-aways in the Western world. Unfortunately, it is often spoiled by cooks who use too much tomato ketchup in the sauce. Here is a classic recipe from Canton, the city of its origin.

Serves four

INGREDIENTS

350g/12oz lean boneless pork

1.5ml/¼ tsp salt

2.5ml/½ tsp ground Szechuan peppercorns

15ml/1 tbsp Chinese rice wine or dry sherry

115g/4oz bamboo shoots

30ml/2 tbsp plain (all-purpose) flour

1 egg, lightly beaten

vegetable oil, for deep-frying

For the sweet and sour sauce

15ml/1 tbsp vegetable oil

1 garlic clove, finely chopped

1 spring onion (scallion), cut into short sections

1 small green (bell) pepper, seeded and diced

1 fresh red chilli, seeded and thinly shredded

15ml/1 tbsp light soy sauce

30ml/2 tbsp light brown sugar

30–45ml/2–3 tbsp rice vinegar

15ml/1 tbsp tomato purée (paste)

about 120ml/4fl oz/½ cup chicken or vegetable stock or water

1 Cut the pork into small bite-sized cubes and place in a shallow dish. Add the salt, peppercorns and rice wine or dry sherry. Cover and set aside to marinate at room temperature for 15–20 minutes. Alternatively, chill if leaving for more than about 30 minutes.

2 Drain the bamboo shoots, if canned, and cut them into small cubes the same size as the pork; if they are thinly sliced, cut in half.

3 Dust the pork with flour, dip in the beaten egg and coat with more flour. Heat the oil in a preheated wok and deep-fry the pork in moderately hot oil for 3–4 minutes, stirring to separate the pieces. Remove and drain.

4 Reheat the oil until hot, return the pork to the wok and add the bamboo shoots. Fry for about 1 minute, or until the pork is golden. Remove and drain well.

5 To make the sauce, heat the oil in a clean wok or frying pan and add the garlic, spring onion, green pepper and red chilli. Stir-fry for 30–40 seconds, then add the soy sauce, sugar, rice vinegar, tomato purée and stock or water. Bring to the boil, stirring constantly, then add the pork and bamboo shoots. Heat through and stir to mix, then serve at once.

Energy 336kcal/1403kJ; Protein 22.7g; Carbohydrate 18.6g, of which sugars 12.2g; Fat 19.1g, of which saturates 3.3g; Cholesterol 103mg; Calcium 40mg; Fibre 1.5g; Sodium 359mg.

black bean sauce for beef

This Chinese beef dish is a quick stir-fry with a richly flavoured marinade that bubbles down into a luscious, dark sauce. Broccoli, baby corn and water chestnuts bring colour, flavour and texture. The sauce can also be used for chicken or duck – try boneless skinless breast fillets.

Serves 4

INGREDIENTS

225g/8oz lean fillet (beef tenderloin) or
    rump (round) steak
15ml/1 tbsp sunflower oil
225g/8oz broccoli
115g/4oz baby corn, halved diagonally
45–60ml/3–4 tbsp water
2 leeks, diagonally sliced
225g/8oz can water chestnuts, sliced

For the marinade

15ml/1 tbsp fermented black beans
30ml/2 tbsp dark soy sauce
30ml/2 tbsp Chinese rice vinegar or
    cider vinegar
15ml/1 tbsp sunflower oil
5ml/1 tsp sugar
2 garlic cloves, crushed
2.5cm/1in piece of fresh root ginger,
    peeled and finely chopped

1 For the marinade and sauce base, mash the fermented black beans in a non-metallic bowl. Add the remaining ingredients and stir well.

2 Cut the steak into thin slices across the grain, then add them to the marinade. Stir the steak well to coat it in the marinade. Cover the bowl and leave for several hours.

3 Heat the oil in a large frying pan. Drain the steak (reserving the marinade). When the oil is hot, add the meat and stir-fry for 3–4 minutes. Transfer it to a plate and set aside.

4 Cut the broccoli into small florets. Add the broccoli, corn and water to the pan and bring to the boil. Cover and cook gently for about 5 minutes, until tender

COOK'S TIP

Fermented black beans are cooked, salted and fermented whole soya beans; buy them in Oriental stores.

5 Add the leeks and water chestnuts to the broccoli mixture and toss over the heat for 1–2 minutes. Return the meat to the pan, pour over the reserved marinade and toss briefly over a high heat before serving.

Energy 219kcal/912kJ; Protein 19.5g; Carbohydrate 8.4g, of which sugars 5.8g; Fat 12g, of which saturates 3.1g; Cholesterol 33mg; Calcium 69mg; Fibre 4.5g; Sodium 907mg.

quick chilli sauce for sizzling steak

This Malaysian method of sizzling richly marinated meat on a cast iron grill can be applied with equal success to sliced chicken or pork – all will pair up well with the dipping sauce.

Serves four to six

INGREDIENTS

1 garlic clove, crushed

2.5cm/1in fresh root ginger, chopped

10ml/2 tsp black peppercorns

15ml/1 tbsp sugar

30ml/2 tbsp tamarind sauce

45ml/3 tbsp dark soy sauce

15ml/1 tbsp oyster sauce

4 rump (round) steaks, each 200g/7oz

vegetable oil, for brushing

shredded spring onion (scallion) and carrot, to garnish

For the dipping sauce

75ml/5 tbsp beef stock

30ml/2 tbsp tomato ketchup

5ml/1 tsp chilli sauce

juice of 1 lime

1 Pound together the garlic, ginger, peppercorns, sugar and tamarind sauce in a mortar with a pestle. Mix in the soy sauce and oyster sauce, then spoon over the steaks. Cover and set aside in the refrigerator to marinate for at least 1 hour and up to 8 hours.

2 Heat a cast iron grilling plate over high heat until very hot. Scrape the marinade from the meat and reserve. Brush the meat with oil and grill for 2 minutes on each side for rare and 3–4 minutes on each side for medium, depending on thickness.

3 Meanwhile, make the dipping sauce. Pour the marinade into a pan and add the stock, tomato ketchup, chilli sauce and lime juice. Set over a low heat and simmer to heat through.

4 Arrange the steaks on a serving platter and garnish with a mixture of shredded spring onion and carrot. Serve at once, handing the dipping sauce separately.

Energy 216kcal/908kJ; Protein 29.8g; Carbohydrate 6.2g, of which sugars 5.9g; Fat 8.2g, of which saturates 2.6g; Cholesterol 79mg; Calcium 9mg; Fibre 0.1g; Sodium 777mg.

sweet curry peanut sauce with beef

This Thai curry sauce is deliciously rich and thicker than most other Thai curries. Serve with boiled jasmine rice and salted duck's eggs for an authentic taste of Thai cooking.

Serves four to six

INGREDIENTS

600ml/1 pint/2½ cups coconut milk
45ml/3 tbsp red curry paste
45ml/3 tbsp fish sauce
30ml/2 tbsp palm sugar (jaggery)
2 stalks lemon grass, bruised
450g/1lb rump steak cut into thin strips
75g/3oz roasted ground peanuts
2 red chillies, sliced
5 kaffir lime leaves, torn
salt and freshly ground black pepper
2 salted eggs, to serve
10–15 Thai basil leaves, to garnish

1 Put half the coconut milk into a heavy-bottomed pan and heat, stirring, until it boils and separates.

2 Add the red curry paste and cook until fragrant. Add the fish sauce, palm sugar and lemon grass.

COOK'S TIP

If you don't have the time to make your own red curry paste, you can buy a ready-made Thai curry paste. Most supermarkets now stock a wide range of these.

3 Continue to cook until the colour deepens. Add the rest of the coconut milk, stirring. Bring back to the boil.

4 Add the beef and ground peanuts. Stir to coat the meat thoroughly in the sauce mixture and continue cooking for 8–10 minutes, or until most of the liquid has evaporated.

5 Add the chillies and kaffir lime leaves to the meat mixture. Mix lightly and taste for seasoning, adding a little extra fish sauce to taste, if necessary. Serve at once, with salted eggs and garnish with Thai basil leaves.

Energy 227kcal/953kJ; Protein 21g; Carbohydrate 14.3g, of which sugars 11.5g; Fat 9.9g, of which saturates 2.6g; Cholesterol 44mg; Calcium 92mg; Fibre 2.5g; Sodium 723mg.

roquefort and walnut butter for steak

Make a roll of this savoury cheese-flavoured butter to keep in the refrigerator, ready to top plain steaks or pork chops. It is also delicious with grilled white fish or baked squash.

Serves four

INGREDIENTS

15ml/1 tbsp finely snipped fresh chives

15ml/1 tbsp olive oil or sunflower oil

4 lean rump (round) steaks, about 130g/ 4½oz each

120ml/4fl oz/½ cup dry white wine

30ml/2 tbsp crème fraîche or double (heavy) cream

salt and ground black pepper

fresh chives, to garnish

For the Roquefort and walnut butter

2 shallots, chopped

75g/3oz/6 tbsp butter, slightly softened

150g/5oz Roquefort cheese

30ml/2 tbsp finely chopped walnuts

1 Sauté the shallots in a third of the butter. Turn the mixture into a bowl. Add half the remaining butter, the cheese, walnuts, snipped chives and pepper to taste. Chill lightly, roll in foil to a sausage shape and chill again until firm.

2 Heat the remaining butter and oil and cook the steaks to your liking. Season and remove from the pan.

3 Pour the wine into the pan and stir to incorporate any sediment. Bubble up the liquid for a minute or two, then stir in the crème fraîche or cream. Season with salt and pepper, and pour the sauce over the steaks.

4 Cut pats of the Roquefort butter from the roll and put one on top of each steak. Garnish with chives and serve. Green beans make an ideal accompaniment to this dish.

COOK'S TIP

The butter can also be stored in the freezer, but it is easier to cut it into rounds before freezing, so you can remove just as many as you need, without thawing the rest.

Energy 567kcal/2355kJ; Protein 38g; Carbohydrate 1.2g, of which sugars 1.1g; Fat 43.6g, of which saturates 22.5g; Cholesterol 155mg; Calcium 216mg; Fibre 0.6g; Sodium 655mg.

smoked cheese sauce with veal

Sheep's milk cheese melted with cream makes a simple sauce for serving with pan-fried veal escalopes. The escalopes are used as purchased, not beaten thin.

Serves four

INGREDIENTS

25g/1oz/2 tbsp butter

15ml/1 tbsp extra virgin olive oil

8 small veal escalopes

2 garlic cloves, crushed

250g/9oz/3½ cups button (white) mushrooms or closed-cup mushrooms, sliced

150g/5oz/1¼ cups frozen peas, thawed

60ml/4 tbsp brandy

250ml/8fl oz/1 cup whipping cream

150g/5oz smoked sheep's milk cheese, diced

ground black pepper

sprigs of flat leaf parsley, to garnish

2 Lift the escalopes on to a serving dish and keep hot.

3 Add the remaining butter to the pan. When it melts, stir-fry the garlic and mushrooms for about 3 minutes.

4 Add the peas, pour in the brandy and cook until all the pan juices have been absorbed. Season lightly. Using a slotted spoon, remove the mushrooms and peas and place on top of the escalopes. Pour the cream into the pan.

5 Stir in the diced cheese. Heat gently until the cheese has melted. Season with pepper and pour over the escalopes and vegetables. Serve garnished with flat leaf parsley.

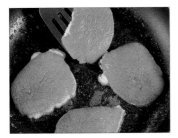

1 Melt half the butter with the oil in a large, heavy-based frying pan. Season the escalopes with plenty of pepper and brown them in batches on each side over a high heat. Reduce the heat and cook for about 5 minutes on each side until just done. The escalopes should feel firm to the touch, with a very light springiness, when tested.

VARIATION

This dish works well with lean pork steaks. Ensure that pork is well cooked, with a slightly longer frying time.

Energy 750kcal/3119kJ; Protein 59.9g; Carbohydrate 6.3g, of which sugars 2.8g; Fat 49.6g, of which saturates 28.9g; Cholesterol 219mg; Calcium 334mg; Fibre 2.5g; Sodium 446mg.

wheat beer sauce for veal

Wheat beers are made in Bavaria, Belgium and northern France, where they are known as bières blanches or white beers. The slight bitterness that the beer gives the sauce in this delectable stew is matched by the sweetness of the caramelized onions and carrots.

Serves four

INGREDIENTS

45ml/3 tbsp plain (all-purpose) flour

900g/2lb boned shoulder or leg of veal, cut into 5cm/2in cubes

65g/2½oz/5 tbsp butter

3 shallots, finely chopped

1 celery stick

fresh parsley sprig

2 fresh bay leaves

5ml/1 tsp caster (superfine) sugar, plus a good pinch

200ml/7fl oz/scant 1 cup wheat beer

450ml/¾ pint/scant 2 cups veal stock

20–25 large silverskin onions or small pickling onions

450g/1lb carrots, thickly sliced

2 large egg yolks

105ml/7 tbsp double (heavy) cream

30ml/2 tbsp chopped fresh parsley

salt and ground black pepper

1 Season the flour and dust the veal in it. Heat 25g/1oz/2 tbsp of the butter in a deep, lidded frying pan, add the veal and quickly seal it on all sides. The veal should be golden but not dark brown. Use a draining spoon to remove the veal from the pan and set aside.

2 Reduce the heat, add another 15g/½oz/1 tbsp butter to the pan and cook the shallots gently for 5–6 minutes, until soft and yellow.

3 Replace the veal. Tie the celery, parsley and 1 bay leaf together in a bundle, then add them to the pan with a good pinch of caster sugar. Increase the heat, pour in the beer and allow to bubble briefly before pouring in the stock. Season, bring to the boil, then cover and simmer gently, stirring once or twice, for 40–50 minutes, or until the veal is cooked and tender.

4 Meanwhile, melt the remaining butter in another frying pan and add the onions, then fry them over a low heat until golden all over. Use a draining spoon to remove the onions from the pan and set aside.

5 Add the carrots and turn to coat them in the butter remaining from the onions. Stir in 5ml/1 tsp caster sugar, a pinch of salt, the remaining bay leaf and enough water to cover the carrots. Bring to the boil and cook uncovered for 10–12 minutes.

6 Return the onions to the pan with the carrots and continue to cook until all but a few tablespoons of the liquid has evaporated and the onions and carrots are slightly caramelized. Keep warm. Transfer the veal to a bowl and discard the celery and herb bundle.

7 Beat the egg yolks and cream together in another bowl, then beat in a ladleful of the hot, but not boiling, carrot liquid. Return this mixture to the pan and cook over a very low heat without boiling, stirring until thickened a little.

8 Add the veal, onions and carrots to the sauce. Reheat and adjust the seasoning, then serve, sprinkled with the parsley.

Energy 660kcal/2752kJ; Protein 52.8g; Carbohydrate 27.8g, of which sugars 16.6g; Fat 37.1g, of which saturates 20.2g; Cholesterol 360mg; Calcium 140mg; Fibre 4.9g; Sodium 399mg.

sauces for fish and shellfish

Fish and shellfish may be delicate but they are also quite distinctive in their flavour. These recipes show just how to combine herbs or spices with the right type of sauce to complement the different strengths of flavour and textures found among fish and shellfish. Spicy and creamy, piquant with horseradish, lively with chilli, or aromatic with Chinese five-spice seasoning, there are plenty of options for producing superb main course meals for all sorts of occasions.

quick parsley sauce for smoked fish

A good, strong, fresh parsley sauce is great with full-flavoured smoked haddock; it is also good with white fish or fish cakes. This recipe is quick to prepare and makes a tasty midweek meal.

Serves four

INGREDIENTS

4 smoked haddock fillets, about
  225g/8oz each

For the quick parsley sauce
75g/3oz/6 tbsp butter, softened
25g/1oz/¼ cup plain (all-purpose) flour
300ml/½ pint/1¼ cups milk
60ml/4 tbsp chopped fresh parsley
salt and ground black pepper
parsley sprigs, to garnish

1 Smear the fish with 50g/2oz/¼ cup butter. Preheat the grill (broiler).

2 Beat the remaining butter and flour together with a wooden spoon to make a smooth, thick paste. Chill the paste to firm it slightly, if necessary, then cut it into lumps.

3 Grill (broil) the fish over a medium high heat for 10–15 minutes, turning when necessary.

4 Meanwhile, heat the milk to just below boiling. Whisk in the lumps of butter and flour. Continue whisking until the sauce boils and thickens. Simmer for 2–3 minutes.

5 Stir in the seasoning and parsley, and serve poured over the fillets, or in a serving jug (pitcher). Serve immediately, garnished with parsley and your choice of vegetables.

Energy 499kcal/2086kJ; Protein 45.6g; Carbohydrate 11.2g, of which sugars 6.4g; Fat 30.6g, of which saturates 18.9g; Cholesterol 157mg; Calcium 228mg; Fibre 0.6g; Sodium 1881mg.

vermouth and chevre sauce for cod

A quick pan sauce of vermouth, creamy goat's cheese, parsley and chervil goes well with chunky cod. Grilled plum tomatoes make the perfect accompaniment.

Serves four

INGREDIENTS

4 pieces cod fillet, about 150g/5oz
   each, skinned

15ml/2 tbsp olive oil

For the vermouth and chevre sauce

15ml/2 tbsp olive oil

4 spring onions (scallions), chopped

150ml/¼ pint/⅔ cup dry vermouth,
   preferably Noilly Prat

300ml/½ pint/1¼ cups fish stock

45ml/3 tbsp crème fraîche or double
   (heavy) cream

65g/2½oz goat's cheese, rind removed,
   and chopped

30ml/2 tbsp chopped fresh parsley

15ml/1 tbsp chopped fresh chervil

salt and ground black pepper

flat leaf parsley, to garnish

grilled plum tomatoes, to serve

1 Remove any stray bones from the cod. Rinse the fillets under cold running water and pat dry with kitchen paper. Season well.

COOK'S TIP

The sauce will taste delicious with a wide variety of fish, including other types or white fish or salmon. The cooking time may change according to the thickness of the fish fillets.

2 Heat a non-stick frying pan, then add 15ml/1 tbsp of the oil, swirling it around to coat the bottom. Add the fish and cook, without turning or moving the pieces, for 4 minutes, or until browned underneath.

3 Turn the pieces of fish and cook the second sides for 3 minutes, or until just firm. Transfer to a serving plate and keep hot.

4 Heat the remaining oil and stir-fry the spring onions for 1 minute. Add the vermouth and cook until reduced by half. Add the stock and cook again until reduced by half.

5 Stir in the crème fraîche or cream and goat's cheese and simmer for 3 minutes. Add salt and pepper to taste, then stir in the herbs and spoon the sauce over the fish. Garnish with parsley and serve with grilled tomatoes.

Energy 360kcal/1497kJ; Protein 31.7g; Carbohydrate 2.1g, of which sugars 2g; Fat 20.9g, of which saturates 7.7g; Cholesterol 97mg; Calcium 68mg; Fibre 0.7g; Sodium 198mg.

tarragon and mushroom sauce for salmon

Tarragon has a distinctive aniseed flavour that is good with fish and mushrooms, especially in a creamy sauce. Oyster mushrooms have been included for their delicate flavour.

2 Heat the remaining butter in the pan and gently fry the shallot to soften it without letting it colour. Add the mushrooms and cook until the juices begin to flow. Add the stock and simmer for 2–3 minutes.

3 Mix the cornflour and mustard to a smooth paste with 15ml/1 tbsp water. Stir into the sauce and bring to the boil, stirring, until thickened. Add the crème fraîche, tarragon, vinegar, and salt and pepper.

Serves four

INGREDIENTS

50g/2oz/¼ cup unsalted (sweet) butter
4 salmon steaks, about 175g/6oz each
1 shallot, finely chopped
175g/6oz/2½ cups assorted wild and cultivated mushrooms, such as oyster mushrooms, saffron milk-caps, bay boletus or cauliflower fungus, trimmed and sliced
200ml/7fl oz/scant 1 cup chicken or vegetable stock
10ml/2 tsp cornflour (cornstarch)
2.5ml/½ tsp mustard
50ml/3½ tbsp crème fraîche
45ml/3 tbsp chopped fresh tarragon
5ml/1 tsp white wine vinegar
salt and cayenne pepper
new potatoes and a green salad, to serve

1 Melt half the butter in a large, non-stick frying pan. Season the salmon and add to the pan. Cook over a moderate heat for 8 minutes, turning once. (You may have to cook the fish in batches if space in the pan is limited.) Transfer to a plate, cover and keep warm.

4 Spoon the mushrooms over the salmon steaks and serve with new potatoes and a green salad.

COOK'S TIP

Fresh tarragon will bruise and darken quickly after chopping, so prepare the herb just before you use it.

Energy 479kcal/1990kJ; Protein 37g; Carbohydrate 4.4g, of which sugars 1.5g; Fat 35g, of which saturates 13.3g; Cholesterol 128mg; Calcium 76mg; Fibre 1.3g; Sodium 165mg.

spinach and lemon sauce for hake

A light but flavourful sauce of spinach and lemon is the perfect accompaniment to this simple but delicious dish of golden hake sautéed in olive oil.

Serves four

INGREDIENTS

500g/1¼lb fresh spinach, trimmed
  of thick stalks

4 hake steaks or pieces cod fillet, about
  200g/7oz each

30ml/2 tbsp plain (all-purpose) flour

75ml/5 tbsp extra virgin olive oil

175ml/6fl oz/¾ cup white wine

3–4 strips pared lemon rind

salt and ground black pepper

For the egg and lemon sauce

2 large (US extra large) eggs, at room
  temperature

juice of ½ lemon

2.5ml/½ tsp cornflour (cornstarch)

1 Place the spinach leaves in a large pan with just the water that clings to the leaves after washing. Cover the pan tightly and cook over a medium heat for 5–7 minutes, or until they are cooked. Turn the leaves occasionally using a wooden spoon. Drain and set aside.

2 Dust the fish lightly with the flour and shake off any excess. Heat the olive oil in a large frying pan, add the pieces of fish and sauté gently for 2–3 minutes on each side until the flesh starts to turn golden.

3 Pour in the wine, add the lemon rind and a little seasoning and carefully shake the pan from side to side to blend the flavourings and coat the flesh of the cooking fish. Lower the heat and simmer gently for a few minutes until the wine has reduced a little.

4 Add the spinach, distributing it evenly around the fish. Let it simmer for 3–4 minutes more, then pull the pan off the heat and let it stand for a few minutes before adding the sauce.

5 To make the sauce, mix the cornflour to a smooth paste with a little water. Beat the eggs. Beat in the lemon juice and the cornflour mixture. Gradually beat in a ladleful of liquid from the fish pan, then beat for 1 minute. Add a second ladleful in the same way, and continue with the rest.

6 Pour the sauce over the fish and spinach, place over very gentle heat and shake to mix the ingredients. If the fish appears too dry, add a little warm water. Allow to cook gently for 2–3 minutes and serve at once.

Energy 441kcal/1839kJ; Protein 43.6g; Carbohydrate 10.6g, of which sugars 2.3g; Fat 22.1g, of which saturates 3.5g; Cholesterol 141mg; Calcium 273mg; Fibre 2.9g; Sodium 413mg.

orange and caper sauce for skate

This wonderfully sweet-sour, creamy sauce adds zest to otherwise plain white fish. Slightly peppery and piquant capers are especially good with skate.

Serves four

INGREDIENTS

4 skate wings, about 200g/7oz each
25g/1oz/2 tbsp butter
350ml/12fl oz/1½ cups fish stock

For the orange and caper sauce
25g/1oz/2 tbsp butter
1 onion, chopped
5ml/1 tsp black peppercorns
fish bones and trimmings
300ml/½ pint/1¼ cups dry white wine
2 small oranges
15ml/1 tbsp capers, drained
60ml/4 tbsp crème fraîche
salt and ground white pepper

1 To make the sauce, melt the butter in a non-stick pan and add the onion. Cook, stirring, over a moderate heat for approximately 5 minutes, or until the onion is lightly browned.

2 Add the peppercorns, fish bones and trimmings, and wine. Bring to the boil, reduce the heat and cover. Simmer gently for 30 minutes.

3 Using a serrated knife, peel the oranges, ensuring all the white pith is removed. Ease the segments away from the membrane.

4 Place the skate in a frying pan, add the butter and the fish stock and poach for 10–15 minutes, depending on thickness.

5 Strain the wine sauce into a clean pan. Add the capers and orange segments with any juice, and heat through. Lower the heat and stir in the crème fraîche and seasoning. Serve the skate wings and the sauce, garnished with parsley.

Energy 360kcal/1507kJ; Protein 31.7g; Carbohydrate 8.5g, of which sugars 8.1g; Fat 17.2g, of which saturates 10.6g; Cholesterol 44mg; Calcium 137mg; Fibre 1.5g; Sodium 326mg.

lemon and chive sauce for fishcakes

A fragrant ginger, lemon and chive sauce is an ideal match for these piquant fishcakes.
Flavoured with horseradish and parsley, they are a cut above the rest.

Serves four

INGREDIENTS

350g/12oz potatoes, peeled

75ml/5 tbsp milk

350g/12oz haddock or hoki fillets, skinned

15ml/1 tbsp lemon juice

15ml/1 tbsp creamed horseradish

30ml/2 tbsp chopped fresh parsley

flour, for dusting

115g/4oz/2 cups fresh wholemeal (whole-wheat) breadcrumbs

salt and ground black pepper

flat leaf parsley sprig, to garnish

mangetouts (snow peas) and a sliced tomato and onion salad, to serve

For the lemon and chive sauce

thinly pared rind and juice of ½ small lemon

120ml/4fl oz/½ cup dry white wine

2 thin slices fresh root ginger

10ml/2 tsp cornflour (cornstarch)

30ml/2 tbsp chopped fresh chives

1 Cook the potatoes in a large pan of boiling water for 15–20 minutes. Drain and mash with the milk, and season with salt and ground black pepper to taste.

2 Purée the fish together with the lemon juice and horseradish sauce in a food processor or blender. Mix together with the potatoes and parsley.

3 With floured hands, shape the mixture into eight fishcakes and coat with the breadcrumbs. Place on a floured plate, cover with clear film (plastic wrap) and chill in the refrigerator for 30 minutes.

4 Preheated the grill (broiler) to medium and cook the fishcakes for 8 minutes each side, until brown.

5 For the sauce, cut the lemon rind into strips and put in a pan with the lemon juice, wine, ginger and seasoning. Simmer for 6 minutes.

6 Blend 15ml/1 tbsp of cold water into the cornflour. Stir into the sauce, bring to the boil and simmer for 2 minutes. Stir in the chives and serve at once with the fishcakes. Garnish with flat leaf parsley and serve mangetouts and a tomato and onion salad as accompaniments.

Energy 280kcal/1191kJ; Protein 22.5g; Carbohydrate 40.7g, of which sugars 3.8g; Fat 2.1g, of which saturates 0.4g; Cholesterol 33mg; Calcium 102mg; Fibre 2.1g; Sodium 335mg.

orange butter sauce for sea bream

This rich butter sauce, sharpened with tangy orange juice, goes well with the firm white flesh of sea bream served on a bed of fresh mixed salad leaves.

3 Place the orange juice concentrate in a heatproof bowl and heat over a pan of simmering water. Remove the pan from the heat and gradually whisk in the butter until creamy. Season well.

Serves two

INGREDIENTS

2 sea bream, about 350g/12oz each, scaled and gutted

10ml/2 tsp Dijon mustard

5ml/1 tsp fennel seeds

30ml/2 tbsp olive oil

50g/2oz watercress

175g/6oz mixed salad leaves

For the orange butter sauce

30ml/2 tbsp frozen orange juice concentrate

175g/6oz/¾ cup unsalted (sweet) butter, diced

salt and cayenne pepper

1 Slash the fish four times on each side. Mix the mustard and fennel seeds, then spread all over the fish.

2 Preheated the grill (broiler). Brush the fish with olive oil and grill (broil) for 10–12 minutes without burning, turning the fish midway through the cooking time.

4 Dress the watercress and salad leaves with the remaining olive oil, and arrange on two plates. Add the fish to the plates. Spoon the sauce over the fish and serve.

COOK'S TIP

Alternatively, barbecue the bream on a medium-hot barbecue. This is much easier if you use a hinged wire rack that holds the fish firmly and enables you to turn the fish without it breaking up.

Energy 969kcal/4007kJ; Protein 37.1g; Carbohydrate 4.3g, of which sugars 4.3g; Fat 89.5g, of which saturates 47.3g; Cholesterol 263mg; Calcium 166mg; Fibre 1.2g; Sodium 768mg.

tahini sauce for baked fish

This tahini sauce contributes a clever twist of complementary seasoning to this north African recipe that evokes all the colour and rich flavours of Mediterranean cuisine.

Serves four

INGREDIENTS

1 whole fish, about 1.2kg/2½ lb, scaled
  and cleaned
10ml/2 tsp coriander seeds
4 garlic cloves, sliced
10ml/2 tsp harissa sauce
90ml/6 tbsp olive oil
6 plum tomatoes, sliced
1 mild onion, sliced
3 preserved lemons or 1 fresh lemon
plenty of fresh herbs, such as bay leaves,
  thyme and rosemary
salt and ground black pepper
extra herbs, to garnish

For the tahini sauce

75ml/2½ fl oz/⅓ cup light tahini
juice of 1 lemon
1 garlic clove, crushed
45ml/3 tbsp finely chopped fresh parsley
  or coriander (cilantro)

1 Preheat the oven to 200°C/400°F/Gas 6. Grease the base and sides of a large, shallow ovenproof dish.

2 Finely crush the coriander seeds in a mortar, using a pestle. Then add and crush the garlic. Mix in the harissa sauce and stir in about 60ml/4 tbsp of the olive oil until all the ingredients are thoroughly combined in a coarse paste.

3 Slash the fish diagonally on both sides with a sharp knife. Spread a little of the harissa, coriander and garlic paste inside the cavity of the fish. Spread the remainder over each side of the fish, pushing it into the slashes, and set aside.

4 Scatter the tomatoes, onion and preserved or quartered fresh lemon in the greased dish. Sprinkle with the remaining oil, and season. Put the fish on top. Tuck plenty of herbs around it.

5 Bake the fish, uncovered, for about 25 minutes, or until its flesh has turned opaque – test by piercing the thickest part with a knife to ease the flakes apart.

6 Meanwhile, to make the sauce, put the tahini, lemon juice, garlic and parsley or coriander in a small pan. Add 120ml/4fl oz/½ cup cold water and a little salt and ground black pepper. Cook gently, stirring occasionally, until smooth and hot.

7 Garnish the fish with the herbs, and serve the sauce separately.

Energy 423kcal/1755kJ; Protein 33.3g; Carbohydrate 1.5g, of which sugars 0.5g; Fat 31.5g, of which saturates 4.6g; Cholesterol 120mg; Calcium 349mg; Fibre 2.4g; Sodium 112mg.

whisky and cream sauce for salmon

This dish combines two of the finest flavours of Scotland – salmon and whisky. It takes very little time to make, so cook it at the last moment. Serve quite plainly.

Serves four

INGREDIENTS

4 thin pieces salmon fillet, about
175g/6oz each

5ml/1 tsp chopped fresh thyme leaves

50g/2oz/¼ cup butter

For the whisky and cream sauce

75ml/5 tbsp whisky

150ml/¼ pint/⅔ cup double
(heavy) cream

juice of ½ lemon (optional)

salt and ground black pepper

fresh dill sprigs, to garnish

VARIATION

Although fresh thyme works particularly
well with this delicious whisky and
cream sauce, you can replace it with
whatever fresh herbs are available.

1 Season the salmon and sprinkle with the thyme. Melt half the butter in a frying pan large enough to hold two pieces of salmon.

2 When the butter is foaming, fry the first two pieces of salmon for 2–3 minutes on each side, until they are golden on the outside and just cooked through.

3 Pour in 30ml/2 tbsp of the whisky and ignite it. When the flames have died down, carefully transfer the salmon to a plate and keep it hot. Heat the remaining butter and repeat with the remaining salmon. Keep hot.

4 Pour the cream into the pan and bring to the boil, stirring constantly and scraping the cooking juices off the pan. Simmer until reduced and slightly thickened. Season and add the last of the whisky and a squeeze of lemon if you like.

5 Place the salmon on warmed plates, pour the sauce over and garnish with dill. New potatoes and green beans are good with this.

Energy 667kcal/2760kJ; Protein 36.1g; Carbohydrate 0.8g, of which sugars 0.8g; Fat 53g, of which saturates 24.5g; Cholesterol 174mg; Calcium 61mg; Fibre 0g; Sodium 164mg.

green peppercorn sauce for salmon

Salmon benefits from being served with a piquant accompaniment. Lemon and lime are the obvious choices, but capers and green peppercorns also serve to counter the rich fish.

Serves four

INGREDIENTS

4 pieces salmon fillet, about
175g/6oz each

salt and ground black pepper

fresh parsley, to garnish

For the green peppercorn sauce

15g/½oz/1 tbsp butter

2–3 shallots, finely chopped

15ml/1 tbsp brandy (optional)

60ml/4 tbsp white wine

90ml/6 tbsp fish or chicken stock

120ml/4fl oz/½ cup whipping cream

30–45ml/2–3 tbsp green peppercorns
in brine, rinsed

15–30ml/1–2 tbsp vegetable oil

1 Melt the butter in a heavy pan. Add the shallots and cook for 1–2 minutes, until just softened.

2 Add the brandy, if using, then pour in the white wine and stock. Bring to the boil and reduce by three-quarters, stirring occasionally.

3 Reduce the heat, then add the cream and half the peppercorns, crushing them slightly against the pan with the back of a spoon. Cook very gently for 4–5 minutes, until thickened slightly,

4 Strain the sauce into a clean pan. Stir in the remaining peppercorns. Keep the sauce warm over a very low heat, stirring occasionally, while you cook the salmon fillets.

5 Heat the oil in a large, heavy frying pan over medium-high heat. Lightly season the salmon. Sear the fillets on both sides, then lower the heat and cook for 4–6 minutes, until the flesh is opaque through. Arrange the fish on warmed plates and pour over the sauce. Garnish with parsley and serve.

COOK'S TIP

Green peppercorns are available pickled in jars or cans for adding to all kinds of sauces and stews. Rinse the peppercorns before use.

Energy 497kcal/2063kJ; Protein 36.2g; Carbohydrate 2.1g, of which sugars 1.8g; Fat 37.2g, of which saturates 13.3g; Cholesterol 127mg; Calcium 60mg; Fibre 0.2g; Sodium 110mg.

tomato coulis for marinated monkfish

A light but well-flavoured sauce, this should be made when Italian plum tomatoes are at their ripest. The lime and herb marinade is offset by the sweet tomatoes in the coulis. Serve this delicious dish with a glass of chilled white wine.

Serves four

INGREDIENTS

30ml/2 tbsp olive oil
finely grated rind and juice of 1 lime
30ml/2 tbsp chopped fresh mixed herbs
5ml/1 tsp Dijon mustard
4 skinless, boneless monkfish fillets
salt and ground black pepper
fresh herb sprigs, to garnish

For the tomato coulis

4 plum tomatoes, peeled and chopped
1 garlic clove, chopped
15ml/1 tbsp olive oil
15ml/1 tbsp tomato purée (paste)
30ml/2 tbsp chopped fresh oregano
5ml/1 tsp light soft brown sugar

1 Place the oil, lime rind and juice, herbs, mustard, and salt and pepper in a small bowl or jug and whisk together until thoroughly mixed.

VARIATION

Tomato coulis is also delicious seasoned with dill and lemon instead of garlic and oregano. Add the grated rind of 1 lemon, and use dill instead of oregano. Omit the garlic. This is good with fine-textured white fish fillets.

2 Place the monkfish fillets in a shallow, non-metallic container and pour the lime mixture over. Turn the fish several times in the marinade to coat the pieces evenly. Cover and chill for 1–2 hours.

3 Preheat the oven to 180°C/350°F/ Gas 4. Cut four pieces of greaseproof (waxed) paper, each large enough to hold a fish fillet. Place the fillets on the papers.

4 Spoon a little marinade over each piece of fish. Gather the paper loosely over the fish and fold over the edges to secure the parcel tightly. Place on a baking sheet. Bake for 20–30 minutes, or until the fish fillets are cooked, tender and just beginning to flake.

5 Meanwhile, make the tomato coulis. Place all the coulis ingredients in a food processor or blender and process until smooth. Season to taste, then pour the mixture into a serving dish. Cover and chill until required.

6 Carefully unwrap the baked fish parcels and transfer the fish fillets to warm serving plates. Add a little of the chilled coulis and garnish with a few fresh herb sprigs. Serve immediately, offering the remaining coulis separately.

COOK'S TIP

The coulis can be served hot, if you prefer. Simply make as directed in the recipe and heat gently in a pan until almost boiling, just before serving.

Energy 197kcal/830kJ; Protein 24.5g; Carbohydrate 4.7g, of which sugars 4.7g; Fat 9.2g, of which saturates 1.4g; Cholesterol 21mg; Calcium 21mg; Fibre 1.1g; Sodium 45mg.

almond and tomato sauce for prawns

Ground almonds add an interesting texture and delicate nutty taste to the creamy, piquant sauce that accompanies these succulent shellfish.

Serves six

INGREDIENTS

900g/2lb cooked, peeled prawns (shrimp)

For the almond and tomato sauce

1 dried chilli

1 onion

3 garlic cloves

30ml/2 tbsp vegetable oil

8 plum tomatoes

5ml/1 tsp ground cumin

120ml/4fl oz/½ cup chicken stock

130g/4½oz/generous 1 cup ground almonds

175ml/6fl oz/¾ cup crème fraîche

½ lime

salt

fresh coriander (cilantro) and spring onion (scallion) strips, to garnish

cooked rice and warm tortillas, to serve

1 Place the dried chilli in a heatproof bowl and cover with boiling water. Leave to soak for 30 minutes. Drain, remove the stalk, then slit the chilli and scrape out the seeds. Chop the flesh roughly and set it aside.

VARIATION

Try this sauce with other fish. Adding a few prawns (shrimp) and serving it over sole makes a very luxurious dish.

2 Chop the onion finely and then crush the garlic. Heat the oil in a frying pan and fry the onion and garlic over a low heat until soft.

3 Cut a cross in the base of each tomato. Place them in a heatproof bowl and cover with boiling water. After 30 seconds, lift them out with a slotted spoon and plunge them into a bowl of cold water. Drain.

4 Skin and seed the tomatoes. Chop the flesh into 1cm/½in cubes and stir them into the onion in the frying pan, with the chopped chilli and ground cumin. Cook for 10 minutes, stirring occasionally.

5 Pour the mixture into a food processor or blender. Add the stock and process until smooth.

6 Pour the mixture into a large pan, then add the ground almonds and stir over a low heat for 2–3 minutes. Stir in the crème fraîche until it has been incorporated completely.

7 Squeeze the juice from the lime into the sauce and stir it in. Season with salt to taste, then increase the heat and bring the sauce to simmering point.

8 Add the prawns to the sauce and heat until warmed through. Do not boil or cook for too long once the prawns are added or they will become very tough. Serve on a bed of hot rice garnished with the coriander and spring onion strips. Offer warm tortillas separately.

Energy 416kcal/1732kJ; Protein 32.7g; Carbohydrate 7.1g, of which sugars 6.2g; Fat 28.7g, of which saturates 9.6g; Cholesterol 325mg; Calcium 199mg; Fibre 3.1g; Sodium 307mg.

sorrel sauce for salmon

The sharp, almost lemon-like flavour of the sorrel is delicious with salmon or trout. Young sorrel has the best flavour, so it is worth growing the herb in a large pot or kitchen garden.

Serves four

INGREDIENTS

25g/1oz/2 tbsp butter

4 shallots, finely chopped

90ml/6 tbsp crème fraîche or double (heavy) cream

100g/3½oz fresh sorrel leaves, washed and patted dry

salt and ground black pepper

1 Melt the butter in a heavy pan over a medium heat. Add the shallots and fry for 2–3 minutes, stirring frequently, until just softened.

2 Stir in the crème fraîche or double (heavy) cream. Add the sorrel to the shallots and cook until the leaves are completely wilted, stirring constantly.

3 Spoon the cream and sorrel mixture into a food processor and process for just long enough to chop the sorrel and distribute the pieces evenly throughout the sauce.

4 Return the sauce to the clean pan, season with salt and pepper and heat gently. Serve hot.

VARIATION

If sorrel is not available, use finely chopped watercress instead.

Energy 147kcal/605kJ; Protein 1.5g; Carbohydrate 3g, of which sugars 2.3g; Fat 14.4g, of which saturates 9.4g; Cholesterol 39mg; Calcium 63mg; Fibre 0.9g; Sodium 79mg.

green tartare sauce for seafood pasta

This colourful sauce is good with all kinds of seafood, particularly fresh scallops, and it looks stunning over black, squid ink pasta.

Serves four

INGREDIENTS

350g/12oz black tagliatelle

12 large scallops

60ml/4 tbsp white wine

150ml/¼ pint/⅔ cup fish stock

lime wedges and parsley sprigs,
  to garnish

For the green tartare sauce

120ml/4fl oz/½ cup crème fraîche

10ml/2 tsp wholegrain mustard

2 garlic cloves, crushed

30–45ml/2–3 tbsp fresh lime juice

60ml/4 tbsp chopped fresh parsley

30ml/2 tbsp chopped chives

salt and ground black pepper

4 Put the white wine and fish stock into a pan. Heat to simmering point. Add the scallops and cook very gently for 3–4 minutes (no longer or they will become tough).

5 Remove the scallops from the pan. Boil the wine and stock to reduce by half and add the tartare sauce to the pan. Heat gently to warm the sauce.

6 Replace the scallops and heat for 1 minute. Spoon the sauce over the pasta and garnish with lime wedges and parsley.

COOK'S TIPS

• If you are removing the scallops from the shells yourself, remember to wash them first in plenty of cold water.

• If the scallops are frozen, defrost them before cooking, as they will probably have been glazed with water and will need to be drained well.

VARIATIONS

• This sauce could be made equally well with fresh mussels.

• Instead of serving over pasta, this sauce would go particularly well with fish dishes, such as monkfish, which has a flavour reminiscent of lobster.

1 To make the tartare sauce, blend the crème fraîche, mustard, garlic, lime juice, parsley, chives and seasoning together in a food processor or blender.

2 Cook the pasta in a large pan of boiling, salted water according to the instructions on the packet until *al dente*. Drain thoroughly.

3 Meanwhile, slice the scallops in half, horizontally. Keep any corals whole.

Energy 508kcal/2144kJ; Protein 26.1g; Carbohydrate 68.5g, of which sugars 3.9g; Fat 15.7g, of which saturates 8.6g; Cholesterol 62mg; Calcium 86mg; Fibre 3.1g; Sodium 121mg.

sauce vierge for grilled halibut

Any thick white fish fillets can be cooked in this versatile dish; turbot, brill and John Dory are especially delicious, but the flavoursome sauce also gives humbler white fish a real lift.

Serves four

INGREDIENTS

2.5ml/½ tsp fennel seeds

2.5ml/½ tsp celery seeds

105ml/7 tbsp olive oil

5ml/1 tsp mixed peppercorns

coarse sea salt

5ml/1 tsp fresh thyme leaves, chopped

5ml/1 tsp fresh rosemary leaves, chopped

5ml/1 tsp fresh oregano or marjoram leaves, chopped

675–800g/1½–1¾lb middle cut of halibut, about 3cm/1¼in thick, cut into 4 pieces

For the sauce vierge

105ml/7 tbsp extra virgin olive oil, plus extra for cooking

juice of 1 lemon

1 garlic clove, finely chopped

2 tomatoes, peeled, seeded and diced

5ml/1 tsp small capers

2 drained canned anchovy fillets, chopped

5ml/1 tsp snipped fresh chives

15ml/1 tbsp shredded fresh basil leaves

15ml/1 tbsp chopped fresh chervil

1 Mix the fennel and celery seeds with the peppercorns in a mortar. Crush with a pestle, and then stir in the coarse sea salt to taste. Spoon the mixture into a shallow dish and stir in the herbs and the olive oil.

2 Heat a ridged grilling pan or preheat the grill (broiler) on high. Brush the grilling pan or grill pan with a little olive oil to prevent the fish from sticking during cooking.

3 Add the halibut pieces to the olive oil mixture, turning them to coat them thoroughly, then arrange them with the dark skin uppermost in the oiled grilling pan or grill pan. Cook for about 6–8 minutes, turning once, until the fish is cooked all the way through and the skin has browned.

4 Combine the sauce ingredients, except the fresh herbs, in a pan and heat gently until warm but not hot. Stir in the chives, basil and chervil.

5 Place the halibut on four warmed plates. Spoon the sauce around and over the fish and serve immediately, with lightly-cooked green cabbage.

Energy 462kcal/1920kJ; Protein 37.4g; Carbohydrate 1.9g, of which sugars 1.8g; Fat 33.9g, of which saturates 4.9g; Cholesterol 60mg; Calcium 82mg; Fibre 1.1g; Sodium 169mg.

spicy pesto for rolled salmon

This is a great way to serve salmon steaks boneless, as a solid piece of fish. The pesto uses sunflower kernels and chilli as its flavouring rather than the classic basil and pine nuts.

Serves four

INGREDIENTS

4 salmon steaks, about 225g/8oz each
30ml/2 tbsp sunflower oil
finely grated rind and juice of 1 lime
salt and ground black pepper

For the spicy pesto

6 fresh mild red chillies, seeded and
  roughly chopped
2 garlic cloves
30ml/2 tbsp pumpkin or sunflower seeds
finely grated rind and juice of 1 lime
75ml/5 tbsp olive oil

1 Place a salmon steak flat on a board. Insert a very sharp knife close to the top of the bone. Staying close to the bone all the time, cut to the end of the steak to release one side of the steak. Repeat with the other side.

2 Place one piece of salmon skin side down and hold it firmly with one hand. Insert a small sharp knife under the skin and, working away from you, cut the flesh off in a single piece. Repeat with the remaining salmon steaks.

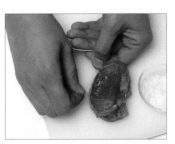

3 Wrap each piece of fish into a circle, with the thinner end wrapped around the fatter end. Tie with string (twine). Place in a shallow bowl.

4 Rub the oil into the boneless fish rounds. Add the lime juice and rind to the bowl. Cover and marinate in the refrigerator for 2 hours.

5 Make the pesto. Process the chillies, garlic, pumpkin or sunflower seeds, lime rind and juice and seasoning in a food processor. until well mixed. With the machine running, gradually add the olive oil. The pesto will slowly thicken and emulsify. Scrape it into a bowl. Preheat the grill (broiler).

6 Drain the salmon and place the rounds in a grill pan. Grill (broil) for 5 minutes on each side or until opaque. Serve with the spicy pesto.

COOK'S TIP

If any small bones remain in the salmon steaks after preparation, remove them with fish tweezers or a pair of new eyebrow tweezers kept for the purpose.

Energy 627kcal/2601kJ; Protein 47.7g; Carbohydrate 1.6g, of which sugars 0.3g; Fat 47.7g, of which saturates 7.3g; Cholesterol 113mg; Calcium 63mg; Fibre 0.5g; Sodium 103mg.

oyster sauce for turbot fillets

This luxurious oyster sauce is perfect for special occasions. It is worth buying a whole turbot and asking the fishmonger to fillet and skin it for you. Keep the head, bones and trimmings for stock. Sole, brill and halibut can all be substituted for the turbot.

2 Melt 25g/1oz/2 tbsp of the butter in a pan, add the vegetables and cook gently until tender but not coloured. Add half the Champagne and cook gently until evaporated, without browning the vegetables.

3 Strain the oyster juices into a small pan. Add the cream and remaining Champagne. Place over a medium heat until reduced to the consistency of thin cream. Dice half the remaining butter and whisk it in, a piece at a time. Season. Whizz in a blender until velvet-smooth.

4 Reheat the sauce to just below boiling. Add and poach the oysters for 1 minute, until warm but barely cooked. Keep warm; do not boil.

5 Season the turbot. Heat the rest of the butter in a large frying pan until foaming. Fry the fish over a medium heat for 2–3 minutes each side until cooked and golden.

6 Cut each fillet into three and arrange on warm plates. Pile the vegetables on top, then add the oysters and sauce around the fillets.

Serves four

INGREDIENTS

1 turbot, about 1.8kg/4lb, filleted
  and skinned
salt and ground white pepper

For the oyster sauce

12 Pacific (rock) oysters
115g/4oz/½ cup butter
2 carrots, cut into julienne strips
200g/7oz celeriac, cut into julienne strips
the white parts of 2 leeks, cut into
  julienne strips
375ml/13fl oz/generous 1½ cups
  Champagne or dry white sparkling wine
  (about ½ bottle)
105ml/7 tbsp whipping cream
salt and ground white pepper

1 Using an oyster knife, open the oysters over a bowl to catch the juices, then carefully remove them from their shells, discarding the shells, and place them in a separate bowl. Set the oysters aside until required.

Energy 784kcal/3263kJ; Protein 72.9g; Carbohydrate 9.6g, of which sugars 7.5g; Fat 44.8g, of which saturates 24g; Cholesterol 132mg; Calcium 330mg; Fibre 1g; Sodium 630mg.

light curry sauce for john dory fillets

This excellent combination of flavours also works well with other flat fish like turbot, halibut and brill, or more exotic species like mahi-mahi or orange roughy. The curry taste should be very subtle, so use a mild curry powder. Serve the fish with pilau rice and mango chutney.

Serves four

INGREDIENTS

4 John Dory fillets, about 175g/6oz each, skinned
15ml/1 tbsp sunflower oil
25g/1oz/2 tbsp butter
salt and ground black pepper

For the curry sauce
30ml/2 tbsp sunflower oil
1 carrot, chopped
1 onion, chopped
1 celery stick, chopped
white of 1 leek, chopped
2 garlic cloves, crushed
50g/2oz creamed coconut, crumbled
2 tomatoes, peeled, seeded and diced
2.5cm/1in piece fresh root ginger, grated
15ml/1 tbsp tomato purée (paste)
5–10ml/1–2 tsp mild curry powder
500ml/17fl oz/generous 2 cups chicken or fish stock

For the garnish
15ml/1 tbsp fresh coriander (cilantro) leaves
4 banana leaves (optional)
1 small mango, peeled and diced

1 Make the sauce. Heat the oil in a pan. Cook the vegetables and garlic gently until soft but not brown.

2 Add the coconut, tomatoes and ginger. Cook for 1–2 minutes. Stir in the tomato purée, curry powder to taste, stock and seasoning.

3 Bring to the boil, then lower the heat, cover the pan and cook the sauce over the lowest heat for about 50 minutes. Stir once or twice to prevent the sauce from burning. Leave to cool.

4 Purée to a smooth sauce in a blender or food processor. Reheat, adding a little water if too thick.

5 Season the fish fillets with salt and pepper. Heat the oil in a large frying pan, add the butter and heat until sizzling. Put in the fish and fry for about 2–3 minutes on each side, until pale golden and cooked through. Drain on kitchen paper.

6 If you have banana leaves, place these on individual warmed plates and arrange the fillets on top. Pour the sauce around the fish and scatter on the finely diced mango. Garnish with coriander leaves and serve at once.

Energy 398kcal/1657kJ; Protein 34.1g; Carbohydrate 6.5g, of which sugars 5.8g; Fat 26.4g, of which saturates 12.3g; Cholesterol 94mg; Calcium 42mg; Fibre 1.9g; Sodium 170mg.

teriyaki sauce for salmon

Marinating the salmon in this teriyaki sauce makes it so wonderfully tender, it just melts in the mouth, and the crunchy condiment provides an excellent foil.

Serves four

INGREDIENTS

675g/1½lb salmon fillet
30ml/2 tbsp sunflower oil
watercress, to garnish

For the teriyaki sauce
5ml/1 tsp caster (superfine) sugar
5ml/1 tsp dry white wine
5ml/1 tsp sake, rice wine or dry sherry
30ml/2 tbsp dark soy sauce

For the condiment
5cm/2in fresh root ginger, grated
pink food colouring (optional)
50g/2oz mooli, grated

1 For the teriyaki sauce, mix together the sugar, white wine, sake or rice wine or dry sherry and soy sauce, stirring until the sugar dissolves.

2 Remove the skin from the salmon using a very sharp filleting knife. Cut the fillet into strips, then place in a non-metallic dish. Pour over the teriyaki sauce and set aside to marinate for 10–15 minutes.

3 To make the condiment, place the ginger in a bowl and add a little pink food colouring if you wish. Stir in the mooli.

4 Transfer the salmon to a sieve to drain off the teriyaki sauce.

5 Heat a wok, then add and heat the oil. Add the salmon in batches and stir-fry for 3–4 minutes, until it is cooked. Transfer to serving plates. Garnish with the watercress and serve with the mooli and ginger condiment.

Energy 364kcal/1515kJ; Protein 34.4g; Carbohydrate 1.9g, of which sugars 1.9g; Fat 24.1g, of which saturates 3.9g; Cholesterol 84mg; Calcium 40mg; Fibre 0.1g; Sodium 612mg.

coconut sauce for salmon

Salmon is quite a robust fish, and responds well to being cooked with a sauce of strong flavours, as in this fragrant blend of spices, garlic and chilli.

Serves four

INGREDIENTS

4 salmon steaks, about 175g/6oz each

5ml/1 tsp ground cumin

10ml/2 tsp chilli powder

2.5ml/½ tsp ground turmeric

30ml/2 tbsp white wine vinegar

1.5ml/¼ tsp salt

For the coconut sauce

45ml/3 tbsp oil

1 onion, chopped

2 fresh green chillies, seeded
  and chopped

2 garlic cloves, crushed

2.5cm/1in piece fresh root ginger, grated

5ml/1 tsp ground cumin

5ml/1 tsp ground coriander

175ml/6fl oz/¾ cup coconut milk

fresh coriander (cilantro) sprigs, to garnish

rice with spring onions (scallions), to serve

1 Arrange the salmon steaks in a single layer in a shallow glass dish. Put 5ml/1 tsp of ground cumin in a bowl and add the chilli powder, turmeric, vinegar and salt. Rub the paste over the salmon steaks and leave to marinate for about 15 minutes.

2 Heat the oil in a large deep frying pan and fry the onion, chillies, garlic and ginger, stirring frequently, for 5–6 minutes, until the onion is softened. Cool slightly.

3 Transfer the onion mixture to a food processor or blender and process to a smooth paste.

4 Return the onion paste to the pan. Add the remaining cumin, the coriander and coconut milk. Bring to the boil, reduce the heat and simmer the sauce for 5 minutes, stirring occasionally.

5 Add the salmon steaks. Cover and cook for 15 minutes, until the fish is tender. Transfer to a serving dish and garnish with the fresh coriander. Serve with the rice and spring onions.

Energy 416kcal/1729kJ; Protein 36.2g; Carbohydrate 5.2g, of which sugars 4.8g; Fat 27.9g, of which saturates 4.4g; Cholesterol 88mg; Calcium 75mg; Fibre 1.1g; Sodium 132mg.

sweet and sour sauce for baked fish

This sweet and sour sauce is light and slightly piquant, with a hint of red chilli – perfect for whole fish and equally delicious with pan-fried fillets, stir-fried prawns or baked fish steaks.

Serves four

INGREDIENTS

1 whole fish, such as red snapper
  or carp, about 1kg/2¼lb, cleaned

30–45ml/2–3 tbsp cornflour (cornstrach)

oil for frying

salt and ground black pepper

boiled rice, to serve

For the spice paste

2 garlic cloves

2 lemon grass stalks

2.5cm/1in fresh lengkuas

2.5cm/1in fresh root ginger

2cm/¾in fresh turmeric or 2.5ml/
  ½ tsp ground turmeric

5 macadamia nuts or 10 almonds

For the sweet and sour sauce

15ml/1 tbsp brown sugar

45ml/3 tbsp cider vinegar

about 350ml/12fl oz/1½ cups water

2 lime leaves, torn

4 shallots, quartered

3 tomatoes, peeled and cut in wedges

3 spring onions (scallions), finely
  shredded

1 fresh red chilli, seeded and shredded

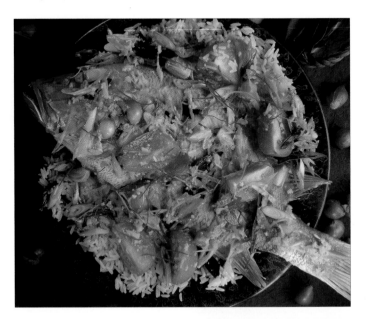

1 Wash and dry the fish thoroughly and then sprinkle it inside and out with salt. Set aside for 15 minutes.

2 Peel and crush the garlic cloves. Use only the lower white part of the lemon grass stems and slice them thinly. Peel and slice the lengkuas, ginger and fresh turmeric, if using. Grind the nuts, garlic, lemon grass, lengkuas, ginger and turmeric to a fine paste in a food processor or blender, or using a pestle and mortar.

3 Scrape the paste into a bowl. Stir in the brown sugar, cider vinegar, seasoning to taste and water. Add the lime leaves. Set this sauce aside.

4 Dust the fish with the cornflour and fry on both sides in hot oil for about 8–9 minutes or until almost cooked through. Drain the fish on kitchen paper and transfer to a serving dish. Keep warm.

5 Pour off most of the oil and then pour in the sauce. Bring to the boil, stirring. Reduce the heat and cook for 3–4 minutes. Add the shallots and tomatoes, followed a minute later by the spring onions and chilli. Taste and adjust the seasoning if necessary.

6 Pour the sauce over the fish. Serve at once, with plenty of rice.

Energy 280kcal/1176kJ; Protein 32.4g; Carbohydrate 8.4g, of which sugars 7.7g; Fat 13.3g, of which saturates 1.8g; Cholesterol 56mg; Calcium 98mg; Fibre 1.8g; Sodium 125mg.

black bean sauce for stir-fried squid

This dish follows the style of Cantonese cooking and it tastes as good as it looks. Use an authentic full-flavoured fermented black bean sauce rather than a "cook-in" type sauce.

Serves four

INGREDIENTS

350–400g/12–14oz squid

1 medium green (bell) pepper, cored and seeded

45–60ml/3–4 tbsp vegetable oil

1 garlic clove, finely chopped

2.5ml/½ tsp finely chopped fresh root ginger

15ml/1 tbsp finely chopped spring onion (scallion)

5ml/1 tsp salt

15ml/1 tbsp black bean sauce

15ml/1 tbsp Chinese rice wine or dry sherry

few drops of sesame oil

3 Cut the green pepper into small triangular pieces. Heat a wok until hot. Add and heat the oil, then add the green pepper and stir-fry for about 1 minute.

4 Add the garlic, ginger, spring onion, salt and squid, then stir for 1 minute. Add the black bean sauce, rice wine or dry sherry and sesame oil and serve.

1 To clean the squid, cut off the tentacles just below the eye. Remove the "quill" from inside the body. Dip your fingers in a little salt, then rub off and discard the mottled skin on the squid. Wash the squid and dry well. Cut open the squid and score the inside in a criss-cross pattern, taking care not to cut right through.

2 Cut the squid into pieces each about the size of an oblong postage stamp. Blanch the squid in a pan of boiling water for a few seconds. Remove and drain. Dry well.

Energy 169kcal/705kJ; Protein 14.3g; Carbohydrate 4.8g, of which sugars 2.9g; Fat 10g, of which saturates 1.6g; Cholesterol 197mg; Calcium 18mg; Fibre 0.9g; Sodium 99mg.

sauces for vegetables

Here is a glorious collection of recipes to
bring out the very best in vegetables. There is
something so vibrant about them that many
cooks simply settle for a hint of butter or a
drizzle of olive oil. But for a superlative
stand-alone dish, try enhancing them with
piquant dressings, braising them in rich wine
marinades or combining them with a creamy
sauce. Even when flanking a meat or fish
course, these fabulous roots, leaves and
vegetable-fruits should be given all the
special treatment they deserve.

light tomato sauce for aubergine rolls

The tomato sauce in this recipe is light and perfect with rich or creamy ingredients. Here it is just right with a rich cheese and rice filling in little rolls of aubergine.

Serves four

INGREDIENTS

2 aubergines (eggplants)

olive oil, or sunflower oil for shallow frying

75g/3oz/scant ½ cup ricotta cheese

75g/3oz/scant ½ cup soft goat's cheese

225g/8oz/2 cups cooked long grain white rice

15ml/1 tbsp chopped fresh basil

5ml/1 tsp chopped fresh mint, plus mint sprigs, to garnish

salt and ground black pepper

For the tomato sauce

15ml/1 tbsp olive oil

1 red onion, finely chopped

1 garlic clove, crushed

400g/14oz can chopped tomatoes

120ml/4fl oz/½ cup vegetable stock or white wine or a mixture

15ml/1 tbsp chopped fresh parsley

1 Make the tomato sauce. Heat the oil in a small pan. Fry the onion and garlic for 3–4 minutes until softened. Add the tomatoes, vegetable stock and/or wine, and parsley. Season well. Bring to the boil, then lower the heat and simmer for 10–12 minutes until slightly thick, stirring occasionally.

2 Preheat the oven to 190°C/375°F/ Gas 5. Slice the aubergines lengthways. Heat the oil in a large frying pan and fry the aubergine slices until they are golden brown on both sides. Drain on kitchen paper. Mix the ricotta, goat's cheese, rice, basil and mint in a bowl. Season well.

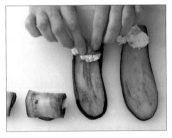

3 Place a generous spoonful of the cheese and rice mixture at one end of each aubergine slice and roll up. Arrange the rolls side by side in a shallow ovenproof dish. Pour the tomato sauce over the top and bake for 10–15 minutes until heated through. Garnish with the mint sprigs and serve.

Energy 233kcal/980kJ; Protein 8.9g; Carbohydrate 24.6g, of which sugars 6.7g; Fat 11.8g, of which saturates 5.8g; Cholesterol 25mg; Calcium 56mg; Fibre 3.3g; Sodium 125mg.

quick tomato sauce on cheese polenta

This quick tomato sauce can be prepared from store-cupboard ingredients. Adding tomato purée enriches its flavour, making it ideal for plain vegetables or baked polenta, as here.

Serves four

INGREDIENTS

5ml/1 tsp salt

250g/9oz/2¼ cups quick-cook polenta

5ml/1 tsp paprika

2.5ml/½ tsp ground nutmeg

75g/3oz/¾ cup grated Gruyère cheese

For the rich tomato sauce

30ml/2 tbsp olive oil

1 large onion, finely chopped

2 garlic cloves, crushed

30ml/2 tbsp brandy or medium sherry

2 x 400g/14oz cans chopped tomatoes

60ml/4 tbsp tomato purée (paste)

5ml/1 tsp sugar

salt and ground black pepper

1 Line a 28 x 18cm/11 x 7in baking tin with clear film (plastic wrap. Bring 1 litre/1¾ pints/4 cups water to the boil with the salt.

2 Add the polenta in a thin stream. Cook, stirring, for 5 minutes. Beat in the paprika and nutmeg. Spread in the tin, smoothing the top. Cool.

3 To make the rich tomato sauce, heat the oil in a pan. Cook the onion and garlic until soft. Add the brandy or sherry, tomatoes, tomato purée and sugar. Bring to the boil. Reduce the heat, season and cover, then simmer gently for 20 minutes. Taste for seasoning and set aside.

4 Preheat the oven to 200°C/400°F/ Gas 6. Turn out the polenta on to a board, and cut into 5cm/2in squares. Place half the squares in a greased ovenproof dish. Spoon over half the tomato sauce, and sprinkle with half the cheese. Repeat the layers. Bake for 25 minutes.

Energy 492kcal/2052kJ; Protein 20g; Carbohydrate 55.8g, of which sugars 8.4g; Fat 20.3g, of which saturates 8.8g; Cholesterol 37mg; Calcium 394mg; Fibre 3.6g; Sodium 861mg.

wild mushroom sauce for polenta

The flavour of wild mushrooms combines well with mascarpone in this sauce to heighten the taste of the polenta. It also makes a delicious topping for baked potatoes.

Serves four to six

INGREDIENTS

900ml/1½ pints/3¾ cups milk
900ml/1½ pints/3¾ cups water
5ml/1 tsp salt
300g/11oz/2¾ cups polenta
50g/2oz/¼ cup butter
115g/4oz Gorgonzola cheese
fresh thyme sprigs, to garnish

For the wild mushroom sauce

40g/1½ oz/scant 1 cup dried
  porcini mushrooms
150ml/¼ pint/⅔ cup hot water
25g/1oz/2 tbsp butter
115g/4oz/1½ cups button (white)
  mushrooms, chopped
60ml/4 tbsp dry white wine
generous pinch of dried thyme
60ml/4 tbsp mascarpone
salt and ground black pepper

1 Pour the milk and water into a large, heavy pan. Add the salt and bring to the boil. Using a long-handled spoon, stir the liquid briskly with one hand while drizzling in the polenta with the other. When the mixture is thick and smooth, lower the heat to a gentle simmer and cook for about 20 minutes, stirring occasionally.

2 Remove from the heat and stir in the butter and Gorgonzola. Spoon the polenta mixture into a shallow dish and level the surface.

3 Let the polenta set until solid, then cut it into wedges.

4 Meanwhile, make the sauce. Soak the porcini in the hot water for 15 minutes. Drain, reserving the liquid. Finely chop the porcini and strain the soaking liquid through a sieve lined with kitchen paper. Discard the kitchen paper.

5 Melt half the butter in a small pan. Sauté the chopped fresh mushrooms for about 5 minutes. Add the wine, porcini and strained soaking liquid, with the dried thyme. Season to taste. Cook for a further 2 minutes. Stir in the mascarpone and simmer for a few minutes, until reduced by a third. Set aside to cool.

6 Heat a ridged griddle pan or grill (broiler), and grill (broil) the polenta until crisp. Brush with melted butter and serve hot with the sauce. Garnish with thyme.

COOK'S TIP

If fresh porcini mushrooms are available, use this nutty-tasting variety instead of the dried mushrooms. You will not need to soak them beforehand. You would need about 175g/6oz fresh porcini for this recipe. They are also sold under the name ceps.

Energy 478kcal/1992kJ; Protein 15.9g; Carbohydrate 47.7g, of which sugars 7.5g; Fat 24.8g, of which saturates 12.7g; Cholesterol 56mg; Calcium 283mg; Fibre 1.4g; Sodium 412mg.

mornay sauce for two-veg gratin

This nursery favourite is enjoying a revival. The secret of a good cheese sauce is not to make it too thick and to stir in the cheese off the heat so that it melts gently.

Serves four to six

INGREDIENTS

1 medium cauliflower

2 heads of broccoli

1 onion, sliced

3 hard-boiled eggs, quartered

6 cherry tomatoes, halved (optional)

30–45ml/2–3 tbsp natural-coloured dried breadcrumbs

For the mornay sauce

40g/1½oz/3 tbsp butter

40g/1½oz/⅓ cup plain (all-purpose) flour

600ml/1 pint/2½ cups milk or a mixture of milk and vegetable water

150g/5oz/1¼ cups grated mature Cheddar cheese

freshly grated nutmeg

salt and ground black pepper

1 Trim the cauliflower and broccoli and cut them into even-size florets, slicing the thinner parts of the stalks if you prefer.

2 Bring a large pan of lightly salted water to the boil and cook the cauliflower, broccoli and onion slices for 5–7 minutes or until just tender. Do not over-cook.

3 Drain the cauliflower and broccoli, reserving some of the vegetable water if you intend using it for the sauce. Arrange the vegetables in a shallow flameproof dish and add the quartered eggs.

4 To make the sauce, melt the butter in a pan and stir in the flour. Cook gently for 1 minute, stirring occasionally, and taking care not to brown the flour.

5 Gradually add the milk, or milk and vegetable water, whisking constantly. Bring to the boil, whisking until smooth and thick. Lower the heat and simmer for 2 minutes. Whisk in three-quarters of the cheese and season with nutmeg, salt and pepper.

6 Preheat the grill (broiler). Pour the sauce over the vegetables and dot with the tomato halves, if using. Mix the remaining cheese with the dried breadcrumbs. Sprinkle the cheese and breadcrumb mixture over the vegetables, and grill (broil) until bubbling and golden brown. Serve immediately.

VARIATION

The sauce can also be used for macaroni cheese. Cook 200g/7oz/ 1¾ cups dried macaroni or pasta shapes according to the package instructions. Drain and mix with the sauce, quartered hard-boiled eggs and tomato halves.

Energy 336kcal/1404kJ; Protein 20.9g; Carbohydrate 18.6g, of which sugars 8.9g; Fat 19.8g, of which saturates 11.1g; Cholesterol 139mg; Calcium 403mg; Fibre 4.1g; Sodium 352mg.

tamarind sauce for stuffed aubergines

The traditional way of cooking with tamarind is in a terracotta dish, which brings out the full fruity tartness of the tamarind. This spicy dish of stuffed aubergines in a tart tamarind sauce will add a refreshing tang to any meal.

Serves four

INGREDIENTS

12 baby aubergines (eggplants)

For the stuffing

15ml/1 tbsp vegetable oil
1 small onion, chopped
10ml/2 tsp grated fresh root ginger
10ml/2 tsp crushed garlic
5ml/1 tsp coriander seeds
5ml/1 tsp cumin seeds
10ml/2 tsp white poppy seeds
10ml/2 tsp sesame seeds
10ml/2 tsp desiccated (dry
  unsweetened shredded) coconut
105ml/7tbsp warm water
15ml/1 tbsp dry-roasted skinned peanuts
2.5–5ml/½–1 tsp chilli powder
5ml/1 tsp salt

For the tamarind sauce

15ml/1 tbsp vegetable oil
6–8 curry leaves
1–2 dried red chillies, chopped
2.5ml/½ tsp concentrated tamarind paste
105ml/7tbsp hot water

COOK'S TIP

Some food processors are too big for grinding spices for sauces, or simply do not have the requisite small blade and bowl attachment. There are alternatives: many cooks keep a coffee grinder especially for grinding spices. Grind spices in small batches and wipe the grinder out with paper after use. Japanese-style ridged mortars are brilliant for grinding spices, particularly moist pastes. They are partnered by special pestles made from very hard wood.

1 Make three deep slits lengthways in each aubergine, without cutting through, then soak in salted water for 20 minutes.

2 Heat 15ml/1 tbsp oil in a pan and sauté the onion for 3–4 minutes. Add the ginger and garlic and cook for 30 seconds.

3 Add the coriander and cumin seeds and sauté for 30 seconds, then add the poppy seeds, sesame seeds and coconut. Sauté for 1 minute, stirring constantly. Allow to cool slightly, then grind the spices in a food processor, adding 105ml/7 tbsp warm water. This mixture is the base for the stuffing and it should form a thick, slightly coarse paste.

4 Mix the peanuts, chilli powder and salt into the spice paste. Drain the aubergines and dry on kitchen paper. Stuff each of the slits with the spice paste and reserve any remaining paste.

5 For the sauce, heat the remaining oil in a wok or large pan over a medium heat. Add the curry leaves and chillies. Let the chillies blacken, then add the aubergines and the tamarind blended with 105ml/7 tbsp hot water. Stir, adding any remaining spice paste.

6 Cover the pan and simmer gently for 15–20 minutes or until the aubergines are tender. Serve with chapatis and a meat or poultry dish, if you like.

Energy 132kcal/549kJ; Protein 2.9g; Carbohydrate 4.7g, of which sugars 3.8g; Fat 11.5g, of which saturates 3.3g; Cholesterol 0mg; Calcium 36mg; Fibre 3.7g; Sodium 5mg.

egg and lemon sauce for asparagus

Eggs and lemons are often found in dishes from Greece, Turkey and the Middle East. This sauce has a fresh, tangy taste and brings out the best in asparagus.

2 Blend the cornflour with the cooled, reserved cooking liquid and place in a small pan. Bring to the boil, stirring constantly, and cook over a low heat until the sauce thickens slightly. Stir in 10ml/2 tsp sugar, then remove the pan from the heat and leave to cool slightly.

3 Beat the egg yolks thoroughly with the lemon juice and then stir gradually into the cooled sauce. Cook over a very low heat, stirring constantly, until the sauce is fairly thick. Be careful not to overheat the sauce or it may curdle.

4 As soon as the sauce has thickened, remove the pan from the heat and continue stirring for 1 minute. Taste and add salt or sugar as necessary. Leave the sauce to cool slightly.

5 Stir the cooled sauce, then pour a little over the asparagus. Cover and chill for at least 2 hours before serving with the rest of the sauce.

Serves four

INGREDIENTS

675g/1½lb asparagus, tough ends removed, and tied in a bundle

For the egg and lemon sauce
15ml/1 tbsp cornflour (cornstarch)
about 10ml/2 tsp sugar
2 egg yolks
juice of 1½ lemons
salt

VARIATION
This sauce goes very well with young vegetables. Try it with baby leeks, cooked whole or chopped.

1 Cook the bundle of asparagus in salted boiling water for 7–10 minutes. Drain well and arrange the asparagus in a serving dish. Reserve 200ml/7fl oz/scant 1 cup of the cooking liquid.

COOK'S TIP
Use only the tiny asparagus spears for a light, elegant first course.

Energy 96kcal/399kJ; Protein 6.4g; Carbohydrate 9.5g, of which sugars 5.8g; Fat 3.8g, of which saturates 1g; Cholesterol 101mg; Calcium 59mg; Fibre 2.9g; Sodium 8mg.

fruity red wine sauce for braised leeks

Fragrant oregano and strong dark vinegar give a distinctive flavour to this dish of braised leeks and fruity wine sauce. Serve it as part of a mixed meze or as a partner for baked white fish.

Serves six

INGREDIENTS

12 baby leeks or 6 thick leeks

15ml/1 tbsp coriander seeds, lightly crushed

5cm/2in piece of cinnamon stick

120ml/4fl oz/½ cup olive oil

3 fresh bay leaves

2 strips pared orange rind

5 or 6 fresh or dried oregano sprigs

5ml/1 tsp sugar

150ml/¼ pint/⅔ cup fruity red wine

10ml/2 tsp balsamic or sherry vinegar

30ml/2 tbsp coarsely chopped fresh oregano or marjoram

salt and ground black pepper

1 If using baby leeks, simply trim the ends, but leave them whole. Cut thick leeks into 5–7.5cm/2–3in lengths.

2 Place the coriander seeds and cinnamon in a pan wide enough to take all the leeks in a single layer. Cook over a medium heat for 2–3 minutes, or until the spices give off a fragrant aroma, then stir in the olive oil, bay leaves, orange rind, oregano, sugar, wine and balsamic or sherry vinegar. Bring to the boil and simmer for 5 minutes.

3 Add the leeks to the pan. Bring back to the boil, reduce the heat and cover the pan. Cook the leeks gently for 5 minutes. Uncover and simmer gently for another 5–8 minutes, or until the leeks are just tender when tested with the tip of a sharp knife.

4 Use a slotted spoon to transfer the leeks to a serving dish. Boil the pan juices rapidly until reduced to about 75–90ml/5–6 tbsp. Add salt and pepper to taste and pour the liquid over the leeks. Set aside and leave to cool.

5 The leeks can be left to stand for several hours. If you chill them, bring them back to room temperature again before serving. Sprinkle the chopped herbs over the leeks just before serving.

COOK'S TIP

Balsamic vinegar is ideal for this dish. It has a high sugar content and wonderfully strong bouquet. It is a very dark brown colour and has a deep, rich flavour with hints of herbs and port. It is expensive, but the flavour is so rich that you only need to use a little.

Energy 151Kcal/621kJ; Protein 1.1g; Carbohydrate 1.7g, of which sugars 1.3g; Fat 13.7g, of which saturates 2g; Cholesterol 0mg; Calcium 29mg; Fibre 1.5g; Sodium 5mg.

tomato and ginger sauce for tofu rosti

In this recipe, the tofu is marinated in a mixture of tamari, honey and oil, flavoured with garlic and ginger. This marinade is then added to the fresh tomatoes to make a thick, creamy tomato sauce with a delicious tang, and the method ensures the tofu is infused with the same flavours.

Serves four

INGREDIENTS

425g/15oz tofu, cut into 1cm/½in cubes
4 large potatoes, about 900g/2lb total weight, peeled
sunflower oil, for frying
salt and ground black pepper
30ml/2 tsp sesame seeds, toasted

For the tomato and ginger sauce
30ml/2 tbsp tamari or dark soy sauce
15ml/1 tbsp clear honey
2 garlic cloves, crushed
4cm/1½in piece fresh root ginger, grated
5ml/1 tsp toasted sesame oil
15ml/1 tbsp olive oil
8 tomatoes, halved, seeded and chopped

1 For the sauce, mix together the tamari or dark soy sauce, clear honey, garlic, root ginger and toasted sesame oil in a large shallow dish.

2 Add the tofu, then spoon the liquid over the tofu and leave to marinate in the fridge for at least 1 hour. Turn the tofu occasionally in the marinade to allow the flavours to infuse.

3 To make the rösti, par-boil the potatoes for 10–15 minutes until almost tender. Leave to cool, then grate coarsely. Season well with salt and freshly ground black pepper.

4 Preheat the oven to 200°C/400°F/Gas 6. Using a slotted spoon, remove the tofu from the marinade and reserve the marinade on one side. Spread out the tofu on a baking tray and bake for about 20 minutes, turning occasionally, until the tofu squares are golden and crisp on all sides.

5 Divide the potato mixture into four equal portions. Take a quarter and shape it into a rough cake by hand. Repeat with the remaining three portions of mixture.

6 Heat a frying pan and pour in just enough oil to cover the base. Heat the oil. Place the cakes in the frying pan and flatten the mixture, using your hands (taking care not to touch the pan) or a metal spatula or palette knife to form rounds about 1cm/½in thick.

7 Cook for about 6 minutes, or until golden and crisp underneath. Carefully turn the rösti over and cook for a further 6 minutes, or until golden brown on both sides.

8 Meanwhile, complete the sauce. Heat the oil in a pan, add the reserved marinade and then the tomatoes and cook for 2 minutes, stirring continuously.

9 Reduce the heat and simmer, covered, for 10 minutes, stirring occasionally, until the tomatoes break down. Press the mixture through a sieve to make a thick, smooth sauce.

10 To serve, place a rösti on each of four warm plates. Scatter the tofu on top and spoon over the tomato sauce. Sprinkle with sesame seeds and serve at once.

COOK'S TIPS
• Tamari is a thick, mellow soy sauce, which is sold in Japanese food shops and some larger health-food stores.
• Tofu can be rather bland so allow it to marinate for 2–3 hours if possible.

Energy 523kcal/2184kJ; Protein 15.2g; Carbohydrate 46.1g, of which sugars 12.4g; Fat 32.1g, of which saturates 4.6g; Cholesterol 0mg; Calcium 620mg; Fibre 4.9g; Sodium 49mg.

walnut and garlic sauce for vegetables

This sauce, which boasts several versions throughout the Mediterranean, is excellent with roast steamed cauliflower or potatoes, or poached chicken. It can also be a dip served with bread.

Serves four

INGREDIENTS

2 x 1cm/½in slices good white bread, crusts removed

60ml/4 tbsp milk

150g/5oz/1¼ cups shelled walnuts

4 garlic cloves, chopped

120ml/4fl oz/½ cup mild olive oil

15–30ml/1–2 tbsp walnut oil (optional)

juice of 1 lemon

salt and ground black pepper

walnut or olive oil, for drizzling

paprika, for dusting (optional)

1 Soak the slices of white bread in the milk for about 5 minutes, then process with the walnuts and chopped garlic in a food processor or blender, to make a rough paste.

2 Gradually add the olive oil to the paste with the motor still running, until the mixture forms a smooth thick sauce. Blend in the walnut oil, if using.

3 Scoop the sauce into a bowl and squeeze in lemon juice to taste. Season with salt and pepper and beat well.

4 Transfer the sauce to a serving bowl, drizzle over a little more walnut or olive oil, then dust lightly with paprika, if using.

COOK'S TIP

Once opened, walnut oil has a fairly short shelf life. Buy it in small bottles and keep it in a cool, dark place. It is delicious in many salad dressings.

VARIATION

For an Italian salsa di noci for pasta, process 90g/3½oz/scant 1 cup walnuts with 2 garlic cloves and 15g/½oz flat leaf parsley. Blend in 1 slice white bread (crusts removed), soaked in milk, and 120ml/4fl oz/½ cup fruity olive oil as above. Season with salt, pepper and lemon juice. Thin with more milk or single (light) cream if very thick.

Energy 474kcal/1958kJ; Protein 7.1g; Carbohydrate 8.1g, of which sugars 2g; Fat 46.2g, of which saturates 5.1g; Cholesterol 1mg; Calcium 67mg; Fibre 1.5g; Sodium 74mg.

garlic sauce for roasted beetroot

In Greece, beetroot is a favourite winter vegetable, either served solo as a salad or with a layer of the flavourful garlic sauce, known as skordalia, on top.

Serves four

INGREDIENTS

675g/1½lb medium or small beetroot (beets)

75–90ml/5–6 tbsp extra virgin olive oil

salt

For the garlic sauce

4 medium slices of bread, crusts removed, soaked in water for 10 minutes

2 or 3 garlic cloves, chopped

15ml/1 tbsp white wine vinegar

60ml/4 tbsp extra virgin olive oil

1 Preheat the oven to 180°C/350°F/ Gas 4. Rinse the beetroot under cold running water and rub off any grit, but be careful not to pierce the skin or the colour will run. If the leaves are still on the beetroot, cut them off leaving short lengths of stalks in place.

2 Line a roasting pan with a large sheet of foil and place the beetroot on top. Drizzle a little of the olive oil over them, sprinkle lightly with salt and fold over both edges of the foil to enclose the beetroot completely. Bake for about 1½ hours until perfectly soft.

3 Meanwhile, make the garlic sauce. Squeeze most of the water out of the soaked bread, but leave it quite moist.

4 Place the bread in a blender or food processor. Add the garlic and vinegar, with salt to taste, and blend until smooth. Scrape the mixture down in the bowl.

5 While the blender or food processor is running, drizzle in the extra virgin olive oil through the lid or feeder tube. The sauce should absorb the oil and become creamy, not runny. Taste the sauce for seasoning. Spoon it into a serving bowl and set it aside.

6 Remove the beetroot from the foil package. When they are cool enough to handle, carefully peel them. Cut them into thin, round slices and arrange these on a flat platter or individual plates.

7 Drizzle with the remaining oil. Either spread a thin layer of garlic sauce on top, or hand it around separately. Serve with fresh bread, if you like.

Energy 342kcal//1425kJ; Protein 5g; Carbohydrate 25.2g, of which sugars 12.5g; Fat 25.4g, of which saturates 3.6g; Cholesterol 0mg; Calcium 61mg; Fibre 3.6g; Sodium 242mg.

classic dressings and marinades

Whereas a dressing was once set aside for tossing into a salad and a marinade seen simply as a seasoned wine for soaking meat, in contemporary cooking they are viewed as exciting and flavourful infusions. Dressings now enhance hot as well as cold dishes, including fish, meat, game and leafy combinations. Herbs, seasonings, citrus fruits and spices come together with oils and vinegars, wine, cider, yogurt or creams in these most eclectic of light meal recipes.

balsamic dressing for fennel and orange

This balsamic dressing is laced with garlic, zesty orange, delicate fennel and peppery rocket.

Serves four

INGREDIENTS

2 oranges, such as Jaffa, Shamouti or
blood oranges
1 fennel bulb
115g/4oz rocket (arugula) leaves
50g/2oz/⅓ cup black olives

For the dressing

30ml/2 tbsp extra virgin olive oil
15ml/1 tbsp balsamic vinegar
1 small garlic clove, crushed
salt and ground black pepper

VARIATION

If you aren't a fan of garlic, you can
leave it out of this dressing.

1 With a vegetable peeler, cut strips
of rind from the oranges, without
pith, and cut into thin julienne
strips. Cook in boiling water for a
few minutes. Drain and set aside.
Peel the oranges, removing all pith.
Slice them thinly and discard seeds.

2 Trim the fennel bulb, then cut in
half lengthways and slice it across
as thinly as possible, preferably in a
food processor fitted with a slicing
disc or using a mandolin.

3 Combine the slices of orange and
fennel in a serving bowl and toss
with the rocket leaves.

4 To make the dressing, mix
together the oil, vinegar, garlic and
seasoning. Pour over the salad, toss
together well and leave to stand for
a few minutes. Sprinkle with the
black olives and julienne strips of
orange. Serve.

Energy 105kcal/434kJ; Protein 2.3g; Carbohydrate 8g, of which sugars 7.7g; Fat 7.3g, of which saturates 1g; Cholesterol 0mg; Calcium 104mg; Fibre 3.5g; Sodium 331mg

lemon, caper and olive dressing

Lemons subtly underline the flavours of vegetables while capers add a touch of a piquancy.

Serves four

INGREDIENTS

1 large aubergine (eggplant), weighing
about 675g/1½lb
60ml/4 tbsp olive oil
grated rind and juice of 1 lemon
30ml/2 tbsp capers, rinsed
12 green olives, pitted
30ml/2 tbsp chopped fresh flat
leaf parsley
salt and ground black pepper

COOK'S TIP

This salad tastes best when made a
day ahead. It will keep well, covered, in
the refrigerator, for up to 4 days. Return
it to room temperature before serving.

1 Cut the aubergine into 2.5cm/1in
cubes. Heat the olive oil in a large,
heavy frying pan and cook the
aubergine for about 10 minutes,
tossing frequently, until golden and
softened. Drain on kitchen paper;
sprinkle with salt.

2 For the dressing, mix the lemon
rind and juice, capers, olives and
parsley with seasoning. Place the
aubergine cubes in a large serving
bowl, add the dressing and mix
well to coat the aubergine. Serve at
room temperature.

Energy 140kcal/580kJ; Protein 1.9g; Carbohydrate 4g, of which sugars 3.6g; Fat 13.2g, of which saturates 2g; Cholesterol 0mg; Calcium 42mg; Fibre 4.2g; Sodium 288mg

lime dressing for stir-fried vegetables

There is nothing quite like crisp, sweet, young vegetables. They are finished to perfection with a zesty dressing – when dressings are bursting with flavour a small quantity goes a long way.

3 Add the sugar-snap peas, asparagus, spring onions and cherry tomatoes, and stir-fry for a further 1–2 minutes. Use two wooden spoons or chopsticks to toss the ingredients, so that they cook evenly on all sides.

4 To make the dressing, mix the lime juice, honey, soy sauce and sesame oil in a small bowl, and stir until thoroughly combined. Add the dressing to the frying pan or wok and stir through.

5 Cover the pan or wok and cook the vegetables for 2–3 minutes more, or until they are just tender but still crisp. Transfer to individual bowls or plates and serve immediately.

Serves four

INGREDIENTS

15ml/1 tbsp groundnut (peanut) oil

1 garlic clove, sliced

2.5cm/1in piece fresh root ginger, peeled and finely chopped

115g/4oz baby carrots

115g/4oz patty pan squash

115g/4oz baby corn

115g/4oz green beans, trimmed

115g/4oz sugar-snap peas, trimmed

115g/4oz young asparagus, cut into 7.5cm/3in pieces

8 spring onions (scallions), cut into 5cm/2in pieces

115g/4oz cherry tomatoes

For the lime dressing

juice of 2 limes

15ml/1 tbsp clear honey

15ml/1 tbsp soy sauce

5ml/1 tsp sesame oil

1 Heat the groundnut oil in a large frying pan or wok. Add the garlic and chopped root ginger and stir-fry over a high heat for 1 minute, until the ingredients are aromatic.

2 Add the baby carrots, patty pan squash, baby corn and green beans and stir-fry for another 3–4 minutes, until the vegetables are beginning to cook.

COOK'S TIP

Stir-fries cook quickly and the trick for success is to have all the ingredients prepared and ready to go before you begin. The preparation can be done in advance, and everything kept covered and chilled. Stir-frying is a pan-to-plate method – last-minute cooking means the dish will be crisp and fresh.

Energy 115kcal/479kJ; Protein 5.9g; Carbohydrate 12.7g, of which sugars 9.4g; Fat 4.9g, of which saturates 0.7g; Cholesterol 0mg; Calcium 93mg; Fibre 4.8g; Sodium 647mg.

coriander dressing for chicken salad

Serve this salad warm to make the most of the wonderful flavour of barbecued chicken basted with a marinade of coriander, sesame and mustard, and finished with a matching dressing.

Serves six

INGREDIENTS

4 boneless chicken breasts, skinned

225g/8oz mangetouts (snow peas)

2 heads lettuce, such as lollo rosso or frisée lettuce

3 carrots, cut into matchstick strips

175g/6oz/2¼ cups button mushrooms, sliced

6 bacon rashers (strips), fried and chopped

15ml/1 tbsp chopped fresh coriander (cilantro), to garnish

For the coriander dressing

120ml/4fl oz/½ cup lemon juice

30ml/2 tbsp wholegrain mustard

5ml/1 tsp coriander seeds, crushed

250ml/8fl oz/1 cup olive oil

75ml/5 tbsp sesame oil

1 To make the coriander dressing, whisk the lemon juice with the mustard and coriander seeds in a bowl. Whisk in the olive and sesame oils.

2 Place the chicken breasts in a dish and pour over half the dressing. Marinate overnight in the refrigerator. Chill the remaining dressing ready for finishing the cooked chicken and salad

3 Cook the mangetouts for about 2 minutes in boiling water, then drain and refresh in cold water.

4 Preheat the grill (broiler) or prepare the barbecue. Tear the lettuces into small pieces and mix with all the carrots, mushrooms and bacon. Divide the salad among six individual bowls.

5 Cook the chicken breasts on a medium barbecue or under the grill (broiler) for 10–15 minutes, basting with the marinade and turning once, until cooked through.

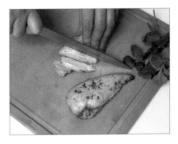

6 Slice the chicken on the diagonal into thin pieces. Divide among the bowls of salad and add some of the reserved dressing to each. Combine quickly and scatter some fresh coriander over each bowl.

Energy 555kcal/2300kJ; Protein 31.3g; Carbohydrate 7.1g, of which sugars 6.4g; Fat 44.8g, of which saturates 7.5g; Cholesterol 83mg; Calcium 68mg; Fibre 3.4g; Sodium 544mg.

ginger and lime marinade for prawns

This fragrant marinade will guarantee a mouth-watering aroma from the barbecue, and is as delicious with chicken or pork as it is with prawns – or salmon.

Serves four

INGREDIENTS

225g/8oz peeled raw tiger prawns (shrimp)
⅓ cucumber
15ml/1 tbsp sunflower oil
15ml/1 tbsp sesame seed oil
175g/6oz mangetouts (snow peas)
4 spring onons (scallions), sliced
a little chopped fresh coriander (cilantro)

For the ginger and lime marinade

15ml/1 tbsp clear honey
15ml/1 tbsp light soy sauce
15ml/1 tbsp dry sherry
2 garlic cloves, crushed
small piece fresh root ginger, peeled and finely chopped
juice of 1 lime

VARIATION

This marinade is also a good one to use with larger pieces of fish for grilling, such as salmon, trout or tuna.

1 To make the marinade, mix the honey, soy sauce and sherry in a bowl. Stir in the garlic, ginger and lime juice. Add the prawns and turn them in the marinade until they are completely coated. Cover and leave to marinate in the refrigerator for 1-2 hours.

2 Prepare the cucumber. Slice it in half lengthways, scoop out the seeds, then slice each half neatly into crescents. Set aside.

3 Heat the sunflower and sesame oils in a large, heavy frying pan or wok. Drain the prawns (reserving the marinade) and stir-fry over a high heat for 4 minutes, or until they begin to turn pink. Add the mangetouts and cucumber and stir-fry for 2 minutes more.

4 Stir in the reserved marinade and heat through until it is boiling. Finally, stir in the spring onions and cook for a few seconds until they are bright green, but not soft.

5 Remove the pan from the heat and sprinkle with chopped fresh coriander. Divide the stir-fry among four warm serving bowls and serve immediately.

Energy 198kcal/831kJ; Protein 12g; Carbohydrate 24.4g, of which sugars 24g; Fat 6g, of which saturates 0.8g; Cholesterol 110mg; Calcium 74mg; Fibre 1.3g; Sodium 113mg.

peppered citrus marinade for monkfish

Monkfish is a firm, meaty fish that cooks well on the barbecue. Its flavour is delicate but not weak and is enhanced by a pepper and uplifting citrus marinade. Serve with a green salad.

Serves four

INGREDIENTS

2 monkfish tails, about 350g/12oz each

1 lime

1 lemon

2 oranges

handful of fresh thyme sprigs

30ml/2 tbsp olive oil

15ml/1 tbsp mixed peppercorns, roughly crushed

salt and ground black pepper

1 Using a sharp kitchen knife, remove any membrane from the monkfish tails. Cut the fish carefully down one side of the backbone, sliding the knife between the bone and flesh, to remove the fillet from one side.

2 Turn the fish and repeat on the other side to remove the second fillet. Repeat on the second tail. Place the four fillets flat on a chopping board.

3 Cut two fine slices from each of the citrus fruit and arrange them over two of the fillets. The tops of the fillets should be covered by the two slices each of lime, lemon and orange, overlapped neatly to fit.

4 Add a few sprigs of fresh thyme, and sprinkle with plenty of salt and ground black pepper. Finely grate the rind from the remaining fruit and sprinkle it over the fish. Press on about half the peppercorns.

5 Lay the other two fillets on top and tie firmly. Place in a dish.

6 Squeeze the juice from the citrus fruits and mix with the olive oil and seasoning. Spoon over the fish. Cover with clear film (plastic wrap) and chill for about 1 hour, spooning the marinade over the fish once or twice.

7 Drain the monkfish, reserving the marinade. Sprinkle the peppercorns over and cook on a medium-hot grill (broiler) for 15–20 minutes, basting with marinade.

Energy 179kcal/753kJ; Protein 31g; Carbohydrate 0g, of which sugars 0g; Fat 6.3g, of which saturates 1g; Cholesterol 28mg; Calcium 32mg; Fibre 0g; Sodium 37mg.

orange-peppercorn marinade for bass

This is an excellent light marinade for whole fish – sea bass here, but salmon trout or sea bream would also be delicious cooked this way. The cooked fish, in the aromatic and delicate marinade, needs only a sprinkling of fresh herbs as a garnish.

Serves four

INGREDIENTS

1 medium whole sea bass, cleaned

For the peppercorn marinade

1 red onion

2 small oranges

90ml/6 tbsp light olive oil

30ml/2 tbsp cider vinegar

30ml/2 tbsp green peppercorns in brine, drained

30ml/2 tbsp chopped fresh parsley

salt and sugar, to taste

COOK'S TIP

If you do not have an ovenproof dish large enough to hold the fish, place it in a serving dish for marinating and transfer it to a baking sheet or roasting pan for cooking.

1 Note the weight of the fish. With a sharp knife, slash the bass three or four times on both sides.

2 Line an ovenproof dish with foil. Peel and slice the onion and oranges. Place half the onion and oranges in the dish, place the fish on top, and cover with the remaining onion and orange.

3 Mix the remaining marinade ingredients and pour over the fish. Fold up the foil to enclose the fish completely and stand for 4 hours.

4 Preheat the oven to 180°C/350°F/ Gas 4. Make sure the foil over the fish is folded to seal in juices. Bake for 15 minutes per 450g/1lb, plus 15 minutes. Serve with the juices.

Energy 329kcal/1369kJ; Protein 34g; Carbohydrate 1.2g, of which sugars 0.9g; Fat 20.9g, of which saturates 3.1g; Cholesterol 140mg; Calcium 231mg; Fibre 0.2g; Sodium 121mg.

summer herb marinade for salmon

Make the best use of summer herbs in this marinade – vary the mixture according to whatever you have available, remembering to use more of the delicate herbs and less of those with a stronger flavour. The marinade is also excellent for veal, chicken, pork or lamb.

Serves four

INGREDIENTS

4 salmon steaks or fillets, about
  175g/6oz each

For the herb marinade

large handful of fresh herb sprigs, such
  as chervil, thyme, parsley, sage, chives
  rosemary, oregano

90ml/6 tbsp olive oil

45ml/3 tbsp tarragon vinegar

1 garlic clove, crushed

2 spring onions (scallions), chopped

salt and ground black pepper

COOK'S TIP

For a smoked herb flavour, keep the
herb stalks to throw on to the barbecue
coals when you cook the fish that way.
Thyme and rosemary stalks are ideal.

1 Discard any coarse stalks or
damaged leaves from the herbs,
then chop them very finely,
especially slightly tough rosemary.

2 Mix the oil, tarragon vinegar,
garlic and spring onions in a bowl.
Add the chopped herbs and stir to
mix thoroughly.

3 Place the salmon in a dish and
spoon the marinade over. Cover
and leave to marinate in the
refrigerator for 4–6 hours.

4 Preheat a grill (broiler) barbecue.
Drain the fish and grill for 2–3
minutes each side, brushing with
the leftover marinade occasionally.

Energy 383kcal/1593kJ; Protein 34.6g; Carbohydrate 0.5g, of which sugars 0.4g; Fat 27g, of which saturates 4.4g; Cholesterol 84mg; Calcium 63mg; Fibre 0.7g; Sodium 81mg.

basil and chilli marinade for sea trout

Sea trout is similar to wild salmon in texture and flavour. This Thai-style marinade is an ideal seasoning, with chillies and lime to complement and cut the richness of the fish.

Serves six

INGREDIENTS

6 sea trout cutlets, about 115g/4oz each, or wild or farmed salmon

For the basil and chilli marinade

2 garlic cloves, chopped

1 fresh long red chilli, seeded and chopped

45ml/3 tbsp chopped Thai basil

15ml/1 tbsp palm sugar (jaggery) or granulated sugar

3 limes

400ml/14fl oz/1⅔ cups coconut milk

15ml/1 tbsp Thai fish sauce

1 Place the sea trout cutlets in a single layer in a large shallow dish.

2 Using a pestle, pound the garlic and chilli in a large mortar to break it up roughly. Then add 30ml/2 tbsp of the Thai basil with the sugar and continue to pound until reduced to a rough paste.

3 Grate the rind from 1 lime and squeeze the juice. Mix the rind and juice into the chilli paste, with the coconut milk. Pour the mixture over the fish cutlets, cover and chill them for about 1 hour. Cut the remaining limes into wedges.

4 Prepare the barbecue. Once the flames have died down, position a lightly oiled grill rack over the coals to heat. The barbecue is ready when the coals are cool to medium-hot, or with a thick to moderate coating of ash. Alternatively, if not cooking the fish on a barbecue, preheat the grill (broiler).

5 Remove the fish from the refrigerator before cooking so that it returns to room temperature. Transfer the cutlets to an oiled, hinged wire fish basket, or directly to the grill rack, reserving the marinade. If cooking indoors, place them on an oiled rack in a grill pan. Cook the fish for 4 minutes on each side. Do not move the cutlets too soon as they tend to stick to the rack until they firm up.

6 Strain the remaining marinade into a pan, reserving the contents of the sieve. Bring the marinade to the boil, simmer gently for 5 minutes, then stir in the contents of the sieve and continue to simmer for 1 minute more. Add the Thai fish sauce and the remaining Thai basil. Lift each fish cutlet on to a plate, pour over the sauce and serve with the lime wedges.

Energy 157kcal/662kJ; Protein 23.1g; Carbohydrate 5.9g, of which sugars 5.9g; Fat 4.7g, of which saturates 0.1g; Cholesterol 0mg; Calcium 46mg; Fibre 0.4g; Sodium 141mg.

soy and star anise marinade for chicken

Chicken cooks quickly and benefits from being marinated first. Aromatic star anise brings clear, punchy flavour to this uncomplicated marinade of soy sauce and olive oil.

Serves four

INGREDIENTS
4 skinless chicken breast fillets
2 whole star anise
45ml/3 tbsp olive oil
30ml/2 tbsp soy sauce
ground black pepper

VARIATION
If you prefer, cook on a barbecue. When the coals are dusted with ash, spread them out evenly. Remove the chicken breasts from the marinade and cook for 8 minutes on each side, spooning over the marinade from time to time, until the chicken is cooked through.

1 Put the chicken breast fillets in a shallow, non-metallic dish and add the star anise.

2 In a small bowl, whisk together the oil and soy sauce and season with black pepper to make the base for marinade.

3 Pour the mixture over the chicken and turn chicken fillets to coat them all over. Cover the dish with clear film (plastic wrap) and set aside for as much time as you have. If you are able to prepare ahead, leave the chicken in the marinade overnight or for about 6–8 hours as the flavour will be improved. Place the covered dish in the refrigerator.

4 Preheat the grill (broiler). Lift the chicken from the marinade and place on a rack in a grill pan. Cook, turning occasionally, for about 8 minutes on each side. Serve immediately.

Energy 206kcal/868kJ; Protein 36g; Carbohydrate 0g, of which sugars 0g; Fat 6.9g, of which saturates 1.2g; Cholesterol 105mg; Calcium 8mg; Fibre 0g; Sodium 90mg.

aromatic marinade for duck

This aromatic marinade makes a delicious alternative to the classic plum sauce that is so often served with duck and pancakes. It takes a long time to prepare but is well worth the effort.

3 Place the duck in a dish with the star anise, peppercorns, cloves, cinnamon, spring onions, ginger and rice wine or dry sherry. Cover and set aside to marinate for at least 4–6 hours.

4 Place the duck with the marinade in a steamer positioned in a wok partly filled with boiling water and steam vigorously for 3–4 hours (longer if possible). Remove the duck from the cooking liquid and leave to cool for at least 5–6 hours. The duck must be completely cold and dry or the skin will not crisp.

5 Heat the oil in a preheated wok until smoking, place the duck pieces in the oil, skin side down, and deep-fry for 5–6 minutes or until crisp and brown, turning just once at the very last moment.

6 Drain the duck well. Take the meat off the bone and pile it, with the skin, on lettuce. Serve with the accompaniments: pancakes spread with a little sauce to wrap a portion of the duck meat, plus the shredded spring onion and cucumber. Eat with your fingers.

Serves six to eight

INGREDIENTS

1.75–2.25kg/4–5¼lb oven-ready duck
10ml/2 tsp salt
5–6 whole star anise
15ml/1 tbsp Szechuan peppercorns
5ml/1 tsp cloves
2–3 cinnamon sticks
3–4 spring onions (scallions)
3–4 slices fresh root ginger, unpeeled
75–90ml/5–6 tbsp Chinese rice wine
  or dry sherry
vegetable oil, for deep-frying

To serve

20–24 thin Chinese pancakes
120ml/4fl oz/½ cup duck sauce or
  plum sauce
6–8 spring onions (scallions), thinly
  shredded
½ cucumber, thinly shredded

1 Remove the wings from the duck. Split the body in half down the backbone. The best way to do this is using a meat cleaver: if you are nervous about using a chopping technique, use a rolling pin to tap the cleaver through the duck.

2 Rub salt all over the two duck halves, taking care to rub it well in.

Energy 337kcal/1411kJ; Protein 18.1g; Carbohydrate 27.2g, of which sugars 5.1g; Fat 17.8g, of which saturates 4.6g; Cholesterol 66mg; Calcium 59mg; Fibre 1.3g; Sodium 438mg.

spicy yogurt marinade for chicken

Plan this dish well in advance; the extra-long marinating time is necessary to develop a really mellow spicy flavour. Use a little less onion if you'd prefer this aspect to be slightly milder.

Serves six

INGREDIENTS

6 chicken pieces

juice of 1 lemon

5ml/1 tsp salt

fresh mint, lemon and lime, to garnish

For the yogurt marinade

5ml/1 tsp coriander seeds

10ml/2 tsp cumin seeds

6 cloves

2 bay leaves

1 onion, quartered

2 garlic cloves

5cm/2in piece fresh root ginger, peeled and roughly chopped

2.5ml/½ tsp chilli powder

5ml/1 tsp turmeric

150ml/¼ pint/⅔ cup natural (plain) yogurt

1 Skin the chicken joints and make deep slashes in the fleshiest parts with a sharp knife. Sprinkle the lemon juice and salt over the chicken, and rub in well.

2 Make the marinade. Spread the coriander and cumin seeds, cloves and bay leaves in the bottom of a large frying pan and dry-fry over a moderate heat until the bay leaves are crispy.

3 Allow the spice mixture to cool, then grind it coarsely in a mortar and pestle.

4 Finely mince the onion, garlic and ginger in a food processor or blender with the ground spices, chilli, turmeric and yogurt. Strain in the lemon from the chicken.

5 Arrange the chicken in a single layer in a roasting pan. Pour the marinade over, then cover and chill for 24–36 hours, turning the chicken pieces occasionally.

6 Preheat the oven to 200°C/400°F/ Gas 6. Cook the chicken for 45 minutes, or until the juices run clear when the meat is pierced. Serve the chicken hot or cold, garnished with fresh mint and slices of lemon or lime.

VARIATION

This marinade will also work well brushed over skewers of lamb or pork fillet prior to grilling or barbecuing.

Energy 156kcal/660kJ; Protein 32.9g; Carbohydrate 2.2g, of which sugars 1.5g; Fat 1.8g, of which saturates 0.5g; Cholesterol 94mg; Calcium 44mg; Fibre 0.5g; Sodium 98mg.

five-spice marinade for quail

This marinade is a Chinese classic. Although the quail is a relatively small bird it is surprisingly meaty. One bird is usually quite sufficient for one serving.

Serves four

INGREDIENTS

4 oven-ready quails

For the five-spice marinade

2 pieces star anise
10ml/2 tsp ground cinnamon
10ml/2 tsp fennel seeds
10ml/2 tsp ground Szechuan or
    Chinese pepper
pinch of ground cloves
1 small onion, finely chopped
1 garlic clove, crushed
60ml/4 tbsp clear honey
30ml/2 tbsp dark soy sauce

To garnish

2 spring onions (scallions), roughly
    chopped
1 mandarin orange or satsuma, finely
    shredded
radish and carrot flowers
banana leaves, to serve

1 Remove the backbones from the quails by cutting down either side with a pair of kitchen scissors.

2 Flatten the birds with the palm of your hand and secure each one with two bamboo skewers.

COOK'S TIP

If you prefer, or if quails are not available, you could use other small poultry such as poussins. Poussins will take around 25–30 minutes to cook.

3 Grind together the star anise, cinnamon, fennel seeds, pepper and cloves in a mortar with a pestle. Add the onion, garlic, honey and soy sauce and combine well.

4 Place the quails on a flat dish, cover with the spice mixture and cover the dish. Set aside to marinate for at least 8 hours.

5 Cook the quails under a preheated grill (broiler) or on a barbecue for 7–8 minutes on each side, basting from time to time with the marinade.

6 Arrange the quails on a bed of banana leaves and garnish with the spring onion, orange rind and radish and carrot "flowers", and serve immediately.

Energy 159kcal/664kJ; Protein 13.2g; Carbohydrate 5.6g, of which sugars 5.6g; Fat 9.5g, of which saturates 2.6g; Cholesterol 68mg; Calcium 7mg; Fibre 0.1g; Sodium 404mg.

lavender balsamic marinade for lamb

Lavender is an unusual flavour to use with meat, but its heady, summery scent works well with barbecued lamb. Use the flower heads for a garnish.

Serves four

INGREDIENTS

4 racks of lamb, with 3–4 cutlets each
lavender flowers, to garnish

For the balsamic marinade

1 shallot, finely chopped
45ml/3 tbsp chopped fresh lavender
15ml/1 tbsp balsamic vinegar
30ml/2 tbsp olive oil
15ml/1 tbsp lemon juice
handful of lavender sprigs
salt and ground black pepper

1 Place the racks of lamb in a large mixing bowl or wide dish and sprinkle the chopped shallot over.

2 Sprinkle the chopped fresh lavender over the lamb in the bowl. Then rub the lavender into the meat, especially into the the fat.

3 Beat together the vinegar, olive oil and lemon juice and pour them over the lamb. Season well with salt and ground black pepper and then turn the meat to coat evenly.

4 Scatter a few lavender sprigs over the coals of a medium-hot barbecue. Alternatively, preheat a grill (broiler) and have a grill pan with a rack in it ready for cooking the lamb.

5 Cook the lamb for 15–20 minutes, turning once and basting with any remaining marinade, until golden outside and slightly pink in the centre. Keep the lamb well away from the source of heat under a grill. Just before serving, garnish with lavender flower heads.

Energy 565kcal/2333kJ; Protein 31.4g; Carbohydrate 1.2g, of which sugars 0.9g; Fat 48.3g, of which saturates 21.5g; Cholesterol 135mg; Calcium 26mg; Fibre 0.2g; Sodium 111mg.

chinese sesame marinade for beef

Toasted sesame seeds bring their distinctive smoky aroma to this Oriental marinade.
It's delicious with lean pork or lamb as well as the beef used in this recipe.

Serves four

INGREDIENTS

450g/1lb rump (round) steak
30ml/2 tbsp sesame seeds
15ml/1 tbsp sesame oil
30ml/2 tbsp vegetable oil
115g/4oz/1½ cups small mushrooms, quartered
1 green (bell) pepper, seeded and diced
4 spring onions (scallions), chopped

For the Chinese sesame marinade

10ml/2 tsp cornflour (cornstarch)
30ml/2 tbsp rice wine or sherry
15ml/1 tbsp lemon juice
15ml/1 tbsp soy sauce
few drops Tabasco sauce
2.5cm/1in piece fresh root ginger, peeled and grated
1 garlic clove, crushed

1 To make the marinade, blend the cornflour with the rice wine or sherry. Add the other marinade ingredients.

2 Trim the steak and cut it into thin strips about 1 x 5cm/½ x 2in. Stir into the marinade, cover and leave in a cool place for 3–4 hours.

3 Place the sesame seeds in a large frying pan or wok. Cook dry over a moderate heat, shaking the pan until the seeds are golden: do not overcook. Set aside.

4 Heat the oils in the frying pan. Drain the beef, reserving the marinade, and brown a few pieces at a time. Remove the meat with a slotted spoon.

5 Add the mushrooms and pepper and fry for 2–3 minutes, stirring continuously. Add the spring onions and cook for about a further minute.

6 Replace the beef and reserved marinade, and stir over a moderate heat for 2 minutes, or until the strips of beef are evenly coated with the glaze. Sprinkle with the toasted sesame seeds, and serve.

VARIATION

This marinade would also be good with lean pork fillet or chicken breast. Instead of the Tabasco, a seeded and diced red chilli may be added with the mushrooms and bell pepper to bring a little chilli heat to the dish.

Energy 290kcal/1208kJ; Protein 27.4g; Carbohydrate 5.8g, of which sugars 3.2g; Fat 17.6g, of which saturates 3.7g; Cholesterol 66mg; Calcium 65mg; Fibre 1.8g; Sodium 252mg.

winter-spiced ale marinade for beef

This marinade can also be used as a flavouring base for a casserole of beef or lamb pieces. It will imbue the meat with a rich malty flavour.

Serves six

INGREDIENTS

1.3kg/3lb top rump beef

For the winter-spiced ale marinade

1 onion, sliced

2 carrots, sliced

2 celery sticks, sliced

2–3 parsley stalks, lightly crushed

large fresh thyme sprig

2 bay leaves

6 cloves, lightly crushed

1 cinnamon stick

8 black peppercorns

300ml/½ pint/1¼ cups brown ale

45ml/3 tbsp vegetable oil

30ml/2 tbsp beurre manié

salt and ground black pepper

1 Put the meat in a polythene bag placed inside a large, deep bowl. For the marinade, add the vegetables, herbs and spices, then pour the ale over the meat in the bag. Gather up the bag and tie or close the end to seal the meat in the marinade. Leave in a cool place for at least 5–6 hours.

2 Remove the beef and set aside. Strain the marinade into a bowl, reserving the vegetables and liquid.

3 Heat the oil in a flameproof casserole. Fry the vegetables until lightly browned, then remove with a slotted spoon and set aside. Brown the beef all over in the remaining oil.

4 Preheat the oven to 160°C/325°F/ Gas 3. Return the vegetables to the casserole and pour the reserved marinade over the beef.

5 Cover the casserole and cook in the oven for 2½ hours. Turn the beef two or three times in the marinade during cooking so that it cooks evenly.

6 To serve, remove and slice the beef. Arrange on plates with the vegetables. Bring the liquor to the boil. Gradually stir in the beurre manié and simmer for 3 minutes. Taste the sauce and adjust the seasoning. Serve with the meat.

Energy 380kcal/1590kJ; Protein 48.4g; Carbohydrate 5.3g, of which sugars 3.8g; Fat 15.8g, of which saturates 5.2g; Cholesterol 131mg; Calcium 27mg; Fibre 0.3g; Sodium 155mg.

berry sauce for baked ricotta cakes

This fabulously fragrant, fruity sauce complements ice creams, custards, sponge puddings and cheesecakes – especially these honey and vanilla-flavoured baked ricotta cheesecakes.

Serves four

INGREDIENTS

250g/9oz/generous 1 cup ricotta cheese
2 egg whites
about 60ml/4 tbsp clear honey
few drops of vanilla extract
fresh mint leaves, to decorate (optional)

For the red berry sauce

450g/1lb/4 cups mixed fresh or frozen
 fruit, such as strawberries, raspberries,
 blackberries and cherries

COOK'S TIPS

• The sauce can be made a day
ahead. Chill until ready to use.

• Frozen fruit doesn't need extra water,
as there will be ice crystals clinging to
the berries.

1 Preheat the oven to 180°C/350°F/ Gas 4. Grease four ramekins.

2 Place the ricotta cheese in a bowl and break it up with a wooden spoon. Lightly whisk the egg whites with a fork to break them up a little, then mix into the cheese with the honey and vanilla until thoroughly combined and smooth.

3 Spoon the ricotta mixture into the prepared ramekins and level the tops. Bake for 20 minutes or until risen and golden.

4 Meanwhile, make the berry sauce. Reserve about a quarter of the fruit for decoration. Place the rest of the fruit in a pan, with a little water if the fruit is fresh, and heat gently until softened. Cool slightly, removing any cherry stones (pits), if necessary.

5 Press the fruit through a sieve, then taste and sweeten with honey if it is too tart. Serve the sauce, warm or cold, with the ricotta cakes. Decorate with the reserved berries and mint leaves, if using.

Energy 186kcal/782kJ; Protein 8.7g; Carbohydrate 18g, of which sugars 18g; Fat 9.4g, of which saturates 5.8g; Cholesterol 26mg; Calcium 27mg; Fibre 2.5g; Sodium 35mg.

papaya sauce for grilled pineapple

This papaya sauce partners slightly tart fruit perfectly – pineapple, redcurrants or gooseberries. It is also excellent with grilled chicken, game birds, pork or lamb.

Serves six

INGREDIENTS

1 sweet pineapple

melted butter, for greasing and brushing

2 pieces drained stem ginger in syrup, cut into fine matchstick pieces

30ml/2 tbsp demerara (raw) sugar

pinch of ground cinnamon

30ml/2 tbsp stem ginger syrup

fresh mint sprigs, to decorate

For the papaya sauce

1 ripe papaya, peeled and seeded

175ml/6fl oz/¾ cup apple juice

VARIATIONS

Try papaya nectar in the sauce, using it half and half with the apple juice.
Try grilled bananas instead of pineapple, adding the grated rind and juice of 1 lime and omitting the ginger.

1 Cut the leaves and stalk end off the pineapple. Peel it and cut out the eyes by removing spiral wedges around the fruit. Then slice it across into six slices, each about 2.5cm/1in thick.

2 Line a baking tray with a sheet of foil, rolling up the edges to make a rim. Grease the foil with melted butter. Preheat the grill (broiler).

3 To make the sauce, cut a few slices from the papaya and set them aside. Then purée the rest with the apple juice in a food processor or blender. Press the purée through a fine sieve and set aside.

4 Arrange the pineapple slices on the foil. Brush with butter, then top with the ginger and sprinkle with the sugar and cinnamon. Drizzle over the ginger syrup. Grill (broil) for 5–7 minutes, or until the slices are lightly charred.

5 Arrange the pineapple slices on warm plates. Stir any cooking juices into the papaya sauce and drizzle a little on each plate. Decorate with the reserved papaya slices and the mint sprigs.

Energy 110kcal/469kJ; Protein 0.9g; Carbohydrate 27.5g, of which sugars 27.5g; Fat 0.4g, of which saturates 0g; Cholesterol 0mg; Calcium 44mg; Fibre 3.1g; Sodium 7mg.

lemon and lime sauce for pancakes

This tangy, refreshing sauce is the perfect foil for pancakes. It is also good with fruit fritters – especially banana fritters – or a lively accompaniment for steamed sponge pudding.

2 Place the rind in a pan with enough water to cover. Bring to the boil, drain and set aside, discarding the water.

3 Mix a little sugar with the arrowroot and stir in enough of the water to give a smooth paste. Heat the remaining water until hot but not boiling. Stir in the paste and bring to the boil, stirring. Remove from the heat at once. Stir in the remaining sugar, citrus juice and reserved rind. Keep the sauce hot but do not boil.

Serves four

INGREDIENTS

90g/3½oz/scant 1 cup plain
  (all-purpose) flour
1 egg
300ml/½ pint/1¼ cups milk
vegetable oil, for frying
mint or lemon balm, to decorate

For the lemon and lime sauce

1 lemon
2 limes
300ml/½ pint/1¼ cups water
50g/2oz/¼ cup caster (superfine) sugar
25ml/1½ tbsp arrowroot

1 First, make the sauce. Using a citrus zester, remove the rind in fine shreds from the lemon and limes, taking care not to cut into the pith. Squeeze the juice from the fruit into a single bowl and and set it aside while you make the pancakes.

4 For the pancakes, sift the flour into a bowl and make a well in the middle. Add the egg and a little milk, then beat together drawing in flour and gradually adding the rest of the milk for a smooth batter.

5 Heat a little oil in a frying pan. Add a thin layer of batter and cook until set. Turn the pancake and lightly brown the other side. Turn out on to a plate and keep warm while you repeat the method with the rest of the batter. To serve, fold the pancakes, drizzle with sauce and decorate with mint.

Energy 181kcal/770kJ; Protein 6.3g; Carbohydrate 34.7g, of which sugars 11.7g; Fat 3g, of which saturates 1.2g; Cholesterol 52mg; Calcium 133mg; Fibre 0.7g; Sodium 51mg.

butterscotch sauce for waffles

This is a deliciously sweet sauce which will be loved by everyone. It is a classic with waffles but also ice cream. Be sure to use dark muscovado for rich success.

Serves four to six

INGREDIENTS

1 pack ready-made waffles
vanilla ice cream, to serve

For the butterscotch sauce
75g/3oz/6 tbsp butter
175g/6oz/¾ cup dark muscovado
   (molasses) sugar
175ml/6fl oz/¾ cup evaporated milk
50g/2oz/⅓ cup hazelnuts

1 Warm the waffles in a preheated oven, according to the packet instructions, while you make the butterscotch sauce.

2 Melt the butter and sugar in a heavy-based pan, bring to the boil and simmer for 2 minutes. Cool for 5 minutes.

3 Heat the evaporated milk to just below boiling point, then gradually stir into the sugar mixture. Cook over a low heat for 2 minutes, stirring the sauce frequently.

VARIATION
Substitute any nut for the hazelnuts. You could also add plump raisins and a dash of rum instead of the nuts.

4 Spread the hazelnuts on a baking sheet and toast under a hot grill until golden brown. Tip on to a clean dish towel and rub briskly to remove the skins.

5 Chop the nuts roughly and stir into the sauce. Serve the sauce hot, poured over scoops of vanilla ice cream and the warm waffles.

Energy 405kcal/1694kJ; Protein 6.6g; Carbohydrate 47.3g, of which sugars 35.1g; Fat 22.3g, of which saturates 7.6g; Cholesterol 32mg; Calcium 192mg; Fibre 1.1g; Sodium 305mg.

caramel sauce for oranges

The appeal of this tasty dessert is the contrast between sweet caramel and tangy oranges. Make it in advance for convenient entertaining – try caramel with pineapple for a classy alternative.

Serves six

INGREDIENTS

6 large seedless oranges, such
 as Navelina, well-scrubbed

90g/3½oz/½ cup sugar

1 With a vegetable peeler, remove wide strips of rind from two of the oranges. Stack two or three strips at a time and cut into very thin julienne strips.

2 Using a sharp knife, cut a thin slice of peel and pith from both ends of each orange. Place cut-side down on a plate and cut off the peel and pith in strips down the side of the fruit. Remove any remaining pith. Slice the peeled fruit crossways into thick rounds about 1cm/½in thick. Put the orange slices in a serving bowl and pour over any juice.

3 Half-fill a large bowl with cold water and set aside. Place the sugar and 45ml/3 tbsp water in a small, heavy pan without a non-stick coating and bring to the boil over a high heat, swirling the pan to dissolve the sugar.

4 Continue to boil, without stirring, until the mixture turns a dark caramel colour. Remove the pan from the heat and, standing well back, dip the base of the pan into the cold water to stop the cooking process.

5 Add about 30ml/2 tbsp water to the caramel, pouring it down the sides of the pan, swirling to mix.

6 Add the strips of orange rind and return the pan to the heat. Simmer gently over a medium-low heat, stirring occasionally, for 8–10 minutes, or until the strips are slightly translucent. Remove the pan from the heat.

7 Pour the caramel and rind over the oranges, turn gently to mix and cool, then chill for at least 1 hour before serving.

Energy 96kcal/410kJ; Protein 1.2g; Carbohydrate 24.2g, of which sugars 24.2g; Fat 0.1g, of which saturates 0g; Cholesterol 0mg; Calcium 55mg; Fibre 1.7g; Sodium 6mg.

hot plum sauce for meringue islands

The plum sauce can be made in advance, then reheated just before you cook the meringues.
This makes an unusual and healthy pudding that is simpler to make than it looks.

Serves four

INGREDIENTS

2 egg whites

30ml/2 tbsp concentrated apple juice
  syrup

freshly grated nutmeg

For the hot plum sauce

450g/1lb red plums

300ml/½ pint/1¼ cups apple juice

1 To make the plum sauce, halve
the plums and remove, and discard,
the stones (pits). Place the plum
halves in a wide pan and pour in
the apple juice.

2 Bring to the boil and then cover
the pan. Reduce the heat and leave
the fruit to simmer very gently for
15–20 minutes, or until the plums
are tender.

3 Meanwhile, whisk the egg whites
into firm, soft peaks. Gradually
whisk in the apple juice syrup, and
continue whisking until the
meringue is stiff and glossy.

COOK'S TIP

Concentrated apple juice or apple juice
syrup is available from health food
shops. Golden (light corn) syrup may be
used instead.

4 Use two spoons to scoop the
meringue in ovals and add them to
the gently simmering sauce. (If the
pan is not big enough, do this in
two batches.)

5 Cover and simmer gently for 2–3
minutes, until the meringues are
just firm and set. Serve the
meringues on the sauce as soon as
they are all cooked. Sprinkled with
a little nutmeg.

Energy 81kcal/347kJ; Protein 2.2g; Carbohydrate 18.8g, of which sugars 18.8g; Fat 0.2g, of which saturates 0g; Cholesterol 0mg; Calcium 22mg; Fibre 1.8g; Sodium 35mg.

lime sabayon for ice cream

Sabayon is a light, foamy sauce. This tangy version is irresistible with chocolate ice cream or it can be served with vanilla or tropical fruit ice cream.

2 Whisk the mixture over a pan of simmering water until the sabayon is smooth and thick, and the mixture leaves a ribbon trail when the whisk is lifted from the bowl.

3 Lightly whisk in the cream. Remove the bowl from the pan and cover with a lid or plate.

4 Working quickly, place scoops of the chocolate ice cream into four chilled sundae glasses or individual serving dishes. Spoon the warm lime sabayon sauce over the ice cream, sprinkle with the strips of lime rind to decorate and serve immediately.

Serves four

INGREDIENTS

2 egg yolks
65g/2½oz/5 tbsp caster (superfine) sugar
finely grated rind and juice of 2 limes
60ml/4 tbsp white wine or apple juice
45ml/3 tbsp single (light) cream
500ml/17fl oz/2¼ cups chocolate
  ice cream
thinly pared strips of lime rind, to decorate

COOK'S TIP
For a special occasion, serve the ice cream in frosted glass. Rub the rim of the glasses with a lime wedge, then dip in a saucer of caster (superfine) sugar. Leave to dry before carefully adding the scoops of ice cream.

1 Put the egg yolks and caster sugar in a heatproof bowl and beat well until thoroughly combined. Beat in the lime rind and juice, then the white wine or apple juice.

VARIATIONS
• You can substitute other citrus fruit for the limes in the sabayon sauce. Orange sabayon, using the rind and juice of one orange, would also go well with chocolate ice cream, while lemon sabayon sauce complements peach sorbet (sherbet).

• For a completely different dessert serve the lime sabayon with fresh strawberries or sliced bananas piled on hot waffles.

Energy 343kcal/1440kJ; Protein 6.4g; Carbohydrate 43.5g, of which sugars 42.1g; Fat 15.7g, of which saturates 9.8g; Cholesterol 137mg; Calcium 157mg; Fibre 0g; Sodium 84mg.

lime and cardamom sauce for bananas

Aromatic cardamom and fresh lime give an exotic hint to the flaked almonds in this delicious sauce for pouring over bananas.

Serves four

INGREDIENTS

6 small bananas
50g/2oz/¼ cup butter
50g/2oz/½ cup flaked (sliced) almonds
seeds from 4 cardamom pods, crushed
thinly pared rind and juice of 2 limes
50g/2oz/¼ cup light muscovado (molasses) sugar
30ml/2 tbsp dark rum
vanilla ice cream, to serve

VARIATIONS

• If you prefer not to use alcohol in your cooking, replace the rum with a fruit juice of your choice, such as orange or even pineapple juice.
• The sauce is equally good poured over folded crêpes.

1 Peel the bananas and cut them in half lengthways. Heat half the butter in a large frying pan. Add half the bananas, and cook until golden. Turn carefully and cook the second side until golden.

2 As they cook, transfer the bananas to a heatproof serving dish. Cook the remaining bananas in the same way.

3 Melt the remaining butter, then add the almonds and cardamom seeds. Cook, stirring until golden.

4 Stir in the lime rind and juice, then the sugar. Cook, stirring, until the mixture is smooth, bubbling and slightly reduced. Stir in the rum. Pour the sauce over the bananas and serve immediately, with vanilla ice cream.

Energy 347kcal/1452kJ; Protein 4.2g; Carbohydrate 41.3g, of which sugars 38.2g; Fat 17.6g, of which saturates 7.2g; Cholesterol 27mg; Calcium 46mg; Fibre 2.2g; Sodium 80mg.

sticky toffee sauce for sponge pudding

Forget the main course because this is gooey and gorgeous for a sweet-course-only meal! The sauce is also fabulous with ice cream or, for a complete change, try it with apple pie or tart.

Serves six

INGREDIENTS

115g/4oz/1 cup walnuts, chopped
175g/6oz/¾ cup butter
175g/6oz/scant 1 cup soft brown sugar
60ml/4 tbsp double (heavy) cream
30ml/2 tbsp lemon juice
2 eggs, beaten
115g/4oz/1 cup self-raising
 (self-rising) flour

1 Toast the walnuts by dry-frying in an ungreased pan. Remove from the heat as soon as they begin to brown. Next, grease a 900ml/1½ pint/¾ cup heatproof bowl. Place half the nuts in the bowl.

2 To make the sauce, heat 50g/2oz/4 tbsp of the butter with 50g/2oz/4 tbsp of the sugar, the cream and 15ml/1 tbsp lemon juice in a small pan, stirring until smooth. Pour half over the nuts, then swirl the bowl to part-coat the sides.

3 For the pudding, beat the remaining butter and sugar until fluffy, then beat in the eggs. Fold in the flour, remaining nuts and lemon juice and spoon into the bowl.

4 Cover with greaseproof (waxed) paper with a pleat folded across the middle, then tie securely with string. Steam the pudding for about 1¼ hours, until risen, springy and set in the centre.

5 Just before serving, gently warm the remaining sauce. Unmould the pudding on to a warm plate and pour over the warm sauce.

Energy 606Kcal/2523kJ; Protein 7.5g; Carbohydrate 46g, of which sugars 31.6g; Fat 44.9g, of which saturates 20.3g; Cholesterol 152mg; Calcium 122mg; Fibre 1.3g; Sodium 279mg.

real custard

Adding cornflour helps to prevent custard from curdling. This recipe uses enough cornflour for sure success – simple to make and seriously good with all sorts of heartwarming hot puddings.

Serves four to six

INGREDIENTS

450ml/¾ pint/scant 2 cups milk

few drops of vanilla extract

2 eggs plus 1 egg yolk

15–30ml/1–2 tbsp caster (superfine) sugar)

15ml/1 tbsp cornflour (cornstarch)

30ml/2 tbsp water

COOK'S TIP

If you are not serving the custard immediately, cover the surface of the sauce with clear film (plastic wrap) to prevent a skin from forming and keep warm in a heatproof bowl over a pan of hot water.

1 In a pan heat the milk with the vanilla extract and remove from the heat just as the milk comes to the boil.

3 Strain the egg and milk mixture back into the pan and heat gently, stirring constantly. Take care not to overheat the mixture or the eggs will curdle.

4 Continue stirring until the custard thickens sufficiently to coat the back of a wooden spoon. Do not allow to boil or it will curdle. Serve immediately.

2 Whisk the eggs and yolk in a bowl with the caster sugar until well combined but not frothy. In a separate bowl, blend together the cornflour with the water and mix into the eggs. Whisk in a little of the hot milk, then mix in all the remaining milk.

Energy 156Kcal/656kJ; Protein 8g; Carbohydrate 17.9g, of which sugars 11g; Fat 6.5g, of which saturates 2.4g; Cholesterol 170mg; Calcium 147mg; Fibre 0g; Sodium 92mg.

orange-almond paste for baked apricots

Take advantage of the short apricot season by making this charming apricot and almond dessert, delicately scented with lemon juice and orange flower water.

Serves six

INGREDIENTS

75g/3oz/6 tbsp caster (superfine) sugar

30ml/2 tbsp lemon juice

300ml/½ pint/1¼ cups water

115g/4oz/1 cup ground almonds

50g/2oz/½ cup icing (confectioners') sugar

a little orange flower water

25g/1oz/2 tbsp unsalted (sweet) butter, melted

2.5ml/½ tsp almond extract

900g/2lb fresh apricots

fresh mint sprigs, to decorate

1 Preheat the oven to 180°C/350°F/ Gas 4. Place the sugar, lemon juice and water in a small pan and bring to the boil, stirring occasionally until the sugar has all dissolved. Simmer gently for 5–10 minutes to make a thin syrup.

COOK'S TIP

Always use a heavy pan when making syrup and stir constantly until the sugar has completely dissolved. Do not let liquid come to the boil before it has dissolved, or the result will be grainy.

2 Place the ground almonds, icing sugar, orange flower water, butter and almond extract in a large bowl and blend together to make a smooth paste.

3 Wash the apricots and then make a slit in the flesh and ease out the stone (pit). Take small pieces of the almond paste, roll into balls and press one into each of the apricots.

4 Arrange the stuffed apricots in a shallow ovenproof dish and carefully pour the sugar syrup around them. Cover with foil and bake in the oven for 25–30 minutes.

5 Serve the apricots with a little of the syrup, and decorated with sprigs of fresh mint.

Energy 277kcal/1164kJ; Protein 5.5g; Carbohydrate 33.9g, of which sugars 33.4g; Fat 14.3g, of which saturates 3g; Cholesterol 9mg; Calcium 80mg; Fibre 4g; Sodium 32mg.

lime cheese for lemon grass skewers

Grilled fruits make a fine finale. Lemon grass skewers and bay leaves add delicate flavour.
Lime cheese is the perfect accompaniment – it is also good with any fresh fruit, grilled or raw.

Serves four

INGREDIENTS

4 long fresh lemon grass stalks

1 mango, peeled, stoned (pitted) and cut into chunks

1 papaya, peeled, seeded and cut into chunks

1 star fruit (carambola), cut into chunks

8 fresh bay leaves

oil, for greasing

a little nutmeg

60ml/4 tbsp maple syrup

50g/2oz/¼ cup demerara (raw) sugar

For the lime cheese

150g/5oz/⅔ cup curd (farmer's) cheese or low-fat soft cheese

120ml/4fl oz/½ cup double (heavy) cream

grated rind and juice of ½ lime

30ml/2 tbsp icing (confectioners') sugar

1 Prepare the barbecue or preheat the grill (broiler). Cut the top of each lemon grass stalk into a point with a sharp knife. Discard the outer leaves, then use the back of the knife to bruise the length of each stalk to release the oils.

2 Thread each lemon grass stalk, skewer-style, with a selection of the fruit pieces and two bay leaves.

3 Support a piece of foil on a baking sheet and roll up the edges to make a rim. Grease the foil, lay the kebabs on top and grate a little nutmeg over each. Drizzle the maple syrup over and dust liberally with the demerara sugar. Grill (broil) or barbecue for 5 minutes, until the kebabs are lightly charred.

4 Meanwhile, make the lime cheese. Mix together the cheese, cream, grated lime rind and juice, and icing sugar in a bowl. Serve at once with the lightly charred fruit kebabs.

COOK'S TIP

The lime cheese can be made in advance and chilled. It makes a great dip for strawberries, apple wedges or chunks of banana.

Energy 390kcal/1634kJ; Protein 7.1g; Carbohydrate 51.3g, of which sugars 51.2g; Fat 19.3g, of which saturates 12g; Cholesterol 50mg; Calcium 102mg; Fibre 3.7g; Sodium 219mg.

rose petal cream for fruit shortcakes

Rose petal cream and fresh raspberries fill this delectable and luxurious dessert. Although they look impressive, these shortcakes are easy to make and are ideal for a dinner party. Offer the rose-flavoured cream as an accompaniment for all sorts of desserts, from ices to hot fruit pies.

Serves six

INGREDIENTS

115g/4oz/½ cup unsalted (sweet) butter, softened

50g/2oz/¼ cup caster (superfine) sugar

½ vanilla pod (bean), split and seeds reserved

115g/4oz/1 cup plain (all-purpose) flour, plus extra for dusting

50g/2oz/⅓ cup semolina

For the filling

300ml/½ pint/1¼ cups double (heavy) cream

15ml/1 tbsp icing (confectioners') sugar, plus extra for dusting

2.5ml/½ tsp rose water

450g/1lb/2⅔ cups raspberries

For the decoration

12 miniature roses, unsprayed

6 mint sprigs

1 egg white, beaten

caster (superfine) sugar, for dusting

COOK'S TIPS

• For best results, serve the shortcakes as soon as possible after assembling them. Otherwise, they are likely to turn soggy from the raspberries' liquid.
• If necessary, ground rice can be substituted for the semolina used for making the shortcakes.
• For the best-flavoured shortcakes, always use butter and not margarine.

1 Cream the butter, sugar and vanilla seeds together in a bowl until the mixture is pale and fluffy. Sift the flour and semolina together, then gradually work the dry ingredients into the creamed mixture to make a dough.

2 Gently knead the dough on a lightly floured surface until smooth. Roll out quite thinly and prick all over with a fork. Using a 7.5cm/3in fluted cutter, cut out 12 rounds. Place these on a baking sheet and then chill them in the refrigerator for 30 minutes.

3 Meanwhile, make the rose petal cream. Whisk the double cream with the icing sugar until soft peaks form. Gently fold the rose water into the mixture. Cover and then chill until required.

4 Preheat the oven to 180°C/350°F/Gas 4. Paint the roses and mint sprigs with the beaten egg white. Dust with sugar; place on a wire rack to dry.

5 Bake the shortcakes in the preheated oven for 15 minutes, or until they are lightly golden. Lift them off the baking sheet with a metal fish slice (spatula) and transfer to a wire rack to cool.

6 To assemble the shortcakes, spoon the rose water cream on to half the shortcakes. Arrange a layer of raspberries on top of the cream, then top with a second shortcake.

7 Dust the filled shortcakes with icing sugar. Decorate with the frosted roses and mint sprigs.

VARIATIONS

Other soft, red summer berries, such as mulberries, loganberries and tayberries, would be equally good in this dessert.

Energy 547kcal/2273kJ; Protein 4.7g; Carbohydrate 37.1g, of which sugars 16g; Fat 43.2g, of which saturates 26.8g; Cholesterol 109mg; Calcium 81mg; Fibre 2.7g; Sodium 132mg.

PERFECTING PRESERVES

Modern preserving has evolved from ancient methods of keeping summer produce edible for winter months. Drying was the earliest method of preserving, relying on summer sun or by using fire and smoking food. Salt, vinegar and alcohol followed as mediums for preventing the growth of micro-organisms and putrification. Sugar followed later as a preservative, once it was sourced from sugar beet. Preserving developed as a culinary "craft", a country pastime, during the eighteenth century.

GROWING POPULARITY

From simple methods, rich products evolved. Vegetables, fruit and spices were combined with vinegar and sugar in complex concoctions, bursting with flavour. The pickled vegetables, store sauces or ketchups, chutneys and mixed pickles of tradition became condiments for plain foods. Sweet or sour, smooth or chunky, chutneys or pickles, and tart, piquant relishes epitomize European savoury preserves. They

Left: A simple addition such as citrus rind may add as much flavour as the fruit itself.

are fabulous served with cold pies or cheese, with grilled meats, or with cold and hot roasts.

The same principles are used for capturing the fresh flavour of fruit and vegetables in different countries. Pickled lemons or limes may be rich with the oils and spices of Indian cooking or salted and aromatic for flavouring Middle-Eastern dishes. There are fiery Indian chutneys or sweet-sour combinations that can be used in Chinese cooking.

SWEET PRESERVES

Every culture has its sweet preserves, including jams, jellies and conserves. Some set, some gently flowing, but all packed with fruit flavour captured in syrup or cooked with sugar. Sweet, fruity and sparkling jellies are classic accompaniments for rich poultry or

Above: Stone fruits, such as plums, figs and cherries, can be pickled whole in wine or cider vinegar.

game. Fruit pickled in sweetened vinegars become plump and juicy asides for savoury dishes.

Alcohol and sugar together act as potent preservatives and they can be used to prevent whole pieces of fruit from decaying when preserved in sauces and syrups. Flowers and fruit rind are also popular in sweet preserves. Spices often enhance flavours, making them richer or warmer. Herbs can also be preserved in fruit jellies for sumptuous sweet-savoury condiments.

SELECTING THE BEST

Only the best ingredients are worth preserving. Vegetables and fruit should be in their prime: well developed and just ripe, at their peak of flavour. They should be perfect, neither bruised nor damaged, neither under- nor over-ripe. Some fruit have a high pectin content, an ingredient that reacts with acid and sugar to make liquids set: this is the foundation of classic jams, jellies and marmalades. Not all fruit are rich in pectin and those that are have most when they are slightly under-ripe, so they are usually combined with fruit that is just peaked for a perfect flavour and set combination.

SIMPLE YET SO GOOD

It is often the chutneys and sauces with sophisticated, quite complex flavours that are easiest to make. Vinegar and sugar together form a formidable preservation partnership that protects sauces, chutneys, pickles and relishes for long-term keeping with the minimum of fuss. As long as the sugar is not added too soon, there is no secret technique for perfect results with these savoury condiments. Spices and flavouring ingredients generally require nothing more critical than long simmering. For sure success all you need is perfectly clean pots and equipment, good lids, and all the time in the world to eat up the rewards of your work – these vinegary preserves will usually keep for at least a year or so.

VERSATILITY

Home-made preserves are far superior to most commercial alternatives. There really is no comparison. The vinegar, sugar and spices in savoury preserves are better. Many are useful for

Right: Who can resist the chunky texture and piquant flavours of a fruity chutney?

enriching gravies and sauces, acting as marinades, or enhancing salad dressings and dips.

Sweet fruit preserves usually have more fruit. As long as the concentration of sugar is high enough and the fruit is fantastic, worrying over the perfect set is not essential because the flavour will always be quite luxurious. When sweet preserves are so fruity, they become hugely versatile. With yogurt or soft, fresh cheeses they become brilliant desserts; thinned with a little brandy, sherry or liqueur they make instant, superior sauces for crêpes or other desserts.

Left: The addition of sugar and a tightly-lidded jar are two essentials for successful storage.

PRACTICALITIES

It is also worth remembering that you do not have to embark on a Victorian-style preserving marathon. Row upon row of glistening pots might have suited country house kitchens catering for large families and regular weekend parties but they may be too much for a typical household. The recipes in these chapters are practical for modern cooks and they reflect realistic servings. Seriously good, spicy relishes and fiery sauces are welcome in most households, so you can present your best efforts as gifts for friends and family.

The microwave can be used for cooking small amounts of preserves, especially relishes, and the freezer can be used for storing sweet or savoury preserves. If finding a cool, dark cupboard for storage is a problem, it is worth remembering the garage, where a clean cupboard can be ideal.

PRESERVING INGREDIENTS

A few special ingredients are essential when making preserves, because they contribute to the keeping quality of the final jam, jelly or pickle. The four main preservatives are sugar, vinegar, salt and alcohol. These all help to prolong the life of the other ingredients used in the preserve by creating an environment in which micro-organisms such as moulds and bacteria cannot grow.

SUGAR

This is the key preservative used in jams, jellies, marmalades, curds and many preserved fruits. A high proportion of sugar is needed and if the sugar content is less than 60 per cent of the total weight of the preserve (for example, in low-sugar

jams), this will affect the keeping quality of the preserve. These low-sugar jams and fruit preserves should be used within a few months or kept in the refrigerator to prevent the growth of mould.

Sugar also plays an important role in the setting of jams, jellies and marmalades. To achieve a good set, sugar should make up between 55 and 70 per cent of the total weight of the preserve. (High acid content in the fruit will also aid the setting of sweet preserves.)

white sugars

Use these refined sugars to produce clarity in sweet, set preserves.
Preserving sugar: This has quite large, irregular crystals and is ideal for jams, jellies and marmalades. The large crystals allow water to percolate between them, which helps to prevent the preserve burning and reduces the need for stirring (which is important to avoid breaking up fruit too much). Use this sugar for the clearest preserves. If preserving sugar is unavailable, granulated sugar can be used instead.
Preserving sugar with pectin: Also known as jam sugar, this sugar is used with low-pectin fruit. The sugar contains natural pectin and citric acid to help overcome setting problems. Preserves made with this sugar tend to have a shorter shelf-life and should be stored for no longer than six months.

Left: White and golden sugars are a key ingredient used in sweet fruit preserves, jams and jellies.

Granulated sugar: This is coarser than caster (superfine) sugar, less expensive and gives a clear result.
Cube sugar: Made from white granulated sugar that has been moistened, moulded into blocks, dried and cubed, this gives the same results as preserving sugar.

brown sugars

These sugars give a pronounced flavour and darker colour to both sweet and savoury preserves.
Demerara/raw sugar: A pale golden sugar with a mild caramel flavour. Traditionally an unrefined sugar with a low molasses content, it may also be made from refined white sugar with molasses added.
Golden granulated sugar: This may be refined or unrefined. It can be used instead of white sugar for a hint of flavour and colour.
Soft brown sugar: Moist, with fine grains and a rich flavour, it may be light or dark in colour and is usually made from refined white sugar with molasses added.
Muscovado/molasses sugar: This may be light or dark and is usually made from unrefined cane sugar. It has a deeper, more pronounced taste than soft brown sugar.
Palm sugar: Made from the sap of palms, this has a fragrant flavour. Sold pressed into blocks, it needs to be chopped before use. Light muscovado (brown) sugar is a good alternative.
Jaggery: This raw sugar from India has a distinctive taste. It must be chopped before use. Use a mixture of light brown muscovado and demerara sugar as an alternative.

Right: Raspberry and white wine vinegar are used both to preserve ingredients and to add a sharp, tangy flavour.

VINEGARS

The word vinegar comes from the French *vin aigre*, meaning sour wine. Vinegar is made by exposing fruit or grain-based alcohol to air; a bacterial reaction then turns the alcohol into acetic acid and it is this acid that helps to prevent the growth of micro-organisms in pickles and preserves. Vinegar used for pickling must have an acetic acid content of at least 5 per cent.

Malt vinegar: Made from a type of beer, this usually has an acetic acid content of 8 per cent, which allows it to be safely diluted by moisture and juices from fruit and vegetables. Malt vinegar usually contains caramel, which turns it a dark brown colour. Its strong flavour makes it ideal for pickles, chutneys and bottled sauces.

Pickling vinegar: Simply malt vinegar flavoured with spices.

Distilled malt vinegar: This has the same strong flavour as ordinary malt vinegar but is colourless and therefore suitable for making clear pickles and light preserves.

Wine vinegar: May be red or white, depending on the colour of the original wine. Most wine vinegars contain about 6 per cent acetic acid. White wine vinegar is mild and better for delicate preserves; red wine vinegar is slightly more robust and good for spiced fruits.

Raspberry vinegar: Made by steeping the fruit in wine vinegar, this is excellent for pickled fruits.

Balsamic vinegar: Has a smooth, mellow flavour. Its low acidity makes it unsuitable for use on its own, but it can be used as a flavouring for mild preserves, stirred in at the end of cooking.

Sherry vinegar: Slightly sweet with a fairly strong flavour.

Cider vinegar: Has a slightly sharp taste and a fruity flavour. It is excellent for fruit preserves.

Rice vinegar: Colourless, mild rice vinegar is made from rice wine and is often used for pickling ginger.

SALT

This is used in preserving both as a seasoning and as a dehydrator. It is often used in a process called brining to draw out moisture from vegetables such as cucumber and marrow, making them crisp while preventing the dilution of the preserve, which would reduce its keeping quality. Ordinary table and cooking salt is fine for this process, but use pure crystal salt, also known as kosher salt, or preserving or rock salt for clear pickles as ordinary table and cooking salts contain anti-caking ingredients that contribute to the clouding of preserves.

ALCOHOL

Spirits, such as brandy and rum, and liqueurs, which are at least 40 per cent ABV (alcohol by volume), can be used. Fortified wine, wine, beer and cider have a lower alcohol content so are not effective alone and should be either heat treated or combined with sugar.

ACIDS

These help to set jams and jellies and prevent discoloration.

Lemon juice: This adds pectin, prevents fruits from turning brown and enhances both flavour and colour. Use either freshly squeezed or bottled lemon juice.

Citric acid is sold as fine white crystals and can be used instead of lemon juice in preserves.

Tamarind: This is a brown, dense spice used both for its acid flavour and its character.

Below: Many different kinds of salt can be used for pickling, from coarse sea salt, prized for its ability to draw out flavour, to preserving, or "kosher", salt.

HERBS AND FLOWERS

Flavourings are an essential part of most preserves and using the right amount is as important as selecting the correct one. In some preserves a subtle hint is all that is needed; in others the flavouring is one of the main ingredients.

HERBS

Fresh and dried herbs are invaluable in savoury preserves, and are included occasionally in sweet ones. They can be added during the initial cooking, then removed, or finely chopped and stirred in towards the end of cooking. If dried herbs are used instead of fresh, then reduce the quantity by a third to half.

Below: Oregano has a lovely, aromatic flavour that is very good with summer squashes.

tender herbs

Herbs with fragile leaves need careful handling to avoid bruising. Once picked, they should be used within a few days. Tie the whole herb stalks in muslin (cheesecloth) and add to the simmering preserve, or stir chopped leaves into the preserve at the end of cooking.

Basil: This highly aromatic herb bruises and discolours easily, so rather than adding it to a preserve, it can be steeped in vinegar until it imparts its flavour, then removed.

Chervil: Use these tiny, soft and lacy leaves soon after picking. They have a flavour similar to parsley with a hint of aniseed, which goes well with mild, delicate vegetables.

Mint: The many varieties of this aromatic herb include peppermint, spearmint, apple mint, lemon mint and pineapple mint. It adds a fresh flavour to preserves, but should be used sparingly.

Parsley: Curly and flat leaf varieties are available. It is an essential herb in a bouquet garni.

Tarragon: This herb is excellent for flavouring vinegars but is rarely used in its fresh form because it darkens and discolours on heating.

robust herbs

Often woody, with pungent leaves, these herbs are added to preserves during cooking to extract and mellow their flavour.

Bay leaf: Essential in bouquet garni, these dark green glossy leaves should be dried for a few days before use. They add a slightly spicy flavour to preserves.

Above: Parsley has a mild flavour and is often used with other herbs.

Marjoram and oregano: Popular in tomato preserves, these herbs are also good with marrow (large zucchini). They should be added towards the end of cooking.

Rosemary: Powerfully aromatic, fresh or dried rosemary should be used in small quantities. It goes very well with citrus fruits.

Sage: A strong herb that often partners garlic and tomatoes.

Thyme: This robust herb works well with preserves made from roasted vegetables and beans.

aromatic and spicy herbs

Some herbs have aromatic citrus flavours, others aniseed tones; a few have a warm, spicy pungency.

Coriander/cilantro Every part of this aromatic herb can be used – from its delicate leaves and sturdier stalks to its hard brown seeds. Also known as Chinese parsley, the leaves resemble slightly rounded flat leaf parsley. They have a warm, spicy taste and add pungency to Middle Eastern, Asian and Indian chutneys and fresh, Mexican-style relishes.

Dill: This delicate herb has dark green, feathery leaves and has a subtle aniseed taste. It is an excellent flavouring for mild-tasting courgette (zucchini) and cucumber relishes and pickles.

Fennel: Part of the same family as dill, with a similar, but stronger flavour, it is particularly good for flavouring vinegars.

Kaffir lime leaf: This strong-tasting, aromatic leaf is used to flavour Thai and Malaysian preserves.

Lemon grass: A tall hard grass, with a distinctive lemony aroma and taste, lemon grass is often used in Thai preserves and should be bruised to release the flavour.

Lovage Similar to celery leaves with a peppery flavour, lovage is good with root vegetables and in mixed vegetable chutneys.

FLOWERS

Many types of edible flowers and their leaves can be used to add fragrance and flavour to preserves, including the flowers of herbs such as rosemary, thyme, marjoram, fennel and chives.

Borage: The tiny, brilliant blue or purple flowers of this plant can be candied or used to decorate jellies. Borage leaves have a fresh cucumber-like taste and can be used to flavour jellies.

Geranium leaves: These give jams and jellies a subtle flavour. There are several different varieties with apple, rose or lemon aromas.

Lavender: Intensely fragrant, sprigs of lavender can be used to flavour sugar, jams and jellies. The sprigs also look very pretty suspended in jelly: dip them in boiling water first, then shake off the excess before putting them in the jar and pouring over the hot jelly.

Rose: Scented red, pink or yellow petals make wonderful jams and jellies. They are often combined with fruit juice, such as grape, and with added pectin, so that the preserve sets quickly without destroying the aroma of the petals. Be sure to use unsprayed roses.

Left: Tender-leafed basil has a fragrant, peppery flavour that goes particularly well with tomato-based preserves.

MAKING A BOUQUET GARNI

This is a bunch of aromatic herbs, tied with a piece of string or in a square of muslin (cheesecloth). A bouquet garni can be added to preserves and simmered until the flavours have infused (steeped) into the mixture, giving a subtle taste and aroma. Fresh herbs will give the best flavour.

1 For jellies or sauces that will be strained after cooking, tie together a sprig of parsley, a sprig of thyme, and a bay leaf with a piece of string. Suspend the bunch of herbs in the preserve, tying it to the pan handle for easy removal.

2 For chutneys and relishes, tie the herbs loosely in a piece of fine muslin (cheesecloth), about 15cm/6in square, so that the liquid can bubble through and extract the herbs' flavour.

PRESERVING EQUIPMENT

While very few specialist items are essential for preserving, having the correct equipment for the job will make the whole process easier and helps to ensure success. You will probably have most of the basic items such as a large heavy pan, weighing scales or calibrated measuring cups, wooden spoons, a chopping board and a few sharp knives. However, a few specific items such as a jam funnel for potting preserves and a jelly bag for straining fruit juices will prove invaluable. The following is a brief outline of the more useful items, all of which are readily available from large department stores and specialist kitchen equipment stores.

PRESERVING PAN

A preserving pan or large, heavy pan is essential. It must be of a sufficient size to allow rapid boiling without bubbling over (a capacity of about 9 litres/ 16 pints/8 quarts is ideal); wide enough to allow rapid evaporation of liquid, so that setting point is reached quickly; and have a thick heavy base to protect the preserve from burning. Preserving pans are fitted with a pair of short-looped handles, or a carrying handle over the top. A non-corrosive preserving pan such as one made of stainless steel is the best choice for making all types of preserves, especially for pickles, chutneys and relishes that contain a high concentration of acid. Traditional copper preserving pans, usually very wide at the top and sloping to a narrow base, are intended only for jam- and jelly-

making and are unsuitable for preserves containing vinegar or lemon juice, or for acidic or red fruit, as both the flavour and colour will be spoilt. Enamel pans do not conduct heat fast enough for preserving and they burn easily.

SUGAR THERMOMETER

Invaluable for cooking preserves to the exact temperature needed for a perfect set. Choose a thermometer that goes up to at least 110°C/ 230°F, and has a clip or a handle that can be attached to the pan, so that it does not slip into the boiling preserve.

JELLY BAG

Used to strain fruit juices from cooked fruit pulp for jelly-making, jelly bags are made from calico, cotton flannel or nylon. The close weave allows only the fruit juice to flow through, leaving the pulp behind. Some jelly bags have their own stands; others have loops with which to suspend the bag.

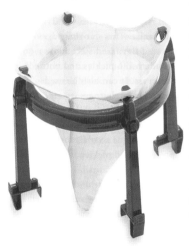

MUSLIN/CHEESECLOTH

Used for making spice and herb bags, muslin is also useful for tying together pips and peel, particularly when making marmalade. It can also be used instead of a jelly bag. To do this, layer three or four squares of muslin together and tie lengths of strong string (twine) securely to each corner. Either knot the ends together to hang from a single support, or make four loops so the bag can be suspended on the legs of an upturned stool or chair. Alternatively, line a large strainer with the muslin squares and place over a bowl to catch the juices.

JARS AND BOTTLES

When making preserves, a selection of containers is needed. Clear glass is ideal because it is non-corrosive, you can easily check for trapped air bubbles when potting preserves, and it looks very pretty when filled. As well as ordinary jam jars and bottles, there are specialist preserving jars that are designed to be heated to a high temperature. Non-corrosive seals are essential, particularly when potting acidic preserves and pickles.

Be sure to choose appropriately shaped and sized containers. Wide-necked jars are essential for recipes using whole or large pieces of fruit or vegetables, but for most preserves it is better to use several smaller jars than one or two large

Left: A jelly bag with its own stand can make an easy job of straining jellies.

ones. Preserves stored in very large jars are likely to deteriorate more quickly once the seal is broken; the preserve is not consumed as quickly and the contents are exposed to the air for longer than a preserve stored in a small jar.

PRESERVE COVERS

The cheapest way to cover jams, jellies and marmalades is to use a waxed paper disc and cellophane cover, secured by an elastic band. The paper discs should be pressed down very lightly over the contents of the jar once filled; they will form a seal to keep out air and moisture. Cellophane covers are available to fit both 450g/1lb and 900g/2lb jars. Do note, however, that paper and cellophane are not vinegar-proof so are unsuitable for preserves containing vinegar. Pot in preserving jars with acid-resistant seals, or use jam jars with plastic-lined lids.

FUNNELS

These make potting preserves considerably easier. A jam funnel with a wide tube (10–13cm/4–5in diameter) that fits into the top of the jar or container can make quick, clean work of filling jars.

An ordinary funnel with a slimmer tube is useful for adding liquid to jars of pickles or fruit as well as for bottling smooth sauces and jellies. Choose funnels made of heat-proof plastic or stainless steel.

HYDROMETER

Also known as a *pese syrop*, a hydrometer measures the density of sugar syrup and is sometimes used when bottling fruit and for jam- and jelly-making. The tube is marked from 0 to 40 and measures the point to which the weighted tube sinks. The more sugar a syrup contains, the higher the hydrometer will float in it.

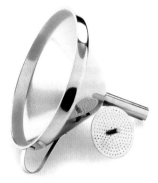

Above: A jam funnel can prove to be a real time-saver when potting jellies, jams and conserves.

SALOMETER

This works in the same way as a hydrometer but is used to measure the amount of salt dissolved in brine. Salometers are marked from 0 to 100, where 1°S is about 0.26% salt by weight, as fully satured brine contains about 26% salt.

Below: A selection of jars with either clamp-top, screw-top or two-piece screw-band lids are perfect for preserving.

7 To check that the peel is cooked, remove a piece from the pan and leave for a few minutes to cool. Once cooled, press the peel between finger and thumb; it should feel very soft.

8 Using a slotted spoon, remove the muslin bag from the pan and set it aside until cool enough to handle. Squeeze as much liquid as possible back into the pan to extract all the pectin from the pips and pith.

9 Add the sugar to the pan and stir over a low heat until the sugar has completely dissolved.

10 Bring the marmalade to the boil, then boil rapidly for about 10 minutes until setting point is reached (105°C/220°F). You may also use the flake or wrinkle test to check the set.

11 Using a slotted spoon, remove any scum from the surface of the marmalade, then leave to cool until a thin skin starts to form on the surface of the preserve.

12 Leave the marmalade to stand for about 5 minutes, then stir gently to distribute the peel evenly. Ladle into hot sterilized jars, then cover and seal.

making orange jelly marmalade

This recipe uses Seville (Temple) oranges, and may be made as a plain jelly marmalade, or a few fine shreds of peel can be added before potting, which can look very pretty and adds an interesting texture. Any marmalade can be made in the same way; use exactly the same ingredients listed in the recipe but use the method below.

Makes about 2kg/4½lb

INGREDIENTS

450g/1lb Seville (Temple) oranges
1.75 litres/3 pints/7½ cups water
1.3kg/3lb/generous 6¾ cups preserving or granulated (white) sugar
60ml/4 tbsp lemon juice

1 Wash and dry the oranges; gently scrub them with a soft brush if they have waxed skins.

2 If you want to add a little peel to the jelly marmalade, thinly pare and finely shred the rind from 2 or 3 of the oranges. Place the shreds in a square of muslin (cheesecloth) and tie it into a neat bag.

3 Halve the oranges and squeeze out the juice and pips (seeds), then tip the juice and pips into a large preserving pan.

4 Roughly chop the orange peel, including all the pith, and add it to the pan. Add the bag of shredded rind, if using, and pour over the water. Cover the pan with a lid and leave to soak for at least 4 hours, or overnight.

5 Bring the mixture to the boil, then reduce the heat and simmer gently for 1½ hours. Using a slotted spoon, remove the bag of peel, and carefully remove a piece of peel to check that it is tender. If not, re-tie the bag and simmer for a further 15–20 minutes. Remove the bag of peel and set aside.

6 Line a large nylon or stainless steel sieve with a double layer of muslin and place over a large bowl. Pour boiling water through the muslin to scald it. Discard the scalding water from the bowl. Alternatively, use a scalded jelly bag suspended over a bowl instead of the muslin-lined sieve.

7 Pour the fruit and juices into the sieve or jelly bag and leave to drain for at least 1 hour. Pour the juices into the cleaned pan.

8 Add the sugar, lemon juice and shredded orange rind, if using, to the pan. Stir over a low heat until the sugar has dissolved, then bring to the boil and boil rapidly for about 10 minutes until setting point is reached (105°C/220°F).

9 Remove any scum from the surface. Leave to cool until a thin skin starts to form on the surface. Stir, then pot, cover and seal.

TOP TIPS FOR SUCCESSFUL MARMALADE-MAKING

• Always wash citrus fruit well. Most citrus fruits have a wax coating that helps to prolong the life of the fruit, which should be removed before making the fruit into marmalade. Alternatively, buy unwaxed fruit, but always rinse before use.

• When shredding peel, always slice it slightly thinner than required in the finished preserve because the rind will swell slightly during cooking.

• Coarse-cut peel will take longer to soften than finely shredded peel. To reduce cooking time, soak the peel for a few hours in the water and juices before cooking.

• If the fruit needs to be peeled, put it in a bowl of boiling water and leave to stand for a couple of minutes. This will help to loosen the skins and make peeling easier. The rind's flavour will leach into the water, so use the soaking water in place of some of the measured water.

• If using small, thin-skinned fruit such as limes, cut the fruit into quarters lengthways, then slice flesh and rind into thin or thick shreds. If using larger, thick-skinned fruit such as grapefruit, pare off the peel, including some white pith, and shred. Cut the fruit into quarters, remove the remaining white pith and roughly chop the flesh.

• To make a coarse-cut preserve, boil the whole fruit for 2 hours until soft; pierce with a skewer to test. Lift out the fruit, halve, prise out the pips, then tie them loosely in muslin (cheesecloth) and add to the hot water. Boil rapidly for 10 minutes, then remove the bag. Slice the fruit and return to the pan. Stir in the sugar until dissolved, then boil to setting point.

• Shredded peel should be simmered gently; fierce cooking can give a tough result. Check that the peel is really soft before adding the sugar because it will not tenderize further after this.

• For easy removal, tie the muslin bag of pith and pips with string and attach it to the pan handle. It can then be lifted out of the boiling mixture easily.

• If the fruit contains a lot of pith, put only a small amount in the muslin bag with the pips (seeds). Put the remaining pith in a small pan, cover with water and boil for 10 minutes. Strain the liquid and use in place of some of the measured water for the recipe.

• To flavour marmalade with liqueur or spirits, add 15–30ml/ 1–2 tbsp for every 450g/1lb/ 2¼ cups sugar – stir it in just before potting. Unsweetened apple juice or dry (hard) cider may be used to replace up to half the water to add flavour to marmalades made with sharper fruits such as kumquats.

FRUIT CURDS, BUTTERS AND CHEESES

These rich, creamy preserves were once the highlight of an English tea during Edwardian and Victorian times. Curds and butters are delicious spread on slices of fresh bread and butter, or used as fillings for cakes; firmer fruit cheeses are usually sliced and can be enjoyed in similar ways. Fruit cheeses and butters are also very good served with roast meat, game or cheese.

Curds are made from fruit juice or purée cooked with eggs and butter. They have a soft texture and short keeping qualities. Fruit butters and cheeses are made from fruit purée boiled with sugar and are good if you have a glut of fruit because they require a relatively high proportion of fruit. Butters are lower in sugar and cooked for a shorter time, producing a soft, fruity preserve with a short shelf-life. Cheeses have a firm texture and may be set in moulds and turned out to serve.

MAKING FRUIT CURDS

Fruit curds are usually made with the juice of citrus fruits, but other acidic fruits such as passion fruit may be used. Smooth purées made from, for example, cooking apples or gooseberries can also be used.

The juice or purée is heated with eggs, butter and sugar until thick. The mixture is always cooked in a double boiler or a bowl set over a pan of simmering water to prevent the eggs curdling. Whole eggs are generally used, but if there is a lot of juice, egg yolks or a combination of whole eggs and yolks give a thicker result.

making lime curd

Makes about 675g/1½lb

INGREDIENTS
5 large, ripe juicy limes
115g/4oz/½ cup butter, cubed,
  at room temperature
350g/12oz/scant 1¾ cups caster
  (superfine) sugar
4 eggs, at room temperature

1 Finely grate the lime rind, ensuring you do not include any of the bitter white pith. Halve the limes and squeeze out the juice.

2 Place the lime rind in a large heatproof bowl set over a pan of barely simmering water, then strain in the lime juice to remove any bits of fruit or pips (seeds).

3 Add the cubed butter and the sugar to the bowl. Heat gently, stirring frequently, until the butter melts; the mixture should be barely warm, not hot.

4 Lightly beat the eggs with a fork, then strain through a fine sieve into the warm fruit mixture.

5 Keeping the water at a very gentle simmer, stir the fruit mixture continuously until the curd is thick enough to coat the back of a wooden spoon. Do not overcook because the curd will thicken on cooling.

6 Spoon the curd into warmed sterilized jars, then cover and seal when cold. Store in a cool, dark place, ideally in the refrigerator. Use within 2 months.

MAKING FRUIT BUTTERS

Smoother and thicker than jam, fruit butters have a spreadable quality not unlike dairy butter. Many recipes also contain a small amount of butter.

making apricot butter

Makes about 1.3kg/3lb

INGREDIENTS
1.3kg/3lb fresh ripe apricots
1 large orange
about 450ml/¾ pint/scant 2 cups water
about 675g/1½lb/scant 3½ cups caster
  (superfine) sugar
15g/½oz/1 tbsp butter (optional)

1 Rinse the apricots, then halve, stone (pit) and roughly chop. Remove the skins, unless you are going to purée the fruit by pressing through a sieve.

2 Scrub the orange and thinly pare 2–3 large strips of rind, avoiding any pith. Squeeze out the juice and put the apricots and the orange rind and juice in a large heavy pan.

3 Pour over enough of the water to cover the fruit. Bring to the boil, half-cover, then reduce the heat and simmer for 45 minutes.

4 Remove the orange rind, then blend the apricot mixture in a food processor until very smooth. Alternatively, press through a fine nylon or stainless steel sieve.

5 Measure the apricot purée and return it to the cleaned pan, adding 375g/13oz/1¾ cups sugar for each 600ml/1 pint/2½ cups purée.

6 Heat the mixture gently, stirring, until the sugar has dissolved, then bring to the boil and boil for about 20 minutes, stirring frequently, until thick and creamy. Remove the pan from the heat.

7 If using, stir the butter into the mixture until melted. (The butter gives a glossy finish.) Spoon into warmed sterilized jars and cover. Store in the refrigerator and use within 6 months.

MAKING FRUIT CHEESES

These sweet, firm preserves are known as cheeses because they are stiff enough to be cut into slices or wedges rather like their dairy counterparts. This name is particularly appropriate when the cheeses are set in moulds and turned out. They may be made either from fresh fruit, or from the pulp left from making jellies.

making cranberry and apple cheese

Makes about 900g/2lb

INGREDIENTS

450g/1lb/4 cups fresh cranberries
225g/8oz cooking apples
600ml/1 pint/2½ cups water
10ml/2 tsp lemon juice
about 450g/1lb/2¼ cups
  granulated (white) sugar
glycerine, for greasing (optional)

1 Rinse the cranberries and place in a large heavy pan. Wash the apples and cut into small pieces (there is no need to peel or core). Add the water and lemon juice.

2 Cover the pan with a lid and bring the mixture to the boil; do not lift the lid until the cranberries stop popping because they often jump out of the pan and can be very hot. Simmer gently for 1 hour, or until the fruit is soft and pulpy.

3 Press the cranberry and apple mixture through a fine nylon or stainless steel sieve into a bowl.

4 Weigh the purée, then return it to the cleaned pan, adding 450g/1lb/ 2¼ cups sugar for every 450g/1lb purée. Gently heat the mixture over a low heat, stirring, until the sugar has dissolved completely.

5 Increase the heat a little and simmer the mixture until it is so thick that the spoon leaves a clean line through the mixture when drawn across the pan. It may take as long as 30 minutes to reduce the purée to this consistency. Stir frequently to stop the mixture burning on the base of the pan.

6 Spoon the fruit cheese into warmed sterilized jars and seal. Alternatively, spoon the mixture into moulds or jars greased with a little glycerine and cover with clear film (plastic wrap) when cool. In sealed jars, the cheese will keep for up to 1 year; in covered moulds, it should be kept in the refrigerator until you are ready to turn it out; eat within 1 month of making.

USING LEFTOVER PULP
The fruit pulp left from jelly-making is perfect for making into fruit cheeses. Remove the pulp from the jelly bag, stir in enough hot water to make a soft purée, then push through a sieve. Place the purée in a clean pan, adding 450g/1lb/2¼ cups sugar for every 450g/1lb purée and cook following the instructions for making fruit cheese above.

MODERN PRESERVING TECHNIQUES

With the advent of new kitchen equipment such as microwaves, pressure cookers and freezers, new ways to make fruit preserves have developed. The increased concern over healthy eating has also led to new types of preserves such as reduced-sugar jams.

PRESERVING IN A MICROWAVE

Preserves can be made using a microwave, but only using specific recipes intended for the appliance. It is difficult to adapt conventional recipes because many rely on the evaporation of liquid to achieve a set or to thicken the preserve.

Make sure the ingredients are at room temperature; if they are not, it will affect cooking times. Frozen fruit and vegetables can be used to make microwave preserves, but they must be defrosted first.

Chop fruit and vegetables into equal-size pieces so that they cook at the same speed, and stir the preserve frequently during cooking to distribute the heat evenly and avoid hot spots. Use a suitable microwave-proof bowl that will withstand very hot temperatures, and that is large enough to hold twice the volume of the ingredients.

When the preserve has finished cooking, leave it to stand for several minutes until it has stopped bubbling. It is essential to protect your hands with oven gloves when lifting the bowl; take care not to place it on a cold surface because this may cause the glass to crack – a wooden board is ideal for protecting the surface and bowl.

making microwave lemon curd

This recipe is based on an 800 watt microwave. For microwaves with a different wattage, adjust cooking times as follows – for a 900 watt oven: subtract 10 seconds per minute; for a 850 watt oven: subtract 5 seconds per minute; for a 750 watt oven: add 5 seconds per minute; for a 700 watt oven: add 10 seconds per minute.

Makes about 450g/1lb

INGREDIENTS
115g/4oz/½ cup butter, cubed

finely grated rind and juice of 3 large lemons

225g/8oz/generous 1 cup caster (superfine) sugar

3 eggs plus 1 egg yolk

1 Put the butter, lemon rind and juice in a large microwave-proof bowl. Cook on high for 3 minutes.

2 Add the sugar and stir until it has almost dissolved. Return to the microwave and cook on full power for 2 minutes, stirring after 1 minute.

3 Beat the eggs and the yolk together, then whisk into the lemon mixture, a little at a time.

4 Cook on 40% power, for 10–12 minutes, whisking every 2 minutes, until the curd thickens. Ladle into hot sterilized jars, cover and seal. When cool, store in the refrigerator. Use within 2 months.

PRESERVING IN A PRESSURE COOKER

Preserves can be made very quickly using a pressure cooker. They are particularly useful for marmalades and for softening whole or hard fruits. Never fill the pan more than half full and always check the manufacturer's instructions.

making pressure-cooker orange marmalade

Makes about 2.5kg/5½lb

INGREDIENTS
900g/2lb Seville (Temple) oranges

1 large lemon

1.2 litres/2 pints/5 cups water

1.8kg/4lb/generous 9 cups preserving or granulated (white) sugar

1 Scrub the fruit, then halve and squeeze out the juice. Quarter the oranges, scrape off the pulp and membranes and tie in a piece of muslin (cheesecloth) with the lemon halves and any pips.

2 Place the orange peel in the pressure cooker with the muslin bag and 900ml/1½ pints/3¾ cups of the water. Bring to medium (4.5kg/10lb) pressure and cook for 10 minutes.

3 Reduce the pressure and leave until the fruit is cool enough to handle. Remove the muslin bag and squeeze it over the pan.

4 Cut the orange peel into fine shreds and return to the pan with the remaining water and the fruit juice. Add the sugar and heat gently until the sugar has dissolved. Bring to the boil, then boil rapidly for about 10 minutes until setting point is reached (105°C/220°F).

5 Remove any scum from the surface using a slotted spoon, then leave the marmalade to cool until a thin skin starts to form on the surface. Stir gently to distribute the peel evenly, then ladle into hot sterilized jars, cover and seal.

MAKING FREEZER JAMS

This type of jam is not cooked, so it has a fresher, fruitier flavour and a brighter colour than cooked jam. Once thawed, it does not keep as well as traditional jam. Commercial pectin is used as a setting agent.

making strawberry freezer jam

Makes about 1.3kg/3lb

INGREDIENTS

800g/1¾lb/7 cups strawberries
900g/2lb/4½ cups caster (superfine) sugar
30ml/2 tbsp lemon juice
120ml/4fl oz/½ cup commercial liquid pectin

1 Wipe the fruit. (Only wash if necessary, then pat dry on kitchen paper.) Hull and cut into quarters, then put in a bowl with the sugar.

2 Lightly mash the fruit with a fork, leaving plenty of lumps of fruit. Cover and leave to stand for 1 hour, stirring once or twice.

3 Add the lemon juice and pectin to the fruit and stir for 4 minutes until thoroughly combined. Ladle the jam into small freezer-proof containers, cover and leave to stand for about 4 hours.

4 Put the jam in the refrigerator and chill for 24–48 hours, or until the jam sets. Freeze the jam for up to 6 months, or until ready to use.

5 To serve, remove the jam from the freezer and leave at room temperature for about 1 hour, or until defrosted. Keep any leftover defrosted jam in the refrigerator and use quickly.

MAKING REDUCED-SUGAR PRESERVES

Sugar is the vital preserving agent in sweet fruit preserves. It helps to prevent fermentation and spoilage, as well as adding sweetness and flavour, and improving the set. The proportion of sugar required for this is about 60 per cent of the final weight of preserve. Although it is possible to make reduced-sugar preserves, the yield is smaller and they will not keep for as long. In most recipes, the sugar content can be reduced by up to half. The jam should be stored in the refrigerator and used within 4 months.

USING FROZEN FRUIT
Freezing is a quick and convenient way to preserve fruit when it is at its best and cheapest. It is especially useful for fruit with a very short season, such as Seville or Temple oranges. Freezing does destroy some of the pectin content, so to compensate for this, an extra 10 per cent of fruit should be used in the recipe. Do a pectin test during cooking to check the set.

BOTTLED FRUITS

Bottling is a traditional method of preserving fruit in syrup. The jars or bottles of fruit and syrup are heated to destroy micro-organisms. Although superseded by freezing, bottling is more suitable for some fruits such as peaches, pears, grapes and oranges; the method is less suitable for preserving soft berries such as raspberries.

MAKING BOTTLED FRESH FRUIT SALAD

Makes about 1.8kg/4lb

INGREDIENTS

250g/9oz/generous 1¼ cups granulated (white) sugar
350ml/12fl oz/1½ cups water
1 lemon
450g/1lb each eating apples, pears, peaches or nectarines
350g/12oz seedless green grapes
4 oranges

1 Put the sugar and water in a pan. Pare off a small strip of lemon rind, avoiding the pith, and add to the pan. Heat gently, stirring, until the sugar has dissolved. Bring to the boil and simmer for 1 minute. Cover and leave to stand.

2 Halve the lemon, then squeeze out the juice and strain.

3 Prepare the fruit, allowing 275g/10oz fruit for each 450g/1lb jar. Peel, core and slice the apples and pears and toss in lemon juice. Peel, halve, stone (pit) and slice the peaches or nectarines; halve the grapes; and segment the oranges.

4 Rinse hot sterilized jars with boiling water. Pack the fruit into the jars tightly, pressing down gently with a wooden spoon.

5 Strain the syrup through a fine sieve and return it to the cleaned pan. Bring to the boil, then pour over the fruit, filling the jars to within 1cm/½in of the top. Cover and heat-treat.

MAKING POACHED PEARS

Fruit is often poached in syrup until just tender before bottling.

Makes about 1.8kg/4lb

INGREDIENTS

225g/8oz/scant 1¼ cups granulated (white) sugar
1.2 litres/2 pints/5 cups water
1 orange
1 cinnamon stick
2kg/4½lb cooking pears

1 Put the sugar and water in a large, wide pan and add a thinly pared strip of orange rind and the cinnamon. Heat gently until the sugar has dissolved, then bring to the boil and simmer for 1 minute.

2 Squeeze the juice from the orange, then strain. Peel and core the pears, then toss in lemon juice as soon as each one is prepared.

3 Add the pears to the syrup in a single layer. Place greaseproof (waxed) paper over the pears to keep them immersed. Poach for 15 minutes until just tender and slightly transluscent; the syrup should hardly bubble so that the fruit holds its shape. Once cooked, bottle and heat-treat.

MAKING SUGAR SYRUPS

Poach whole and slightly hard fruits such as pears and plums in a light syrup; poach figs, peaches, nectarines and apricots in a medium syrup; and poach soft fruits such as strawberries and raspberries in a heavy syrup.

To make a light syrup, use 115g/4oz/generous ½ cup sugar to 600ml/1 pint/2½ cups water; to make a medium syrup, use 175g/6oz/scant 1 cup sugar to 600ml/1 pint/2½ cups water; to make a heavy syrup, use 350g/12oz/1¾ cups sugar to 600ml/1 pint/2½ cups water.

Put the sugar and water in a pan and heat gently, stirring, until the sugar has dissolved. Bring to the boil and simmer for 1 minute. Use hot or cool.

HEAT TREATMENTS

There are several ways to heat-treat bottled fruit. The filled jars may be heated in hot water, in the oven, or in a pressure cooker. As the fruit cools, a vacuum is created.

Use jars specifically designed for heat treatment. Preserving jars with clamp tops should be sealed once filled; the clamps expand slightly to allow steam to escape. Screw tops on preserving jars should not be tightened until after heating because the steam will not be able to escape and the jars may burst. Heat-treated preserves may be kept for up to 2 years.

water bath method

This is suitable for fruits bottled in either hot or cold syrup; the latter will take a little longer to process.

1 Wrap folded newspaper or cloth around each filled container, then stand them on a metal trivet or a thick layer of paper or cloth in a large heavy pan. (Containers placed directly on the pan may crack.)

2 Pour tepid water around the jars, right up to the neck, then cover the pan. Bring slowly to the boil (this should take 25–30 minutes), then simmer for the required time.

3 Turn off the heat and ladle out some of the hot water. Using tongs or oven gloves, lift the containers out of the pan and place on a wooden board. If they have screw-band lids, tighten immediately.

4 Leave the containers to cool for 24 hours, then remove the screw bands or clips. Holding the rim of the lid, carefully lift the container; it should hold its own weight. Containers with one-piece lids should have a very slight dip in the lid to indicate that they are sealed. If a jar is not sealed properly, it should be stored in the refrigerator and used as soon as possible.

HEATING TIMES FOR THE WATER BATH METHOD
The following times are for fruit packed in hot syrup after boiling. Allow 5 minutes more for fruit packed in cold syrup.

Fruit	Minutes
Soft berries and redcurrants	2
Blackcurrants, gooseberries, rhubarb, cherries, apricots and plums	10
Peaches and nectarines	20
Figs and pears	35

moderate oven method

This is only suitable for fruits covered with hot syrup; cold-filled jars may crack in the warm oven.

1 Preheat the oven to 150°C/300°F/Gas 2. Put the rubber rings and lids on the filled jars, but do not seal. Place in a roasting pan lined with newspaper or cloth, spacing the jars about 5cm/2in apart. Pour 1cm/½in boiling water into the pan.

2 Place the pan in the middle of the oven. Cook 500–600ml/17–20fl oz jars for 30–35 minutes and 1 litre/1¾ pint jars for 35–55 minutes. If there are more than four jars, allow a little extra time.

3 Remove from the oven and seal the lids immediately. Cool on a wooden board. Test the seals as for the water bath method.

pressure cooker method

If using clip-top jars, move the clips slightly to the side of the lid to reduce the pressure. Check the instructions for the pressure cooker.

1 Stand the jars on the trivet in the pressure cooker, ensuring they do not touch each other or the pan.

2 Pour in 600ml/1 pint/2½ cups hot water. Put on the lid with a low (2.25kg/5lb) weight and slowly bring to pressure. Maintain this pressure for 4 minutes. Leave to stand until the pressure drops.

3 Transfer the jars to a board and seal. Leave for 12 hours, then test as for the water bath method.

PICKLES

These can be sharp or sweet or a combination of the two. They are made by preserving raw or lightly cooked fruit or vegetables in spiced vinegar. They may be eaten alone or as a condiment with cheese or cold meat. There are two types of pickles: clear pickles or sweet pickles. To make clear pickles such as pickled onions, salt or brine is used to extract water from the vegetables to give them a crisp texture before they are bottled in vinegar. To make sweet pickles, fruit or vegetables are usually cooked until tender, then bottled in a sweet vinegar syrup.

Fruit and vegetables used for pickling should be firm and young. Small varieties such as baby (pearl) onions, beetroot (beets), gherkins, plums and cherries, which can be pickled whole, are particularly good. Large vegetables such as cucumbers, marrows (large zucchini), cabbage and cauliflower should be sliced or chopped.

Most pickles have to be matured in a cool dark place for a minimum of 3 weeks and preferably for at least 2 months to develop and mellow their flavour before eating. Pickled cabbage loses its crisp texture after 2–3 months, so it should be eaten within 2 months of making.

Take care when packing the fruit or vegetables into jars – they should be well packed, but not too tightly because the vinegar must surround each piece. It is important to fill jars to the brim and avoid trapping air in the pickles because this will cause discoloration and may encourage the growth of bacteria and moulds.

Large, wide-necked jars are recommended for pickling. Screw-top jars with lids that have plastic-coated linings such as those used for commercial pickles are an ideal choice. Vinegar reacts with metal, causing it to corrode and flavour the pickle, so metal tops should always be avoided when pickling.

MAKING CLEAR PICKLES

When making clear pickles, the ingredients are usually prepared first by soaking them in a brine. The salt draws out the moisture from the vegetables, making them more receptive to vinegar and preventing vegetable juices from diluting the preserving vinegar. Pure or kosher salt should always be used because iodized salt will taint the pickle with an iodine flavour and the additives in table salt will make it cloudy. There are two types of brine: dry brine, where the salt is sprinkled over the vegetables; and wet brine, where the salt is dissolved in water first.

making pickled peppers using dry brine

For this method, salt is rubbed into the vegetables or, more simply, sprinkled between layers of vegetables to draw out the juices. This then produces a brine. Salting vegetables makes them firmer and crunchier. It is particularly suitable for vegetables with a high water content such as (bell) peppers. Other vegetables that suit this method include cucumbers and courgettes (zucchini).

Makes about 1.8kg/4lb

INGREDIENTS

1.3kg/3lb red and yellow (bell) peppers
60ml/4 tbsp salt
750ml/1¼ pints/3 cups distilled
   malt vinegar
2 fresh bay leaves
2 thyme sprigs
5ml/1 tsp black peppercorns

1 Wash the peppers and pat them dry on kitchen paper. Cut each one into quarters lengthways, remove the seeds and cores, then cut each quarter in half to make long wide strips. If the peppers are very large, cut each quarter into three strips rather than two.

2 Layer the peppers in a large, non-corrosive bowl, fleshy side up, lightly sprinkling salt between each layer. Cover the bowl with clear film (plastic wrap) and leave to stand in a cool place for 8 hours or overnight to extract the moisture. If the weather is warm, place the bowl in the refrigerator.

3 Tip the peppers into a colander or large sieve and rinse thoroughly in cold water to remove the salt. The easiest way to check for salt is to taste one of the peppers: if it is too salty, rinse again.

4 Drain the peppers well and pat dry with kitchen paper. This is important because excess water will dilute the vinegar.

5 Pour the vinegar into a pan and add the herbs and peppercorns. Slowly bring to the boil, then simmer for 2 minutes.

6 Meanwhile, pack the peppers into hot sterilized jars. Remove the herbs from the pickling vinegar and tuck them into the jars.

7 Pour the vinegar and peppercorns over the peppers, filling the jars almost up to the brim. (To make an even crunchier pickle, allow the vinegar to cool first.)

8 Gently tap the jars on the work surface to release any trapped air bubbles, then seal with vinegar-proof lids. Store in a cool, dark place for 4 weeks before eating. Use within 1 year.

making vegetable pickle using wet brine

For this method, salt is mixed with water to make a brine solution. The ingredients are then immersed in the brine, sometimes for several days before pickling in vinegar. Wet brine may be used hot but it is more often used cold. For most pickles, a 10 per cent salt solution is used; this requires 50g/2oz/¼ cup salt to every 600ml/1 pint/2½ cups water. In some preserves where vinegar is used with sugar, this may be reduced to a 5 per cent solution.

Pickling using wet brine is suitable for ingredients with a very dense texture or thick skin such as whole lemons, watermelon rind and green walnuts, or where a softer result is required.

Makes about 1.3kg/3lb

INGREDIENTS

1.3kg/3lb mixed vegetables such as baby (pearl) onions, carrots, cauliflower and green beans

175g/6oz/¾ cup salt

1.75 litres/3 pints/7½ cups water

2 bay leaves

0.75–1 litre/1¼–1¾ pints/3–4 cups spiced vinegar

1 Prepare the vegetables: skin, peel, and trim as necessary. Leave the onions whole, thickly slice the carrots, break the cauliflower into small florets and cut the beans into 2.5cm/1in lengths. Place the vegetables in a large glass bowl.

2 Put the salt and water in a large pan and warm over a low heat until the salt has dissolved completely. Leave to cool, then pour enough over the prepared vegetables to cover completely.

3 Place a plate, slightly smaller than the diameter of the bowl, on top of the vegetables to keep them submerged in the brine. Leave to stand for 24 hours.

4 Tip the vegetables into a colander or sieve to drain, then rinse well in cold water to remove the excess brine. Drain again and pat dry using kitchen paper.

5 Put the bay leaves and vinegar in a pan and slowly bring to the boil over a low heat.

6 Meanwhile, pack the brined vegetables into hot sterilized jars. Tuck in the bay leaves and pour in the hot vinegar, filling the jars almost to the top.

7 Gently tap the jars to release any trapped air bubbles, cover and seal. Store the vegetables in a cool, dark place for 4 weeks before eating. Use within 1 year.

making unbrined pickled mushrooms

Not all clear pickles are brined before bottling in vinegar. The moisture can be removed from mushrooms by simmering them gently in water with a little salt until just tender. This method is also suitable for beetroot (beets).

Makes about 450g/1lb

INGREDIENTS

1 small onion
1 garlic clove
300ml/½ pint/1¼ cups
  white wine vinegar
6 black peppercorns
sprig of fresh thyme
275g/10oz/3¼ cups small button
  (white) mushrooms
600ml/1 pint/2½ cups water
10ml/2 tsp salt

1 Thinly slice the onion and bruise the garlic clove and place in a pan with the vinegar, peppercorns and thyme. Bring the mixture slowly to the boil over a low heat, then half cover the pan with a lid. Simmer for 15 minutes. Remove from the heat, cover completely with the lid and leave to cool.

2 Meanwhile, wipe the mushrooms clean with damp kitchen paper and trim the stems if necessary.

3 Place the mushrooms in a pan with the water and salt. Bring to the boil and simmer for 1 minute. Remove from the heat, cover and leave to cool for 4 minutes, stirring a couple of times, so that all sides of the mushrooms are immersed in the hot water.

4 Tip the mushrooms into a colander or sieve, leave to drain, then pat dry using kitchen paper.

5 Pack the mushrooms into clean sterilized jars, then strain the vinegar mixture into the jars, covering the mushrooms and filling the jars almost to the top.

6 Seal the jars and store in a cool dark place for at least 3 weeks before eating. Use within 1 year.

PICKLING GREEN VEGETABLES

The colour of green vegetables tends to be lost if stored for more than a few months, although their flavour remains the same. Blanching them in boiling water mixed with 5ml/ 1 tsp bicarbonate of soda (baking soda) for 30 seconds helps to retain their colour, but destroys the vitamin C content.

MAKING SPICED PICKLING VINEGAR

Ready-spiced pickling vinegar and jars or packets of mixed pickling spices are readily available from supermarkets. However, you can make your own, adapting the combination of spices according to personal preference and the ingredients to be preserved. You can use any variety of vinegar, but make sure that it has an acetic acid content of at least 5 per cent.

making basic spiced pickling vinegar

Makes 1.2 litres/2 pints/5 cups

INGREDIENTS

15ml/1 tbsp allspice berries
15ml/1 tbsp cloves
5cm/2in piece fresh root ginger, peeled
  and sliced
1 cinnamon stick
12 whole black peppercorns
1.2 litres/2 pints/5 cups vinegar

1 Put all the spices in a jar and pour over the vinegar. Cover the jar and leave to steep for 1–2 months, shaking occasionally.

2 After this time, strain the vinegar and return it to the cleaned jar and store it in a cool dark place until ready to use.

COOK'S TIP

To make quick pickling vinegar for immediate use, put all the ingredients in a pan and heat gently to boiling point. Simmer for about 1 minute, then remove from the heat, cover and leave to infuse (steep) for 1 hour. Strain and use.

MAKING SWEET PICKLES

For these pickles, fruit and some vegetables such as cucumbers are preserved in sweetened vinegar. They are excellent served as an accompaniment to cold meats, poultry and cheeses. Pickled apples or pears are also delicious served with hot baked ham or grilled (broiled) meat such as lamb chops. Sweet pickles are always made with distilled malt, wine or cider vinegar rather than brown malt vinegar, which would overpower the flavour and affect the colour of the fruit.

To offset the sharpness of the vinegar, a fairly large amount of sugar is added, usually between 350g/12oz/scant 1¾ cups and 450g/1lb/2¼ cups to every 300ml/½ pint/1¼ cups vinegar. Unlike vegetables, fruits do not need to be brined before pickling. Fruits that are pickled whole such as plums and cherries should be pricked before the initial cooking to allow the vinegar syrup to penetrate the skin and stop the fruit shrivelling. Some fruits such as berries become very soft when pickled and are therefore better preserved in sugar syrup or alcohol.

Spices and flavourings add zest to sweet pickles. They are best infused in the vinegar at the start of cooking, but also look attractive added to the bottle when packing the preserve. Use whole spices such as cinnamon, cloves, allspice, ginger, nutmeg and mace; ground spices will make the pickle murky. Citrus rind and vanilla pods (beans) also add a wonderful taste and aroma. Robustly flavoured herbs such as rosemary and bay leaves work well in sweet pickles.

making pickled apples

Makes about 1.3kg/3lb

INGREDIENTS

750ml/1¼ pints/3 cups raspberry, cider or white wine vinegar

1 cinnamon stick

5cm/2in piece fresh root ginger, peeled and sliced

6 whole cloves

1.3kg/3lb eating apples, peeled, cored and halved

800g/1¾lb/4 cups granulated (white) sugar

1 Put the vinegar in a stainless steel pan with the cinnamon, ginger and cloves, and bring to the boil. Reduce the heat and simmer gently for about 5 minutes.

2 Add the apples to the vinegar and simmer for 5–10 minutes until they are almost tender. Be careful not to overcook the fruit; it will continue to cook in the hot syrup and should still be firm when packed into the jars.

3 Using a slotted spoon, lift the apples out of the vinegar and pack them into hot sterilized jars, adding the cloves and the cinnamon stick, if you like.

4 Add the sugar to the vinegar and heat gently over a low heat, stirring until dissolved completely.

5 Increase the heat and boil the syrup rapidly for 5 minutes, or until the syrup has reduced and thickened slightly.

6 Strain the syrup through a sieve into a jug (pitcher), then pour it over the apples to cover them completely. Seal and label. Store the jars in a cool dark place and use within 1 year.

RASPBERRY VINEGAR

Fruit vinegars are perfect for making sweet pickles and are very easy to make at home.

To make about 750ml/1¼ pints/3 cups raspberry vinegar, put 450g/1lb/generous 2½ cups fresh raspberries in a bowl with 600ml/1 pint/2½ cups white wine or cider vinegar. Cover the bowl with a cloth and leave in a cool place for 4–5 days, stirring each day.

Strain the vinegar through a nylon or stainless-steel sieve and discard the raspberries. Pour the liquid into a jelly bag suspended over a large bowl or jug (pitcher). Leave to drain, then pour the vinegar into sterilized bottles and seal. Store in a cool dark place and use within 1 year.

PICKLING DRIED FRUITS

All sorts of dried fruits can be made into excellent pickles. The fruits soak up the pickling syrup, becoming soft, succulent and juicy. Dried apricots, peaches, pears, figs, prunes and mango slices are all perfect for pickling.

Pickles made with dried fruit do not need as much sugar as pickles made with fresh fruit; dried fruits are already packed with sugar. A small amount of liquid such as apple juice or water may be used to rehydrate the fruit before pickling. This prevents the fruit soaking up too much vinegar and the flavour becoming overpowering.

When pickling light-coloured dried fruits such as apricots, pears or apples, use light-coloured sugars and vinegars. Dark-coloured fruits such as figs and prunes can be pickled using malt or red wine vinegar and darker sugars.

SWEET PICKLING VINEGAR
When choosing vinegar for sweet pickles, it is important to think about the colour as well as the flavour of the vinegar. For green fruits such as green figs or red fruits such as plums, choose a light-coloured vinegar and spices or flavourings that won't alter the colour. Using a dark vinegar will turn the fruits a sludgy brown colour. Yellow fruits such as nectarines and apricots, and white or creamy fruits such as pears look stunning pickled in a coloured vinegar such as raspberry.

making pickled prunes

Makes about 1.3kg/3lb

INGREDIENTS
675g/1½lb/3 cups prunes
150ml/¼ pint/⅔ cup clear apple juice
750ml/1¼ pints/3 cups pickling malt vinegar
strip of pared orange rind
350g/12oz/1½ cups light muscovado (brown) sugar

1 Put the prunes in a non-corrosive pan, pour over the apple juice and cover. Leave to soak for 2 hours, or until the prunes have absorbed most of the juice.

2 Uncover the pan, add the vinegar and orange rind and bring slowly to the boil over a gentle heat. Reduce the heat and simmer gently for 10–15 minutes until the prunes are plump and juicy.

3 Remove the strip of orange rind from the pan and discard. Using a slotted spoon, lift the prunes out of the vinegar and pack well into hot sterilized jars.

4 Add the sugar to the vinegar and heat gently, stirring, until the sugar has dissolved completely. Bring the mixture to a rapid boil and cook for about 5 minutes, or until slightly reduced and thickened.

5 Carefully pour the hot vinegar syrup over the prunes and seal. Store in a cool dark place for at least 2 weeks before eating. Use within 1 year.

USING DRIED FRUITS IN PRESERVES
Dried fruits can be used in many types of preserve. They absorb liquid readily, so are often added to chutneys to help thicken the mixture. Raisins and sultanas (golden raisins) are particularly popular for this. Chopped dried apricots, peaches, dates and figs can also be used and contribute a substantial texture as well as a lovely sweet flavour.

Dried fruit is widely used to impart a full, fruity flavour to cooked relishes and savoury preserves made with mildly flavoured vegetables such as pumpkin, squash and green (unripe) tomatoes.

When choosing dried fruit for pickling, select the fully dried type, rather than the softer ready-to-eat variety that is popular for general cooking. The former has a better texture when soaked for a long time in pickling vinegar.

FRUITS PRESERVED IN ALCOHOL

Fruits preserved in alcohol make luxurious instant desserts, served with crème fraîche or ice cream. One of the best-known fruit and alcohol preserves is German *rumtopf*, which means rum pot. It consists of summer and early autumn fruits bottled in alcohol, usually rum, but not always, with a little sugar. Traditionally, this preserve is made in a large jar with a wide neck and tight-fitting lid.

Pure alcohol is the best preservative because bacteria and moulds are unable to grow in it. Clear liqueurs, such as eau de vie, orange liqueur, Kirsch and amaretto, or spirits such as brandy, rum and vodka, which are at least 40 per cent ABV, may be used.

The alcohol content of table wine and dry (hard) cider is too low and so these are not effective preservatives on their own unless the bottles are heat-treated. Fruits preserved in wine or cider should be stored in the refrigerator and used within 1 month of making.

When using alcohol to preserve, it is usually best to combine it with sugar syrup because high-alcohol liqueurs and spirits tend to shrink the fruit. Most fruits are first simmered in syrup, which helps to tenderize the fruit and kills the bad enzymes.

The type of syrup used for preserving fruits in alcohol varies depending on the sweetness and juiciness of the fruit, as well as the desired result. A typical syrup would be 600ml/1 pint/2½ cups alcohol, blended with a syrup of 150ml/¼ pint/⅔ cup water and 150g/5oz/¾ cup sugar.

MAKING NECTARINES IN BRANDY SYRUP

For extra flavour, you can add whole spices such as vanilla or cinnamon to the syrup.

Makes about 900g/2lb

INGREDIENTS

350g/12oz/1¾ cups preserving or granulated (white) sugar
150ml/¼ pint/⅔ cup water
450g/1lb firm, ripe nectarines
2 bay leaves
150ml/¼ pint/⅔ cup brandy

1 Put the sugar in a large heavy pan with the water and heat gently, stirring until dissolved completely. Bring to the boil, then reduce the heat and simmer for 10 minutes.

2 Halve and stone (pit) the nectarines. (If liked, you may also peel them.) Add them to the syrup.

3 Reduce the heat so that the syrup is barely simmering and poach the nectarines until almost tender. Add the bay leaves 1 minute before the end of the cooking. Turn off the heat and leave them to stand for 5 minutes; they will cook a little more as it cools.

4 Using a slotted spoon, lift the fruit out of the pan and pack into hot sterilized jars.

5 Bring the syrup to a rapid boil and cook for 3–4 minutes. Leave to cool for a few minutes, then stir in the brandy. (Do not add the brandy to the boiling syrup because the alcohol will evaporate and the syrup will lose its preserving qualities.) Pour the syrup into the jars, covering the fruit completely. Tap the jars to release any air and seal. Store in a cool dark place and use within 1 year.

CHUTNEYS

These are made from finely cut ingredients, cooked slowly with vinegar, a sweetener and frequently spices or other flavourings to make a thick, savoury jam-like mixture. Onions and apples are popular, but almost any fruits and vegetables can be used. Chutneys should be matured in a cool dark place for at least 2 months before eating.

MAKING TOMATO CHUTNEY

Makes about 2.25kg/5lb

INGREDIENTS

450g/1lb onions, chopped

900ml/1½ pints/3¾ cups malt vinegar

50g/2oz whole pickling spices, such as peppercorns, allspice berries, dried chillies, dried ginger and celery seeds

1kg/2¼lb ripe tomatoes, skinned and chopped

450g/1lb cooking apples, peeled, cored and chopped

350g/12oz/1½ cups soft light brown sugar

10ml/2 tsp salt

225g/8oz/1 cup sultanas (golden raisins)

1 Put the onions and vinegar in a large pan. Tie the pickling spices in a muslin (cheesecloth) bag and add to the pan. Bring slowly to the boil, then simmer gently for 30 minutes until the onions are almost tender.

2 Add the tomatoes and apples to the pan, and simmer for 10 minutes until the fruit is softened and starts to break down slightly.

3 Add the sugar and salt to the pan, and stir over a low heat until the sugar has dissolved completely, then stir in the sultanas.

4 Gently simmer the chutney for 1½–2 hours, stirring occasionally to prevent the mixture sticking. The chutney is ready when it is thick and there is no liquid on the surface. Draw a wooden spoon across the base of the pan: it should leave a clear line in the mixture.

5 Remove the pan from the heat and leave to cool for 5 minutes. Remove the spice bag and discard. Stir the mixture to ensure the chutney is evenly mixed, then spoon into warmed, sterilized jars.

6 Use the handle of a wooden spoon to release any trapped air bubbles and ensure the chutney is packed down well. Seal the jars immediately and leave to cool. Store the chutney in a cool, dark place and leave to mature for at least 1 month before eating. Use within 2 years.

TOP TIPS FOR SUCCESSFUL CHUTNEY-MAKING

• Use malt vinegar for its intense flavour. Wine vinegar or cider vinegar are better for preserving colourful or light-coloured vegetables because they will not spoil the colour of the vegetables.

• The choice of sugar will affect the end result: brown sugar gives the richest flavour and colour; demerara (raw) sugar and golden granulated sugar give a caramel flavour; and white sugar helps to retain the colour of light ingredients.

• Never cover the pan when making chutney. Cooking the preserve uncovered allows the liquid to evaporate and the chutney to thicken. Towards the end, stir the chutney frequently to prevent it from catching and burning on the base of the pan.

• Always store chutney in a cool dark place: warmth can cause it to ferment, and bright sunlight can affect the colour.

RELISHES

These are similar to chutneys, but cooked for less time to give a fresher result. The fruits and vegetables are usually cut into smaller, neater pieces, and wine or cider vinegar is more frequently used than malt vinegar. Relishes contain a low proportion of vinegar and sugar, so do not keep for long. They can be eaten immediately or chilled and used within 2–3 months.

MAKING HOT PEPPER RELISH

Makes about 1.3kg/3lb

INGREDIENTS

900g/2lb red (bell) peppers, quartered, cored and seeded

10ml/2 tsp salt

4 fresh red chillies, seeded

450g/1lb red (Italian) onions, finely chopped

400ml/14fl oz/1¾ cups red wine vinegar

5ml/1 tsp celery seeds

6 black peppercorns

200g/7oz/1 cup granulated (white) sugar

1 Cut the peppers into 1cm/½in pieces and layer them in a colander or sieve placed over a large bowl, sprinkling salt between each layer. Leave the peppers to drain for at least 30 minutes.

2 Tip the red peppers into a large heavy pan and add the chillies, onions and vinegar.

3 Tie the celery seeds and black peppercorns in a square of muslin (cheesecloth) and add to the pan. Slowly bring to the boil over a low heat. Reduce the heat and simmer for about 25 minutes, or until the peppers are just tender.

4 Add the sugar and stir over a low heat until dissolved. Bring to the boil and simmer for 15 minutes, or until the relish is thick.

5 Remove the spice bag from the pan and discard. Spoon the relish into warmed, sterilized jars and seal. Store in the refrigerator and use within 3 months.

RELISHES WITH THICKENED SAUCES

Some relishes have a sauce base thickened with flour or cornflour (cornstarch). Mustard or turmeric may be added to the relish to give it a yellow colour. Corn relish, piccalilli and chow-chow are examples. The vegetables should retain their shape and be slightly crunchy, rather than soft.

making mustard relish

Makes about 1.3kg/3lb

INGREDIENTS

900g/2lb mixed vegetables, such as cauliflower, green beans, courgettes (zucchini), carrots, (bell) peppers and green (unripe) tomatoes

225g/8oz shallots, finely sliced

750ml/1¼ pints/3 cups malt vinegar

1 garlic clove, crushed

50g/2oz/½ cup plain (all-purpose) flour

25g/1oz/¼ cup English mustard powder

200g/7oz/1 cup caster (superfine) sugar

2.5ml/½ tsp ground coriander

5ml/1 tsp salt

1 Break the cauliflower into small florets, cut the beans into 2.5cm/1in lengths and dice the courgettes, carrots, peppers and tomatoes.

2 Put the shallots in a large heavy pan with 600ml/1 pint/2½ cups of the vinegar. Simmer, uncovered, for 10 minutes. Add the vegetables and garlic and simmer for 10 minutes.

3 Mix together the flour, mustard, sugar, coriander, salt and remaining vinegar to make a smooth paste, then stir into the vegetables. Simmer for 10 minutes, stirring. Pot and store for 2 weeks before eating. Use within 6 months.

DRIED FRUITS AND VEGETABLES

Removing moisture from foods is one of the oldest methods of preserving. Traditional techniques depend on the correct proportions of sunlight, heat and humidity for successful results. If food is dried too fast, moisture can get trapped and spoil it; if it is dried too slowly, micro-organisms may start to grow. Most commercially dried fruits and vegetables, such as apricots, figs and tomatoes, which are high both in sugar and acid, are still wind- and sun-dried in the way they have been for centuries.

To re-create these conditions, an airy place with a steady temperature is needed. A very warm room or cupboard may be used if the temperature is constant, but the most efficient way is to use an oven on the lowest setting.

A fan oven is ideal because of the constant circulation of air. If using a conventional oven, leave the door open with the tiniest possible gap, or open frequently during the drying process to let steam escape. Be careful that the temperature does not become too high, or the fruit or vegetables will cook and shrivel. If necessary, turn off the oven occasionally and leave it to cool down.

Choose firm, fresh and ripe fruit and vegetables for drying. Citrus fruits and melons consist mainly of water, so do not dry well, nor do berry fruits because they discolour and become very seedy. To help preserve the dried fruit and prevent discoloration, the prepared pieces should be dipped into a very weak brine solution, or acidulated water, before drying.

making dried apple rings

INGREDIENTS

15ml/1 tbsp salt, or 90ml/6 tbsp lemon juice, or 30ml/2 tbsp ascorbic acid (vitamin C) powder

1.2 litres/2 pints/5 cups water

900g/2lb firm, ripe apples

1 Put the salt, lemon juice or ascorbic acid powder in a large bowl and pour in the water. Stir until dissolved.

2 Peel and core the apples, then cut into rings slightly thicker than 5mm/¼in. As soon as each apple is cut, put the rings in the bowl of water and leave for 1 minute before lifting out. Pat the rings dry using kitchen paper.

3 Thread the apple rings on to wooden skewers, leaving a small space between each ring, or spread the apple rings out on wire racks. (Baking sheets are not suitable because air needs to circulate around the fruit.)

4 If using skewers, rest them on the oven shelves, allowing the apple rings to hang between the gaps. If using wire racks, simply place the racks in the oven. Leave the door very slightly ajar.

5 Dry the apples at 110°C/225°F/Gas ¼ for about 5 hours, or until the apple rings resemble soft, pliable leather.

6 Remove the fruit from the oven and leave to cool completely. Very crisp fruits and vegetables should be stored in airtight containers, but leathery, pliable fruits are better stored in paper bags or cardboard boxes; storing them in plastic bags may make them go mouldy.

7 To reconstitute the dried apple slices, put them in a bowl and pour over boiling water. Leave to soak for at least 5 minutes, then place in a pan and gently cook in the soaking liquid.

COOK'S TIPS

• Dried apple slices make a healthy snack and are popular with children.
• They are also good chopped and added to desserts and bakes.

PREPARING FRUITS AND VEGETABLES FOR DRYING

The time taken for fruit and vegetables to dry depends greatly on their size, so cut them into equal-size pieces.

Apples and pears: Peel and core. Cut apples into 5mm/¼in slices; halve or quarter pears, depending on size.

Apricots, plums and figs: These may be dried whole, but are better if halved and stoned (pitted). Place on the racks with the cut sides uppermost, so that the juices do not run out. If the oven has a lower setting, dry on this for 1 hour, before turning up to 110°C/ 225°C/Gas ¼, to prevent the skins from bursting.

Grapes: Use seedless grapes. These can be dried whole: prick a tiny hole in each one to stop the skins bursting.

Onions and leeks: Slice thinly crossways. The pieces may fall through wire racks, so cover the racks with muslin (cheesecloth) first.

Mushrooms and chillies: Tie these up on to fine string or cotton thread and hang up to air-dry in the sun or in an airy room for 2–3 weeks until dry and shrivelled. The dried strings of mushrooms and chillies can look very pretty hung in the kitchen.

Plum tomatoes: Split these lengthways and arrange cut side up. Sprinkle lightly with salt before placing in the oven to dry out.

FRUIT LEATHER

This unusual delicacy is made from slightly sweetened fruit pulp that has been spread out thinly and dried. The final result is a sweet, chewy fruit "leather" that can be eaten as confectionery or a snack. Most ripe fruits can be used; mangoes, peaches and apricots work particularly well and produce an intensely flavoured, orange-coloured confection.

making apricot leather

Makes about 115g/4oz

INGREDIENTS
900g/2lb ripe apricots
10ml/2 tsp lemon juice
45ml/3 tbsp caster
 (superfine) sugar

1 Put the apricots in a bowl and pour over boiling water. Leave to stand for about 30 seconds, then drain and peel off the skins. Halve the fruits and remove the stones (pits). Using a sharp knife, roughly chop the flesh.

2 Put the chopped apricots, lemon juice and sugar in a food processor or blender and process for about 3 minutes, or until the fruit has formed a smooth purée.

3 Line a large baking sheet with a piece of baking parchment. Pour the purée on to the middle of the baking parchment, then, using a palette knife (metal spatula), spread the purée out to a thickness of 5mm/¼in, leaving a 2cm/¾in margin. Tap the baking sheet on the work surface to level the purée.

4 Put the baking sheet in the oven, leaving the door slightly ajar, and dry at 110°C/225°F/Gas ¼ for about 8 hours, or until the purée is dry, but still pliable.

5 Leave the apricot leather to cool on the baking sheet, then roll it up, still on the baking parchment, and store in an airtight container for up to 3 months.

6 To eat, carefully unroll the fruit leather and cut into squares or 5cm/2in lengths while still on the baking parchment, then peel off the baking parchment.

CANDIED FRUIT

Sugar is an excellent preservative. Candying is a method by which fruit or citrus peel is preserved by steeping in syrup. The fruit or peel becomes so saturated in sugar that natural deterioration is virtually halted. The process works by gradually replacing the fruit's moisture with a saturated sugar solution. This has to be done slowly and takes at least 15 days, but is well worth it. Candied fruit is expensive to buy and, although you need to plan ahead when making candied fruit or peel, it requires only a little time each day.

making candied fruit

You can candy as much or as little fruit as you like, working with the basic proportions of fruit to sugar given in the recipe below. Always candy different fruits separately, so that each type retains its own flavour. Choose firm, fresh fruits that are free of blemishes.

INGREDIENTS

fresh, firm, just-ripe fruit, such as pineapples, peaches, pears, apples, plums, apricots, kiwi fruit or cherries

granulated (white) sugar

caster (superfine) sugar, for sprinkling

Day 1

1 Prepare the fruit. Thickly peel and core pineapples, then slice into rings; peel, stone (pit) or core peaches, pears and apples, then halve or cut into thick slices; plums and apricots can be left whole (prick them all over with a fine skewer) or halve and stone; skin and quarter kiwi fruit, or thickly slice; stone cherries.

2 Weigh the fruit, then put in a pan and just cover with water. Bring to the boil and simmer until just tender. Do not overcook because the flavour and shape will be lost; do not undercook because the fruit will be tough when candied.

3 Using a slotted spoon, lift the cooked fruit into a large wide bowl; avoid piling the fruit up high. Retain the cooking liquid.

4 For every 450g/1lb prepared (uncooked) fruit, use 300ml/½ pint/ 1¼ cups of the cooking liquid and 175g/6oz/scant 1 cup sugar. Gently heat the sugar and liquid in a pan, stirring, until the sugar has dissolved, then bring to the boil.

5 Pour the boiling syrup over the fruit, making sure that the fruit is completely immersed. Cover and leave to stand for 24 hours.

Day 2

1 Drain the syrup from the fruit back into a pan, being careful not to damage the fruit as you do so. Return the fruit to the bowl.

2 Add 50g/2oz/¼ cup granulated sugar to the syrup and heat gently, stirring until dissolved completely, then bring to the boil.

3 Pour the hot syrup over the fruit. Allow to cool, then cover and leave to stand for 24 hours.

Days 3–7

Repeat the instructions for day 2 every day for the next 5 days. The concentration of sugar will become much stronger.

Days 8–9

1 Drain the syrup from the fruit into a large wide pan and add 90g/3½oz/½ cup sugar. Heat gently, stirring, until dissolved.

2 Carefully add the fruit to the syrup and simmer gently for about 3 minutes. Return the fruit and syrup to the bowl, cool, then cover and leave to stand for 48 hours.

Days 10–13

Repeat the instructions for days 8–9, leaving the fruit to soak for 4 days rather than 2.

COOK'S TIP

The final soaking stage from days 10–13 can be extended another 6 days, if you like – to a total of 10 days. The longer the fruit is left to soak in the syrup, the sweeter and more intense its flavour will become.

Days 14–15

1 Drain the fruit, discarding the syrup. Carefully spread the fruit out, spacing each piece slightly apart, on a wire rack placed over a baking sheet.

2 Cut a sheet of baking parchment or foil slightly larger than the baking sheet. Using a fine skewer, prick about 12 tiny holes at equal intervals in the sheet.

3 Cover the fruit with the baking parchment or foil, being very careful not to touch the fruit. The parchment or foil is simply to keep off any dust; air should still be able to circulate around the fruit.

4 Leave the fruit in a warm place such as a sunny windowsill or airing cupboard for 2 days, turning each piece of fruit occasionally until all the fruit is thoroughly dry.

5 Sprinkle the fruit with a little caster sugar, then store in an airtight container in single layers between sheets of baking parchment. Eat within 1 year.

COOK'S TIP

Candied fruits are very pretty, retaining the colour of the original fruits. They make great sweetmeats for serving after a meal, particularly at Christmas.

making candied peel

Citrus peel contains less moisture than the fruit, making candying simpler and less time-consuming.

INGREDIENTS

5 small oranges, 6 lemons or 7 limes, or a combination

granulated (white) sugar

caster (superfine) sugar, for sprinkling

1 Scrub the fruit. Remove the peel in quarters, scraping away the pith. Place in a pan, cover with cold water and simmer for 1¼–1½ hours. Drain, reserving 300ml/½ pint/ 1¼ cups of the cooking water.

2 Pour the reserved water into the pan and add 200g/7oz/1 cup sugar. Heat gently, stirring until dissolved, then bring to the boil. Add the peel and simmer for 1 minute. Leave to cool, tip into a bowl, cover and leave for 48 hours.

3 Remove the peel and tip the syrup back into the pan. Add 150g/ 5oz/¾ cup sugar and heat gently, stirring until dissolved. Add the peel, bring to the boil, then simmer until transparent. Cool, tip into a bowl, cover and leave for 2 weeks.

4 Drain the peel, then dry, sprinkle and store in the same way as candied fruit.

making glacé fruit

Glacé, or crystallized, fruit is made from candied fruit, dipped in heavy syrup to give it a glossy coating.

INGREDIENTS

candied fruit

400g/14oz/2 cups granulated (white) sugar

120ml/4fl oz/½ cup water

1 Make sure the candied fruit is dry and dust off any sugar coating. Put the sugar and water in a pan and heat gently, stirring, until the sugar has dissolved. Bring to the boil and simmer for 2 minutes.

2 Pour one-third of the syrup into a small bowl. Fill a second bowl with boiling water. Using a slotted spoon or fork, first dip the fruit into the boiling water for 15 seconds, then shake and dip into the syrup for 15 seconds. Place on a wire rack.

3 Repeat with the remaining fruit, topping up the bowl of syrup when necessary (return the syrup to the boil before doing this).

4 Dry the fruit on wire racks placed over baking sheets in a very warm place for 2–3 days, turning the fruit occasionally. Store in the same way as candied fruit.

preserved sauces and mustards

Also known as "store sauces" these long-keeping sauces are condiments rather than pouring sauces. Often serving up a spicy punch, they are accompaniments for poultry, meat or game, and also pep up gravies and deglazed juices. They can also be whisked into a salad dressing or marinade, or introduced to a basting sauce, especially for a piquant, sweet-sour and caramelized result. The mustards are delicious with plain-cooked sausages and meats, and smoked fish.

moutarde aux fines herbes

This classic, fragrant mustard may be used either as a delicious condiment or for coating meats such as chicken and pork, or oily fish such as mackerel, before cooking.

Makes about 300ml/½ pint/1¼ cups

INGREDIENTS

75g/3oz/scant ½ cup white mustard seeds

50g/2oz/¼ cup soft light brown sugar

5ml/1 tsp salt

5ml/1 tsp whole peppercorns

2.5ml/½ tsp ground turmeric

200ml/7fl oz/scant 1 cup distilled
  malt vinegar

60ml/4 tbsp chopped fresh mixed
  herbs, such as parsley, sage, thyme
  and rosemary

COOK'S TIP

Stir a spoonful of this fragrant mustard into creamy savoury sauces and salad dressings to enhance their flavour.

1 Put the mustard seeds, sugar, salt, whole peppercorns and ground turmeric into a food processor or blender and process for about 1 minute, or until the peppercorns are coarsely chopped.

2 Gradually add the vinegar to the mustard mixture, 15ml/1 tbsp at a time, processing well between each addition, then continue processing until a coarse paste forms.

3 Add the chopped fresh herbs to the mustard and mix well, then leave to stand for 10–15 minutes until the mustard thickens slightly.

4 Spoon the mustard into a 300ml/ ½ pint/1¼ cup sterilized jar. Cover the surface of the mustard with a waxed disc, then seal with a screw-top lid or a cork, and label. Store in a cool, dark place.

Energy 553kcal/2324kJ; Protein 23.4g; Carbohydrate 69.1g, of which sugars 53.4g; Fat 34.5g, of which saturates 1.1g; Cholesterol 3mg; Calcium 374mg; Fibre 2.5g; Sodium 23mg.

honey mustard

Delicious home-made mustards mature to make the most aromatic of condiments. This honey mustard is richly flavoured and is wonderful served with meats and cheeses or stirred into sauces and salad dressings to give an extra, peppery bite.

Makes about 500g/1¼lb

INGREDIENTS

225g/8oz/1 cup mustard seeds

15ml/1 tbsp ground cinnamon

2.5ml/½ tsp ground ginger

300ml/½ pint/1¼ cups white
  wine vinegar

90ml/6 tbsp dark clear honey

COOK'S TIP

Make sure you use well-flavoured clear honey for this recipe. Set (crystallized) honey does not have the right consistency and will not work well.

1 Put the mustard seeds in a bowl with the spices and pour over the vinegar. Stir well to mix, then leave to soak overnight.

2 The next day, put the mustard mixture in a mortar and pound with a pestle, adding the honey very gradually.

3 Continue pounding and mixing until the mustard resembles a stiff paste. If the mixture is too stiff, add a little extra vinegar to achieve the desired consistency.

4 Spoon the mustard into four sterilized jars, seal and label, then store in the refrigerator and use within 4 weeks.

COOK'S TIP

This sweet, spicy mustard is perfect for adding extra flavour to cheese tarts or quiches. Spread a very thin layer of mustard across the base of the pastry case before adding the filling, then bake according to the recipe. The mustard will really complement the cheese, giving a mouth-watering result.

Energy 1276kcal/5345kJ; Protein 65.4g; Carbohydrate 115.3g, of which sugars 68.8g; Fat 101.5g, of which saturates 3.4g; Cholesterol 9mg; Calcium 747mg; Fibre 0g; Sodium 21mg.

spiced tamarind mustard

Tamarind has a distinctive sweet and sour flavour, a dark brown colour and sticky texture. Combined with spices and ground mustard seeds, it makes a wonderful condiment.

Makes about 200g/7oz

INGREDIENTS

115g/4oz tamarind block
150ml/¼ pint/⅔ cup warm water
50g/2oz/¼ cup yellow mustard seeds
25ml/1½ tbsp black or brown
  mustard seeds
10ml/2 tsp clear honey
pinch of ground cardamom
pinch of salt

COOK'S TIP

The mustard will be ready to eat in
3–4 days. It should be stored in a cool,
dark place and used within 4 months.

1 Put the tamarind in a small bowl and pour over the water. Leave to soak for 30 minutes. Mash to a pulp with a fork, then strain through a fine sieve into a bowl.

2 Grind the mustard seeds in a spice mill or coffee grinder and add to the tamarind with the remaining ingredients. Spoon into sterilized jars, cover and seal.

Energy 376kcal/1570kJ; Protein 22.3g; Carbohydrate 24.2g, of which sugars 8.7g; Fat 34.1g, of which saturates 1.1g; Cholesterol 3mg; Calcium 295mg; Fibre 1.3g; Sodium 74mg.

clove-spiced mustard

This spicy mustard is the perfect accompaniment to robust red meats such as sausages and steaks, particularly when they are cooked on the barbecue.

Makes about 300ml/½ pint/1¼ cups

INGREDIENTS

75g/3oz/scant ½ cup white
   mustard seeds
50g/2oz/¼ cup soft light brown sugar
5ml/1 tsp salt
5ml/1 tsp black peppercorns
5ml/1 tsp cloves
5ml/1 tsp turmeric
200ml/7fl oz/scant 1 cup distilled
   malt vinegar

COOK'S TIP

Cloves add a lovely, warming taste to this mustard. Make sure you use whole cloves in this mustard – ground cloves tend to have less flavour.

1 Put all the ingredients except the malt vinegar into a food processor or blender and process. Gradually add the vinegar, 15ml/1 tbsp at a time, processing well between each addition. Continue processing the mustard until it forms a fairly thick, coarse paste.

2 Leave the mustard to stand for 10–15 minutes to thicken slightly. Spoon into a 300ml/½ pint/1¼ cup sterilized jar or several smaller jars, using a funnel. Cover the surface with a waxed paper disc, then seal with a screw-top lid or a cork, and label.

Energy 536kcal/2254kJ; Protein 21.9g; Carbohydrate 67.8g, of which sugars 52.3g; Fat 33.8g, of which saturates 1.1g; Cholesterol 3mg; Calcium 275mg; Fibre 0g; Sodium 1972mg.

kashmir chutney

In the true tradition of the Kashmiri country store, this is a typical family recipe passed down from generation to generation. It is wonderful served with plain or spicy grilled sausages.

Makes about 2.75kg/6lb

INGREDIENTS

1kg/2¼lb green eating apples
15g/½oz garlic cloves
1 litre/1¾ pints/4 cups malt vinegar
450g/1lb dates
115g/4oz preserved stem ginger
450g/1lb/3 cups raisins
450g/1lb/2 cups soft light brown sugar
2.5ml/½ tsp cayenne pepper
30ml/2 tbsp salt

COOK'S TIP

This sweet, chunky, spicy chutney is perfect served with cold meats for an informal buffet lunch.

1 Quarter the apples, remove the cores and chop coarsely. Peel and chop the garlic.

2 Place the apple and garlic in a pan with enough vinegar to cover. Bring to the boil and boil for 10 minutes.

3 Chop the dates and ginger and add them to the pan, together with the rest of the ingredients. Cook gently for 45 minutes.

4 Spoon the mixture into warmed sterilized jars and seal immediately.

Energy 3920kcal/16737kJ; Protein 22.6g; Carbohydrate 1014.4g, of which sugars 1012.2g; Fat 3.3g, of which saturates 0g; Cholesterol 0mg; Calcium 599mg; Fibre 33.7g; Sodium 12139mg.

fiery bengal chutney

Not for timid tastebuds, this fiery chutney is the perfect choice for lovers of hot and spicy food. Although it can be eaten a month after making, it is better matured for longer.

Makes about 2kg/4½lb

INGREDIENTS

115g/4oz fresh root ginger

1kg/2¼lb cooking apples

675g/1½lb onions

6 garlic cloves, finely chopped

225g/8oz/1½ cups raisins

450ml/¾ pint/scant 2 cups malt vinegar

400g/14oz/1¾ cups demerara
  (raw) sugar

2 fresh red chillies

2 fresh green chillies

15ml/1 tbsp salt

5ml/1 tsp turmeric

1 Peel and finely shred the fresh root ginger. Peel, core and roughly chop the apples. Peel and quarter the onions, then slice as thinly as possible. Place in a preserving pan with the garlic, raisins and vinegar.

2 Bring to the boil, then simmer steadily for 15–20 minutes, stirring occasionally, until the apples and onions are thoroughly softened. Add the sugar and stir over a low heat until the sugar has dissolved. Simmer the mixture for about 40 minutes, or until thick and pulpy, stirring frequently towards the end of the cooking time.

3 Halve the chillies and remove the seeds, then slice them finely. (Always wash your hands with soapy water immediately after handling chillies.)

4 Add the chillies to the pan and cook for a further 5–10 minutes, or until no excess liquid remains. Stir in the salt and turmeric.

5 Spoon the chutney into warmed sterilized jars, cover and seal them immediately, then label when cool.

6 Store the chutney in a cool, dark place and leave to mature for at least 2 months before eating. Use within 2 years of making. Once opened, store in the refrigerator and use within 1 month.

Energy 2789kcal/11889kJ; Protein 18.4g; Carbohydrate 717.3g, of which sugars 701.8g; Fat 3.5g, of which saturates 0g; Cholesterol 0mg; Calcium 573mg; Fibre 31.2g; Sodium 6163mg.

pickled peach and chilli chutney

This is a spicy, rich chutney with a succulent texture. It is great served traditional-style, with cold roast meats such as ham, pork or turkey; it is also good with pan-fried chicken served in warm wraps. Try it with ricotta cheese as a filling for pitta bread.

Makes about 450g/1lb

INGREDIENTS

475ml/16fl oz/2 cups cider vinegar

275g/10oz/1¼ cups light muscovado (brown) sugar

225g/8oz/1⅓ cups dried dates, stoned (pitted) and finely chopped

5ml/1 tsp ground allspice

5ml/1 tsp ground mace

450g/1lb ripe peaches, stoned and cut into small chunks

3 onions, thinly sliced

4 fresh red chillies, seeded and finely chopped

4 garlic cloves, crushed

5cm/2in piece fresh root ginger, peeled and finely grated

5ml/1 tsp salt

1 Place the vinegar, sugar, dates, allspice and mace in a large pan and heat gently, stirring, until the sugar has dissolved. Bring to the boil, stirring occasionally.

2 Add the peaches, sliced onions, chopped chillies, crushed garlic, grated ginger and salt, and bring the mixture back to the boil, stirring occasionally.

3 Reduce the heat and simmer for 40–50 minutes, or until the chutney has thickened. Stir frequently to prevent the mixture sticking to the bottom of the pan.

4 Spoon the hot cooked chutney into warmed sterilized jars and seal immediately. When cold, store the jars in a cool, dark place and leave the chutney to mature for at least 2 weeks before eating. Use within 6 months.

COOK'S TIP

To test the consistency of the chutney before bottling, spoon a little of the mixture on to a plate; the chutney should hold its shape.

Energy 2039kcal/8684kJ; Protein 20.9g; Carbohydrate 517.3g, of which sugars 502.9g; Fat 2g, of which saturates 0.2g; Cholesterol 0mg; Calcium 407mg; Fibre 23.6g; Sodium 59mg.

hot yellow plum chutney

It is well worth seeking out yellow plums to make this hot, fragrant chutney. They give it a slightly tart flavour and make it the perfect accompaniment to deep-fried Asian-style snacks such as spring rolls and wontons, or battered vegetables and shellfish.

Makes 1.3kg/3lb

INGREDIENTS

900g/2lb yellow plums, halved and stoned (pitted)

1 onion, finely chopped

7.5cm/3in piece fresh root ginger, peeled and grated

3 whole star anise

350ml/12fl oz/1 ½ cups white wine vinegar

225g/8oz/1 cup soft light brown sugar

5 celery sticks, thinly sliced

3 green chillies, seeded and finely sliced

2 garlic cloves, crushed

1 Put the halved plums, onion, ginger and star anise in a large pan and pour over half the white wine vinegar. Bring to the boil and simmer gently over a low heat for about 30 minutes, or until the plums have softened.

2 Stir the remaining vinegar, sugar, sliced celery, chillies and crushed garlic into the plum mixture. Cook very gently over a low heat, stirring frequently, until the sugar has completely dissolved.

3 Bring the mixture to the boil, then simmer for 45–50 minutes, until there is no excess liquid. Stir frequently during the final stages to prevent the chutney sticking.

4 Spoon the plum chutney into warmed sterilized jars, then cover and seal immediately.

5 Store the chutney in a cool, dark place and allow to mature for at least 1 month before using. Use within 2 years.

COOK'S TIPS

• Once opened, store the chutney in the refrigerator and use within 3 months.

• Be sure to use jars with non-metallic lids to store the chutney.

Energy 1243kcal/5312kJ; Protein 8g; Carbohydrate 320.4g, of which sugars 319g; Fat 1.3g, of which saturates 0g; Cholesterol 0mg; Calcium 313mg; Fibre 16.9g; Sodium 123mg.

bloody mary relish

This fresh-tasting relish with contrasting textures of tomatoes, celery and cucumber is perfect for al fresco *summer eating. For a special occasion, serve it with freshly shucked oysters.*

Makes about 1.3kg/3lb

INGREDIENTS

1.3kg/3lb ripe well-flavoured tomatoes
1 large cucumber
30–45ml/2–3 tbsp salt
2 celery sticks, chopped
2 garlic cloves, peeled and crushed
175ml/6fl oz/¾ cup white wine vinegar
15ml/1 tbsp sugar
60ml/4 tbsp vodka
5ml/1 tsp Tabasco sauce
10ml/2 tsp Worcestershire sauce

COOK'S TIP

To peel the tomatoes, plunge them in a bowl of just-boiled water for 30 seconds. The skins will split and will be easy to peel off.

1 Peel and chop the tomatoes. Peel the cucumber and slice the flesh from around the seeds. Discard the seeds and chop the flesh. Layer the vegetables in a colander placed over a bowl, lightly sprinkling each layer with salt. Cover, put in the refrigerator and leave to drain overnight.

2 The next day, rinse the tomatoes and cucumber thoroughly under cold running water to remove as much salt as possible. Drain well, then place in a pan. (Discard the salty vegetable juices in the bowl.)

3 Add the celery, garlic, vinegar and sugar to the pan and slowly bring to the boil over a low heat.

4 Cook the vegetables, uncovered, for about 30 minutes, stirring occasionally, until the vegetables have softened and most of the liquid has evaporated.

5 Remove the pan from the heat and leave to cool for about 5 minutes. Add the vodka, and Tabasco and Worcestershire sauces and stir well to combine.

6 Spoon the hot relish into warmed sterilized jars, cool, cover and seal. Store in the refrigerator for at least 1 week.

COOK'S TIP

Use the relish within 3 months. Once opened, store it in the refrigerator and use within 1 month.

Energy 430kcal/1814kJ; Protein 13.1g; Carbohydrate 65.6g, of which sugars 65g; Fat 4.5g, of which saturates 1.3g; Cholesterol 0mg; Calcium 233mg; Fibre 16.7g; Sodium 289mg.

yellow pepper and coriander relish

Fresh relishes are quick and easy to make although they do not have a long shelf life. Try this relish with mild, creamy cheeses or with grilled tuna or other firm fish, poultry or meat.

Serves four

INGREDIENTS

1 large yellow (bell) pepper
45ml/3 tbsp sesame oil
1 large mild fresh red chilli
small handful of fresh coriander (cilantro)
salt

1 Seed and coarsely chop the yellow pepper. Heat the oil in a pan, add the pepper and cook, stirring frequently, for 8–10 minutes, until lightly coloured.

2 Meanwhile, seed the chilli, slice it very thinly and set aside. Transfer the pepper to a food processor and process until chopped, but not puréed. Transfer half the pepper to a bowl, leaving the rest in the food processor.

3 Using a sharp knife, chop the fresh coriander, then add it to the mixture in the food processor and process briefly to combine. Tip the mixture into the bowl with the rest of the pepper, add the sliced chilli and stir well to combine.

4 Season the relish with salt to taste and stir well to combine. Cover the bowl with clear film (plastic wrap) and chill in the refrigerator until ready to serve.

COOK'S TIPS

• Red and orange sweet peppers work just as well as yellow, though green peppers are unsuitable as they are not sweet enough in flavour.
• This relish does not keep well, so use within 3 or 4 days of making.
• If you find the flavour of chilli too hot, use only half a chilli and chop into tiny pieces.

Energy 91kcal/374kJ; Protein 0.8g; Carbohydrate 2.9g, of which sugars 2.8g; Fat 8.5g, of which saturates 1.3g; Cholesterol 0mg; Calcium 8mg; Fibre 0.7g; Sodium 3mg.

sweet piccalilli

Undoubtedly one of the most popular relishes, piccalilli can be eaten with grilled sausages, ham or chops, cold meats or a strong, well-flavoured cheese such as Cheddar. It should contain a good selection of fresh crunchy vegetables in a smooth, mustard sauce.

Makes about 1.8kg/4lb

INGREDIENTS

1 large cauliflower

450g/1lb pickling (pearl) onions

900g/2lb mixed vegetables, such as marrow (large zucchini), cucumber, French (green) beans

225g/8oz/1 cup salt

2.4 litres/4 pints/10 cups cold water

200g/7oz/1 cup sugar

2 garlic cloves, peeled and crushed

10ml/2 tsp mustard powder

5ml/1 tsp ground ginger

1 litre/1¾ pints/4 cups distilled (white) vinegar

25g/1oz/¼ cup plain (all-purpose) flour

15ml/1 tbsp turmeric

1 Prepare the vegetables. Divide the cauliflower into small florets; peel and quarter the pickling onions; seed and finely dice the marrow and cucumber; top and tail the French beans, then cut them into 2.5cm/1in lengths.

2 Layer the vegetables in a large glass or stainless steel bowl, generously sprinkling each layer with salt. Pour over the water, cover the bowl with clear film (plastic wrap) and leave to soak for about 24 hours.

3 Drain the soaked vegetables, and discard the brine. Rinse well in several changes of cold water to remove as much salt as possible, then drain them thoroughly.

4 Put the sugar, garlic, mustard, ginger and 900ml/1½ pints/3¾ cups of the vinegar in a preserving pan. Heat gently, stirring occasionally, until the sugar has dissolved.

5 Add the vegetables to the pan, bring to the boil, reduce the heat and simmer for 10–15 minutes, or until they are almost tender.

6 Mix the flour and turmeric with the remaining vinegar and stir into the vegetables. Bring to the boil, stirring, and simmer for 5 minutes, until the piccalilli is thick.

7 Spoon the piccalilli into warmed sterilized jars, cover and seal. Store in a cool, dark place for at least 2 weeks. Use within 1 year.

Energy 1358kcal/5757kJ; Protein 34.1g; Carbohydrate 300.8g, of which sugars 266g; Fat 12g, of which saturates 1.2g; Cholesterol 0mg; Calcium 555mg; Fibre 20.6g; Sodium 4011mg.

corn relish

When golden corn cobs are in season, try preserving their kernels in this delicious relish. It has a lovely crunchy texture and a wonderfully bright, appetizing appearance.

Makes about 1kg/2¼lb

INGREDIENTS

6 large fresh corn on the cob

½ small white cabbage, weighing about 275g/10oz, very finely shredded

2 small onions, halved and very finely sliced

475ml/16fl oz/2 cups distilled malt vinegar

200g/7oz/1 cup golden granulated sugar

1 red (bell) pepper, seeded and finely chopped

5ml/1 tsp salt

15ml/1 tbsp plain (all-purpose) flour

5ml/1 tsp mustard powder

2.5ml/½ tsp turmeric

1 Put the corn cob in a pan of boiling water and cook for 2 minutes. Drain and, when cool enough to handle, use a sharp knife to slice the kernels from the cobs.

2 Put the corn kernels in a pan with the cabbage and onions. Reserve 30ml/2 tbsp of the vinegar, then add the rest to the pan with the sugar. Slowly bring to the boil, stirring occasionally until the sugar dissolves. Simmer for 15 minutes. Add the red pepper and simmer for a further 10 minutes.

3 Blend the salt, flour, mustard and turmeric with the reserved vinegar to make a smooth paste.

4 Stir the paste into the vegetable mixture and bring back to the boil. Simmer for 5 minutes, until the mixture has thickened.

5 Spoon the relish into warmed sterilized jars, cover and seal. Store in a cool dark place. Use within 6 months of making. Once opened, store in the refrigerator and use within 2 months.

COOK'S TIP

This tangy relish is the perfect barbecue preserve. It is perfect for enlivening barbecued meats such as chicken, sausages and burgers.

Energy 1479kcal/6291kJ; Protein 20.3g; Carbohydrate 356.7g, of which sugars 275.1g; Fat 6.4g, of which saturates 1g; Cholesterol 0mg; Calcium 307mg; Fibre 15.5g; Sodium 3086mg.

pineapple relish

This fruity sweet-and-sour relish is excellent with grilled chicken, gammon, sausages or bacon.
It is not a long-keeping preserve but a clever 'fresh' relish made with canned pineapple.

Serves four

INGREDIENTS

400g/14oz can crushed pineapple in
  natural juice
30ml/2 tbsp light muscovado (brown)
  sugar
30ml/2 tbsp wine vinegar
1 garlic clove, finely chopped
4 spring onions (scallions), finely chopped
2 red chillies, seeded and chopped
10 fresh basil leaves, finely shredded
salt and ground black pepper

VARIATION

This relish can be made with fresh
pineapple: remove the leafy top, peel
and eyes, and cut out the core. Then
chop the fruit, reserving all juices.

1 Drain the pineapple and reserve
60ml/4 tbsp of the juice.

2 Place the juice in a small pan
with the sugar and vinegar. Heat
gently, stirring, until the sugar
dissolves. Remove from the heat
and season with salt and pepper.

3 Place the pineapple, garlic, spring
onions and chillies in a bowl. Mix
well and stir in the juice. Allow to
cool for at least 5 minutes.

4 Taste the relish for seasoning
when cool. Stir in the basil just
before serving.

Energy 83kcal/351kJ; Protein 1g; Carbohydrate 20.6g, of which sugars 20.6g; Fat 0.2g, of which saturates 0g; Cholesterol 0mg; Calcium 22mg; Fibre 0.7g; Sodium 4mg.

toffee onion relish

Slow, gentle cooking reduces onions to a soft, caramelized golden brown in this recipe. This sweet relish complements mature cheese, savoury tarts or quiches, and will keep for a week.

Serves four

INGREDIENTS

3 large onions
50g/2oz/¼ cup butter
30ml/2 tbsp olive oil
30ml/2 tbsp light muscovado (brown) sugar
30ml/2 tbsp pickled capers
30ml/2 tbsp chopped fresh parsley
salt and ground black pepper

COOK'S TIP

Choose a heavy pan that does not burn easily to cook the relish – this is essential for an evenly browned toffee mixture that does not begin to burn.

1 Peel the onions and cut them in half vertically, down through the core, then slice them thinly. Keep the slices as even as possible – they will cook and brown evenly, and the relish will have a good texture.

2 Heat the butter and oil together in a large, heavy-based saucepan. Add the sliced onions and sugar. Then cook very gently for about 30 minutes over a low heat, stirring occasionally, until the onions are reduced to a soft rich-brown, toffee-like mixture.

3 Roughly chop the capers and stir into the browned onion mixture. Allow to cool completely and transfer to a bowl.

4 Stir in the chopped parsley and add salt and freshly ground black pepper to taste. Cover and chill until ready to serve.

VARIATION

Make this recipe with red (Italian) onions or shallots for a subtly different flavour.

Energy 239kcal/992kJ; Protein 2.6g; Carbohydrate 22.1g, of which sugars 18g; Fat 16.3g, of which saturates 7.3g; Cholesterol 27mg; Calcium 75mg; Fibre 3.1g; Sodium 86mg.

cool cucumber and green tomato relish

This is a great way to use up those green tomatoes that seem as though they're never going to ripen. Combined with cucumber, they make a pale green relish that is good for barbecues.

Makes about 1.6kg/3½lb

INGREDIENTS

2 cucumbers

900g/2lb green (unripe) tomatoes

4 onions

7.5ml/1½ tsp salt

350ml/12fl oz/1½ cups distilled (white) vinegar

150g/5oz/scant ¾ cup demerara (raw) sugar

200g/7oz/1 cup sugar

15ml/1 tbsp plain (all-purpose) flour

2.5ml/½ tsp mustard powder

1 Wash the cucumbers and green tomatoes. Cut into 1cm/½in cubes. Peel and finely chop the onions.

2 Layer the vegetables in a strainer or colander placed over a bowl, lightly sprinkling each layer with salt, then cover and leave to drain for at least 6 hours, or overnight.

3 Discard the salty liquid and tip the salted vegetables into a large heavy pan. Reserve 30ml/2 tbsp of the vinegar and add the rest to the pan with the demerara and granulated sugars.

4 Slowly bring the vegetable mixture to the boil, stirring occasionally until the sugar has dissolved completely. Reduce the heat slightly and cook, uncovered, for about 30 minutes, or until the vegetables are tender.

5 In a small bowl, blend the flour and mustard to a paste with the reserved vinegar. Stir the mixture into the relish and simmer for about 20 minutes, or until the mixture is very thick.

6 Spoon the relish into warmed sterilized jars, cover and seal. Store in a cool, dark place for at least 1 week. Use the relish within 6 months. Once opened, keep in the refrigerator and use within 2 months.

Energy 1803kcal/7668kJ; Protein 18.3g; Carbohydrate 450.8g, of which sugars 427.5g; Fat 4.3g, of which saturates 0.9g; Cholesterol 0mg; Calcium 467mg; Fibre 18.9g; Sodium 129mg.

malay mixed vegetable relish

This traditional, full-flavoured relish, with its crunchy texture and spicy kick, is known as acar kuning *in Malaysia. It is served in very generous portions, almost like a side salad.*

Makes about 900g/2lb

INGREDIENTS

12 small pickling (pearl) onions, quartered

225g/8oz French (green) beans, cut into 2.5cm/1in lengths

225g/8oz carrots, cut into 2.5cm/1in long thin sticks

225g/8oz cauliflower, cut into small florets

5ml/1 tsp mustard powder

5ml/1 tsp salt

10ml/2 tsp sugar

60ml/4 tbsp sesame seeds

For the spice paste

2 shallots, finely chopped

2 garlic cloves, crushed

2 fresh green chillies, seeded and finely chopped

115g/4oz/1 cup dry-roasted peanuts

5ml/1 tsp turmeric

5ml/1 tsp chilli powder

60ml/4 tbsp distilled (white) vinegar

30ml/2 tbsp vegetable oil

175ml/6fl oz/¾ cup boiling water

1 Make the spice paste. Put the shallots, garlic, chillies, peanuts, turmeric, chilli powder, vinegar and oil in a food processor or blender and process to a fairly smooth paste.

2 Transfer the mixture to a large heavy pan and slowly bring to the boil. Reduce the heat and simmer gently for 2 minutes, stirring all the time. Gradually stir in the water and simmer the mixture for a further 3 minutes.

3 Add the onions to the pan, cover and simmer for 5 minutes, then add the beans and carrots. Cover the pan again and cook for a further 3 minutes.

4 Finally, add the cauliflower, mustard, salt and sugar to the pan and simmer, uncovered, for about 5 minutes, or until the vegetables are tender and have absorbed most of the sauce. Remove the pan from the heat and set aside to cool for a few minutes.

5 Meanwhile, toast the sesame seeds in a non-stick pan over a medium heat until golden, stirring frequently. Stir the seeds into the vegetable mixture.

6 Spoon the relish into warmed sterilized jars, cover and seal. Leave until completely cold, then store in the refrigerator.

COOK'S TIP

The relish can be served immediately and should be used within 4 weeks.

Energy 1200kcal/4978kJ; Protein 48g; Carbohydrate 77.7g, of which sugars 57.8g; Fat 79.6g, of which saturates 13.5g; Cholesterol 0mg; Calcium 348mg; Fibre 27.4g; Sodium 92mg.

carrot and almond relish

This is a Middle Eastern classic, usually made with long fine strands of carrot, available from many supermarkets. Alternatively, grate large carrots lengthways on a medium grater.

2 Put the lemon juice, vinegar, water, honey and salt in a jug (pitcher) and stir until the salt has dissolved. Pour over the carrot mixture. Mix well, cover and leave in the refrigerator for 4 hours.

3 Transfer the chilled mixture to a preserving pan. Slowly bring to the boil, then reduce the heat and simmer for 15 minutes until the carrots and ginger are tender.

4 Increase the heat and boil for 15 minutes, or until most of the liquid has evaporated and the mixture is thick. Stir frequently towards the end of the cooking time to prevent the mixture from sticking to the pan.

5 Put the almonds in a frying pan and toast over a low heat until just beginning to colour. Gently stir into the relish, taking care not to break the almonds.

Makes about 675g/1½lb

INGREDIENTS

15ml/1 tbsp coriander seeds
500g/1¼lb carrots, grated
50g/2oz fresh root ginger,
 finely shredded
200g/7oz/1 cup caster (superfine) sugar
finely grated rind and juice
 of 1 lemon
120ml/4fl oz/½ cup white wine vinegar
75ml/5 tbsp water
30ml/2 tbsp clear honey
7.5ml/1½ tsp salt
50g/2oz/½ cup flaked (sliced) almonds

1 Crush the coriander seeds using a mortar and pestle. Put them in a bowl with the carrots, ginger, sugar and lemon rind and mix together well to combine.

6 Spoon the relish into warmed sterilized jars, cover and seal. Leave for at least 1 month and use within 18 months. Once opened, store in the refrigerator.

Energy 1359kcal/5743kJ; Protein 14.9g; Carbohydrate 275.3g, of which sugars 271.5g; Fat 29.5g, of which saturates 2.7g; Cholesterol 0mg; Calcium 374mg; Fibre 16.3g; Sodium 3125mg.

lemon and garlic relish

This powerful relish is flavoured with North African spices and punchy preserved lemons, which are widely available in Middle Eastern stores. It is great served with Moroccan tagines.

Serves six

INGREDIENTS

45ml/3 tbsp olive oil

3 large red onions, sliced

2 heads of garlic, separated into cloves and peeled

10ml/2 tsp coriander seeds, crushed

10ml/2 tsp light muscovado (brown) sugar, plus a little extra

pinch of saffron threads

5cm/2in piece cinnamon stick

2–3 small whole dried red chillies (optional)

2 fresh bay leaves

30–45ml/2–3 tbsp sherry vinegar

juice of ½ small orange

30ml/2 tbsp chopped preserved lemon

salt and ground black pepper

1 Gently heat the oil in a large heavy pan. Add the onions and stir, then cover and cook on the lowest setting for 10–15 minutes, stirring occasionally, until soft.

2 Add the garlic cloves and the coriander seeds. Cover and cook for 5–8 minutes, until soft.

3 Add a pinch of salt, lots of ground black pepper and the sugar to the onions and cook, uncovered, for a further 5 minutes.

4 Soak the saffron threads in about 45ml/3 tbsp warm water for 5 minutes, then add to the onions, with the soaking water. Add the cinnamon stick, dried chillies, if using, and bay leaves. Stir in 30ml/2 tbsp of the sherry vinegar and the orange juice.

5 Cook very gently, uncovered, until the onions are very soft and most of the liquid evaporated. Stir in the preserved lemon and cook gently for 5 minutes.

6 Taste the relish and adjust the seasoning, adding more salt, sugar and/or vinegar to taste.

7 Serve warm or cold (not hot or chilled). The relish tastes best if left to stand for 24 hours.

COOK'S TIP

You can store the relish in a tightly covered bowl or jar for up to a week in the refrigerator. Allow it to stand at room temperature for about an hour before serving.

Energy 102kcal/422kJ; Protein 1.9g; Carbohydrate 11.4g, of which sugars 7.8g; Fat 5.8g, of which saturates 0.8g; Cholesterol 0mg; Calcium 28mg; Fibre 1.8g; Sodium 4mg.

papaya and lemon relish

This chunky relish is best made with a firm, unripe papaya. Leave for a week before eating to allow all the flavours to mellow. Serve with roast meats or with a robust cheese and crackers.

2 Bring the liquid to the boil, then immediately lower the heat and allow to simmer for 10 minutes.

3 Add all the remaining ingredients to the pan and bring to the boil, stirring all the time. Check that all the sugar has dissolved, then lower the heat and simmer for 50–60 minutes, or until the relish is thick and syrupy.

Makes about 450g/1lb

INGREDIENTS

1 large unripe papaya
1 onion, thinly sliced
40g/1½ oz/⅓ cup raisins
250ml/8fl oz/1 cup red wine vinegar
juice of 2 lemons
150ml/¼ pint/⅔ cup elderflower cordial
150g/5oz/¾ cup golden granulated sugar
1 cinnamon stick
1 fresh bay leaf
2.5ml/½ tsp hot paprika
2.5ml/½ tsp salt

1 Peel the papaya and cut in half lengthways. Remove the seeds with a teaspoon. Use a sharp knife to cut the flesh into small chunks and place them in a saucepan. Add the onion slices and raisins, then stir in the red wine vinegar.

4 Remove and discard the bay leaf. Ladle the relish into hot, sterilized jars. Seal and label, and store in a cool, dark place for 1 week before using. Keep the relish chilled after opening.

COOK'S TIP

The seeds of papaya have a peppery taste and are good in a salad dressing.

Energy 1069kcal/4559kJ; Protein 5g; Carbohydrate 277.9g, of which sugars 276.5g; Fat 0.8g, of which saturates 0g; Cholesterol 0mg; Calcium 241mg; Fibre 12.6g; Sodium 72mg.

mango and papaya relish

Brightly coloured pieces of dried papaya add flavour and texture to this anise-spiced mango preserve. The fruit is cooked for only a short time to retain its juicy texture and fresh flavour.

Makes about 800g/1¾lb

INGREDIENTS

115g/4oz/½ cup dried papaya

30ml/2 tbsp orange or
  apple juice

2 large slightly under-ripe mangoes

2 shallots, very finely sliced

4cm/1½in piece fresh root
  ginger, grated

1 garlic clove, crushed

2 whole star anise

150ml/¼ pint/⅔ cup cider vinegar

75g/3oz/scant ½ cup light muscovado
  (brown) sugar

1.5ml/¼ tsp salt

1 Using a sharp knife or scissors, roughly chop the papaya and place in a small bowl. Sprinkle over the orange or apple juice and leave to soak for at least 10 minutes.

2 Meanwhile, peel and slice the mangoes, cutting the flesh away from the stone (pit) in large slices. Cut into 1cm/½in chunks, then set the flesh aside.

3 Put the sliced shallots, ginger, garlic and star anise in a large pan. Pour over the vinegar. Slowly bring to the boil, then reduce the heat, cover and simmer for 5 minutes, or until the shallots are just beginning to soften.

4 Add the sugar and salt to the pan and stir over a low heat until dissolved. When the mixture is simmering, add the papaya and mango and cook for a further 20 minutes, or until the fruit is just tender and the relish mixture has reduced and thickened.

5 Allow the relish to cool for about 5 minutes, then spoon into warmed sterilized jars. Allow to cool completely before covering and sealing. Store in a cool, dark place and use within 3 months of making. Once opened, keep the jars in the refrigerator and use within 1 month.

Energy 621kcal/2654kJ; Protein 4.6g; Carbohydrate 158.5g, of which sugars 157.6g; Fat 1g, of which saturates 0.3g; Cholesterol 0mg; Calcium 171mg; Fibre 16.6g; Sodium 623mg.

cranberry and red onion relish

This wine-enriched relish is perfect for serving with hot roast turkey at Christmas or Thanksgiving. It can be made several months in advance of the festive season.

Makes about 900g/2lb

INGREDIENTS

450g/1lb small red (Italian) onions
30ml/2 tbsp olive oil
225g/8oz/1 cup soft light
  brown sugar
450g/1lb/4 cups fresh or
  frozen cranberries
120ml/4fl oz/½ cup red wine vinegar
120ml/4fl oz/½ cup red wine
15ml/1 tbsp mustard seeds
2.5ml/½ tsp ground ginger
30ml/2 tbsp orange liqueur or port
salt and ground black pepper

1 Halve and thinly slice the red onions. Heat the oil in a large pan, add the onions and cook gently for about 15 minutes, stirring often, until softened. Add 30ml/2 tbsp of the sugar. Cook for 5 minutes, or until the onions are caramelized.

2 Meanwhile, put the cranberries in a pan with the remaining sugar, and the vinegar, red wine, mustard seeds and ginger. Heat gently until the sugar has dissolved. Bring to the boil, reduce the heat and cover.

3 Simmer the relish mixture for 12–15 minutes, until the berries have burst and are tender, then stir in the caramelized onions.

4 Increase the heat slightly and cook uncovered for a further 10 minutes, stirring the mixture frequently until it is well reduced and thickened. Remove the pan from the heat, then season with salt and pepper to taste.

5 Transfer the relish to warmed sterilized jars. Spoon a little of the orange liqueur or port over the top of each, then cover and seal. Store in a cool place for up to 6 months. Store in the refrigerator once opened and use within 1 month.

COOK'S TIP

It is important to cover the pan when cooking the cranberries because they can sometimes pop out of the pan during cooking and are very hot.

VARIATION

Redcurrants work well instead of cranberries – they produce a relish with a slightly less tart flavour and a very pretty colour.

Energy 1532kcal/6486kJ; Protein 8g; Carbohydrate 314.6g, of which sugars 304.2g; Fat 23.3g, of which saturates 3.1g; Cholesterol 0mg; Calcium 259mg; Fibre 13.5g; Sodium 46mg.

sweet and sour pineapple relish

This simple preserve is an excellent condiment for perking up grilled chicken or bacon chops. Using canned pineapple means it can be made mainly from store-cupboard ingredients.

Makes about 675g/1½lb

INGREDIENTS

2 x 400g/14oz cans pineapple rings
  or pieces in natural juice

1 lemon

115g/4oz/½ cup sugar

45ml/3 tbsp white wine vinegar

6 spring onions (scallions),
  finely chopped

2 fresh red chillies, seeded and
  finely chopped

salt and ground black pepper

1 Drain the pineapple, reserving 120ml/4fl oz/½ cup of the juice. Pour the juice into a preserving pan. Finely chop the pineapple, if necessary, and place in a sieve (strainer) set over a bowl.

2 Pare a strip of rind from the lemon. Squeeze the lemon juice and add to the pan with the lemon rind, sugar and vinegar.

3 Heat over a low heat, stirring occasionally, until the sugar has dissolved, then bring to the boil. Cook, uncovered, over a medium heat for about 10 minutes, or until the sauce has thickened slightly.

4 Add the chopped onions and chillies to the pan, together with any juice that has been drained from the chopped pineapple.

5 Cook the sauce for 5 minutes, until thick and syrupy, stirring frequently towards the end of the cooking time.

6 Increase the heat slightly, add the pineapple and cook for about 4 minutes, or until most of the liquid has evaporated. Season.

7 Spoon the relish into warmed sterilized jars, cover and seal. Store in the refrigerator and eat within 3 months of making.

Energy 859kcal/3659kJ; Protein 4.7g; Carbohydrate 222.8g, of which sugars 222.5g; Fat 0.5g, of which saturates 0.1g; Cholesterol 0mg; Calcium 152mg; Fibre 5.7g; Sodium 21mg.

plum and cherry relish

This luxurious sweet-sour fruity relish complements rich poultry, game or meat, including roast duck or grilled duck breasts. Sieve a few spoonfuls into a sauce or gravy to add fruity zest and flavour, as well as for uplifting colour when a sauce looks a little dull.

Makes about 350g/12oz

INGREDIENTS

350g/12oz dark-skinned red plums

350g/12oz/2 cups cherries

2 shallots, finely chopped

15ml/1 tbsp olive oil

30ml/2 tbsp dry sherry

60ml/4 tbsp red wine vinegar

15ml/1 tbsp balsamic vinegar

1 bay leaf

90g/3½oz/scant ½ cup demerara (raw) sugar

1 Halve and stone (pit) the plums, then roughly chop the flesh. Stone all the cherries.

2 Cook the shallots gently in the oil for 5 minutes, or until soft. Add the fruit, sherry, vinegars, bay leaf and sugar.

3 Slowly bring the mixture to the boil, stirring until the sugar has dissolved completely. Increase the heat and cook briskly for about 15 minutes, or until the relish is very thick and the fruit tender.

4 Remove the bay leaf and spoon the relish into warmed sterilized jars. Cover and seal. Store the relish in the refrigerator and use within 3 months.

Energy 804kcal/3407kJ; Protein 6.5g; Carbohydrate 170.3g, of which sugars 168.9g; Fat 11.8g, of which saturates 1.6g; Cholesterol 0mg; Calcium 156mg; Fibre 9.6g; Sodium 21mg.

nectarine relish

This sweet and tangy fruit relish goes very well with hot roast meats such as pork and game birds such as guinea fowl and pheasant. Make it while nectarines are plentiful and keep tightly covered in the refrigerator to serve for Christmas, or even to give as a seasonal gift.

Makes about 450g/1lb

INGREDIENTS

45ml/3 tbsp olive oil

2 Spanish (Bermuda) onions, thinly sliced

1 fresh green chilli, seeded and finely chopped

5ml/1 tsp finely chopped fresh rosemary

2 bay leaves

450g/1lb nectarines, stoned (pitted) and cut into chunks

150g/5oz/1 cup raisins

10ml/2 tsp crushed coriander seeds

350g/12oz/1½ cups demerara (raw) sugar

200ml/7fl oz/scant 1 cup red wine vinegar

1 Heat the oil in a large pan. Add the onions, chilli, rosemary and bay leaves. Cook, stirring frequently, for about 15 minutes, or until the onions are soft.

COOK'S TIP
Pots of this relish make lovely gifts. Store it in pretty jars and add colourful labels identifying the relish, and reminding the recipient that it should be stored in the refrigerator, and when it should be used by.

2 Add the nectarines, raisins, coriander seeds, sugar and vinegar to the pan, then slowly bring to the boil, stirring frequently.

3 Reduce the heat under the pan and simmer gently for 1 hour, or until the relish is thick and sticky. Stir occasionally during cooking, and more frequently towards the end of cooking time to prevent the relish sticking to the pan.

4 Spoon the relish into warmed, sterilized jars and seal. Leave the jars to cool completely, then store in the refrigerator. The relish will keep well in the refrigerator for up to 5 months.

Energy 2408kcal/10211kJ; Protein 16g; Carbohydrate 541.8g, of which sugars 532.6g; Fat 34.8g, of which saturates 4.7g; Cholesterol 0mg; Calcium 386mg; Fibre 14g; Sodium 128mg.

pickles and preserved fruits

Pickles are king of the preserves, and this selection of savoury and sweet items draws on culinary traditions from all over the world. There are sweet-sour fruits to enhance hot or cold meats or cheese, or spiced fruit and vegetables to complement Asian or Middle-Eastern main courses. Italian-style pickled vegetables make appetizing first courses, plus you have the classics: pickled cucumbers, sweet onions, dill pickles, and delicious fruits preserved in alcohol.

dill pickles

Redolent of garlic and piquant with fresh chilli, salty dill pickles can be supple and succulent or crisp and crunchy. Every pickle aficionado has a favourite type.

Makes about 900g/2lb

INGREDIENTS

20 small, ridged or knobbly pickling (small) cucumbers
2 litres/3½ pints/8 cups water
175g/6oz/¾ cup coarse sea salt
15–20 garlic cloves, unpeeled
2 bunches fresh dill
15ml/1 tbsp dill seeds
30ml/2 tbsp mixed pickling spice
1 or 2 hot fresh chillies

1 Scrub the cucumbers and rinse well in cold water. Leave to dry.

2 Put the measured water and salt in a large pan and bring to the boil. Turn off the heat and leave to cool to room temperature.

3 Using the flat side of a knife blade or a wooden mallet, lightly crush each garlic clove, breaking the papery skin.

4 Pack the cucumbers tightly into one or two wide-necked, sterilized jars, layering them with the garlic, fresh dill, dill seeds and pickling spice. Add one chilli to each jar. Pour over the cooled brine, making sure that the cucumbers are completely covered. Tap the jars on the work surface to dispel any trapped air bubbles.

5 Cover the jars with lids and then leave to stand at room temperature for 4–7 days before serving. Store in the refrigerator.

COOK'S TIP

If you cannot find ridged or knobbly pickling (small) cucumbers, use any kind of small cucumbers instead.

Energy 45kcal/180kJ; Protein 3.1g; Carbohydrate 6.8g, of which sugars 6.3g; Fat 0.5g, of which saturates 0g; Cholesterol 0mg; Calcium 83mg; Fibre 2.7g; Sodium 5909mg.

pickled mushrooms with garlic

This method of preserving mushrooms is popular throughout Europe. The pickle is good made with cultivated mushrooms, but it is worth including a couple of sliced ceps for their flavour.

Makes about 900g/2lb

INGREDIENTS

500g/1¼lb/8 cups mixed mushrooms, such as small ceps, chestnut mushrooms, shiitake and girolles

300ml/½ pint/1¼ cups white wine vinegar or cider vinegar

15ml/1 tbsp sea salt

5ml/1 tsp caster (superfine) sugar

300ml/½ pint/1¼ cups water

4–5 fresh bay leaves

8 large fresh thyme sprigs

15 garlic cloves, peeled, halved, with any green shoots removed

1 small red (Italian) onion, halved and thinly sliced

2–3 small dried red chillies

5ml/1 tsp coriander seeds, lightly crushed

5ml/1 tsp black peppercorns

a few strips of lemon rind

250–350ml/8–12fl oz/1–1½ cups extra virgin olive oil

1 Trim and wipe the mushrooms and cut any large ones in half.

2 Put the vinegar, salt, sugar and water in a pan and bring to the boil. Add the bay leaves, thyme, garlic, onion, chillies, coriander seeds, peppercorns and lemon rind and simmer for 2 minutes.

3 Add the mushrooms to the pan and simmer for 3–4 minutes. Drain the mushrooms through a seive, retaining all the herbs and spices, then set aside for a few minutes more until the mushrooms are thoroughly drained.

4 Fill one large or two small cool sterilized jars with the mushrooms. Distribute the garlic, onion, herbs and spices evenly among the layers of mushrooms, then add enough olive oil to cover by at least 1cm/½in. You may need to use extra oil if you are making two jars.

5 Leave the pickle to settle, then tap the jars on the work surface to dispel any air bubbles. Seal the jars, then store in the refrigerator. Use within 2 weeks.

Energy 579kcal/2392kJ; Protein 9g; Carbohydrate 7.2g, of which sugars 6.2g; Fat 57.4g, of which saturates 8.4g; Cholesterol 0mg; Calcium 33mg; Fibre 5.5g; Sodium 25mg.

pickled red cabbage

This delicately spiced and vibrant-coloured pickle is an old-fashioned favourite to serve with bread and cheese for an informal lunch, or to use to accompany cold ham, duck or goose.

Makes about 1–1.6kg/2¼–3½lb

INGREDIENTS

675g/1½lb/6 cups red
  cabbage, shredded

1 large Spanish onion, sliced

30ml/2 tbsp sea salt

600ml/1 pint/2½ cups red wine vinegar

75g/3oz/6 tbsp light muscovado
  (brown) sugar

15ml/1 tbsp coriander seeds

3 cloves

2.5cm/1in piece fresh root ginger

1 whole star anise

2 bay leaves

4 eating apples

1 Put the cabbage and onion in a bowl, add the salt and mix well until thoroughly combined. Tip the mixture into a colander over a bowl and leave to drain overnight.

2 The next day, rinse the salted vegetables, drain well and pat dry using kitchen paper.

3 Pour the vinegar into a pan, add the sugar, spices and bay leaves and bring to the boil. Remove from the heat and leave to cool.

4 Core and chop the apples, then layer with the cabbage and onions in sterilized preserving jars. Pour over the cooled spiced vinegar. (If you prefer a milder pickle, strain out the spices first). Seal the jars and store for 1 week before eating. Eat within 2 months. Once opened, store in the refrigerator.

Energy 674kcal/2869kJ; Protein 12g; Carbohydrate 161.4g, of which sugars 159.3g; Fat 2g, of which saturates 0g; Cholesterol 0mg; Calcium 406mg; Fibre 23g; Sodium 64mg.

pickled turnips and beetroot

This delicious pickle is a Middle Eastern speciality. The turnips turn a rich red in their beetroot-spiked brine and look gorgeous stacked on shelves in the storecupboard.

2 Put the salt and water in a bowl, stir and leave to stand until the salt has completely dissolved.

3 Sprinkle the beetroot with lemon juice and place in the bottom of four 1.2 litre/2 pint sterilized jars. Top with sliced turnip, packing them in very tightly, then pour over the brine, making sure that the vegetables are covered.

4 Seal the jars and leave in a cool place for 7 days before serving.

Makes about 1.6kg/3½lb

INGREDIENTS

1kg/2¼lb young turnips
3–4 raw beetroot (beets)
about 45ml/3 tbsp coarse sea salt
about 1.5 litres/2½ pints/6¼ cups water
juice of 1 lemon

COOK'S TIP

Be careful when preparing the beetroot because their bright red juice can stain clothing.

1 Wash the turnips and beetroot, but do not peel them, then cut into slices about 5mm/¼in thick.

Energy 338kcal/1442kJ; Protein 14.1g; Carbohydrate 69.8g, of which sugars 66g; Fat 3.3g, of which saturates 0g; Cholesterol 0mg; Calcium 541mg; Fibre 29.7g; Sodium 4278mg.

english pickled onions

These powerful pickles are traditionally served with a plate of cold meats and bread and cheese. They should be made with malt vinegar and stored for at least 6 weeks before eating.

Makes about four jars

INGREDIENTS

1kg/2¼lb pickling onions
115g/4oz/½ cup salt
750ml/1¼ pints/3 cups malt vinegar
15ml/1 tbsp sugar
2–3 dried red chillies
5ml/1 tsp brown mustard seeds
15ml/1 tbsp coriander seeds
5ml/1 tsp allspice berries
5ml/1 tsp black peppercorns
5cm/2in piece fresh root ginger, sliced
2–3 blades mace
2–3 fresh bay leaves

1 To peel the onions, trim off the root ends, but leave the onion layers attached. Cut a thin slice off the top (neck) end of the onion. Place the onions in a bowl, then cover with boiling water. Leave to stand for about 4 minutes, then drain. The skin should then be easy to peel using a small, sharp knife.

2 Place the peeled onions in a bowl and cover with cold water, then drain the water into a large pan. Add the salt and heat slightly to dissolve it, then cool before pouring the brine over the onions.

3 Place a plate inside the top of the bowl and weigh it down slightly so that it keeps all the onions submerged in the brine. Leave to stand for 24 hours.

4 Meanwhile, place the vinegar in a large pan. Wrap all the remaining ingredients, except the bay leaves, in a piece of muslin (cheesecloth). Bring to the boil, simmer for about 5 minutes, then remove the pan from the heat. Set aside and leave to infuse overnight.

5 The next day, drain the onions, rinse and pat dry. Pack them into sterilized 450g/1lb jars. Add some or all of the spice from the vinegar, except the ginger slices. The pickle will become hotter if you add the chillies. Pour the vinegar over to cover and add the bay leaves. (Store leftover vinegar in a bottle for another batch of pickles.)

6 Seal the jars with non-metallic lids and store in a cool, dark place for at least 6 weeks before eating.

Energy 105kcal/438kJ; Protein 3g; Carbohydrate 23.7g, of which sugars 17.9g; Fat 0.5g, of which saturates 0g; Cholesterol 0mg; Calcium 65mg; Fibre 3.5g; Sodium 8mg.

instant pickle of mixed vegetables

This fresh, salad-style pickle doesn't need lengthy storing so makes the perfect choice if you need a bowl of pickle immediately. However, it does not have good storing properties.

Makes about 450g/1lb

INGREDIENTS

½ cauliflower head, cut into florets

2 carrots, sliced

2 celery sticks, thinly sliced

¼–½ white cabbage, thinly sliced

115g/4oz/scant 1 cup runner (green) beans, cut into bitesize pieces

6 garlic cloves, sliced

1–4 fresh chillies, whole or sliced

5cm/2in piece fresh root ginger, sliced

1 red (bell) pepper, sliced

2.5ml/½ tsp turmeric

105ml/7 tbsp white wine vinegar

15–30ml/1–2 tbsp granulated (white) sugar

60–90ml/4–6 tbsp olive oil

juice of 2 lemons

salt

1 Toss the cauliflower, carrots, celery, cabbage, beans, garlic, chillies, ginger and pepper with salt and leave them to stand in a colander over a bowl for 4 hours.

2 Shake the vegetables well to remove any excess juices.

3 Transfer the salted vegetables to a bowl. Add the turmeric, vinegar, sugar to taste, oil and lemon juice. Toss to combine, then add enough water to distribute the flavours. Cover the bowl and leave to chill for at least 1 hour, or until you are ready to serve.

Energy 776kcal/3211kJ; Protein 19.1g; Carbohydrate 42.5g, of which sugars 38.3g; Fat 59.6g, of which saturates 8.7g; Cholesterol 0mg; Calcium 302mg; Fibre 17.8g; Sodium 109mg.

preserved lemons

These richly flavoured fruits are widely used in Middle Eastern cooking. Only the rind, which contains the essential flavour of the lemon is used in recipes. Traditionally whole lemons are preserved, but this recipe uses wedges, which can be packed into jars more easily.

2 Pack the salted lemon wedges into two 1.2 litre/2 pint/5 cup warmed sterilized jars. To each jar, add 30–45ml/2–3 tbsp sea salt and half the lemon juice, then top up with boiling water to cover the lemon wedges. Seal the jars and leave to stand for 2–4 weeks before using.

3 To use, rinse the preserved lemons well to remove some of the salty flavour, then pull off and discard the flesh. Cut the lemon rind into strips or leave in chunks and use as desired.

Makes about two jars

INGREDIENTS

10 unwaxed lemons

about 200ml/7fl oz/scant 1 cup fresh lemon juice or a combination of fresh and preserved juice

boiling water

sea salt

COOK'S TIP

The salty, well-flavoured juice that is used to preserve the lemons can be used to flavour salad dressings or added to hot sauces.

1 Wash the lemons well and cut each into six to eight wedges. Press a generous amount of salt on to the cut surface of each wedge.

Energy 95kcal/395kJ; Protein 5g; Carbohydrate 16g, of which sugars 16g; Fat 1.5g, of which saturates 0.5g; Cholesterol 0mg; Calcium 425mg; Fibre 0g; Sodium 25mg.

pickled limes

This hot, pungent pickle comes from the Punjab in India. Salting softens the rind and intensifies the flavour of the limes, while they mature in the first month or two of storage. Pickled limes are extremely salty so are best served with slightly under-seasoned dishes.

Makes about 1kg/2¼lb

INGREDIENTS

1kg/2¼lb unwaxed limes
75g/3oz/⅓ cup salt
seeds from 6 green cardamom pods
6 whole cloves
5ml/1 tsp cumin seeds
4 fresh red chillies, seeded
  and sliced
5cm/2in piece fresh root ginger, peeled
  and finely shredded
450g/1lb/2¼ cups preserving or
  granulated (white) sugar

1 Put the limes in a large bowl and pour over cold water to cover. Leave to soak for 8 hours, or overnight, if preferred.

2 The next day, remove the limes from the water. Using a sharp knife, cut each lime in half from end to end, then cut each half into 5mm/¼in-thick slices.

3 Place the lime slices in the bowl, sprinkling the salt between the layers. Cover and leave to stand for a further 8 hours.

4 Drain the limes, catching the juices in a preserving pan. Crush the cardamom seeds with the cumin seeds. Add to the pan with the chillies, ginger and sugar. Bring to the boil, stirring until the sugar dissolves. Simmer for 2 minutes and leave to cool.

5 Mix the limes in the syrup. Pack into sterilized jars, cover and seal. Store in a cool, dark place for at least 1 month before eating. Use within 1 year.

Energy 1963kcal/8355kJ; Protein 12.3g; Carbohydrate 502.3g, of which sugars 502.3g; Fat 3g, of which saturates 1g; Cholesterol 0mg; Calcium 1089mg; Fibre 0g; Sodium 2042mg.

pickled plums

This preserve is popular in Central Europe and works well for all varieties of plums, from small wild bullaces and astringent damsons to the more delicately flavoured yellow or red-flushed mirabelle. Plums soften easily, so make sure that you choose very firm fruit.

Makes about 900g/2lb

INGREDIENTS

900g/2lb firm plums

150ml/¼ pint/⅔ cup clear apple juice

450ml/¾ pint/scant 2 cups cider vinegar

2.5ml/½ tsp salt

8 allspice berries

2.5cm/1in piece fresh root ginger, peeled and cut into matchstick strips

4 bay leaves

675g/1½lb/scant 3½ cups preserving or granulated (white) sugar

VARIATION

Juniper berries can be used instead of the allspice berries.

1 Wash the plums, then prick them once or twice using a wooden cocktail stick (toothpick). Put the apple juice, vinegar, salt, allspice berries, ginger and bay leaves in a preserving pan.

2 Add the plums to the pan and slowly bring to the boil. Reduce the heat and simmer gently for 10 minutes, or until the plums are just tender. Remove the plums with a slotted spoon and pack them into hot sterilized jars.

3 Add the sugar to the pan and stir over a low heat until dissolved. Boil steadily for 10 minutes, or until the mixture is syrupy.

4 Leave the syrup to cool for a few minutes, then pour over the plums. Cover and seal. Store for at least 1 month before using and use within 1 year of making.

Energy 3041kcal/12988kJ; Protein 8.9g; Carbohydrate 799.4g, of which sugars 799.4g; Fat 1.1g, of which saturates 0g; Cholesterol 0mg; Calcium 485mg; Fibre 14.4g; Sodium 62mg.

italian mustard fruit pickles

This traditional and popular Italian preserve is made from late summer and autumn fruits, and then left to mature in time for Christmas when it is served with Italian steamed sausage. The fruits can be mixed together, or arranged in layers in the jars for a stunning effect.

Makes about 1.2kg/2½lb

INGREDIENTS

450ml/¾ pint/scant 2 cups white wine vinegar

30ml/2 tbsp mustard seeds

1kg/2¼lb mixed fruit, such as peaches, nectarines, apricots, plums, melon, figs and cherries

675g/1½lb/scant 3½ cups preserving or granulated (white) sugar

VARIATION

If you prefer a slightly less tangy pickle, use cider vinegar instead of the white wine vinegar used here.

1 Put the vinegar and mustard seeds in a pan, bring to the boil, then simmer for 5 minutes. Remove from the heat, cover and leave to infuse for 1 hour. Strain the vinegar into a clean pan and discard the mustard seeds.

2 Prepare the fruit. Wash and pat dry the peaches, nectarines, apricots and plums, then stone (pit) and thickly slice or halve. Cut the melon in half, discard the seeds (pips), then slice into 1cm/½in pieces or scoop into balls using a melon baller. Cut the figs into quarters and remove the stalks from the cherries.

3 Add the sugar to the mustard vinegar and heat gently, stirring occasionally, until the sugar has dissolved completely. Bring to the boil, reduce the heat and simmer for 5 minutes, or until syrupy.

4 Add the fruit to the syrup and poach it over a gentle heat for 5–10 minutes. Some fruit will be ready sooner than others, so lift out as soon as each variety is tender, using a slotted spoon.

5 Pack the fruit into hot sterilized jars. Ladle the hot mustard syrup over the fruit. Cover and seal. Allow the pickles to mature for at least 1 month before eating. Use within 6 months.

Energy 3140kcal/13399kJ; Protein 20.2g; Carbohydrate 813.4g, of which sugars 813.4g; Fat 1.2g, of which saturates 0g; Cholesterol 0mg; Calcium 442mg; Fibre 14.4g; Sodium 53mg.

sweet pickled watermelon rind

This unusual pickle has a slightly aromatic melon flavour and a crunchy texture. It's the perfect way to use up the part of the fruit that is normally discarded.

Makes about 900g/2lb

INGREDIENTS

900g/2lb watermelon rind
  (from 1 large fruit)
50g/2oz/¼ cup salt
900ml/1½ pints/3¾ cups water
450g/1lb/2¼ cups preserving or
  granulated (white) sugar
300ml/½ pint/1¼ cups white wine vinegar
6 whole cloves
7.5cm/3in cinnamon stick

COOK'S TIP

Leave the watermelon rind to mature for at least 4 weeks before eating. This really helps the flavours to develop.

1 Remove the dark green skin from the watermelon rind, leaving a thin layer, no more than 3mm/⅛in thick, of the pink fruit. Cut the rind into slices about 5cm × 5mm/2 × ¼in thick, and place in a large bowl.

2 Dissolve the salt in 600ml/1 pint/2½ cups of the water. Pour over the watermelon rind, cover and leave for at least 6 hours or overnight.

3 Drain the watermelon rind and rinse under cold water. Put the rind in a pan and cover with fresh water. Bring the boil, reduce the heat and simmer for 10–15 minutes until just tender. Drain well.

4 Put the sugar, vinegar and remaining water in a clean pan. Tie the cloves and cinnamon in muslin (cheesecloth) and add to the pan. Heat gently, stirring occasionally, until the sugar has dissolved, then bring to the boil and simmer for 10 minutes. Turn off the heat. Add the rind, cover and leave to stand for about 2 hours.

5 Slowly bring the mixture back to the boil, then reduce the heat and simmer gently for 20 minutes, or until the rind has a translucent appearance. Remove and discard the spice bag. Place the rind in hot sterilized jars. Pour over the hot syrup, tapping the jar to release any trapped air. Cover and seal.

Energy 1836kcal/7835kJ; Protein 6.8g; Carbohydrate 478.4g, of which sugars 478.4g; Fat 1.8g, of which saturates 0g; Cholesterol 0mg; Calcium 608mg; Fibre 9.9g; Sodium 567mg.

blushing pears

As this pickle matures, the fruits absorb the colour of the vinegar, giving them a glorious pink hue. They're especially good served with cold turkey, game pie, well-flavoured cheese or pâté.

Makes about 1.3kg/3lb

INGREDIENTS

1 small lemon
450g/1lb/2¼ cups golden
  granulated sugar
475ml/16fl oz/2 cups raspberry
  vinegar
7.5cm/3in cinnamon stick
6 whole cloves
6 allspice berries
150ml/¼ pint/⅔ cup water
900g/2lb firm pears

1 Using a sharp knife, thinly pare a few strips of rind from the lemon. Squeeze out 30ml/2 tbsp of the juice and put it in a large pan with the strips of rind.

2 Add the sugar, vinegar, spices and water to the pan. Heat gently, stirring occasionally, until the sugar has completely dissolved, then slowly bring to the boil.

VARIATION

Nectarines and peaches may be pickled using the same method. Blanch and skin the fruits, then halve and stone (pit). Add a strip of orange rind to the syrup instead of lemon rind.

3 Meanwhile, prepare the pears. Peel and halve the pears, then scoop out the cores using a melon baller or small teaspoon. If the pears are very large, cut them into quarters rather than halves.

4 Add the pears to the pan and simmer very gently for about 20 minutes, or until tender and translucent but still whole. Check the pears frequently towards the end of the cooking time. Using a slotted spoon, remove the pears from the pan and pack into hot sterilized jars, adding the spices and strips of lemon rind.

5 Boil the syrup for 5 minutes, or until slightly reduced. Skim off any scum, then ladle the syrup over the pears. Cover and seal. Store for at least 1 month before eating.

Energy 2133kcal/9086kJ; Protein 5g; Carbohydrate 560.3g, of which sugars 560.3g; Fat 0.9g, of which saturates 0g; Cholesterol 0mg; Calcium 338mg; Fibre 19.8g; Sodium 54mg.

mulled pears

These pretty pears in a warming spiced syrup make a tempting dessert, particularly during the cold winter months. Serve them with crème fraîche or vanilla ice cream, or in open tarts.

Makes about 1.3kg/3lb

INGREDIENTS

1.8kg/4lb small firm pears

1 orange

1 lemon

2 cinnamon sticks, halved

12 whole cloves

5cm/2in piece fresh root ginger, peeled and sliced

300g/11oz/1½ cups granulated (white) sugar

1 bottle fruity light red wine

COOK'S TIP

Pears have a delicate flavour, so use a light, fruity wine such as Beaujolais or Merlot to make the syrup.

1 Peel the pears leaving the stalks intact. Peel very thin strips of rind from the orange and lemon, using a vegetable peeler. Pack the pears and citrus rind into large sterilized preserving jars, dividing the spices evenly between the jars.

2 Preheat the oven to 120°C/250°F/Gas ½. Put the sugar and wine in a large pan and heat gently, stirring, until the sugar has completely dissolved. Bring the mixture to the boil, then cook for 5 minutes.

3 Pour the wine syrup over the pears, making sure that there are no air pockets and that the fruits are completely covered with the syrup.

4 Cover the jars with their lids, but do not seal. Place them in the oven and cook for 2½–3 hours.

5 Carefully remove the jars from the oven, place on a dry dishtowel and seal. Leave the jars to cool completely, then label and store in a cool, dark place.

COOK'S TIP

To check that jars are properly sealed, leave them to cool for 24 hours, then loosen the clasp. Very carefully, try lifting the jar by the lid alone: if the jar is sealed properly, the lid should be fixed firmly enough to take the weight of the pot. Replace the clasp and store until ready to use.

Energy 2412kcal/10208kJ; Protein 7.7g; Carbohydrate 495g, of which sugars 495g; Fat 1.8g, of which saturates 0g; Cholesterol 0mg; Calcium 410mg; Fibre 39.6g; Sodium 125mg.

poached spiced plums in brandy

Bottling plums in a spicy syrup is a great way to preserve the flavours of autumn and provide a store of instant desserts during the winter months. Serve them with whipped cream.

Makes about 900g/2lb

INGREDIENTS

600ml/1 pint/2½ cups brandy

rind of 1 lemon, peeled in a long strip

350g/12oz/1¾ cups caster
  (superfine) sugar

1 cinnamon stick

900g/2lb plums

VARIATION

Any member of the plum family can be preserved using this recipe. Try bottling damsons or wild yellow plums as a delicious alternative. Cherries will also work very well.

1 Put the brandy, lemon rind, sugar and cinnamon in a large pan and heat gently until the sugar dissolves. Add the plums and poach for 15 minutes until soft. Remove the fruit and pack in sterilized jars.

2 Boil the syrup rapidly until reduced by a third, then strain over the plums to cover. Seal the jars tightly. Label when cold and store for up to 6 months in a cool, dark place.

Energy 3035kcal/12793kJ; Protein 7.2g; Carbohydrate 444.9g, of which sugars 444.9g; Fat 0.9g, of which saturates 0g; Cholesterol 0mg; Calcium 303mg; Fibre 14.4g; Sodium 39mg.

apricots in amaretto syrup

Amaretto brings out the delicious flavour of apricots. Try serving the drained fruit on top of a tart filled with crème patissière, using some of the amaretto syrup to glaze the apricots.

2 Add the apricots to the syrup and bring almost to the boil. Cover and simmer gently for 5 minutes. Remove the apricots with a slotted spoon and drain in a colander.

3 Add the remaining sugar to the pan and heat gently, stirring until the sugar has dissolved, then boil rapidly until the syrup reaches 104°C/219°F. Cool slightly, then remove the vanilla pod and stir in the amaretto.

Makes about 900g/2lb

INGREDIENTS

1.3kg/3lb firm apricots

1 litre/1¾ pints/4 cups water

800g/1¾lb/4 cups granulated (white) sugar

1 vanilla pod (bean)

175ml/6fl oz/¾ cup amaretto liqueur

4 Pack the apricots loosely in large, warmed sterilized jars. Pour the syrup over, twisting and tapping the jars to expel any air. Seal and store in a cool, dark place for 2 weeks before eating.

COOK'S TIP

For the best results, make this preserve when apricots are in season. Choose firm, unblemished fruits blushed with pink, that give slightly when squeezed gently in the palm of the hand.

1 Cut a slit in each apricot and remove the stone (pit), keeping the fruit intact. Put the water, half the sugar and the vanilla pod in a large pan, heat gently, stirring, until the sugar dissolves. Increase the heat and simmer for 5 minutes.

Energy 3890kcal/16577kJ; Protein 12.1g; Carbohydrate 958.2g, of which sugars 958.2g; Fat 0.9g, of which saturates 0g; Cholesterol 0mg; Calcium 568mg; Fibre 15.3g; Sodium 87mg.

figs infused with earl grey

The aromatic flavour of Earl Grey tea in this syrup permeates the figs to create a sweet and intriguing flavour. They are delicious spooned over creamy Greek yogurt.

Makes about 1.8kg/4lb

INGREDIENTS

900g/2lb ready-to-eat dried figs

1.2 litres/2 pints/5 cups Earl Grey tea

pared rind of 1 orange
1 cinnamon stick

275g/10oz/1¼ cups granulated (white) sugar

250ml/8fl oz/1 cup brandy

VARIATION

Use Grand Marnier or Cointreau instead of brandy to emphasize the flavour of zesty orange in the syrup.

1 Put the figs in a pan and add the tea, orange rind and cinnamon stick. Bring to the boil, cover and simmer for 10–15 minutes, or until the figs are tender.

2 Using a slotted spoon, remove the figs from the pan and leave to drain. Add the sugar to the tea and heat gently, stirring, until the sugar has dissolved. Boil rapidly for 2 minutes until syrupy.

3 Remove the pan from the heat, then stir in the brandy. Pack the figs and orange rind into warmed sterilized jars and pour in the hot syrup to cover. Twist and gently tap the jars to expel any air bubbles, then seal and store in a cool, dark place for 1 month.

Energy 3520kcal/14921kJ; Protein 31.1g; Carbohydrate 724.8g, of which sugars 724.8g; Fat 13.5g, of which saturates 0g; Cholesterol 0mg; Calcium 2216mg; Fibre 62.1g; Sodium 530mg.

peaches in peach schnapps

The fragrant taste of peaches is complemented and intensified by the addition of the schnapps.
Serve with whipped cream flavoured with some of the syrup and a squeeze of lemon juice.

Makes about 1.3kg/3lb

INGREDIENTS

1.3kg/3lb firm peaches
1 litre/1¾ pints/4 cups water
900g/2lb/4½ cups granulated (white)
 sugar
8 green cardamom pods
50g/2oz/½ cup whole blanched
 almonds, toasted
120ml/4fl oz/½ cup peach schnapps

VARIATION

Amaretto can be used instead of
peach schnapps.

1 Put the peaches in a bowl and
pour over boiling water. Drain
immediately and peel, then halve
and remove the stones (pits).

2 Put the water and half the sugar
in a large pan and heat gently until
the sugar has dissolved. Increase
the heat and boil for 5 minutes.

3 Add the peaches to the syrup
and return to the boil. Reduce the
heat, cover and simmer gently for
5–10 minutes, or until tender but
not too soft. Using a slotted spoon,
remove the peaches and set aside
to drain.

4 Put the cardamom pods and
almonds in a large pan, then add
900ml/1½ pints/3¾ cups of the
syrup and the remaining sugar.

5 Gently heat the syrup, stirring
until the sugar has dissolved. Bring
to the boil and boil until the syrup
reaches 104°C/219°F. Leave to cool
slightly, remove the cardamom
pods, then stir in the schnapps.

6 Pack the peaches loosely in
warmed sterilized jars. Pour the
syrup and almonds over the fruit,
twisting and gently tapping the jars
to release any air bubbles. Seal and
store in a cool, dark place for
2 weeks before eating.

Energy 4595kcal/19561kJ; Protein 28.1g; Carbohydrate 1082.1g, of which sugars 1080.8g; Fat 29.2g, of which saturates 2.2g; Cholesterol 0mg; Calcium 694mg; Fibre 23.2g; Sodium 88mg.

pineapple in coconut rum

The tropical flavour of pineapple is enhanced by the addition of coconut rum. For a really special treat, serve topped with whipped cream and grated bitter chocolate.

Makes about 900g/2lb

INGREDIENTS

1 orange
1.2 litres/2 pints/5 cups water
900g/2lb/4½ cups granulated (white)
   sugar
2 pineapples, peeled, cored and cut
   into small chunks
300ml/½ pint/1¼ cups coconut rum

COOK'S TIP

Choose plump pineapples that feel heavy for their size, with fresh, stiff plumes. To test for ripeness, gently pull out one of the bottom leaves; it should come out easily.

1 Thinly pare strips of rind from the orange, then slice into thin matchsticks. Put the water and half the sugar in a large pan with the orange rind and heat gently until the sugar has dissolved. Increase the heat and boil for 5 minutes.

2 Carefully add the pineapple pieces to the syrup and return to the boil. Reduce the heat and simmer gently for 10 minutes. Using a slotted spoon, remove the pineapple from the pan and set aside to drain.

3 Add the remaining sugar to the syrup and heat, stirring, until the sugar has dissolved completely. Bring to the boil and boil for about 10 minutes, or until the syrup has thickened. Remove from the heat and set aside to cool slightly, then stir in the coconut rum.

4 Pack the drained pineapple loosely into warmed sterilized jars. Pour in the syrup until the fruit is completely covered, tapping and twisting the jars to release any air bubbles before sealing. Seal, label and store in a cool, dark place for 2 weeks before eating.

Energy 4660kcal/19834kJ; Protein 7.7g; Carbohydrate 1119.7g, of which sugars 1119.7g; Fat 1.6g, of which saturates 0g; Cholesterol 0mg; Calcium 636mg; Fibre 9.6g; Sodium 106mg.

forest berries in kirsch

This preserve captures the essence of the season in its rich, dark colour and flavour. Adding the
sweet cherry liqueur Kirsch to the syrup intensifies the flavour of the bottled fruit.

Makes about 1.3kg/3lb

INGREDIENTS

1.3kg/3lb/12 cups mixed prepared
  summer berries, such as blackberries,
  raspberries, strawberries, redcurrants
  and cherries

225g/8oz/generous 1 cup
  granulated sugar

600ml/1 pint/2½ cups water

120ml/4fl oz/½ cup Kirsch

COOK'S TIP

Be careful not to overcook the fruits
because they will lose their beautiful
colour and fresh flavour.

1 Preheat the oven to 120°C/
250°F/Gas ½. Pack the prepared
fruit loosely into sterilized jars.
Cover without sealing and place
in the oven for 50–60 minutes, or
until the juices start to run.

2 Meanwhile, put the sugar and
water in a large pan and heat
gently, stirring, until the sugar has
dissolved. Increase the heat, bring
to the boil and boil for 5 minutes.
Stir in the Kirsch and set aside.

3 Carefully remove the jars from
the oven and place on a dishtowel.
Use the fruit from one of the jars
to top up the rest.

4 Pour the boiling syrup into each
jar, twisting and tapping each one
to ensure that no air bubbles have
been trapped. Seal, then store in
a cool, dark place.

Energy 1518kcal/6487kJ; Protein 19.3g; Carbohydrate 334g, of which sugars 334g; Fat 3.9g, of which saturates 1.3g; Cholesterol 0mg; Calcium 444mg; Fibre 32.5g; Sodium 53mg.

cherries in eau de vie

These potent cherries should be consumed with respect as they pack quite an alcoholic punch.
Serve them with rich, dark chocolate torte or as a wicked topping for creamy rice pudding.

2 Spoon the sugar over the fruit, then pour in the eau de vie to cover and seal tightly.

3 Store for at least 1 month before serving, shaking the bottle now and then to help dissolve the sugar.

COOK'S TIP

Eau de vie actually refers to all spirits distilled from fermented fruits. Eau de vie is always colourless, with a high alcohol content (sometimes 45% ABV) and a clean, pure scent and the flavour of the founding fruit. Popular eaux de vie are made from cherries and strawberries.

Makes about 1.3kg/3lb

INGREDIENTS

450g/1lb/generous 3 cups ripe cherries
8 blanched almonds
75g/3oz/6 tbsp granulated (white) sugar
500ml/17fl oz/scant 2¼ cups eau de vie

VARIATIONS

Strawberries, raspberries and blackcurrants are all excellent preserved in eau de vie. They will all produce fine fruity liqueurs as well as the macerated fruit.

1 Wash and stone (pit) the cherries then pack them into a sterilized, wide-necked bottle along with the blanched almonds.

Energy 1479kcal/6142kJ; Protein 9.3g; Carbohydrate 53.5g, of which sugars 52.8g; Fat 14.4g, of which saturates 1.1g; Cholesterol 0mg; Calcium 119mg; Fibre 5.9g; Sodium 8mg.

blackcurrant brandy

Spoon a little of the brandy into a wine glass and top up with chilled white wine or champagne.

Makes about 1 litre/1¾ pints/4 cups

INGREDIENTS

900g/2lb/8 cups blackcurrants, washed

600ml/1 pint/2½ cups brandy

350g/12oz/1¾ cups granulated (white) sugar

COOK'S TIP

When you have strained off the brandy, reserve the blackcurrants and freeze for later use. They are great added to fruit salads and trifles, or make a delicious richly flavoured ice cream topping. Be careful though, because they pack quite a boozy punch.

1 Strip the blackcurrants off their stems and pack the fruit into a sterilized 1.5 litre/2½ pint/6¼ cup preserving jar. Using the back of a wooden spoon, crush the blackcurrants lightly.

2 Add the brandy and sugar to the jar, ensuring the fruit is completely covered by the brandy. Twist and gently tap the jar to ensure there are no trapped air bubbles.

3 Seal the jar, then store in a cool, dark place for about 2 months, shaking the jar occasionally.

4 Pour the liquor through a sieve lined with a double layer of muslin (cheesecloth) into a sterilized jug (pitcher). Pour into sterilized bottles, seal, label and store in a cool, dark place.

Energy 2963kcal/12487kJ; Protein 9.8g; Carbohydrate 425.1g, of which sugars 425.1g; Fat 0g, of which saturates 0g; Cholesterol 0mg; Calcium 726mg; Fibre 32.4g; Sodium 48mg.

blueberries in gin syrup

This syrup turns a fabulous blue colour and the distinctive flavour of the gin complements, rather than masks, the essence of the blueberries.

Makes about 1.8kg/4lb

INGREDIENTS

1.3kg/3lb/12 cups blueberries

225g/8oz/1 cup granulated (white) sugar

600ml/1 pint/2½ cups water

120ml/4fl oz/½ cup gin

1 Preheat the oven to 120°C/250°F/Gas ½. Pack the blueberries into sterilized jars and cover, without sealing. Put the jars in the oven and bake for 50–60 minutes until the juices start to run.

2 Meanwhile, put the sugar and water in a pan and gently heat, stirring continuously, until the sugar has dissolved completely. Increase the heat and boil for 5 minutes. Stir in the gin.

3 Carefully remove the jars from the oven and place on a dry dishtowel. Use the fruit from one of the jars to top up the others.

4 Carefully pour the boiling gin syrup into the jars to completely cover the fruit. Twist and gently tap the jars to ensure that no air bubbles have been trapped.

5 Seal, then store in a cool, dark place until ready to serve.

Energy 1478kcal/6237kJ; Protein 12.8g; Carbohydrate 301.4g, of which sugars 301.4g; Fat 2.6g, of which saturates 0g; Cholesterol 0mg; Calcium 652mg; Fibre 40.3g; Sodium 40mg.

rumtopf

This fruit preserve originated in Germany, where special earthenware rumtopf pots are traditionally filled with fruits as they come into season. It is not necessary to use the specific pot; you can use a large preserving jar instead. Store in a cool, dark place.

Makes about 3 litres/5 pints/12½ cups

INGREDIENTS

900g/2lb fruit, such as strawberries, blackberries, blackcurrants, redcurrants, peaches, apricots, cherries and plums

250g/9oz/1¼ cups granulated (white) sugar

1 litre/1¾ pints/4 cups white rum

1 Prepare the fruit: remove stems, skins, cores and stones (pits) and cut larger fruit into pieces. Put the fruit and sugar in a bowl, cover and leave to stand for 30 minutes.

2 Spoon the fruit and juices into a sterilized 3 litre/5 pint/12½ cup preserving or earthenware jar and pour in the white rum to cover.

3 Cover the jar with clear film (plastic wrap), then seal and store in a cool, dark place.

4 As space allows, and as different fruits come into season, add more fruit, sugar and rum in appropriate proportions, as described above.

5 When the jar is full, store in a cool, dark place for 2 months. Serve the fruit spooned over ice cream or other desserts and enjoy the rum in glasses as a liqueur.

Energy 3448kcal/14410kJ; Protein 8.4g; Carbohydrate 315.3g, of which sugars 315.3g; Fat 0.9g, of which saturates 0g; Cholesterol 0mg; Calcium 277mg; Fibre 9.9g; Sodium 69mg.

spiced apple mincemeat

This fruity mincemeat is traditionally used to fill little pies at Christmas but it is great at any time. Try it as a filling for large tarts finished with a lattice top and served with custard. To make a lighter mincemeat, add some extra grated apple just before using.

Makes about 1.8kg/4lb

INGREDIENTS

500g/1¼lb tart cooking apples, peeled, cored and finely diced

115g/4oz/½ cup ready-to-eat dried apricots, coarsely chopped

900g/2lb/5⅓ cups luxury dried mixed fruit

115g/4oz/1 cup whole blanched almonds, chopped

175g/6oz/1 cup shredded beef or vegetarian suet (chilled, grated shortening)

225g/8oz/generous 1 cup dark muscovado (molasses) sugar

grated rind and juice of 1 orange

grated rind and juice of 1 lemon

5ml/1 tsp ground cinnamon

2.5ml/½ tsp grated nutmeg

2.5ml/½ tsp ground ginger

120ml/4fl oz/½ cup brandy

1 Put the apples, apricots, dried fruit, almonds, suet and sugar in a large non-metallic bowl and stir together until thoroughly combined.

2 Add the orange and lemon rind and juice, cinnamon, nutmeg, ginger and brandy and mix well. Cover the bowl with a clean dishtowel and leave to stand in a cool place for 2 days, stirring occasionally.

3 Spoon the mincemeat into cool sterilized jars, pressing down well, and being very careful not to trap any air bubbles. Cover and seal.

4 Store the jars in a cool, dark place for at least 4 weeks before using. Once opened, store in the refrigerator and use within 4 weeks. Unopened, the mincemeat will keep for 1 year.

COOK'S TIP

If, when opened, the mincemeat seems dry, pour a little extra brandy or orange juice into the jar and gently stir in. You may need to remove a spoonful or two of the mincemeat from the jar to do this.

Energy 6071kcal/25579kJ; Protein 52.2g; Carbohydrate 963.6g, of which sugars 939.7g; Fat 227.3g, of which saturates 92.4g; Cholesterol 144mg; Calcium 1156mg; Fibre 44.4g; Sodium 488mg.

savoury and sweet jellies

Jellies are sumptuously slow preserves, not to be rushed in the preparation, but to gently drip their juicy yield through old-fashioned jelly bags. Then a miraculous transformation turns the cloudy, dull and tart liquid into a bright, exciting firm fruit gem as sugar is added. As well as sweet fruit, herbs and spices bring glorious flavour to savoury jellies. They may be sharp with citrus or with vinegar, can also be added to sauces and gravies, or used to glaze fruity fillings in tarts and pastries.

lemon grass and ginger jelly

This aromatic jelly is delicious with Asian-style roast meat and poultry such as Chinese crispy duck. It is also the perfect foil for rich fish, especially cold smoked trout or mackerel.

2 Put the chopped lemon grass in a preserving pan and pour over the water. Add the lemons and ginger. Bring to the boil, then reduce the heat, cover and simmer for 1 hour, or until the lemons are pulpy.

3 Pour the fruit and juices into a sterilized jelly bag suspended over a large bowl. Leave to drain for at least 3 hours, or until the juice stops dripping.

4 Measure the juice into the cleaned preserving pan, adding 450g/1lb/2¼ cups sugar for every 600ml/1 pint/2½ cups juice.

5 Heat the mixture gently, stirring occasionally, until the sugar has dissolved completely. Boil rapidly for about 10 minutes until the jelly reaches setting point (105°C/220°F). Remove from the heat.

Makes about 900g/2lb

INGREDIENTS

2 lemon grass stalks

1.5 litres/2½ pints/6¼ cups water

1.3kg/3lb lemons, washed and cut into small pieces

50g/2oz fresh root ginger, unpeeled, thinly sliced

about 450g/1lb/2¼ cups preserving or granulated (white) sugar

1 Using a rolling pin, bruise the lemon grass, then chop roughly.

6 Skim any scum off the surface using a slotted spoon, then pour the jelly into warmed sterilized jars, cover and seal. Store in a cool, dark place and use within 1 year. Once opened, keep in the refrigerator. Eat within 3 months.

Energy 1715kcal/7304kJ; Protein 27.4g; Carbohydrate 417.1g, of which sugars 231.8g; Fat 4.5g, of which saturates 0.7g; Cholesterol 0mg; Calcium 63mg; Fibre 14.4g; Sodium 41mg.

roasted red pepper and chilli jelly

The hint of chilli in this glowing red jelly makes it ideal for spicing up hot or cold roast meat, sausages or hamburgers. The jelly is also good stirred into sauces or used as a glaze for poultry.

Makes about 900g/2lb

INGREDIENTS

8 red (bell) peppers, quartered
  and seeded
4 fresh red chillies, halved and seeded
1 onion, roughly chopped
2 garlic cloves, roughly chopped
250ml/8fl oz/1 cup water
250ml/8fl oz/1 cup white wine vinegar
7.5ml/1½ tsp salt
450g/1lb/2¼ cups preserving
  or granulated (white) sugar
25ml/1½ tbsp powdered pectin

4 Scrape the purée into a large stainless steel pan, then stir in the white wine vinegar and salt.

5 In a bowl, combine the sugar and pectin, then stir it into the pepper mixture. Heat gently, stirring, until the sugar and pectin have dissolved completely, then bring to a rolling boil. Cook the jelly, stirring frequently, for exactly 4 minutes, then remove the pan from the heat.

6 Pour the jelly into warmed, sterilized jars. Leave to cool and set, then cover, label and store.

1 Arrange the peppers, skin side up, on a rack in a grill (broiling) pan and grill (broil) until the skins blister and blacken.

2 Put the peppers in a polythene bag until they are cool enough to handle, then remove the skins.

3 Put the skinned peppers, chillies, onion, garlic and water in a food processor or blender and process to a purée. Press the purée through a nylon sieve set over a bowl, pressing hard with a wooden spoon, to extract as much juice as possible. There should be about 750ml/1¼ pints/3 cups.

Energy 2275kcal/9665kJ; Protein 18g; Carbohydrate 571g, of which sugars 565.1g; Fat 6.1g, of which saturates 1.5g; Cholesterol 0mg; Calcium 374mg; Fibre 24.8g; Sodium 89mg.

tomato and herb jelly

This dark golden jelly is delicious served with roast and grilled meats, especially lamb. It is also great for enlivening tomato-based pasta sauces: stirring a couple of teaspoons of the jelly into sauces helps to heighten their flavour and counteract acidity.

Makes about 1.3kg/3lb

INGREDIENTS

1.8kg/4lb tomatoes

2 lemons

2 bay leaves

300ml/½ pint/1¼ cups cold water

250ml/8fl oz/1 cup malt vinegar

bunch of fresh herbs such as rosemary, thyme, parsley and mint, plus a few extra sprigs for the jars

about 900g/2lb/4½ cups preserving or granulated (white) sugar

COOK'S TIP

Once you have opened a jar of this jelly, store it in the refrigerator and use within 3 months.

1 Wash the tomatoes and lemons well, then cut the tomatoes into quarters and the lemons into small pieces. Put the chopped tomatoes and lemons in a large heavy pan with the bay leaves and pour over the water and vinegar.

2 Add the herbs, either one herb or a mixture if preferred. (If you are using pungent woody herbs such as rosemary and thyme, use about six sprigs; if you are using milder leafy herbs such as parsley or mint, add about 12 large sprigs.)

3 Bring the mixture to the boil, then reduce the heat. Cover the pan with a lid and simmer for about 40 minutes, or until the tomatoes are very soft.

4 Pour the tomato mixture and all the juices into a sterilized jelly bag suspended over a large bowl. Leave to drain for about 3 hours, or until the juices stop dripping.

5 Measure the juice into the cleaned pan, adding 450g/1lb/ 2¼ cups sugar for every 600ml/ 1 pint/2½ cups juice. Heat gently, stirring, until the sugar dissolves. Boil rapidly for 10 minutes, to setting point (105°C/220°F), then remove from the heat. Skim off any scum.

6 Leave the jelly for a few minutes until a skin forms. Place a herb sprig in each warmed sterilized jar, then pour in the jelly. Cover and seal when cold. Store in a cool, dark place and use within 1 year.

Energy 3767kcal/16078kJ; Protein 13.6g; Carbohydrate 980.8g, of which sugars 980.8g; Fat 3.9g, of which saturates 1.3g; Cholesterol 0mg; Calcium 568mg; Fibre 13g; Sodium 171mg.

citrus thyme jelly

You can vary the sharpness of this jelly by altering the proportions of fruit. Use more oranges and fewer lemons and limes to obtain a milder, sweeter-tasting jelly.

2 Bring the mixture to the boil, then reduce the heat, cover and simmer for 1 hour, or until pulpy. Discard the bay leaves, then pour the fruit and juices into a sterilized jelly bag suspended over a large bowl. Leave to drain for 3 hours, or until the juices stop dripping.

3 Measure the juice into the cleaned pan, adding 450g/1lb/ 2¼ cups sugar for every 600ml/ 1 pint/2½ cups juice. Heat gently until the sugar has dissolved. Bring to the boil, then boil rapidly for about 10 minutes, or until setting point is reached (105°C/220°F). Remove the pan from the heat.

Makes about 1.3kg/3lb

INGREDIENTS

675g/1½lb lemons
675g/1½lb limes
450g/1lb oranges
2 bay leaves
2 litres/3½ pints/8¾ cups water
about 800g/1¾lb/4 cups preserving or granulated (white) sugar
60ml/4 tbsp fresh thyme leaves

COOK'S TIP

It is important to stir the jelly before potting to re-distribute the herbs.

1 Wash all the fruit, then cut into small pieces. Place in a large heavy pan with the bay leaves and pour over the water.

4 Skim any scum off the surface, then stir in the thyme leaves. Leave to cool for a few minutes until a thin skin forms, then gently stir again to make sure the thyme is evenly distributed.

5 Pour the jelly into warmed sterilized jars. Cover and seal when cold. Store in a cool, dark place and use within 1 year. Once opened, store in the refrigerator and eat within 3 months.

Energy 3154kcal/13455kJ; Protein 4.2g; Carbohydrate 836.1g, of which sugars 836.1g; Fat 0.1g, of which saturates 0g; Cholesterol 0mg; Calcium 434mg; Fibre 0.3g; Sodium 50mg.

bitter lime and juniper jelly

In this sharp, aromatic jelly the distinctive taste of zesty lime and the rich, resinous flavour of juniper berries is enhanced with a hint of aniseed from the splash of Pernod.

Makes about 1.6kg/3½lb

INGREDIENTS

6 limes

1.3kg/3lb tart cooking apples

6 juniper berries, crushed

1.75 litres/3 pints/7½ cups water

about 800g/1¾lb/4 cups preserving
or granulated (white) sugar

45ml/3 tbsp Pernod (optional)

1 Wash the limes and apples, then cut them into small pieces. Put them in a large heavy pan with the juniper berries. Pour over the water, then bring to the boil and simmer for about 1 hour, or until the fruit is very tender and pulpy.

2 Pour the fruit and juices into a sterilized jelly bag suspended over a large bowl. Leave the fruit to drain for at least 3 hours, until the juices stop dripping.

3 Measure the juice into the cleaned pan, adding 450g/1lb/ 2¼ cups sugar for every 600ml/ 1 pint/2½ cups juice. Heat gently, stirring occasionally, until the sugar has dissolved. Boil rapidly for about 10 minutes, to setting point (105°C/220°F), then remove the pan from the heat.

4 Skim any scum off the surface using a slotted spoon, then stir in the Pernod, if using. Pour the jelly into warmed sterilized jars, cover and seal immediately.

5 Store the jelly in a cool, dark place and use within 1 year. Once opened, keep in the refrigerator and eat within 3 months.

COOK'S TIP

When using citrus fruits for preserves, try to use unwaxed ones. If they are unavailable, scrub waxed fruits well.

Energy 3152kcal/13448kJ; Protein 4g; Carbohydrate 836g, of which sugars 836g; Fat 0g, of which saturates 0g; Cholesterol 0mg; Calcium 424mg; Fibre 0g; Sodium 48mg.

apple, orange and cider jelly

A spoonful or two of this tangy amber jelly adds a real sparkle to a plate of cold meats, especially ham and pork or rich game pâtés. Tart cooking apples make the best-flavoured jelly, while the addition of cloves gives it a wonderfully warm, spicy taste and aroma.

Makes about 1.8kg/4lb

INGREDIENTS

1.3kg/3lb tart cooking apples

4 oranges

4 whole cloves

1.2 litres/2 pints/5 cups sweet cider

about 600ml/1 pint/2½ cups cold water

about 800g/1¾lb/4 cups preserving or granulated (white) sugar

VARIATION

Replace some of the apples with crab apples for a more distinctive taste.

1 Wash and chop the apples and oranges, then put in a preserving pan with the cloves, cider and water to barely cover the fruit.

2 Bring the mixture to the boil, cover and simmer gently for 1 hour, stirring occasionally.

3 Pour the fruit and juices into a sterilized jelly bag suspended over a large bowl. Leave to drain for at least 4 hours, or overnight, until the juices stop dripping.

4 Measure the juice into the cleaned preserving pan, adding 450g/1lb/2¼ cups sugar for every 600ml/1 pint/2½ cups juice.

5 Heat the mixture gently stirring, until the sugar has dissolved. Boil rapidly for about 10 minutes until setting point is reached (105°C/220°F). Remove from the heat.

6 Skim any scum off the surface, then pour the jelly into warmed sterilized jars. Cover and seal. Store in a cool, dark place and use within 18 months. Once opened, store in the refrigerator and eat within 3 months.

Energy 3442kcal/14691kJ; Protein 10.4g; Carbohydrate 905.2g, of which sugars 905.2g; Fat 0.8g, of which saturates 0g; Cholesterol 0mg; Calcium 671mg; Fibre 13.3g; Sodium 79mg.

quince and rosemary jelly

The amount of water needed for this jelly varies according to the ripeness of the fruit. For a good set, hard under-ripe quinces should be used as they contain the most pectin. If the fruit is soft and ripe, add a little lemon juice along with the water.

Makes about 900g/2lb

INGREDIENTS

900g/2lb quinces, cut into small pieces, with bruised parts removed

900ml–1.2 litres/1½–2 pints/ 3¾–5 cups water

lemon juice (optional)

4 large sprigs of fresh rosemary

about 900g/2lb/4½ cups preserving or granulated (white) sugar

1 Put the chopped quinces in a large heavy pan with the water, using the smaller volume if the fruit is ripe and the larger volume plus lemon juice if it is hard.

2 Reserve a few small sprigs of rosemary, then add the rest to the pan. Bring to the boil, reduce the heat, cover with a lid and simmer gently until the fruit becomes pulpy.

3 Remove and discard all the rosemary sprigs. (Don't worry about any tiny leaves that have fallen off during cooking). Pour the fruit and juices into a sterilized jelly bag suspended over a large bowl. Leave for 3 hours, or until the juices stop dripping.

4 Measure the drained juice into the cleaned pan, adding 450g/1lb/ 2¼ cups sugar for every 600ml/ 1 pint/2½ cups juice.

5 Heat the mixture gently over a low heat, stirring occasionally, until the sugar has dissolved completely. Bring to the boil, then boil rapidly for about 10 minutes until the jelly reaches setting point (105°C/220°F). Remove the pan from the heat.

6 Skim any scum from the surface using a slotted spoon, then leave the jelly to cool for a few minutes until a thin skin begins to form on the surface.

7 Place a sprig of rosemary in each warmed sterilized jar, then pour in the jelly. Cover and seal when cold. Store in a cool, dark place and use within 1 year. Once the jelly is opened, keep it in the refrigerator and use within 3 months.

Energy 3666kcal/15636kJ; Protein 5.4g; Carbohydrate 970.5g, of which sugars 970.5g; Fat 0.3g, of which saturates 0g; Cholesterol 0mg; Calcium 510mg; Fibre 6.6g; Sodium 63mg.

minted gooseberry jelly

The colour of this tart jelly is often a surprise as the gooseberry juice turns pink during cooking.

Makes about 1.2kg/2½lb

INGREDIENTS

1.3kg/3lb/12 cups gooseberries
1 bunch fresh mint
750ml/1¼ pints/3 cups cold water
400ml/14fl oz/1⅔ cups white wine vinegar
about 900g/2lb/4½ cups preserving or
   granulated (white) sugar
45ml/3 tbsp chopped fresh mint

1 Place the gooseberries, mint and water in a preserving pan. Bring to the boil, reduce the heat, cover and simmer for about 30 minutes, until the gooseberries are soft. Add the vinegar and simmer uncovered for a further 10 minutes.

2 Pour the fruit and juices into a sterilized jelly bag suspended over a large bowl. Leave to drain for at least 3 hours, or until the juices stop dripping, then measure the strained juices back into the cleaned preserving pan.

3 Add 450g/1lb/2½ cups sugar for every 600ml/1 pint/2½ cups juice, then heat gently, stirring, until the sugar has dissolved. Bring to the boil and cook for 15 minutes, or to setting point (105°C/220°F). Remove the pan from the heat.

4 Skim any scum from the surface. Leave to cool until a thin skin forms, then stir in the mint.

5 Pour the jelly into warmed sterilized jars, cover and seal. Store and use within 1 year. Once opened, store in the refrigerator and eat within 3 months.

Energy 3641kcal/15534kJ; Protein 10g; Carbohydrate 955.5g, of which sugars 955.5g; Fat 2g, of which saturates 0g; Cholesterol 0mg; Calcium 617mg; Fibre 12g; Sodium 64mg.

plum and apple jelly

This sweet jelly complements savoury dishes such as rich roast meats like lamb and pork.

Makes about 1.3kg/3lb

INGREDIENTS

900g/2lb plums
450g/1lb tart cooking apples
150ml/¼ pint/⅔ cup cider vinegar
750ml/1¼ pints/3 cups water
about 675g/1½lb/scant 3½ cups
   preserving or granulated (white) sugar

COOK'S TIPS

• Use dark red cooking plums, damsons or wild plums to offset the sweetness of this jelly.
• It can be stored for up to 2 years. However, once opened, it should be stored in the refrigerator and eaten within 3 months.

1 Cut the plums in half along the crease, twist the two halves apart, then remove the stones (pits) and roughly chop the flesh. Chop the apples, including the cores and skins. Put the fruit in a large heavy pan with the vinegar and water.

2 Bring the mixture to the boil, reduce the heat, cover and simmer for 30 minutes or until the fruit is soft and pulpy.

3 Pour the fruit and juices into a sterilized jelly bag suspended over a large bowl. Leave to drain for at least 3 hours, or until the fruit juices stop dripping.

4 Measure the juice into the cleaned pan, adding 450g/1lb/ 2¼ cups sugar for every 600ml/ 1 pint/2½ cups juice.

5 Bring the mixture to the boil, stirring occasionally, until the sugar has dissolved, then boil rapidly for about 10 minutes, or until the jelly reaches setting point (105°C/220°F). Remove the pan from the heat.

6 Skim any scum from from the surface, then pour the jelly into warmed sterilized jars. Cover and seal while hot. Store in a cool, dark place and use within 2 years.

Energy 2803kcal/11963kJ; Protein 5.5g; Carbohydrate 740.7g, of which sugars 740.7g; Fat 0.4g, of which saturates 0g; Cholesterol 0mg; Calcium 401mg; Fibre 6.4g; Sodium 49mg.

blackberry and sloe gin jelly

Although they have a wonderful flavour, blackberries are full of pips, so turning them into a deep-coloured jelly is a good way to make the most of this full-flavoured hedgerow harvest. This preserve is delicious served with richly flavoured roast meats such as lamb.

Makes about 1.3kg/3lb

INGREDIENTS

450g/1lb sloes (black plums)

600ml/1 pint/2½ cups cold water

1.8kg/4lb/16 cups blackberries

juice of 1 lemon

about 900g/2lb/4½ cups preserving or granulated (white) sugar

45ml/3 tbsp gin

VARIATION

Sloes (black plums) are much harder to come by than blackberries and you will usually need to find them growing in the wild. If you can't find sloes, use extra blackberries in their place.

1 Wash the sloes and prick with a fine skewer. Put them in a large heavy pan with the water and bring to the boil. Reduce the heat, cover and simmer for 5 minutes.

2 Briefly rinse the blackberries in cold water and add them to the pan with the lemon juice.

3 Bring the fruit mixture back to a simmer and cook gently for about 20 minutes, or until the sloes are tender and the blackberries very soft, stirring once or twice.

4 Pour the fruit and juices into a sterilized jelly bag suspended over a large bowl. Leave to drain for at least 4 hours or overnight, until the juices have stopped dripping.

5 Measure the fruit juice into the cleaned preserving pan, adding 450g/1lb/2¼ cups sugar for every 600ml/1 pint/2½ cups juice.

6 Heat the mixture gently, stirring occasionally, until the sugar has dissolved completely. Bring to the boil, then boil rapidly for about 10 minutes until the jelly reaches setting point (105°C/220°F). Remove the pan from the heat.

7 Skim off any scum from the surface of the jelly using a slotted spoon, then stir in the gin.

8 Pour the jelly into warmed sterilized jars, cover and seal. Store in a cool, dark place and use within 2 years. Once opened, keep the jelly in the refrigerator and eat within 3 months.

COOK'S TIP

Sloes (black plums) bring a good level of pectin to the jelly. If all blackberries are used without sloes, select some under-ripe fruit and use preserving sugar with added pectin.

Energy 3750kcal/15986kJ; Protein 10.8g; Carbohydrate 984.3g, of which sugars 984.3g; Fat 1.3g, of which saturates 0g; Cholesterol 0mg; Calcium 743mg; Fibre 21g; Sodium 69mg.

cranberry and claret jelly

The slight sharpness of cranberries makes this a superb jelly for serving with rich meats such as lamb or game. Together with claret, the cranberries give the jelly a beautiful deep red colour.

Makes about 1.2kg/2½lb

INGREDIENTS

900g/2lb/8 cups fresh or
  frozen cranberries

350ml/12fl oz/1½ cups water

about 900g//2lb/4½ cups preserving
  or granulated (white) sugar

250ml/8fl oz/1 cup claret

COOK'S TIP

When simmering the cranberries,
keep the pan covered until they stop
"popping", as they can occasionally
explode and jump out of the pan.

1 Wash the cranberries, if fresh, and put them in a large heavy pan with the water. Cover the pan and bring to the boil.

2 Reduce the heat under the pan and simmer for about 20 minutes, or until the cranberries are soft.

3 Pour the fruit and juices into a sterilized jelly bag suspended over a large bowl. Leave to drain for at least 3 hours or overnight, until the juices stop dripping.

4 Measure the juice and wine into the cleaned preserving pan, adding 400g/14oz/2 cups preserving or granulated sugar for every 600ml/1 pint/2½ cups liquid.

5 Heat the mixture gently, stirring occasionally, until the sugar has dissolved, then bring to the boil and boil rapidly for 10 minutes until the jelly reaches setting point (105°C/220°F). Remove the pan from the heat.

6 Skim any scum from the surface using a slotted spoon and pour the jelly into warmed sterilized jars. Cover and seal. Store in a cool, dark place and use within 2 years. Once opened, keep the jelly in the refrigerator and eat within 3 months.

Energy 3821kcal/16290kJ; Protein 5.7g; Carbohydrate 967.7g, of which sugars 967.7g; Fat 0.3g, of which saturates 0g; Cholesterol 0mg; Calcium 507mg; Fibre 4.8g; Sodium 78mg.

red grape, plum and cardamom jelly

Enhance the flavour of roast beef and steaks with a spoonful of deep ruby-coloured jelly.
You may need to add a little pectin to the jelly to ensure you achieve a really good set.

Makes about 1.3kg/3lb

INGREDIENTS

1.8kg/4lb plums
450g/1lb/3 cups red grapes
15ml/1 tbsp cardamom pods
600ml/1 pint/2½ cups cold water
350–450ml/12fl oz–¾ pint/1½ cups–
    scant 2 cups pectin stock (optional)
about 1kg/2¼lb/5 cups preserving
    or granulated (white) sugar

1 Cut the plums in half, then twist
the two halves apart and remove
the stone (pit). Roughly chop the
flesh and halve the grapes. Remove
the cardamom seeds from the pods
and crush them in a mortar.

2 Put the fruit and cardamom
seeds in a large heavy pan and
pour over the water. Slowly bring
to the boil, then simmer for about
30 minutes, or until very tender.

3 Check the pectin content of the
fruit (see below); if it is low, stir
the pectin stock into the fruit
mixture and simmer for 5 minutes.

COOK'S TIP

To check the pectin content of the fruit,
spoon 5ml/1 tsp of the juices into a
glass. Add 15ml/1 tbsp of methylated
spirits (denatured alcohol) and shake
gently. After about a minute a clot
should form. If the clot is large and jelly-
like or if two or three smaller clots form,
the pectin content should be sufficient
for a set. If there are lots of small clots,
or none at all, the pectin content is low
and additional pectin will be needed.

4 Pour the fruit into a sterilized
jelly bag suspended over a large
bowl. Leave to drain for 3 hours,
or until the juices stop dripping.
Measure the juice into a clean pan,
adding 450g/1lb/2¼ cups sugar for
every 600ml/1 pint/2½ cups juice.

5 Heat the mixture gently, stirring
occasionally, until the sugar has
completely dissolved.

6 Bring the mixture to the boil,
then boil rapidly for 10 minutes
until setting point is reached
(105°C/220°F). Remove the pan
from the heat.

7 Skim off any scum from the
surface, then pour the jelly into
warmed sterilized jars, cover and
seal. Store in a cool, dark place
and use within 2 years. Keep in the
refrigerator once opened, and eat
within 3 months.

Energy 4246kcal/18126kJ; Protein 9.2g; Carbohydrate 1120.9g, of which sugars 1120.9g; Fat 0.8g, of which saturates 0g; Cholesterol 0mg; Calcium 628mg; Fibre 10.7g; Sodium 75mg.

pear and pomegranate jelly

This delicate jelly has a faintly exotic perfume. Pears are not naturally rich in pectin so liquid pectin needs to be added to the jelly during cooking to help it achieve a good set.

4 While the pears are simmering, cut the pomegranates in half horizontally, and use a lemon squeezer to extract all the juice: there should be about 250ml/ 8fl oz/1 cup.

5 Add the pomegranate juice to the pan and bring back to the boil. Reduce the heat and simmer for 2 minutes. Pour the fruit and juices into a sterilized jelly bag suspended over a large bowl. Leave to drip for at least 3 hours.

6 Measure the strained juice into the cleaned pan, adding 450g/1lb/ 2¼ cups sugar for every 600ml/ 1 pint/2½ cups juice.

Makes about 1.2kg/2½lb

INGREDIENTS

900g/2lb pears
pared rind and juice of 2 lemons
1 cinnamon stick
750ml/1¼ pints/3 cups water
900g/2lb red pomegranates
about 900g/2lb/4½ cups preserving or
  granulated (white) sugar
250ml/8fl oz/1 cup liquid pectin
15ml/1 tbsp rose water (optional)

COOK'S TIP

Once opened, store the jelly in the refrigerator and use within 3 months.

1 Wash and remove the stalks from the pears and chop the fruit roughly. Put the chopped fruit in a large heavy pan with the lemon rind and juice, cinnamon stick and measured water.

2 Bring the mixture to the boil, then reduce the heat to low, cover with a lid and simmer gently for about 15 minutes.

3 Remove the lid from the pan, stir the fruit mixture, then leave to simmer, uncovered, for a further 15 minutes.

7 Heat gently, stirring occasionally, until the sugar has dissolved. Bring to the boil, then boil rapidly for 3 minutes. Remove the pan from the heat and stir in the liquid pectin.

8 Skim any scum from the surface, then stir in the rose water, if using. Pour the jelly into warmed sterilized jars. Cover and seal. Store in a cool, dark place and use within 18 months.

Energy 3756kcal/16022kJ; Protein 6g; Carbohydrate 993.6g, of which sugars 993.6g; Fat 0.4g, of which saturates 0g; Cholesterol 0mg; Calcium 530mg; Fibre 7.6g; Sodium 66mg.

guava jelly

Fragrant guava makes an aromatic, pale rust-coloured jelly with a soft set and a slightly sweet-sour flavour that is enhanced by lime juice. Guava jelly goes well with goat's cheese.

Makes about 900g/2lb

INGREDIENTS

900g/2lb guavas
juice of 2–3 limes
about 600ml/1 pint/2½ cups cold water
about 500g/1¼lb/2½ cups preserving
  or granulated (white) sugar

1 Thinly peel and halve the guavas. Using a spoon, scoop out the seeds (pips) from the centre of the fruit and discard them.

2 Place halved guavas in a large heavy pan with 15ml/1 tbsp lime juice and the water – there should be just enough to cover the fruit. Bring the mixture to the boil, then reduce the heat, cover with a lid and simmer for 30 minutes, or until the fruit is tender.

3 Pour the fruit and juices into a sterilized jelly bag suspended over a large bowl. Leave to drain for at least 3 hours.

COOK'S TIP

Do not be tempted to squeeze the jelly bag while the fruit juices are draining from it; this will result in a cloudy jelly.

4 Measure the juice into the cleaned preserving pan, adding 400g/14oz/2 cups sugar and 15ml/ 1 tbsp lime juice for every 600ml/ 1 pint/2½ cups guava juice.

5 Heat gently, stirring occasionally, until the sugar has dissolved. Boil rapidly for about 10 minutes. When the jelly reaches setting point, remove the pan from the heat.

6 Skim any scum from the surface of the jelly using a slotted spoon, then pour the jelly into warmed sterilized jars. Cover and seal.

7 Store the jelly in a cool, dark place and use within 1 year. Once opened, keep in the refrigerator and eat within 3 months.

Energy 2090kcal/8912kJ; Protein 3.4g; Carbohydrate 552.5g, of which sugars 552.5g; Fat 0.3g, of which saturates 0g; Cholesterol 0mg; Calcium 298mg; Fibre 6.6g; Sodium 39mg.

hedgerow jelly

In the autumn, hedgerows are laden with damsons, blackberries and elderberries and it is well worth spending an afternoon in the countryside picking fruit to make into this delightful jelly.

2 Mash the fruit and leave to cool slightly. Pour into a scalded jelly bag suspended over a non-metallic bowl and leave to drain overnight.

3 Measure the strained juice into a preserving pan. Add 450g/1lb/ 2¼ cups sugar for every 600ml/ 1 pint/2½ cups strained fruit juice.

4 Heat the mixture, stirring, over a low heat until the sugar has dissolved. Increase the heat and boil rapidly without stirring for 10–15 minutes, or until the jelly reaches setting point (105°C/220°F).

Makes about 1.3kg/3lb

INGREDIENTS

450g/1lb damsons, washed
450g/1lb/4 cups blackberries, washed
225g/8oz/2 cups raspberries
225g/8oz/2 cups elderberries, washed
juice and pips (seeds) of 2 large lemons
about 1.3kg/3lb/6½ cups preserving
 or granulated (white) sugar, warmed

COOK'S TIP

If you do not have enough of one fruit, you can vary the quantities as long as the total weight of fruit is the same.

1 Put the fruit, lemon juice and pips in a large pan. Pour over just enough water to cover. Put a lid on the pan and simmer for 1 hour.

5 Remove the pan from the heat and skim off any scum using a slotted spoon. Ladle into warmed, sterilized jars and seal. Leave to cool, then label and store.

Energy 5229kcal/22307kJ; Protein 9.3g; Carbohydrate 1382.9g, of which sugars 1382.9g; Fat 0.4g, of which saturates 0.1g; Cholesterol 0mg; Calcium 799mg; Fibre 8.6g; Sodium 86mg.

mulberry jelly

Deep red mulberries are not often available but if you have access to a tree you will find they make the most wonderful jellies and jams. For a good set, pick the fruits when they are red.

Makes about 900g/2lb

INGREDIENTS
900g/2lb/8 cups unripe red mulberries
grated rind and juice of 1 lemon
600ml/1 pint/2½ cups water
about 900g/2lb/4½ cups preserving
    or granulated (white) sugar, warmed

1 Put the mulberries in a pan with the lemon rind and juice and the water. Bring to the boil, cover and simmer for 1 hour, then remove from the heat and leave to cool.

2 Pour the fruit into a scalded jelly bag suspended over a non-metallic bowl and leave to drain overnight.

3 Measure the strained juice into a preserving pan. Add 450g/1lb/ 2¼ cups sugar for every 600ml/ 1 pint/2½ cups fruit juice.

4 Heat the mixture over a low heat, stirring, until the sugar has completely dissolved. Increase the heat and boil rapidly, without stirring, for 5–10 minutes, or to setting point (105°C/220°F).

5 Skim off any scum from the surface of the jelly using a slotted spoon. Ladle into warmed, sterilized jars, cover and seal. When the jars are completely cool, label, then store in a cool, dark place.

COOK'S TIPS
• To test for the set, spoon a little jelly on to a chilled saucer. Chill for about 3 minutes, then gently push the jelly with your finger; if the surface wrinkles, the jelly has reached setting point and it is ready to bottle.
• To make redcurrant jelly using the method here, measure the same quantity of fruit, but add slightly less sugar to the strained juice: 450g/ 1lb/1¼ cups sugar for every 600ml/ 1 pint/2½ cups juice.

Energy 3621kcal/15456kJ; Protein 8.7g; Carbohydrate 954.3g, of which sugars 954.3g; Fat 0.9g, of which saturates 0.3g; Cholesterol 0mg; Calcium 552mg; Fibre 7.5g; Sodium 63mg.

cranberry jelly

This clear, well-flavoured preserve has a tart flavour and is absolutely delicious served with freshly baked scones, toasted tea cakes and crumpets, or as a glaze for fruit tarts. It can also be served at Christmas with a festive roast turkey, pheasant or guinea fowl.

Makes about 900g/2lb

INGREDIENTS

900g/2lb/8 cups cranberries

450g/1lb sweet eating apples, washed and chopped with skins and cores intact

grated rind and juice of 1 orange

600ml/1 pint/2½ cups water

about 900g/2lb/4½ cups preserving or granulated (white) sugar, warmed

COOK'S TIP

Do not be tempted to squeeze the jelly bag while it is draining or the jelly will become cloudy.

1 Put the cranberries and apples in a pan with the orange rind, juice and water. Bring to the boil then cover and simmer for 1 hour.

2 Remove the pan from the heat and set aside to cool slightly. Pour the fruit and juices into a scalded jelly bag suspended over a non-metallic bowl and leave to drain overnight.

3 Measure the strained juice into a preserving pan. Add 450g/1lb/ 2¼ cups sugar for every 600ml/ 1 pint/2½ cups strained juice.

4 Heat, stirring, over a low heat until the sugar has dissolved completely. Increase the heat and boil rapidly, without stirring, for 5–10 minutes, or until the jelly reaches setting point (105°C/220°F).

5 Remove the pan from the heat and skim off any scum from the surface using a slotted spoon. Ladle into warmed, sterilized jars, cover and seal. Leave to cool, then label and store in a cool, dark place.

Energy 3721kcal/15884kJ; Protein 6g; Carbohydrate 985g, of which sugars 985g; Fat 0.5g, of which saturates 0g; Cholesterol 0mg; Calcium 497mg; Fibre 8g; Sodium 64mg.

red plum and cardamom jelly

The fragrance of warm, spicy cardamom combines wonderfully with all varieties of plum – red plums with a good tart flavour are perfect for making into this sweet, fruity, aromatic jelly. Serve it with plain rich ice creams and custards or spread it on toast for breakfast.

Makes about 1.8kg/4lb

INGREDIENTS

1.8kg/4lb red plums, stoned (pitted)

10ml/2 tsp crushed green
  cardamom pods

600ml/1 pint/2½ cups red grape juice

150ml/¼ pint/⅔ cup water

about 1.3kg/3lb/6½ cups preserving
  or granulated (white) sugar, warmed

1 Put the plums, cardamom pods, grape juice and water in a large pan. Bring to the boil, then cover and simmer gently for 1 hour. Leave to cool slightly, then pour into a scalded jelly bag suspended over a non-metallic bowl and leave to drain overnight.

2 Measure the strained juice into a preserving pan. Add 450g/1lb/2¼ cups sugar for every 600ml/1 pint/2½ cups strained juice.

3 Heat the mixture over a low heat, stirring constantly until the sugar has dissolved completely. Increase the heat and boil, without stirring, for 10–15 minutes, or until the jelly reaches setting point (105°C/220°F).

4 Remove the pan from the heat and skim off any scum. Spoon the jelly into warmed sterilized jars, cover and seal. When cool, label and store in a cool, dark place.

Energy 5338kcal/22783kJ; Protein 10.1g; Carbohydrate 1411.3g, of which sugars 1411.3g; Fat 0.6g, of which saturates 0g; Cholesterol 0mg; Calcium 767mg; Fibre 9.6g; Sodium 90mg.

rhubarb and mint jelly

The speckling of this jelly with tiny pieces of chopped fresh mint makes it a very pretty gift.

Makes about 2kg/4½lb

INGREDIENTS

1kg/2¼lb rhubarb

about 1.3kg/3lb/6½ cups preserving
  or granulated (white) sugar, warmed

large bunch fresh mint

30ml/2 tbsp finely chopped
  fresh mint

COOK'S TIPS

• This recipe is a good way to use
up older dark red or green-stemmed
rhubarb, which is usually too tough to
use for desserts.

• As well as serving as a delightful
sweet preserve, this jelly is also very
good served with fatty roast meats
such as lamb and goose.

1 Using a sharp knife, cut the
rhubarb into chunks and place in
a large, heavy pan. Pour in just
enough water to cover, cover the
pan with a lid and cook until the
rhubarb is soft.

2 Remove the pan from the heat
and leave to cool slightly. Pour the
stewed fruit and juices into a
scalded jelly bag suspended over
a non-metallic bowl and leave to
drain overnight.

3 Measure the strained juice into
a preserving pan and add 450g/
1lb/2¼ cups warmed sugar for
each 600ml/1 pint/2½ cups
strained juice.

4 Add the bunch of mint to the
pan. Bring to the boil, stirring
until the sugar has dissolved. Boil
to setting point (105°C/220°F).
Remove the mint.

5 Leave to stand for 10 minutes,
stir in the chopped mint, then pot
and seal. Label when cold.

Energy 5165kcal/22040kJ; Protein 11.1g; Carbohydrate 1363.6g, of which sugars 1360.9g; Fat 0.6g, of which saturates 0g; Cholesterol 0mg; Calcium 1073mg; Fibre 4.2g; Sodium 95mg.

red gooseberry jelly

*This delicious jelly is perfect for spreading on toast at any time of the day. Choose small dark
red gooseberries to produce a jelly with the best colour and flavour.*

Makes about 2kg/4½lb

INGREDIENTS

1.3kg/3lb/12 cups red gooseberries

2 red-skinned eating apples, washed
  and chopped with skins and cores intact

2.5cm/1in piece fresh root ginger, sliced

about 1.3kg/3lb/6½ cups preserving
  or granulated (white) sugar, warmed

COOK'S TIPS

The amount of pectin in gooseberries
diminishes as the fruit ripens so select
firm, just ripe fruit when making this jelly
to achieve a really good set.

1 Put the fruit and ginger in a pan
and pour over just enough water
to cover the fruit. Cover and
simmer for 45 minutes.

2 Remove from the heat, cool
slightly, then pour the fruit and
juices into a scalded jelly bag
suspended over a non-metallic
bowl and leave to drain overnight.

3 Measure the strained juice into
a preserving pan and add 450g/1lb/
2¼ cups warmed sugar for every
600ml/1 pint/2½ cups juice.

4 Stir over a low heat until the
sugar has dissolved. Boil for about
10 minutes, or to setting point
(105°C/220°F). Skim off any scum,
then pot, seal and label.

Energy 5233kcal/22327kJ; Protein 11.8g; Carbohydrate 1378.3g, of which sugars 1378.3g; Fat 1.9g, of which saturates 0g; Cholesterol 0mg; Calcium 820mg; Fibre 12.1g; Sodium 89mg.

rosehip and apple jelly

This economical jelly is made with windfall apples and wild rosehips. It is still rich in vitamin C, full of flavour, and excellent spread on freshly toasted crumpets or scones.

Makes about 2kg/4½lb

INGREDIENTS

1kg/2¼lb windfall apples, peeled, trimmed and quartered

450g/1lb firm, ripe rosehips

about 1.3kg/3lb/6½ cups preserving or granulated (white) sugar, warmed

1 Place the quartered apples in a large pan with just enough water to cover, plus 300ml/½ pint/ 1¼ cups of extra water.

COOK'S TIP

There is no need to remove all the peel from the apples: simply cut out any bruised, damaged or bad areas.

2 Bring the mixture to the boil and cook gently until the apples soften and turn to a pulp. Meanwhile, chop the rosehips coarsely. Add the rosehips to the pan with the apple and simmer for 10 minutes.

3 Remove from the heat and stand for 10 minutes, then pour the mixture into a scalded jelly bag suspended over a non-metallic bowl and leave to drain overnight.

4 Measure the juice into a preserving pan and bring to the boil. Add 400g/14oz/2 cups warmed sugar for each 600ml/ 1 pint/2½ cups of liquid. Stir until the sugar has completely dissolved. Boil to setting point (105°C/220°F).

5 Pour the jelly into warmed, sterilized jars and seal. Label and store when completely cold.

Energy 5684kcal/24259kJ; Protein 8.4g; Carbohydrate 1505.7g, of which sugars 1505.7g; Fat 0.5g, of which saturates 0g; Cholesterol 0mg; Calcium 761mg; Fibre 7.7g; Sodium 94mg.

spiced cider and apple jelly

This wonderful spicy jelly has a rich, warming flavour, making it ideal to serve during the cold winter months. Serve as a spread or use it to sweeten apple pies and desserts.

Makes about 1.3kg/3lb

INGREDIENTS

900g/2lb tart cooking apples, washed and coarsely chopped with skins and cores intact

900ml/1¼ pints/3¾ cups sweet (hard) cider

juice and pips (seeds) of 2 oranges

1 cinnamon stick

6 whole cloves

150ml/¼ pint/⅔ cup water

about 900g/2lb/4½ cups preserving or granulated (white) sugar, warmed

2 Leave to cool slightly, then pour the fruit into a scalded jelly bag suspended over a non-metallic bowl and leave to drain overnight.

3 Measure the strained juice into a preserving pan. Add 450g/1lb/ 2¼ cups warmed sugar for every 600ml/1 pint/2½ cups juice.

4 Heat, stirring, over a low heat until the sugar has dissolved. Increase the heat and boil, without stirring, for 10 minutes, or until the jelly reaches setting point (105°C/220°F).

5 Remove from the heat and skim off any scum. Ladle into warmed sterilized jars. Cover, seal and label.

1 Put the apples, cider, juice and pips, cinnamon, cloves and water in a large pan. Bring to the boil, cover and simmer for about 1 hour.

Energy 3975kcal/16950kJ; Protein 5.4g; Carbohydrate 990.6g, of which sugars 990.6g; Fat 0.3g, of which saturates 0g; Cholesterol 0mg; Calcium 561mg; Fibre 4.8g; Sodium 123mg.

quince and coriander jelly

When raw, quinces are inedible but once cooked and sweetened they become aromatic and have a wonderful flavour, which is enhanced here by the addition of warm, spicy coriander seeds.

2 Leave the fruit to cool slightly, then pour into a scalded jelly bag suspended over a non-metallic bowl and leave to drain overnight.

3 Measure the strained juice into a preserving pan. Add 450g/1lb/ 2¼ cups warmed sugar for every 600ml/1 pint/2½ cups juice.

4 Heat, stirring, over a low heat until the sugar has completely dissolved. Increase the heat and boil rapidly, without stirring, for 5–10 minutes or until the jelly reaches setting point (105°C/220°F).

5 Remove the pan from the heat and skim off any scum from the surface using a slotted spoon. Ladle into warmed sterilized jars, cover and seal. When cold, label and store in a cool, dark place.

Makes about 900g/2lb

INGREDIENTS

1kg/2¼lb quinces, washed and coarsely chopped with skins and cores intact

15ml/1 tbsp coriander seeds

juice and pips (seeds) of 2 large lemons

900ml/1½ pints/3¾ cups water

about 900g/2lb/4½ cups preserving or granulated (white) sugar, warmed

1 Put the quinces in a pan with the coriander seeds, lemon juice and pips, and the water. Bring to the boil, cover and simmer gently for about 1½ hours.

VARIATION

If you don't have enough quinces, you can make up the quantity with apples. The flavour won't be quite the same but the jelly will still be delicious.

COOK'S TIP

Jellies can look very pretty served in decorative glasses. Bottle the jelly in jars as above, then, when ready to serve, gently heat the jelly in a pan with a very small amount of water until melted. Pour the jelly into a heatproof glass and leave to set before serving.

Energy 3678kcal/15687kJ; Protein 5.5g; Carbohydrate 973.5g, of which sugars 973.5g; Fat 0.3g, of which saturates 0g; Cholesterol 0mg; Calcium 513mg; Fibre 7.3g; Sodium 64mg.

geranium and pear jelly

This jelly uses the leaves of scented geranium to give an aromatic lift to the pears. Use rose-scented leaves if you have them, otherwise add a couple of drops of rose water to the strained juice.

Makes about 900g/2lb

INGREDIENTS

900g/2lb Comice pears, washed and coarsely chopped with skins and cores intact

7 rose-scented geranium leaves, plus extra for storing

juice and pips (seeds) of 1 lemon

60ml/4 tbsp clear honey

900ml/1½ pints/3¾ cups water

about 900g/2lb/4½ cups preserving or granulated (white) sugar, warmed

2 Remove the pan from the heat and leave to cool slightly. Pour the fruit into a scalded jelly bag suspended over a non-metallic bowl and leave to drain overnight.

3 Measure the strained juice into a preserving pan. Add 450g/1lb/ 2¼ cups warmed sugar for every 600ml/1 pint/2½ cups juice.

4 Heat, stirring, over a low heat until the sugar has dissolved. Increase the heat and boil rapidly, without stirring, for 10 minutes, or to setting point (105°C/220°F).

5 Remove the pan from the heat and skim off any scum using a slotted spoon. Place a blanched geranium leaf into each warmed sterilized jar, Then ladle in the jelly. Cover and seal, then label.

1 Put the pears, geranium leaves, lemon juice, honey and water in a large pan. Bring to the boil, then cover and simmer for 1 hour.

Energy 3851kcal/16424kJ; Protein 5.7g; Carbohydrate 1019.3g, of which sugars 1019.3g; Fat 0.3g, of which saturates 0g; Cholesterol 0mg; Calcium 516mg; Fibre 7.3g; Sodium 71mg.

pineapple and passion fruit jelly

This exotic jelly has a wonderful warming glow to its taste and appearance. For the best-flavoured jelly, use a tart-tasting, not too ripe pineapple rather than a very ripe, sweet one.

Makes about 900g/2lb

INGREDIENTS

1 large pineapple, peeled, topped and tailed and coarsely chopped

4 passion fruit, halved, with seeds and pulp scooped out

900ml/1½ pints/3¾ cups water

about 900g/2lb/4½ cups preserving or granulated (white) sugar, warmed

COOK'S TIP

For the best flavour, choose passion fruit with dark, wrinkled skins.

1 Place the pineapple and the passion fruit seeds and pulp in a large pan with the water.

2 Bring the mixture to the boil, cover and simmer for 1½ hours. Remove from the heat and leave to cool slightly. Transfer the fruit to a food processor and process briefly.

3 Tip the fruit pulp and any juices from the pan, into a scalded jelly bag suspended over a non-metallic bowl and leave to drain overnight.

4 Measure the strained juice into a preserving pan and add 450g/1lb/2¼ cups warmed sugar for every 600ml/1 pint/2½ cups juice.

5 Heat gently, stirring, until the sugar has dissolved. Increase the heat and boil rapidly, without stirring, for 10–15 minutes or to setting point (105°C/220°F).

6 Remove the pan from the heat and skim off any scum using a slotted spoon. Ladle the jelly into warmed sterilized jars, cover and seal. When cool, label and store in a cool, dark place.

Energy 3633kcal/15504kJ; Protein 5.7g; Carbohydrate 961.6g, of which sugars 961.6g; Fat 0.5g, of which saturates 0g; Cholesterol 0mg; Calcium 515mg; Fibre 2.9g; Sodium 61mg.

pomegranate and grenadine jelly

The slightly tart flavoured, jewel-like flesh of the pomegranate makes the most wonderful jelly.
Be careful though, because pomegranate juice can stain indelibly when spilt on clothing.

Makes about 900g/2lb

INGREDIENTS

6 ripe red pomegranates, peeled and
   seeds removed from membranes

120ml/4fl oz/½ cup grenadine syrup

juice and pips (seeds) of 2 oranges

300ml/½ pint/1¼ cups water

about 900g/2lb/4½ cups preserving
   or granulated (white) sugar, warmed

1 Put the pomegranate seeds in
bowl and crush to release their
juice. Transfer them to a pan and
add the grenadine, orange juice,
pips and water.

2 Bring the mixture to the boil,
cover and simmer for 1½ hours.
Mash the fruit and leave to cool
slightly, then pour into a scalded
jelly bag suspended over a bowl
and leave to drain overnight.

3 Measure the juice into a pan and
add 450g/1lb/2¼ cups sugar for
every 600ml/1 pint/2½ cups juice.

4 Heat, stirring, over a low heat
until the sugar has dissolved.
Increase the heat and boil rapidly,
without stirring, for 5–10 minutes,
or until the jelly reaches setting
point (105°C/220°F).

5 Remove the pan from the heat
and skim off any scum. Ladle into
warmed sterilized jars, cover, seal
and label. Store in a cool place.

Energy 3776kcal/16114kJ; Protein 5.5g; Carbohydrate 1000.5g, of which sugars 1000.5g; Fat 0.2g, of which saturates 0g; Cholesterol 0mg; Calcium 511mg; Fibre 0.8g; Sodium 76mg.

seedless raspberry and passion fruit jam

The pips in raspberry jam can often put people off this wonderful preserve. This version has none of the pips and all of the flavour, and is enhanced by the tangy addition of passion fruit.

Makes about 1.3kg/3lb

INGREDIENTS

1.6kg/3½lb/14 cups raspberries

4 passion fruit, halved

1.3kg/3lb/6½ cups preserving sugar
  with pectin, warmed

juice of 1 lemon

COOK'S TIPS

• Check the instructions on the sugar packet for details of the boiling time.
• If you cannot find preserving sugar with pectin, use the same quantity of regular sugar and add powdered or liquid pectin. Check the instructions on the packet for quantities.

1 Place the raspberries in a large pan, then scoop out the passion fruit seeds and pulp and add to the raspberries. Cover and cook over a low heat for 20 minutes, or until the juices begin to run.

2 Remove the pan from the heat and leave to cool slightly, then, using the back of a spoon, press the fruit through a coarse sieve into a preserving pan.

3 Add the sugar and lemon juice to the pan and stir over a low heat until the sugar has dissolved. Bring to the boil and cook for 4 minutes, or until the jam reaches setting point (105°C/220°F).

4 Remove the pan from the heat and skim off any scum. Leave to cool slightly, then pour into warmed sterilized jars. Seal and label, then store in a cool place.

Energy 5544kcal/23688kJ; Protein 30.5g; Carbohydrate 1435.6g, of which sugars 1435.6g; Fat 5g, of which saturates 1.7g; Cholesterol 0mg; Calcium 1096mg; Fibre 42g; Sodium 137mg.

wild strawberry and rose petal conserve

This fragrant jam is ideal served with summer cream teas. Rose water complements the strawberries beautifully, but only add a few drops because the flavour can easily become over-powering.

Makes about 900g/2lb

INGREDIENTS

900g/2lb/8 cups wild Alpine strawberries

450g/1lb/4 cups strawberries, hulled and mashed

2 dark pink rose buds, petals only

juice of 2 lemons

1.3kg/3lb/6½ cups granulated (white) sugar, warmed

a few drops of rose water

1 Put all the strawberries in a non-metallic bowl with the rose petals, lemon juice and warmed sugar. Cover and leave overnight.

2 The next day, tip the fruit into a preserving pan and heat gently, stirring, until all the sugar has dissolved. Boil for 10–15 minutes, or to setting point (105°C/220°F).

3 Stir the rose water into the jam, then remove the pan from the heat. Skim off any scum and leave to cool for 5 minutes, then stir and pour into warmed sterilized jars. Seal and label, then store.

COOK'S TIPS

• If you are unable to find wild berries, use ordinary strawberries instead. Leave the smaller berries whole but mash any large ones.

• To make plain strawberry jam, make in the same way but leave out the rose petals and rose water.

Energy 5487kcal/23379kJ; Protein 17.3g; Carbohydrate 1439.5g, of which sugars 1439.5g; Fat 1.4g, of which saturates 0g; Cholesterol 0mg; Calcium 905mg; Fibre 14.9g; Sodium 159mg.

cherry-berry conserve

Tart cranberries enliven the taste of cherries and also add an essential dose of pectin to this pretty conserve, which is fabulous spread on crumpets or toast. It is also delicious stirred into meaty gravies and sauces served with roast duck, poultry or pork.

2 Add the water to the pan. Cover and bring to the boil, then simmer for 20–30 minutes, or until the cranberries are very tender.

3 Add the sugar to the pan and heat gently, stirring, until the sugar has dissolved. Bring to the boil, then cook for 10 minutes, or to setting point (105°C/220°F).

4 Remove the pan from the heat and skim off any scum using a slotted spoon. Leave to cool for 10 minutes, then stir gently and pour into warmed sterilized jars. Seal, label and store.

Makes about 1.3kg/3lb

INGREDIENTS

350g/12oz/3 cups fresh cranberries
1kg/2¼lb/5½ cups cherries, pitted
120ml/4fl oz/½ cup blackcurrant
  or raspberry syrup
juice of 2 lemons
250ml/8fl oz/1 cup water
1.3kg/3lb/6½ cups preserving
  or granulated (white) sugar, warmed

COOK'S TIP

The cranberries must be cooked until very tender before the sugar is added, otherwise they will become tough.

1 Put the cranberries in a food processor and process until coarsely chopped. Scrape into a pan and add the cherries, fruit syrup and lemon juice.

Energy 5859kcal/24986kJ; Protein 16.7g; Carbohydrate 1540.4g, of which sugars 1540.4g; Fat 1.4g, of which saturates 0g; Cholesterol 0mg; Calcium 844mg; Fibre 14.6g; Sodium 105mg.

summer berry and juniper jam

In late summer, there is a moment when all the different varieties of berries suddenly seem to be ripe at the same time. Combine them in jam as the flavours work well together, particularly when blended with juniper, which produces a taste reminiscent of gin.

Makes about 1.3kg/3lb

INGREDIENTS

675g/1½lb/6 cups raspberries
675g/1½lb/6 cups blackberries
10ml/2 tsp juniper berries,
  crushed
300ml/½ pint/1¼ cups water
1.3kg/3lb/6½ cups granulated (white)
  sugar, warmed
juice of 2 lemons

COOK'S TIP

Juniper berries are quite soft and are
easily broken down into coarsely
crushed pieces. Put the berries in
a mortar and crush with a pestle.

1 Put the raspberries, blackberries and juniper berries in a large heavy pan with the water. Set over a low heat, cover and cook gently for about 15 minutes, or until the juices begin to run.

2 Add the sugar and lemon juice to the pan and cook over a low heat, stirring frequently, until the sugar has dissolved. (Be careful not to break up the berries too much.)

3 Bring to the boil and cook for 5–10 minutes, or until the jam reaches setting point (105°C/220°F). Remove the pan from the heat and skim off any scum from the surface using a slotted spoon. Leave to cool for about 5 minutes, then stir gently and pour into warmed sterilized jars. Seal and label, then store in a cool, dark place.

Energy 5460kcal/23325kJ; Protein 25.4g; Carbohydrate 1420.6g, of which sugars 1420.6g; Fat 4g, of which saturates 1.4g; Cholesterol 0mg; Calcium 1027mg; Fibre 33.8g; Sodium 119mg.

blueberry and lime jam

The subtle yet fragrant flavour of blueberries can be illusive on its own. Adding a generous quantity of tangy lime juice enhances their flavour and gives this jam a wonderful zesty taste.

Makes about 1.3kg/3lb

INGREDIENTS

1.3kg/3lb/12 cups blueberries

finely pared rind and juice
    of 4 limes

1kg/2¼lb/5 cups preserving sugar
    with pectin

COOK'S TIP

Blueberries are not naturally high in pectin, so extra pectin is needed for a good set. If you prefer, used granulated sugar and add pectin according to the instruction on the packet in place of the preserving sugar with pectin.

1 Put the blueberries, lime juice and half the sugar in a large, non-metallic bowl and lightly crush the berries using a potato masher. Set aside for about 4 hours.

2 Tip the crushed berry mixture into a pan and stir in the finely pared lime rind and the remaining preserving sugar. Heat slowly, stirring continuously, until the sugar has completely dissolved.

3 Increase the heat and bring to the boil. Boil rapidly for about 4 minutes, or until the jam reaches setting point (105°C/220°F).

4 Remove the pan from the heat and set aside for 5 minutes. Stir the jam gently, then pour into warmed sterilized jars. Seal the jars, then label when completely cool. Store in a cool, dark place.

Energy 4265kcal/18162kJ; Protein 16.7g; Carbohydrate 1111.3g, of which sugars 1111.3g; Fat 2.6g, of which saturates 0g; Cholesterol 0mg; Calcium 1063mg; Fibre 40.3g; Sodium 86mg.

blackcurrant jam

This jam has a rich, fruity flavour and a wonderfully strong dark colour. It is punchy and delicious with scones for tea or spread on croissants for a continental-style breakfast.

Makes about 1.3kg/3lb

INGREDIENTS

1.3kg/3lb/12 cups blackcurrants
grated rind and juice of 1 orange
475ml/16fl oz/2 cups water
1.3kg/3lb/6½ cups granulated (white)
   sugar, warmed
30ml/2 tbsp cassis (optional)

1 Place the blackcurrants, orange rind and juice and water in a large heavy pan. Bring to the boil, reduce the heat and simmer for 30 minutes.

2 Add the warmed sugar to the pan and stir over a low heat until the sugar has dissolved.

3 Bring the mixture to the boil and cook for about 8 minutes, or until the jam reaches setting point (105°C/220°F).

4 Remove the pan from the heat and skim off any scum from the surface using a slotted spoon. Leave to cool for 5 minutes, then stir in the cassis, if using.

5 Pour the jam into warmed sterilized jars and seal. Leave the jars to cool completely, then label and store in a cool, dark place.

Energy 5504kcal/23503kJ; Protein 18.4g; Carbohydrate 1448.7g, of which sugars 1448.7g; Fat 0.1g, of which saturates 0g; Cholesterol 0mg; Calcium 1474mg; Fibre 46.8g; Sodium 122mg.

dried apricot jam

This richly flavoured jam can be made at any time of year, so even if you miss the short apricot season, you can still enjoy the delicious taste of sweet, tangy apricot jam all year round.

Makes about 2kg/4½lb

INGREDIENTS

675g/1½lb dried apricots

900ml/1½ pints/3¾ cups apple juice

juice and grated rind of
  2 unwaxed lemons

675g/1½lb/scant 3½ cups preserving
  or granulated (white) sugar, warmed

50g/2oz/½ cup blanched almonds,
  coarsely chopped

COOK'S TIP

Use the best quality traditional dried apricots to make this jam. They have a more suitable texture than the soft ready-to-eat dried apricots and will produce a better end result.

1 Put the apricots in a bowl, pour over the apple juice and leave to soak overnight.

2 Pour the soaked apricots and juice into a preserving pan and add the lemon juice and rind. Bring to the boil, then lower the heat and simmer for 15–20 minutes until the apricots are soft.

3 Add the warmed sugar to the pan and bring to the boil, stirring until the sugar has completely dissolved. Boil for 15–20 minutes, or until setting point is reached (105°C/220°F).

4 Stir the chopped almonds into the jam and leave to stand for about 15 minutes, then pour the jam into warmed, sterilized jars. Seal, then leave to cool completely before labelling. Store in a cool, dark place.

Energy 4032kcal/17163kJ; Protein 40.9g; Carbohydrate 955.2g, of which sugars 953.9g; Fat 31.9g, of which saturates 2.2g; Cholesterol 0mg; Calcium 971mg; Fibre 46.2g; Sodium 142mg.

peach and amaretto jam

Adding amaretto (almond liqueur) produces a luxurious jam that's perfect served on warm buttered toast or English muffins. You can use peach schnapps in place of the amaretto if you prefer.

Makes about 1.3kg/3lb

INGREDIENTS

1.3kg/3lb peaches
250ml/8fl oz/1 cup water
juice of 2 lemons
1.3kg/3lb/6½ cups granulated (white)
  sugar, warmed
45ml/3 tbsp amaretto liqueur

1 Carefully peel the peaches using a vegetable peeler, or blanch briefly in boiling water, then peel with a knife. Reserve the skins.

2 Halve and stone the fruit, dice the flesh and put in a pan with the water. Place the peach skins in a small pan with water to cover. Boil until the liquid is reduced to 30ml/2 tbsp. Press the skins and liquid through a sieve into the peaches. Cover and simmer for 20 minutes, or until soft.

3 Add the lemon juice and sugar to the pan. Heat, stirring, until the sugar has dissolved completely. Bring to the boil and cook for 10–15 minutes, or to setting point (105°C/220°F). Remove from the heat and skim off any scum from the surface using a slotted spoon.

4 Leave the jam to cool for about 10 minutes, then stir in the amaretto and pour into warmed sterilized jars. Seal, then leave to cool completely before labelling. Store in a cool, dark place.

Energy 5669kcal/24194kJ; Protein 19.5g; Carbohydrate 1472.1g, of which sugars 1472.1g; Fat 1.3g, of which saturates 0g; Cholesterol 0mg; Calcium 782mg; Fibre 19.5g; Sodium 96mg.

gooseberry and elderflower jam

Pale green gooseberries and fragrant elderflowers make perfect partners in this aromatic jam.

Makes about 2kg/4½lb

INGREDIENTS

1.3kg/3lb/12 cups firm gooseberries,
  topped and tailed

300ml/½ pint/1¼ cups water

1.3kg/3lb/6½ cups granulated (white)
  sugar, warmed

juice of 1 lemon

2 handfuls of elderflowers removed
  from their stalks

COOK'S TIP

The time taken to reach setting point
will vary depending on the ripeness of
the gooseberries. The riper the fruit, the
longer the jam will need to be cooked
to reach setting point.

1 Put the gooseberries into a large preserving pan, add the water and bring the mixture to the boil.

2 Cover the pan with a lid and simmer gently for 20 minutes until the fruit is soft. Using a potato masher, gently mash the fruit to crush it lightly.

3 Add the sugar, lemon juice and elderflowers to the pan and stir over a low heat until the sugar has dissolved. Boil for 10 minutes, or to setting point (105°C/220°F). Remove from the heat, skim off any scum and cool for 5 minutes, then stir. Pot and seal, then leave to cool before labelling.

Energy 5369kcal/22906kJ; Protein 20.8g; Carbohydrate 1397.5g, of which sugars 1397.5g; Fat 5.2g, of which saturates 0g; Cholesterol 0mg; Calcium 1053mg; Fibre 31.2g; Sodium 104mg.

damson jam

Dark, plump damsons produce a deeply coloured and richly flavoured jam that makes a delicious treat spread on toasted English muffins or warm crumpets at tea time.

Makes about 2kg/4½lb

INGREDIENTS

1kg/2¼lb damsons or wild plums

1.4 litres/2¼ pints/6 cups water

1kg/2¼lb/5 cups preserving
  or granulated (white) sugar, warmed

COOK'S TIP

It is important to seal the jars as soon
as you have filled them to ensure the
jam remains sterile. However, you
should then leave the jars to cool
completely before labelling and storing
them to avoid the risk of burns.

1 Put the damsons in a preserving pan and pour in the water. Bring to the boil. Reduce the heat and simmer gently until the damsons are soft, then stir in the sugar.

2 Bring the mixture to the boil, skimming off stones as they rise. Boil to setting point (105°C/220°F). Leave to cool for 10 minutes, then pot. Seal, then label and store when cool.

Energy 4320kcal/18430kJ; Protein 10g; Carbohydrate 1141g, of which sugars 1141g; Fat 0g, of which saturates 0g; Cholesterol 0mg; Calcium 770mg; Fibre 18g; Sodium 80mg.

greengage and almond jam

This is the perfect preserve to make when greengages are readily available in stores, or if you find you have a glut of the fruit. It has a gloriously rich, golden honey colour and a smooth texture that contrasts wonderfully with the little slivers of almond.

Makes about 1.3kg/3lb

INGREDIENTS

1.3kg/3lb greengages, stoned (pitted)

350ml/12fl oz/1½ cups water

juice of 1 lemon

50g/2oz/½ cup blanched almonds,
  cut into thin slivers

1.3kg/3lb/6½ cups granulated (white)
  sugar, warmed

COOK'S TIP

Greengages look like unripened plums. However, despite their appearance, they have a wonderfully aromatic flavour that is captured perfectly in this delicious jam.

1 Put the greengages and water in a preserving pan with the lemon juice and almond slivers. Bring to the boil, then cover and simmer for 15–20 minutes, or until the greengages are really soft.

2 Add the sugar to the pan and stir over a low heat until the sugar has dissolved. Bring to the boil and cook for 10–15 minutes, or until the jam reaches setting point (105°C/220°F).

3 Remove the pan from the heat and skim off any scum from the surface using a slotted spoon.

4 Leave to cool for 10 minutes, then stir gently and pour into warmed sterilized jars. Seal, then leave to cool completely before labelling. Store in a cool place.

Energy 5896kcal/25135kJ; Protein 24.9g; Carbohydrate 1476.3g, of which sugars 1475g; Fat 29.2g, of which saturates 2.2g; Cholesterol 0mg; Calcium 978mg; Fibre 24.5g; Sodium 111mg.

rhubarb and ginger jam

Late summer is the time to make this preserve, when rhubarb leaves are enormous and the stalks thick and green. It has a wonderfully tart, tangy flavour and is delicious spooned over plain cake, or used as a filling with whipped cream.

Makes about 2kg/4½lb

INGREDIENTS

1kg/2¼lb rhubarb

1kg/2¼lb/5 cups preserving
or granulated (white) sugar

25g/1oz fresh root ginger, bruised

115g/4oz crystallized ginger

50g/2oz/¼ cup candied orange
peel, chopped

COOK'S TIP

The young, slender rhubarb stems that are available in the spring are more suitable for making tarts and pies. Their delicate flavour does not shine through in preserves, so it is worth waiting until later in the season for mature rhubarb.

1 Cut the rhubarb into short pieces and layer with the sugar in a glass bowl. Leave to stand overnight.

2 The next day, scrape the rhubarb and sugar mixture into a large, heavy preserving pan.

3 Tie the bruised ginger root in a piece of muslin (cheesecloth) and add it to the rhubarb. Cook gently for 30 minutes, or until the rhubarb has softened.

4 Remove the root ginger from the pan and stir in the crystallized ginger and candied orange peel.

5 Bring the mixture to the boil, then cook over a high heat until setting point is reached (105°C/ 220°F). Leave to cool for a few minutes, then pour into warmed sterilized jars and seal. When completely cool, label and store.

Energy 4135kcal/17664kJ; Protein 14.9g; Carbohydrate 1083.8g, of which sugars 1083.8g; Fat 1.7g, of which saturates 0g; Cholesterol 0mg; Calcium 1582mg; Fibre 17.9g; Sodium 314mg.

papaya and apricot jam

Apricots and papaya make perfect partners in this tantalizing jam. However, if you prefer plain apricot jam, simply replace the papaya with the same weight of apricots.

2 Slice the apricots and place in a preserving pan with the kernels, papaya, grated lemon rind and juice and the water. Bring to the boil then cover and simmer for 20–30 minutes, or until the fruit is really tender.

3 Add the sugar to the pan and stir continuously over a low heat until the sugar has dissolved. Bring to the boil and cook for about 15 minutes, or until the jam reaches setting point (105°C/220°F).

Makes about 1.3kg/3lb

INGREDIENTS

900g/2lb stoned (pitted) apricots, 6 stones (pits) reserved

450g/1lb papaya, peeled, seeded and cut into small chunks

grated rind and juice of 2 lemons

250ml/8fl oz/1 cup water

1.3kg/3lb/6½ cups granulated (white) sugar, warmed

COOK'S TIP

The bitter kernels from apricot stones (pits) contribute an almond-like flavour to the jam. Only a few should be used as they have a strong flavour. They are blanched to remove natural toxins.

1 Using a nut cracker or wooden mallet, crack the reserved apricot stones and remove the kernels inside. Put the kernels in a pan, pour over boiling water and cook for 2 minutes, then drain and slide off their skins.

4 Remove the pan from the heat and skim off any scum from the surface using a slotted spoon. Cool for 5 minutes, then stir gently and pour into warmed sterilized jars and seal. When cool, label the jars, then store in a cool, dark place.

Energy 5599kcal/23901kJ; Protein 17.4g; Carbohydrate 1471.7g, of which sugars 1471.7g; Fat 1.5g, of which saturates 0g; Cholesterol 0mg; Calcium 938mg; Fibre 25.3g; Sodium 129mg.

melon and star anise jam

The delicate flavour of melon is brought out by spicy ginger and perfectly complemented by aromatic star anise. Once opened, store this delicious jam in the refrigerator.

Makes about 1.3kg/3lb

INGREDIENTS

2 Charentais or cantaloupe melons,
peeled and seeded

450g/1lb/2¼ cups granulated (white) sugar

2 star anise

4 pieces preserved stem ginger in syrup,
drained and finely chopped

finely grated rind and juice of 2 lemons

2 Tip the melon and sugar mixture into a large pan and add the star anise, chopped ginger, lemon rind and juice and stir to combine.

3 Bring the mixture to the boil, then lower the heat. Simmer for 25 minutes, or until the melon has become transparent and the setting point reached (105°C/220°F).

4 Spoon the jam into hot sterilized jars and seal. Leave to cool, then label and store in a cool, dark place.

COOK'S TIP

To test for the set, spoon a little jam on to a chilled plate. It should wrinkle when pushed with a finger.

1 Cut the melons into small cubes and layer with the granulated sugar in a large non-metallic bowl. Cover with clear film (plastic wrap) and leave overnight, or until the melons release their juices.

Energy 2133kcal/9095kJ; Protein 9.8g; Carbohydrate 554.3g, of which sugars 554.3g; Fat 1.5g, of which saturates 0g; Cholesterol 0mg; Calcium 434mg; Fibre 6g; Sodium 492mg.

oxford marmalade

The characteristic caramel colour and rich flavour of a traditional Oxford marmalade is obtained by cutting the fruit coarsely and cooking it for several hours before adding the sugar.

Makes about 2.25kg/5lb

INGREDIENTS

900g/2lb Seville (Temple) oranges
1.75 litres/3 pints/7½ cups water
1.3kg/3lb/6½ cups granulated
  (white) sugar, warmed

COOK'S TIP

Traditionalists say that only bitter oranges such as Seville (Temple) should be used to make marmalade. Although this isn't always true, it is certainly the case when making Oxford marmalade.

1 Scrub the orange skins, then remove the rind using a vegetable peeler. Thickly slice the rind and put in a large pan.

2 Chop the fruit, reserving the pips (seeds), and add to the rind in the pan, along with the water. Tie the orange pips in a piece of muslin (cheesecloth) and add to the pan. Bring to the boil, then cover and simmer for 2 hours. Add more water during cooking to maintain the same volume. Remove the pan from the heat and leave overnight.

3 The next day, remove the muslin bag from the oranges, squeezing well, and return the pan to the heat. Bring to the boil, then cover and simmer for 1 hour.

4 Add the warmed sugar to the pan, then slowly bring the mixture to the boil, stirring until the sugar has dissolved completely. Increase the heat and boil rapidly for about 15 minutes, or until setting point is reached (105°C/220°F).

5 Remove the pan from the heat and skim off any scum from the surface. Leave to cool for about 5 minutes, stir, then pour into warmed sterilized jars and seal. When cold, label, then store in a cool, dark place.

Energy 5455kcal/23275kJ; Protein 16.4g; Carbohydrate 1435g, of which sugars 1435g; Fat 0.9g, of which saturates 0g; Cholesterol 0mg; Calcium 1112mg; Fibre 15.3g; Sodium 123mg.

st clement's marmalade

This classic preserve made from oranges and lemons has a lovely citrus tang. It has a light, refreshing flavour and is perfect for serving for breakfast, spread on freshly toasted bread.

Makes about 2.25kg/5lb

INGREDIENTS
450g/1lb Seville (Temple) oranges

450g/1lb sweet oranges

4 lemons

1.5 litres/2½ pints/6¼ cups water

1.2kg/2¼lb/5½ cups granulated (white) sugar, warmed

1 Wash the oranges and lemons, then halve and squeeze the juice into a large pan. Tie the pips (seeds) and membranes in a muslin (cheesecloth) bag, shred the orange and lemon rind and add to the pan.

2 Add the water to the pan, bring to the boil, then cover and simmer for 2 hours. Remove the muslin bag, leave to cool, then squeeze any liquid back into the pan.

3 Add the warmed sugar to the pan and stir over a low heat until completely dissolved. Bring to the boil and boil rapidly for about 15 minutes or until the marmalade reaches setting point (105°C/220°F).

4 Remove the pan from the heat and skim off any scum from the surface. Leave to cool for about 5 minutes, stir, then pour into warmed sterilized jars and seal. When cold, label, then store in a cool, dark place.

Energy 5061kcal/21594kJ; Protein 15.9g; Carbohydrate 1330.5g, of which sugars 1330.5g; Fat 0.9g, of which saturates 0g; Cholesterol 0mg; Calcium 1059mg; Fibre 15.3g; Sodium 117mg.

pink grapefruit and cranberry marmalade

Cranberries give this glorious marmalade an extra tartness and a full fruit flavour, as well as an inimitable vibrant colour. The resulting preserve makes a lively choice for breakfast or a brilliant accompaniment for cold roast turkey during the festive season.

Makes about 2.25kg/5lb

INGREDIENTS

675g/1½lb pink grapefruit
juice and pips (seeds) of 2 lemons
900ml/1½ pints/3¾ cups water
225g/8oz/2 cups cranberries
1.3kg/3lb/6½ cups granulated (white),
  sugar, warmed

COOK'S TIP

You can use fresh or frozen cranberries to make this marmalade. Either gives equally good results.

1 Wash, halve and quarter the grapefruit, then slice them thinly, reserving the pips (seeds) and any juice that runs out.

2 Tie the grapefruit and lemon pips in a muslin (cheesecloth) bag and place in a large pan with the grapefruit slices and lemon juice.

3 Add the water and bring to the boil. Cover and simmer gently for 1½–2 hours, or until the grapefruit rind is very tender. Remove the muslin bag, leave to cool, then squeeze over the pan.

4 Add the cranberries to the pan, then bring to the boil. Simmer for 15–20 minutes, or until the berries have popped and softened.

5 Add the sugar to the pan and stir over a low heat until the sugar has completely dissolved. Bring to the boil and boil rapidly for about 10 minutes, or until setting point is reached (105°C/220°F).

6 Remove the pan from the heat and skim off any scum from the surface using a slotted spoon. Leave to cool for 5–10 minutes, then stir and pour into warmed sterilized jars. Seal, then label when the marmalade is cold.

Energy 5403kcal/23043kJ; Protein 12.6g; Carbohydrate 1424.4g, of which sugars 1424.4g; Fat 0.9g, of which saturates 0g; Cholesterol 0mg; Calcium 853mg; Fibre 12.4g; Sodium 103mg.

ruby red grapefruit marmalade

If you prefer a really tangy marmalade, grapefruit is the perfect choice. To achieve a wonderfully red-blushed preserve, look for the red variety rather than pink. They have a lovely flavour and make a really delicious, sweet, jewel-coloured preserve.

Makes about 1.8kg/4lb

INGREDIENTS

900g/2lb ruby red grapefruit
1 lemon
1.2 litres/2 pints/5 cups water
1.3kg/3lb/6½ cups granulated (white) sugar, warmed

1 Wash the grapefruit and lemon and remove the rind in thick pieces using a vegetable peeler. Cut the fruit in half and squeeze the juice into a preserving pan, reserving all the pips (seeds).

2 Put the pips and membranes from the fruit in a muslin (cheesecloth) bag and add to the pan. Discard the grapefruit and lemon shells.

3 Using a sharp knife, cut the grapefruit and lemon rind into thin or coarse shreds, as preferred, and place in the pan.

COOK'S TIP

Although you can use yellow grapefruit to make this marmalade, it tends to give a very pale result with more tang than the ruby red variety, but a much less fruity flavour.

4 Add the water to the pan and bring to the boil. Cover and simmer for 2 hours, or until the rind is very tender.

5 Remove the muslin bag from the pan, leave to cool, then squeeze it over the pan. Add the sugar and stir over a low heat until it has dissolved. Bring to the boil, then boil rapidly for 10–15 minutes, or to setting point (105°C/220°F).

6 Remove the pan from the heat and skim off any scum using a slotted spoon. Leave to cool for about 10 minutes, then stir and pour into warmed sterilized jars. Seal, then label when cold.

Energy 5392kcal/22987kJ; Protein 13.7g; Carbohydrate 1419.7g, of which sugars 1419.7g; Fat 0.9g, of which saturates 0g; Cholesterol 0mg; Calcium 896mg; Fibre 11.7g; Sodium 105mg.

lemon and ginger marmalade

This zesty marmalade makes an excellent basis for meat glazes. Simply mix a few spoonfuls with a little soy sauce and brush over the meat before grilling.

Makes about 1.8kg/4lb

INGREDIENTS

1.2kg/2½lb lemons
150g/5oz fresh root ginger, peeled and finely grated
1.2 litres/2 pints/5 cups water
900g/2lb/4½ cups granulated (white) sugar, warmed

COOK'S TIP

When choosing fresh root ginger, select young, firm, fine-skinned pieces. For the best results, grate only the tender, juicy parts of the root and discard any tough, hairy parts.

1 Quarter and slice the lemons. Tie the pips (seeds) in a muslin (cheesecloth) bag and place in a preserving pan with the lemons, ginger and water. Bring to the boil, cover with a lid and simmer for 2 hours, or until the fruit is tender.

2 Remove the muslin bag from the pan, leave to cool then squeeze over the pan to release all the juice and pectin. Stir in the sugar over a low heat until dissolved, then increase the heat and boil for 5–10 minutes, or until setting point is reached (105°C/220°F).

3 Remove the pan from the heat and skim off any scum from the surface using a slotted spoon.

4 Leave to cool for 5 minutes, stir, then pour into warmed sterilized jars and seal. When cold, label and store in a cool place.

Energy 3785kcal/16122kJ; Protein 17.3g; Carbohydrate 980.3g, of which sugars 980.3g; Fat 3.9g, of which saturates 1.2g; Cholesterol 0mg; Calcium 1559mg; Fibre 1.6g; Sodium 204mg.

orange and coriander marmalade

This marmalade made with bitter Seville oranges has the added zing of warm, spicy coriander.

Makes about 1.8kg/4lb

INGREDIENTS

675g/1½lb Seville (Temple) oranges
2 lemons
15ml/1 tbsp crushed coriander seeds
1.5 litres/2½ pints/6¼ cups water
900g/2lb/4½ cups granulated (white) sugar, warmed

1 Cut the oranges and lemons in half and squeeze out all the juice. Place the orange and lemon pips (seeds) in a muslin (cheesecloth) bag. Using a sharp knife, cut the rind into shreds and place in a preserving pan with the juice.

2 Put the coriander seeds in the muslin bag with the pips and place in the pan. Add the water and bring to the boil. Cover and simmer for 2 hours, or until the mixture has reduced by half and the peel is soft.

3 Remove the muslin bag from the pan. Set it aside to cool, then squeeze it over the pan to release all the juices and pectin.

4 Add the sugar to the pan and stir over a low heat until it has dissolved. Bring to the boil and boil rapidly for 5–10 minutes, or to setting point (105°C/220°F).

5 Remove the pan from the heat and skim off any scum from the surface using a slotted spoon. Leave to cool for 5 minutes, stir then pour into warmed sterilized jars. Seal, then label when cold.

Energy 3807kcal/16244kJ; Protein 12.4g; Carbohydrate 999.2g, of which sugars 997.9g; Fat 1.2g, of which saturates 0g; Cholesterol 0mg; Calcium 826mg; Fibre 12.6g; Sodium 110mg.

orange and whisky marmalade

Adding whisky to orange marmalade gives it a fantastic warmth and flavour. The whisky is stirred in after the marmalade is cooked, to retain its strength and slightly bitter edge, which would be lost if boiled. Whisky marmalade is great spooned over a steamed sponge pudding.

3 Remove the muslin bag from the pan, leave to cool, then squeeze it over the pan to release any juice and pectin. Add the sugar, then stir over a low heat until the sugar has dissolved. Increase the heat and boil for 5–10 minutes until setting point is reached (105°C/220°F).

4 Remove the pan from the heat and skim off any scum from the surface using a slotted spoon. Stir in the whisky, then leave to cool for 5 minutes. Stir and pour the marmalade into warmed sterilized jars. Seal, then label when cold. Store in a cool dark place.

Makes about 2.25kg/5lb

INGREDIENTS

900g/2lb Seville (Temple) oranges
juice and pips (seeds) of 1 large lemon
1.2 litres/2 pints/5 cups water
1.5kg/3lb 6oz/7½ cups granulated (white) sugar, warmed
60ml/4 tbsp whisky

1 Scrub the oranges and cut in half. Squeeze the juice into a large pan, reserving the pips (seeds) and any membranes. Place these in a muslin (cheesecloth) bag with the lemon pips and add to the juice.

2 Using a sharp knife, thinly slice the orange rind and put in the pan along with the water. Bring to the boil, then cover and simmer for 1½–2 hours, or until the citrus rind is very tender.

Energy 5588kcal/23826kJ; Protein 16.4g; Carbohydrate 1435g, of which sugars 1435g; Fat 0.9g, of which saturates 0g; Cholesterol 0mg; Calcium 1112mg; Fibre 15.3g; Sodium 123mg.

fine lime shred marmalade

There is something about lime marmalade that really captures the flavour and essence of the fruit. It is important to cut the slices very finely though, because lime skins tend to be tougher than those on any other citrus fruit and can result in a chewy marmalade if cut thickly.

Makes about 2.25kg/5lb

INGREDIENTS

12 limes

4 kaffir lime leaves

1.2 litres/2 pints/5 cups water

1.3kg/3lb/6½ cups granulated (white) sugar, warmed

1 Halve the limes lengthways, then slice thinly, reserving any pips (seeds). Tie the pips and lime leaves in a muslin (cheesecloth) bag and place the bag in a large pan with the sliced fruit.

2 Add the water to the pan and bring to the boil. Cover and simmer gently for 1½–2 hours, or until the rind is very soft. Remove the muslin bag, leave to cool, then squeeze it over the pan to release any juice and pectin.

COOK'S TIP

To check whether the rind is cooked, remove a piece from the pan (before the sugar is added) and leave it to cool briefly. When cool enough to handle, press the rind between finger and thumb – it should be very soft.

3 Add the sugar to the pan, and stir over a low heat until the sugar has dissolved. Bring to the boil, then boil rapidly for 15 minutes, stirring occasionally, until setting point is reached (105°C/220°F).

4 Remove the pan from the heat and skim off any scum. Leave to cool for 5 minutes, stir, then pour into warmed sterilized jars. Seal, then label when cold. Store in a cool, dark place.

COOK'S TIPS

• To check for setting, spoon a little marmalade on to a chilled saucer and chill for 2 minutes. Push the surface with your finger; if wrinkles form, the marmalade is ready to bottle.

• Stirring marmalade after standing and before potting distributes the fruit rind evenly as the preserve begins to set.

Energy 5250kcal/22386kJ; Protein 13.3g; Carbohydrate 1380.1g, of which sugars 1380.1g; Fat 2g, of which saturates 0.7g; Cholesterol 0mg; Calcium 1263mg; Fibre 0g; Sodium 112mg.

spiced pumpkin marmalade

The bright orange colour and warm flavour of this marmalade is guaranteed to banish the winter blues. The addition of pumpkin gives the preserve more body and a lovely, satisfying texture. It is perfect for spreading on hot buttered toast or serving with warm croissants.

Makes about 2.75kg/6lb

INGREDIENTS

900g/2lb Seville (Temple) oranges, washed and halved

450g/1lb lemons, halved and thinly sliced, pips (seeds) reserved

2 cinnamon sticks

2.5cm/1in piece fresh root ginger, peeled and thinly sliced

1.5ml/¼ tsp grated nutmeg

1.75 litres/3 pints/7½ cups water

800g/1¾lb squash or pumpkin, peeled, seeds (pips) removed and thinly sliced

1.3kg/3lb/6½ cups granulated (white) sugar, warmed

1 Squeeze the juice from the oranges and pour into a preserving pan. Remove the white membranes and reserve with the pips.

2 Thinly slice the orange rind and place in the pan, along with the sliced lemons. Tie the orange and lemon pips and membranes in a muslin (cheesecloth) bag with the spices and add to the pan with the water. Bring to the boil, then cover and simmer for 1 hour.

3 Add the pumpkin to the pan and continue cooking for 1–1½ hours. Remove the muslin bag, leave to cool, then squeeze over the pan.

4 Stir in the sugar over a low heat until completely dissolved. Bring to the boil, then boil rapidly for 15 minutes, or until the marmalade becomes thick and reaches setting point (105°C/220°F). Stir once or twice to ensure the marmalade does not stick to the pan.

5 Remove the pan from the heat and skim off any scum. Leave to cool for 5 minutes, then stir and pour into warmed sterilized jars. Cover the surface of the preserve with wax discs, then seal. Label when the marmalade is cold and store in a cool, dark place.

Energy 5645kcal/24071kJ; Protein 26.5g; Carbohydrate 1467g, of which sugars 1463g; Fat 3.9g, of which saturates 1.3g; Cholesterol 0mg; Calcium 1727mg; Fibre 23.3g; Sodium 146mg.

clementine and liqueur marmalade

Small, tart clementines make a particularly full-flavoured preserve, which can be put to a wide variety of culinary uses. Stir it into yogurt or warm it with a little water to make a zesty sauce for pancakes or crêpes. It is also superlative served with smooth ripe brie and crisp crackers.

Makes about 1.8kg/4lb

INGREDIENTS

900g/2lb clementines, washed and halved

juice and pips (seeds) of 2 lemons

900ml/1½ pints/3¾ cups water

900g/2lb/4½ cups granulated (white) sugar, warmed

60ml/4 tbsp Grand Marnier or Cointreau

COOK'S TIP

Any member of the mandarin family can be used to make this preserve, but clementines give the best result.

1 Slice the clementines, reserving any pips. Tie the pips in a muslin (cheesecloth) bag with the lemon pips and place in a large pan with the sliced fruit.

2 Add the lemon juice and water to the pan and bring to the boil, then cover and simmer for about 1½ hours, or until the rind is very tender. Remove the muslin bag, cool, then squeeze over the pan.

3 Stir in the sugar over a low heat until dissolved, then bring to the boil and cook 5–10 minutes, or to setting point (105°C/220°F).

4 Remove the pan from the heat and skim off any scum. Cool for 5 minutes, then stir in the liqueur and pour into warmed sterilized jars. Seal, then label when cold.

Energy 4036kcal/17210kJ; Protein 12.6g; Carbohydrate 1038.5g, of which sugars 1038.5g; Fat 0.9g, of which saturates 0g; Cholesterol 0mg; Calcium 759mg; Fibre 10.8g; Sodium 97mg.

tangerine and lemon grass marmalade

The subtle flavours of lemon grass and kaffir lime leaves add an exotic edge to this marmalade.
You can also stir in thinly shredded lime leaf before bottling, which gives a very pretty result.

2 Tie all the pips, lemon grass and lime leaves in a piece of muslin (cheesecloth) and add to the pan. Boil, then simmer for 1½–2 hours, or until the tangerine rind is soft. Remove the bag, leave to cool, then squeeze over the pan.

3 Stir in the sugar over a low heat until completely dissolved, then boil for 5–10 minutes, or to setting point (105°C/220°F).

4 Remove the pan from the heat and skim off any scum. Leave to cool for 5 minutes, then stir and pour into warmed sterilized jars. Seal, then label when cold.

Makes about 1.8kg/4lb

INGREDIENTS

900g/2lb tangerines, washed and halved

juice and pips (seeds) of 2 Seville (Temple) oranges

900ml/1½ pints/3¾ cups water

2 lemon grass sticks, halved and crushed

3 kaffir lime leaves

900g/2lb/4½ cups granulated (white) sugar, warmed

COOK'S TIP

If you can't find kaffir lime leaves, you can substitute the finely pared rind of one lime.

1 Using a sharp knife, slice the tangerines thinly, reserving the pips. Place the sliced fruit in a preserving pan, along with juice from the Seville oranges and the measured water.

Energy 3935kcal/16768kJ; Protein 14.8g; Carbohydrate 1029.5g, of which sugars 1029.5g; Fat 1.1g, of which saturates 0g; Cholesterol 0mg; Calcium 949mg; Fibre 15.1g; Sodium 82mg.

pomelo and pineapple marmalade

Slightly larger than a grapefruit, pomelos have lime-green skin and a sharp, refreshing flavour and are delicious combined with tangy pineapple. Serve as a spread or spoon over desserts.

Makes about 2.75kg/6lb

INGREDIENTS

2 pomelos

900ml/1½ pints/3¾ cups water

2 x 432g/14½oz cans crushed pineapple in fruit juice

900g/2lb/4½ cups granulated (white) sugar, warmed

1 Wash and halve the pomelos. Squeeze out the juice, reserving any pips (seeds), and pour into a large pan. Remove the membranes and any excess pith and tie in muslin (cheesecloth) with the pips. Slice the peel thinly and add to the pan along with the muslin bag and water. Bring to the boil.

2 Cover the pan and simmer for 1½–2 hours, stirring occasionally, or until the fruit is soft. Add the pineapple and juice and simmer for a further 30 minutes.

3 Remove the muslin bag from the pan, leave to cool, then squeeze over the pan. Add the sugar and stir over a low heat until it has dissolved. Increase the heat and boil for 10 minutes, or to setting point (105°C/220°F).

4 Remove the pan from the heat and skim off any scum from the surface using a slotted spoon. Leave to cool for 10 minutes, then stir and pour into warmed sterilized jars. Seal, then label the jars when they are cold.

Energy 4042kcal/17233kJ; Protein 10.1g; Carbohydrate 1065.3g, of which sugars 1065.3g; Fat 0.4g, of which saturates 0g; Cholesterol 0mg; Calcium 633mg; Fibre 9.2g; Sodium 74mg.

peach and kumquat marmalade

Combined with sweet, scented peaches, kumquats make a wonderful, fresh-tasting preserve.

Makes about 1.8kg/4lb

INGREDIENTS

675g/1½lb kumquats, sliced thinly, pips (seeds) and juice reserved

juice and pips (seeds) of 1 lime

900g/2lb peaches, skinned and thinly sliced, skins reserved

900ml/1½ pints/3¾ cups water

900g/2lb/4½ cups granulated (white) sugar, warmed

1 Tie the pips and the peach skins in a muslin (cheesecloth) bag and put in a pan with the kumquats, juices and water. Bring to the boil, then cover and simmer for 50 minutes.

2 Add the peaches to the pan, bring to the boil, then simmer for 40–50 minutes, or until the fruit has become very soft. Remove the muslin bag, leave to cool, then squeeze over the pan.

3 Add the sugar to the pan and stir over a low heat until it has dissolved. Bring the mixture to the boil, then boil rapidly for about 15 minutes, stirring occasionally, to setting point (105°C/220°F).

4 Remove the pan from the heat and skim off any scum from the surface using a slotted spoon.

5 Leave to cool for 5–10 minutes, then stir and pour into warmed sterilized jars. Seal, then label when the jars are cold. Store in a cool, dark place.

Energy 4093kcal/17474kJ; Protein 19.6g; Carbohydrate 1067.6g, of which sugars 1067.6g; Fat 1.6g, of which saturates 0g; Cholesterol 0mg; Calcium 749mg; Fibre 21.6g; Sodium 90mg.

apricot and orange marmalade

This combination of oranges and rich-tasting apricots is a winner with strong coffee.

Makes about 1.5kg/3lb 6oz

INGREDIENTS

2 Seville (Temple) oranges, washed and quartered

1 lemon, washed and quartered,

1.2 litres/2 pints/5 cups water

900g/2lb apricots, stoned (pitted) and thinly sliced

900g/2lb/4½ cups granulated (white) sugar, warmed

COOK'S TIP

It is important to use a food processor to chop the oranges and lemon for this recipe. Chopping them this finely igves the marmalade its wonderful consistency. Preparing the fruits by hand will not give the same result.

1 Remove the pips (seeds) from the citrus fruit and tie in a muslin (cheesecloth) bag. Finely chop the oranges and lemons in a food processor and put in a large pan with the muslin bag and water.

2 Bring the mixture to the boil, then simmer, covered, for 1 hour.

3 Add the apricots to the pan, bring to the boil, then simmer for 30–40 minutes, or until the fruits are very tender.

4 Add the sugar to the pan and stir over a low heat until the sugar has dissolved. Bring to the boil, then boil rapidly for 15 minutes, stirring occasionally, until setting point is reached (105°C/220°F).

5 Remove the pan from the heat and skim off any scum using a slotted spoon. Leave to cool for about 5 minutes, then stir and pour into warmed sterilized jars. Seal, then label when cold and store in a cool, dry place.

Energy 3936kcal/16809kJ; Protein 15.9g; Carbohydrate 1030.8g, of which sugars 1030.8g; Fat 1.2g, of which saturates 0g; Cholesterol 0mg; Calcium 753mg; Fibre 20.4g; Sodium 87mg.

lemon curd

This classic tangy, creamy curd is still one of the most popular of all the curds. It is delicious spread thickly over freshly baked white bread or served with American-style pancakes, and also makes a wonderfully rich, zesty sauce spooned over fresh fruit tarts.

Makes about 450g/1lb

INGREDIENTS

3 lemons

200g/7oz/1 cup caster (superfine) sugar

115g/4oz/8 tbsp unsalted (sweet) butter, diced

2 large (US extra large) eggs

2 large (US extra large) egg yolks

1 Wash the lemons, then finely grate the rind and place in a large heatproof bowl. Using a sharp knife, halve the lemons and squeeze the juice into the bowl. Set over a pan of gently simmering water and add the sugar and butter. Stir until the sugar has dissolved and the butter melted.

2 Put the eggs and yolks in a bowl and beat together with a fork. Pour the eggs through a sieve into the lemon mixture, and whisk well until thoroughly combined.

3 Stir the mixture constantly over the heat until the lemon curd thickens and lightly coats the back of a wooden spoon.

4 Remove the pan from the heat and pour the curd into small, warmed sterilized jars. Cover, seal and label. Store in a cool, dark place, ideally in the refrigerator. Use within 3 months. (Once opened, store in the refrigerator.)

COOK'S TIP

If you are really impatient when it comes to cooking, it is possible to cook the curd in a heavy pan directly over a low heat. However, you really need to watch it like a hawk to avoid the mixture curdling. If the curd looks as though it's beginning to curdle, plunge the base of the pan in cold water and beat vigorously.

Energy 1942kcal/8119kJ; Protein 22.5g; Carbohydrate 209.7g, of which sugars 209.7g; Fat 118.8g, of which saturates 66.8g; Cholesterol 1105mg; Calcium 242mg; Fibre 0g; Sodium 895mg.

seville orange curd

Using flavoursome Seville oranges gives this curd a fantastic orange flavour and a real citrus tang. It is perfect for spreading on toast for breakfast or at tea time, and is also superlative folded into whipped cream and used as a filling for cakes, roulades and scones.

Makes about 450g/1lb

INGREDIENTS

2 Seville (Temple) oranges

115g/4oz/8 tbsp unsalted (sweet) butter, diced

200g/7oz/1 cup caster (superfine) sugar

2 large (US extra large) eggs

2 large (US extra large) egg yolks

1 Wash the oranges, then finely grate the rind and place in a large heatproof bowl. Halve the oranges and squeeze the juice into the bowl with the rind.

2 Place the bowl over a pan of gently simmering water and add the butter and sugar. Stir until the sugar has completely dissolved and the butter melted.

3 Put the eggs and yolks in a small bowl and lightly whisk, then pour into the orange mixture through a sieve. Whisk them together until thoroughly combined.

4 Stir the orange and egg mixture constantly over the heat until the mixture thickens and lightly coats the back of a wooden spoon.

5 Pour the orange curd into small, warmed sterilized jars, cover and seal. Store in a cool, dark place, preferably in the refrigerator.

WATCHPOINTS

• The very young, the elderly, pregnant women, and those with a compromised immune system are advised against eating raw eggs or food containing raw eggs. Although the eggs in fruit curds are lightly cooked, they may still be unsuitable for these groups of people.

• Fruit curds do not have the shelf-life of many other preserves and should be used within 3 months of making.

• Once opened, always store fruit curds in the refrigerator.

Energy 2053kcal/8593kJ; Protein 25.8g; Carbohydrate 235.2g, of which sugars 235.2g; Fat 119.1g, of which saturates 66.8g; Cholesterol 1105mg; Calcium 383mg; Fibre 5.1g; Sodium 910mg.

grapefruit curd

If you favour tangy and refreshing preserves, this grapefruit curd is the one to try. Really fresh free-range eggs give the best results and flavour when making curd.

Makes about 675g/1½lb

INGREDIENTS

finely grated rind and juice of 1 grapefruit

115g/4oz/8 tbsp unsalted (sweet) butter, diced

200g/7oz/1 cup caster (superfine) sugar

4 large (US extra large) eggs, lightly beaten

1 Put the grapefruit rind and juice in a large heatproof bowl with the butter and sugar, and set over a pan of gently simmering water. Heat the mixture, stirring occasionally, until the sugar has dissolved and the butter melted.

2 Add the beaten eggs to the fruit mixture, straining them through a sieve. Whisk together, then stir constantly over the heat until the mixture thickens and lightly coats the back of a wooden spoon.

3 Pour the curd into small, warmed sterilized jars, cover and seal. Once the jars are cold you can label and store them in a cool, dark place, preferably in the refrigerator. They should be used within 3 months. (Once opened, store the curd in the refrigerator.)

VARIATION

Tangy grapefruit and sweet orange marry particularly well in creamy fruit curds. Add the grated rind of a small orange to this grapefruit recipe for an extra zingy, zesty alternative.

Energy 1971kcal/8244kJ; Protein 27.1g; Carbohydrate 218g, of which sugars 218g; Fat 116.8g, of which saturates 66.1g; Cholesterol 1006mg; Calcium 255mg; Fibre 0g; Sodium 996mg.

passion fruit curd

The tropical flavour and aroma of passion fruit fills this curd with a gloriously sunny character. It is perfect spread on toasted English muffins or little American pancakes.

Makes about 675g/1½lb

INGREDIENTS

grated rind and juice of 2 lemons

115g/4oz/8 tbsp unsalted (sweet) butter, diced

275g/10oz/1¼ cups caster (superfine) sugar

4 passion fruit

4 eggs

2 egg yolks

1 Place the lemon rind and juice in a large heatproof bowl and add the butter and sugar.

2 Halve the passion fruit and scoop the seeds into a sieve set over the bowl. Press out all the juice and discard the seeds.

3 Place the bowl over a pan of gently simmering water and stir occasionally until the sugar has dissolved and the butter melted.

4 Beat the eggs and yolks together and add to the bowl, pouring them through a sieve, then whisk well to combine. Stir constantly until the mixture thickens and lightly coats the back of a spoon.

5 Pour the curd into small, warmed sterilized jars, cover and seal. Store in a cool, dark place, preferably in the refrigerator and use within 3 months. (Once opened, store in the refrigerator.)

Energy 2377kcal/9961kJ; Protein 34.4g; Carbohydrate 291.5g, of which sugars 291.5g; Fat 128g, of which saturates 69.3g; Cholesterol 1409mg; Calcium 334mg; Fibre 2g; Sodium 1023mg.

apple and cinnamon butter

Fans of apple pies and crumbles will love this luscious apple butter. Serve on toast or with warmed brioche for a breakfast treat or with pancakes and cream for tea.

Makes about 1.8kg/4lb

INGREDIENTS

475ml/16fl oz/2 cups dry (hard) cider

450g/1lb tart cooking apples, peeled, cored and sliced

450g/1lb eating apples, peeled, cored and sliced

grated rind and juice of 1 lemon

675g/1½lb/scant 3½ cups granulated (white) sugar, warmed

5ml/1 tsp ground cinnamon

COOK'S TIP

Leaving the butter to stand for 2 days give the flavours a chance to develop.

1 Pour the cider into a large pan and bring to the boil. Boil hard until the volume is reduced by half, then add the apples and lemon rind and juice.

2 Cover the pan and cook for 10 minutes. Uncover and continue cooking for 20–30 minutes, or until the apples are very soft.

3 Leave the mixture to cool slightly, then pour into a food processor or blender and blend to a purée. Press through a fine sieve into a bowl.

4 Measure the purée into a large heavy pan, adding 275g/10oz/ 1⅓ cups warmed sugar for every 600ml/1 pint/2½ cups of purée. Add the ground cinnamon and stir well to combine.

5 Gently heat the mixture, stirring continuously, until the sugar has completely dissolved. Increase the heat and boil steadily for about 20 minutes, stirring frequently, until the mixture forms a thick purée that hold its shape when spooned on to a cold plate.

6 Spoon the apple and cinnamon butter into warmed sterilized jars. Seal and label, then store in a cool, dark place for 2 days to allow the flavours to develop before serving.

Energy 3146kcal/13428kJ; Protein 6.1g; Carbohydrate 797.8g, of which sugars 797.8g; Fat 0.9g, of which saturates 0g; Cholesterol 0mg; Calcium 432mg; Fibre 14.4g; Sodium 92mg.

pear and vanilla butter

The delicate flavour of pears is enhanced by vanilla in this butter that really captures the essence of the fruit. It is well worth allowing it to mature for a few days before eating.

Makes about 675g/1½lb

INGREDIENTS

900g/2lb pears, peeled, cored and chopped

juice of 3 lemons

300ml/½ pint/1¼ cups water

1 vanilla pod (bean), split

675g/1½lb/scant 3½ cups granulated (white) sugar, warmed

1 Place the pears in a large pan with the lemon juice, water and vanilla pod. Bring to the boil, then cover and simmer for 10 minutes. Uncover the pan and continue cooking for a further 15–20 minutes, or until the pears are very soft.

2 Remove the vanilla pod from the pan, then carefully scrape the seeds into the fruit mixture using the tip of a knife.

3 Tip the fruit and juices into a food processor or blender and blend to a purée. Press the purée through a fine sieve into a bowl.

4 Measure the purée into a large heavy pan, adding 275g/10oz/1⅓ cups warmed sugar for every 600ml/1 pint/2½ cups of purée.

5 Stir the mixture over a low heat until the sugar dissolves. Increase the heat and boil for 15 minutes, stirring, until the mixture forms a thick purée that holds its shape when spooned on to a cold plate.

6 Spoon the pear butter into small, warmed sterilized jars. Seal, label and store in a cool, dark place for at least 2 days before serving.

COOK'S TIPS

• Fruit butters have a soft spreading consistency – thicker than fruit curds, but softer than fruit cheeses. They make an excellent tea time preserve.

• Fruit butters keep well in sealed jars and can be stored for up to 3 months. Once opened, they should be stored in the refrigerator.

Energy 3020kcal/12868kJ; Protein 6.1g; Carbohydrate 795.4g, of which sugars 795.4g; Fat 0.9g, of which saturates 0g; Cholesterol 0mg; Calcium 457mg; Fibre 19.8g; Sodium 68mg.

plum butter

Simmering plums down creates a preserve with a rich, red colour and a smooth texture.

Makes about 900g/2lb

INGREDIENTS

900g/2lb red plums, stoned (pitted)

grated rind and juice of 1 orange

150ml/¼ pint/⅔ cup water

450g/1lb/2¼ cups granulated (white)
sugar, warmed

1 Place the plums in a large, heavy pan with the orange rind and juice and the water. Bring to the boil, then cover with a lid and cook for 20–30 minutes, or until the plums are very soft. Set aside to cool.

2 Press the fruit through a fine sieve. Measure the purée into a pan and add 350g/12oz/1¾ cups sugar for every 600ml/1 pint/2½ cups purée. Gently heat, stirring.

3 When the sugar has dissolved, increase the heat and boil for 10–15 minutes, stirring frequently, until the mixture holds its shape when spooned on to a cold plate.

4 Spoon the mixture into warmed sterilized jars. Seal and label, then store in a cool, dark place for 2 days to mature before serving.

COOK'S TIP

Serve the plum butter on toasted walnut and raisin bread for a delicious breakfast, at tea time or just as a snack.

Energy 2115kcal/9036kJ; Protein 7.9g; Carbohydrate 553.9g, of which sugars 553.9g; Fat 1g, of which saturates 0g; Cholesterol 0mg; Calcium 361mg; Fibre 14.5g; Sodium 50mg.

golden peach butter

The rich, dark golden colour and delicate, spicy flavour of this butter makes it a real treat.

Makes about 2.25kg/5lb

INGREDIENTS

1.3kg/3lb ripe peaches, stoned (pitted)

600ml/1 pint/2½ cups water

675g/1½lb/scant 3½ cups granulated
(white) sugar, warmed

grated rind and juice of 1 lemon

2.5ml/½ tsp ground cinnamon

2.5ml/½ tsp ground nutmeg

1 Slice the peaches and place in a large pan with the water. Bring to the boil, then cover and simmer for about 10 minutes.

2 Remove the lid from the pan and simmer gently for a further 45 minutes, or until the peaches are quite soft.

3 Leave the fruit mixture to cool slightly, then transfer to a food processor or blender and process to a purée. Press the purée through a fine sieve into a bowl.

4 Measure the purée into a large heavy pan, adding 275g/10oz/ 1⅓ cups warmed sugar for every 600ml/1 pint/2½ cups of purée.

5 Add the lemon rind and juice and spices to the pan and stir to combine. Gently heat, stirring, until the sugar has dissolved.

6 Bring the mixture to the boil and cook for 15–20 minutes, stirring frequently, until the mixture forms a thick purée that holds its shape when spooned on to a cold plate.

7 Spoon the butter into small, warmed sterilized jars and seal and label, then store in a cool, dark place for 2 days before eating.

COOK'S TIP

For a really special treat, spoon this sweet, fragrant butter into tiny tart cases or on to bite-size brioches.

Energy 3089kcal/13193kJ; Protein 16.4g; Carbohydrate 804.2g, of which sugars 804.2g; Fat 1.3g, of which saturates 0g; Cholesterol 0mg; Calcium 449mg; Fibre 19.5g; Sodium 54mg.

pumpkin and maple butter

This all-American butter has a lovely bright, autumnal colour and flavour. It is perfect served spread on little pancakes fresh from the griddle, or used as a filling or topping for cakes.

Makes about 675g/1½lb

INGREDIENTS

1.2kg/2½lb pumpkin or butternut squash, peeled, seeded and chopped

450ml/¾ pint/scant 2 cups water

grated rind and juice of 1 orange

5ml/1 tsp ground cinnamon

120ml/4fl oz/½ cup maple syrup

675g/1½lb/scant 3½ cups granulated (white) sugar, warmed

VARIATION

This butter is also delicious made with clear honey instead of maple syrup. It adds a distinct flavour.

1 Put the pumpkin or squash in the pan with the water and cook for 30–40 minutes, or until it is very tender. Drain and, using the back of a spoon, press the cooked pumpkin or squash through a fine sieve into a bowl.

2 Stir the orange rind and juice, cinnamon and maple syrup into the purée, then measure the purée into a large pan, adding 275g/10oz/1⅓ cups warmed sugar for every 600ml/1 pint/2½ cups purée.

3 Gently heat the purée, stirring, until the sugar has dissolved. Increase the heat and boil for 10–20 minutes, stirring frequently, until the mixture forms a thick purée that holds its shape when spooned on to a cold plate.

4 Spoon the butter into small, warmed sterilized jars. Seal and label, then store in a cool, dark place for 2 days before eating.

Energy 3191kcal/13606kJ; Protein 12.4g; Carbohydrate 831g, of which sugars 825g; Fat 2.4g, of which saturates 1.2g; Cholesterol 0mg; Calcium 730mg; Fibre 12.1g; Sodium 370mg.

mango and cardamom butter

You need to use really ripe mangoes for this recipe. If the mangoes are not ripe enough, they will need much longer cooking and will not produce such a richly flavoured butter.

Makes about 675g/1½lb

INGREDIENTS

900g/2lb ripe mangoes, peeled

6 green cardamom pods, split

120ml/4fl oz/½ cup freshly squeezed lemon juice

120ml/4fl oz/½ cup freshly squeezed orange juice

50ml/2fl oz/¼ cup water

675g/1½lb/scant 3½ cups granulated (white) sugar, warmed

1 Cut the mango flesh away from the stones and chop, then place it in a pan with the cardamom pods, fruit juices and water.

2 Cover and simmer for 10 minutes. Remove the lid and simmer for a further 25 minutes, or until the mangoes are very soft and there is very little liquid left in the pan.

3 Remove the cardamom pods from the pan and discard. Transfer the fruit to a food processor and blend to a purée. Press the purée through a fine sieve into a bowl.

4 Measure the purée into a large, heavy pan, adding 275g/10oz/1⅓ cups warmed sugar for every 600ml/1 pint/2½ cups purée. Gently heat, stirring, until the sugar has dissolved. Increase the heat and boil for 10–20 minutes, stirring, until a thick butter forms that holds its shape when spooned on to a cold plate.

5 Spoon the mango and cardamom butter into small, warmed sterilized jars. Seal and label, then store in a cool, dark place for at least 2 days before eating. (The butter can be stored for up to 3 months.)

Energy 3216kcal/13735kJ; Protein 10.3g; Carbohydrate 842.8g, of which sugars 840.1g; Fat 1.9g, of which saturates 0.9g; Cholesterol 0mg; Calcium 478mg; Fibre 23.5g; Sodium 71mg.

damson and vanilla cheese

This cheese is good with roast lamb, duck and game, or semi-soft cheese.

Makes about 900g/2lb

INGREDIENTS

1.5kg/3lb 6oz damsons
1 vanilla pod (bean), split
800g/1¾lb/4 cups granulated (white)
  sugar, warmed

COOK'S TIPS

• When the cheese is ready, you
should be able to see the base of the
pan when a wooden spoon is drawn
through the mixture. To test the set,
spoon a small amount of the damson
mixture on to a chilled plate; it should
form a firm jelly.

• To make cheese shapes, spoon the
mixture into greased moulds, and leave
to set before turning out and serving.

1 Wash the damsons and place in
a large pan with the vanilla pod
and pour in enough water to come
halfway up the fruit. Cover and
simmer for 30 minutes.

2 Remove the vanilla pod from the
pan and scrape the seeds back into
the pan using the point of a knife.

3 Press the fruit and juices
through a sieve into a bowl.
Measure the purée into a large,
heavy pan, adding 400g/14oz/
2 cups sugar for every 600ml/
1 pint/2½ cups purée.

4 Gently heat the purée, stirring,
until the sugar has dissolved.
Increase the heat slightly and cook
for about 45 minutes, stirring
frequently with a wooden spoon,
until very thick.

5 Spoon the damson cheese into
warmed, sterilized jars. Seal and
label, then store in a cool, dark
place for 2–3 months to dry out
slightly before eating.

Energy 3722kcal/15878kJ; Protein 11.5g; Carbohydrate 980g, of which sugars 980g; Fat 0g, of which saturates 0g; Cholesterol 0mg; Calcium 784mg; Fibre 27g; Sodium 78mg.

quince cheese

This wonderfully fragrant fruit cheese is particularly good served as a sweetmeat.

Makes about 900g/2lb

INGREDIENTS

1.3kg/3lb quinces
800g/1¾lb/4 cups granulated (white)
  sugar, warmed
caster (superfine) sugar, for dusting

COOK'S TIP

Rather than setting the cheese and
cutting it into squares, simply
spoon the mixture into warmed,
sterilized, straight-sided jars. Seal
and label, then store in a cool,
dark place for 2–3 months to dry
out slightly before eating.

1 Wash the quinces, then chop
and place in a large pan. Pour in
enough water to nearly cover the
fruit, then cover with a lid and
simmer for 45 minutes, or until the
fruit is very tender. Cool slightly.

2 Press the mixture through a fine
sieve into a bowl. Measure the
purée into a large, heavy pan,
adding 400g/14oz/2 cups sugar for
every 600ml/1 pint/2½ cups purée.
Heat gently, stirring, until the sugar
has dissolved. Increase the heat and
cook for 40–50 minutes, stirring
frequently, until very thick (see
Cook's Tip left).

3 Pour the mixture into a small
oiled baking tin (pan) and leave
to set for 24 hours. Cut into small
squares, dust with sugar and store
in an airtight container.

Energy 3672kcal/15645kJ; Protein 7.9g; Carbohydrate 966g, of which sugars 966g; Fat 1.3g, of which saturates 0g; Cholesterol 0mg; Calcium 567mg; Fibre 28.6g; Sodium 87mg.

spiced cherry cheese

For the best results, try to use cherries that have a good tart flavour and dark red flesh.
Serve as an accompaniment to strong cheese, or sliced with roast duck or pork.

Makes about 900g/2lb

INGREDIENTS

1.5kg/3lb 6oz/8¼ cups cherries,
  stoned (pitted)

2 cinnamon sticks

800g/1¾lb/4 cups granulated (white)
  sugar, warmed

COOK'S TIPS

• Store the cheese in a cool, dark
place for 2–3 months before eating.

• To serve a fruit cheese in slices, turn
it out of its container and slice using a
sharp knife. The slices may be cut into
smaller portions. Try to use a straight-
sided container so that the cheese can
slide out easily.

1 Place the cherries in a large pan
with the cinnamon sticks. Pour in
enough water to almost cover the
fruit. Bring to the boil, then cover
and simmer for 20–30 minutes, or
until the cherries are very tender.
Remove the cinnamon sticks from
the pan and discard.

2 Tip the fruit into a sieve and
press into a bowl, using the back
of a spoon. Measure the purée into
a large, heavy pan, adding 350g/
12oz/1¼ cups warmed sugar for
every 600ml/1 pint/2½ cups purée.

3 Gently heat the purée, stirring,
until the sugar dissolves. Increase
the heat and cook for 45 minutes,
stirring frequently, until very thick.
To test, spoon a little of the cheese
on to a cold plate; it should form
a firm jelly.

4 Spoon into warmed, sterilized
jars or oiled moulds. Seal, label,
and store in a cool, dark place.

Energy 3872kcal/16493kJ; Protein 17.5g; Carbohydrate 1008.5g, of which sugars 1008.5g; Fat 1.5g, of which saturates 0g; Cholesterol 0mg; Calcium 619mg; Fibre 13.5g; Sodium 63mg.

blackberry and apple cheese

This rich, dark preserve has an incredibly intense flavour and fabulous colour. For a fragrant twist, add a few raspberries – or even strawberries – in place of some of the blackberries.

Makes about 900g/2lb

INGREDIENTS

900g/2lb/8 cups blackberries

450g/1lb tart cooking apples, cut into chunks, with skins and cores intact

grated rind and juice of 1 lemon

800g/1¾lb/4 cups granulated (white) sugar, warmed

1 Put the blackberries, apples and lemon rind and juice in a pan and pour in enough water to come halfway up the fruit. Bring to the boil, then uncover and simmer for 15–20 minutes or until the fruit is very soft.

2 Leave the fruit to cool slightly, then tip the mixture into a sieve and press into a bowl, using the back of a spoon. Measure the purée into a large, heavy pan, adding 400g/14oz/2 cups warmed sugar for every 600ml/1 pint/ 2½ cups purée.

3 Gently heat the purée, stirring, until the sugar dissolves. Increase the heat slightly and cook for 40–50 minutes, stirring frequently, until very thick (see Cook's Tip).

4 Spoon the blackberry and apple cheese into warmed, sterilized straight-sided jars or oiled moulds. Seal and label the jars or moulds, then store in a cool, dark place for 2–3 months to dry out slightly.

COOK'S TIP

When the cheese is ready, you should be able to see the base of the pan when a wooden spoon is drawn through the mixture. Spoon a small amount of the mixture on to a chilled plate; it should form a firm jelly.

Energy 3535kcal/15064kJ; Protein 13.4g; Carbohydrate 921.9g, of which sugars 921.9g; Fat 2.3g, of which saturates 0g; Cholesterol 0mg; Calcium 811mg; Fibre 35.1g; Sodium 75mg.

INDEX